New Perspectives on

Blended HTML, XHTML, and CSS

Introductory

New Perspectives on

Blended HTML, XHTML, and CSS

Introductory

Henry Bojack

THOMSON

COURSE TECHNOLOGY

Australia • Canada • Mexico • Singapore • Spain • United Kingdom • United States

THOMSON

COURSE TECHNOLOGY

New Perspectives on Blended HTML, XHTML, and CSS—Introductory
is published by Thomson Course Technology.

Director of Learning Solutions:
Marie Lee

Senior Product Manager:
Kathy Finnegan

Product Manager:
Erik Herman

Associate Product Manager:
Brandi Henson

Editorial Assistant:
Leigh Robbins

Senior Marketing Manager:
Joy Stark

Marketing Coordinator:
Jennifer Hankin

Developmental Editor:
Lisa Ruffolo

Content Project Manager:
Danielle Chouhan

Composition:
GEX Publishing Services

Art Director:
Marissa Falco

Text Designer:
Steve Deschene

Cover Designer:
Elizabeth Paquin

Cover Art:
Bill Brown

Preface

The New Perspectives Series' critical-thinking, problem-solving approach is the ideal way to prepare students to transcend point-and-click skills and take advantage of all that HTML, XHTML, and Cascading Style Sheets (CSS) have to offer.

In developing the New Perspectives Series, our goal was to create books that give students the software concepts and practical skills they need to succeed beyond the classroom. We've updated our proven case-based pedagogy with more practical content to make learning skills more meaningful to students.

With the New Perspectives Series, students understand *why* they are learning *what* they are learning, and are fully prepared to apply their skills to real-life situations.

I really love the Margin Tips, which add 'tricks of the trade' to students' skills package. In addition, the Reality Check exercises provide for practical application of students' knowledge. I can't wait to use them in the classroom...."

—Terry Morse Colucci
Institute of Technology, Inc.

About This Book

This text offers a new approach to teaching HTML, XHTML, and Cascading Styles Sheets (CSS).

- Presents an easy-to-understand, non-technical style that lets novice learners quickly grasp the material.
- Builds a strong foundation in Cascading Style Sheets (CSS) so that students can migrate to and learn about HTML editors such as Microsoft® Expression® Web and Adobe® Creative® Suite 3 Web Standard.
- Focuses on achieving page layouts through CSS positioning, which more closely reflects the way "real-world applications" are created.
- Integrates CSS right from the start so that students feel confident about their knowledge of CSS when they complete the course.
- Provides case scenarios, review assignments, and case problems that allow students to reinforce concepts and skills learned.

System Requirements

This book assumes a typical installation of Microsoft Windows Vista Ultimate with the Aero feature turned off (or Windows Vista Home Premium or Business edition). Note that you can also complete the tutorials in this book using Windows XP; you will notice only minor differences if you are using Windows XP.

The New Perspectives Approach

Context
Each tutorial begins with a problem presented in a "real-world" case that is meaningful to students. The case sets the scene to help students understand what they will do in the tutorial.

Hands-on Approach
Each tutorial is divided into manageable sessions that combine reading and hands-on, step-by-step work. Colorful screenshots help guide students through the steps. **Trouble?** tips anticipate common mistakes or problems to help students stay on track and continue with the tutorial.

InSight

InSight Boxes
InSight boxes offer expert advice and best practices to help students better understand how to work with the software. With the information provided in the InSight boxes, students achieve a deeper understanding of the concepts behind the software features and skills.

Tip

Margin Tips
Margin Tips provide helpful hints and shortcuts for more efficient use of the software. The Tips appear in the margin at key points throughout each tutorial, giving students extra information when and where they need it.

Reality Check

Reality Checks
Comprehensive, open-ended Reality Check exercises give students the opportunity to practice skills by creating practical, real-world documents, such as resumes and budgets, which they are likely to use in their everyday lives at school, home, or work.

Review

In New Perspectives, retention is a key component to learning. At the end of each session, a series of Quick Check questions helps students test their understanding of the concepts before moving on. Each tutorial also contains an end-of-tutorial summary and a list of key terms for further reinforcement.

Apply

Assessment
Engaging and challenging Review Assignments and Case Problems have always been a hallmark feature of the New Perspectives Series. Colorful icons and brief descriptions accompany the exercises, making it easy to understand, at a glance, both the goal and level of challenge a particular assignment holds.

Reference Window

Reference
While contextual learning is excellent for retention, there are times when students will want a high-level understanding of how to accomplish a task. Within each tutorial, Reference Windows appear before a set of steps to provide a succinct summary and preview of how to perform a task. Each book includes a combination Glossary/Index to promote easy reference of material.

Our Complete System of Instruction

Coverage To Meet Your Needs

Whether you're looking for just a small amount of coverage or enough to fill a semester-long class, we can provide you with a textbook that meets your needs.

- Brief books typically cover the essential skills in just 2 to 4 tutorials.
- Introductory books build and expand on those skills and contain an average of 5 to 8 tutorials.
- Comprehensive books are great for a full-semester class, and contain 9 to 12+ tutorials.

So if the book you're holding does not provide the right amount of coverage for you, there's probably another offering available. Go to our Web site or contact your Thomson Course Technology sales representative to find out what else we offer.

Student Online Companion

This book has an accompanying online companion Web site designed to enhance learning. This Web site includes:

- Internet Assignments for selected tutorials
- Student Data Files
- PowerPoint presentations

CourseCasts – Learning on the Go. Always available…always relevant.

Want to keep up with the latest technology trends relevant to you? Visit our site to find a library of podcasts, CourseCasts, featuring a "CourseCast of the Week," and download them to your mp3 player at http://coursecasts.course.com.

Our fast-paced world is driven by technology. You know because you're an active participant—always on the go, always keeping up with technological trends, and always learning new ways to embrace technology to power your life.

Ken Baldauf, host of CourseCasts, is a faculty member of the Florida State University Computer Science Department where he is responsible for teaching technology classes to thousands of FSU students each year. Ken is an expert in the latest technology trends; he gathers and sorts through the most pertinent news and information for CourseCasts so your students can spend their time enjoying technology, rather than trying to figure it out. Open or close your lecture with a discussion based on the latest CourseCast.

Visit us at http://coursecasts.course.com to learn on the go!

Instructor Resources

We offer more than just a book. We have all the tools you need to enhance your lectures, check students' work, and generate exams in a new, easier-to-use and completely revised package. This book's Instructor's Manual, ExamView testbank, PowerPoint presentations, data files, solution files, figure files, and a sample syllabus are all available on a single CD-ROM or for downloading at www.course.com.

Blackboard

Online Content

Blackboard is the leading distance learning solution provider and class-management platform today. Thomson Course Technology has partnered with Blackboard to bring you premium online content. Content for use with *New Perspectives on Blended HTML, XHTML, and CSS, Introductory* is available in a Blackboard Course Cartridge and may include topic reviews, case projects, review questions, test banks, practice tests, custom syllabi, and more.

Thomson Course Technology also has solutions for several other learning management systems. Please visit http://www.course.com today to see what's available for this title.

Acknowledgments

I would sincerely like to thank the people that worked so hard to make this book a reality. I am grateful to Production Editor Danielle Chouhan and Product Manager Erik Herman for keeping this project on track and on schedule. I would also like to thank Developmental Editor Amanda Brodkin, who helped to shape this project in its early stages. In particular, I want to express my heartfelt thanks and deepest appreciation to Developmental Editor Lisa Ruffolo, who applied her vast knowledge of and experience with the New Perspectives series to morph this text from an awkward signet into a graceful swan. I also want to express my thanks to the six eagle eyes of Copy Editor Mark Goodin, Quality Assurance Tester Susan Whalen, and Validator Serge Palladino.

I would like to dedicate this book to my reasons for being: my loving wife Liliana; my handsome son Mark; and my "favorite daughter," Lauren.

—Henry Bojack

Brief Contents

Table of Contents

Objectives

Session 1.1
- Describe the Internet and the World Wide Web
- Identify and use tags on a Web page
- Document HTML code using comments
- Save a text document as an HTML file

Session 1.2
- Specify headings
- Format Web page text
- Identify deprecated tags
- Insert special characters, superscripts, and subscripts

Session 1.3
- Insert a scaled image
- Create a horizontal rule
- Create ordered and unordered lists
- Format address text

Using HTML Tags to Create Web Pages

Creating a Basic Web Page

Case | Less Sodas and Beverages

The Less Sodas and Beverages Company is a start-up business that manufactures, sells, and distributes its brand of healthy sodas and beverages. Andy Chanos and Warren Metzger founded Less Sodas and Beverages Company in Sheffield Ridge, Illinois, earlier this year to meet consumer demand for refreshing, natural beverages. Andy and Warren are dedicated to not using any artificial sweeteners, food coloring, or artificial ingredients of any kind in their products. Less Sodas have substantially less carbonation and sugar than most soft drinks, but enough of each to appeal to most consumers. In addition, Less Sodas contain several vitamins and minerals to enhance product appeal, especially to parents who traditionally discourage their children from drinking soft drinks. After starting with a product line of three basic flavors—cola, lemon-lime, and ginger ale—Andy and Warren recently introduced new flavors including orange nut cream, mango mint, and passion fruit cola, which are proving to be very popular.

Andy and Warren hired you as an assistant in the marketing and sales department. Besides designing print ads, flyers, and other sales materials, you are helping Andy and Warren launch an advertising campaign that features the new slogan, "Tired of more? Drink Less." Andy wants to develop a Web page that features this slogan and highlights the new soda flavors. You are comfortable creating basic Web pages that combine text and graphics and offer to work with Andy to create one for the Less Sodas and Beverages Company. Current and potential customers can then view the Web page to learn about the company and its beverages.

In this tutorial, you develop an HTML template that you can use as the basis for other HTML documents. You also create a basic Web page for Less Sodas that includes headings, text, and an image, and then format the text to make it more appealing and meaningful.

Starting Data Files

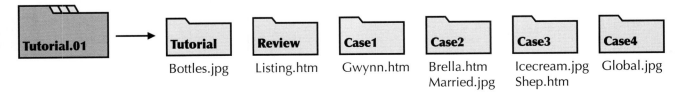

Tutorial.01 → Tutorial Review Case1 Case2 Case3 Case4

Bottles.jpg Listing.htm Gwynn.htm Brella.htm Icecream.jpg Global.jpg
                                                  Married.jpg Shep.htm

Session 1.1

Understanding the Internet and the World Wide Web

Whether you are interested in creating Web pages for personal use or training to become a professional Web developer, you need to know how the Internet and the World Wide Web work. Start by taking a brief look behind the technologies that make the Internet and the World Wide Web what they are today.

The **Internet** is a global network of computers linked by high-speed data lines and wireless systems. The Internet was established in 1969 as a collaborative project between the Department of Defense and several large colleges on the West Coast. National security concerns during the Cold War era sparked interest in developing better communications systems. At that time, the concept of a local area network was a new one, and the idea of linking individual networks to create a "network of networks" was uncharted territory. During the 1970s and 1980s, the primary users of the Internet were educational and research institutions. They used the Internet to freely share and exchange research information, but they did so by sending and receiving short text-only messages. Today, millions of people use the Internet to transfer not only text, but also data, voice, images, and video.

The **World Wide Web** (Web or **WWW** for short) is just one of several services provided by the Internet, which consists of a system of interconnected networks. The software you use to view and browse, or "surf," Web pages is called a **Web browser**. It is this software that lets you navigate from one document, page, or topic to another.

The Web uses a graphical user interface to deliver content. Until the early 1990s, the Internet had a character-based (nongraphical) user interface. As such, the Internet did not enjoy widespread popularity outside of academia. That changed in November 1993, with the introduction of Mosaic, the first widely adopted browser with a graphical user interface. In 1994, Marc Andreessen, who developed Mosaic at the National Center for Supercomputing Applications at the University of Illinois at Urbana-Champaign, introduced the first commercially available browser, Netscape Navigator. The most popular browsers in use today are Microsoft Internet Explorer, Mozilla Firefox (which is a spin-off of Netscape Navigator), and Apple Safari. Opera is a popular browser used mostly outside the United States.

Tip

Because most authors capitalize the words Internet and Web, do the same when you are writing about these topics.

Exploring Hypertext and Markup

To display a Web page in a browser, the text and graphics on the Web page must be formatted using **Hypertext Markup Language (HTML)**. **Hypertext** is a way to organize information so that you can click links to jump from one piece of information to another. You can then view a document in a nonlinear fashion, viewing only the pages or sections that are of greatest interest to you. Instead of viewing pages from the first page through the last, the way you read a book, you can view topics or pages in any order, according to your preferences. **Markup** refers to the symbols that indicate how the text or images should be displayed in a browser. Although *language* is part of HTML's name, it's not correct to say that HTML is a programming language. Although HTML has syntax—specific rules for the way code should be written—HTML is just a series of instructions for displaying (rendering) text and images on a Web page. The instructions are included as tags. Figure 1-1 shows HTML in its code form, and Figure 1-2 shows the Web page generated by that code.

Sample of HTML code ◄ **Figure 1-1**

tag

comment

heading

subheading

code for displaying an image stored in Bottles.jpg

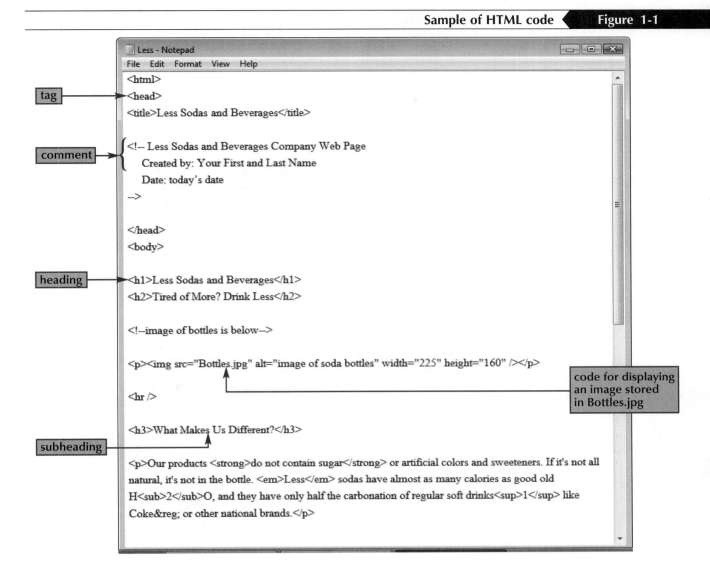

Figure 1-2 | **Resulting Web page as viewed in the browser**

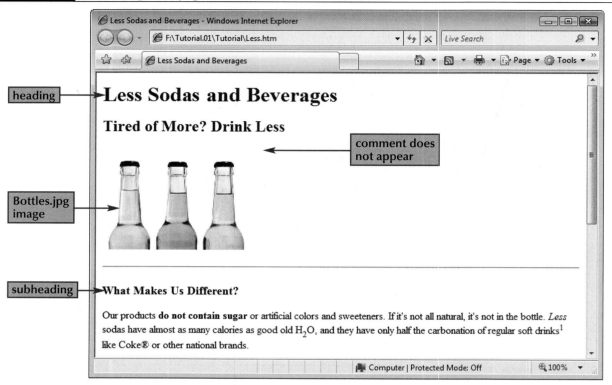

The appearance of a Web page depends on both the HTML code and the Web browser. HTML code has changed since its introduction. New tags have been added, but browsers have generally not kept up with all these changes. Some tags are not displayed at all because a browser usually ignores any code it does not understand. Furthermore, several versions of HTML have been released over the years. The current version of HTML is version 4.01. Future versions and new features for HTML are under development by the **World Wide Web Consortium (W3C)**, the recognized keeper of the HTML standard. The W3C Web site is *www.w3.org*.

| InSight | | **Designing Web Pages for Multiple Browsers** |

One Web browser sometimes displays the same HTML code differently from another Web browser. These differences in rendering a page are called cross-browser incompatibilities. When designing your Web pages, you should always use several browsers to compare how they display the pages. Although you might not be able to achieve identical results in all browsers, your goal should be to display your Web pages properly no matter what browser is being used.

To see an example of how different browsers render the same Web page in different ways, compare the Web pages shown in Figure 1-3.

Comparing a Web page in Mozilla Firefox and Microsoft Internet Explorer   Figure 1-3

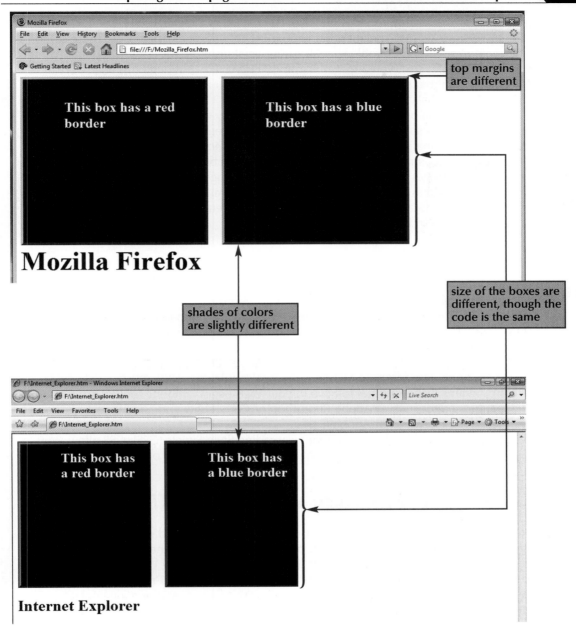

Both browsers shown in Figure 1-3 are displaying the same HTML document. The size of the black text boxes differs, as does the top margin. The colors on the borders of the boxes are also slightly different. On a simple Web page, these discrepancies might not affect the viewer's experience of the Web page, though it might on a more complex Web page. To anticipate how your HTML documents will appear in various browsers, you should be sure to display your Web pages on the browsers your viewers are likely to use.

Introducing XHTML

XHTML is an acronym for **Extensible Hypertext Markup Language**. XHTML 1.1 is the current version. XHTML specifies that code must be written a certain way. These strict rules help to solve some problems with earlier versions of HTML. When you are learning HTML 4.01 in this text, you are also learning XHTML 1.1. Although this text refers to HTML code without specifying a version number, keep in mind that HTML 4.01 and XHTML 1.1 are the same.

A newer version of XHTML, version 2.0, is currently being developed. XHTML 2.0 is still a draft, and as such, is not supported fully by current versions of Web browsers. When the W3C finalizes a draft, it is called a *recommendation*. When the W3C makes XHTML 2.0 a recommendation, you can expect much better browser support for the new features and changes in XHTML 2.0. Many of the changes in XHTML 2.0 require that users migrate (adopt) the new releases of browsers. Similarly, there have also been several versions of Cascading Style Sheets (CSS). The current version, and the one you will be learning about in this text, is version 2.1.

Understanding What HTML Is Not

HTML's sole focus is to uniformly and consistently deliver content. Complex text formatting, composing images, and manipulating data are not strengths or even features of HTML. Fairly simple formatting tasks such as line spacing and tab indents don't exist in HTML, nor do footnotes, headers and footers, and automatic column and table layout.

To compose and edit a Web page, you need a text editor such as Microsoft Notepad or WordPad or HTML-editing software such as Adobe Dreamweaver or Microsoft Expression Web. If you use an Apple Macintosh, you also might use BBEdit as your text editor. Other programs that are useful to have in your Web page-authoring tool kit are a photo and graphics editor such as Adobe Photoshop or Corel Draw and an animation editor such as Adobe Fireworks or Adobe Flash.

Later in this text, you will learn about Cascading Style Sheets (CSS). CSS allows you to format documents in ways that you cannot when you use HTML only.

Creating a Web Page with Basic HTML Tags

Before you start composing a Web page using HTML, you should sketch or design the page freehand or using a software tool. You meet with Andy Chanos and Warren Metzger to discuss their goals for the Less Sodas and Beverages Company Web page. They want to feature their logo and slogan prominently, briefly explain what makes their company different from other beverage manufacturers, list their flavors, and provide contact information. After collaborating with Andy and Warren, you create the sketch shown in Figure 1-4, which you can use as the model for the completed Web page.

Sketch of the Web page for Less Sodas and Beverages | **Figure 1-4**

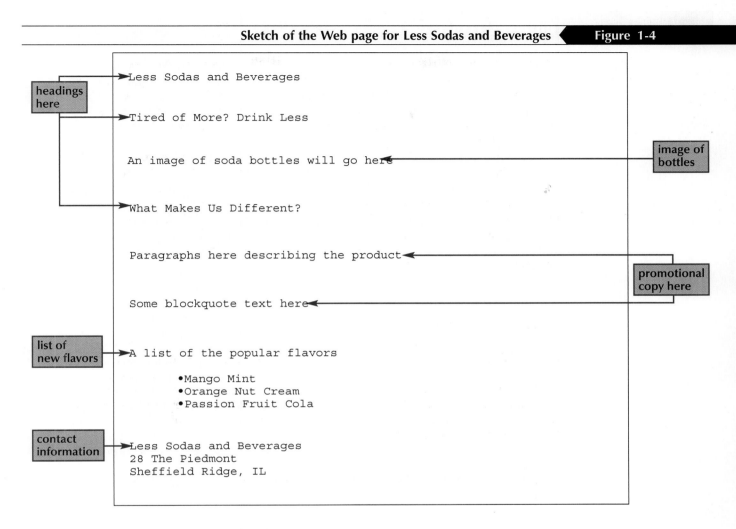

To begin creating this Web page, you distinguish the content—the text and images that appear on the Web page in a browser—from the HTML code. Recall that HTML is composed of formatting codes, more commonly known as tags. Although some tags do not contain formatting instructions and are used only to contain information about a Web page, most tags define how a browser should display text or graphics. Tags begin and end with angle brackets, which surround elements. An element is a structure or a behavior. Elements can be headings, paragraphs, links, tables, or images. Each element type declaration usually has three parts—a start tag, content, and an end tag—in the following format:

```
<start tag>content</end tag>
```

A tag looks like this: <blockquote>. Prior to HTML version 4.01, you could enter code using uppercase or lowercase text, or a mix of the two. HTML 4.01/XHTML 1.1 requires that you enter all of your code in lowercase.

Reference Window | **Entering HTML Tags**

- To enter an element with a start tag and an end tag, use the following format:
  ```
  <tag>content</tag>
  ```
- To enter an empty element, use the following format:
  ```
  content
  <tag />
  ```
- To nest tags, use the following format:
  ```
  <tag1><tag2>content</tag2></tag1>
  ```

Most tags are paired—they include both a start tag and an end tag. End tags are differentiated from start tags by including a forward slash at the beginning of the end tag, as in </blockquote>. It is good coding practice to type the start and end tags first, before entering text or information between the tags, like this: <blockquote> </blockquote>. Typing the tags side by side means you are less likely to accidentally omit the closing tag. It's also easier to notice spelling or coding errors in the tags themselves.

Some elements only describe a behavior. For example, the HTML element <br /> creates a line break and has no content. Because this element, called a line break tag, or break tag, has no content, it is called an **empty element**. Besides having no content, empty elements do not include a corresponding end tag. For example, there is a *single* break tag, and it ends with a space followed by a slash.

Sometimes tags are used together to create more complex formatting. For example, you have used word processing software to create text that is both bold and italic. To produce the same formatting in an HTML document, you nest tags, which means that you use more than one pair of tags at the same time. For example, to make a book title italic, you code the text as follows:

```
<em>Wizard of Oz</em>
```

To make the same title bold, you code the text as follows:

```
<strong>Wizard of Oz</strong>
```

To make text both bold and italic, you code it as follows:

```
<strong><em>Wizard of Oz</em></strong>
```

When nesting tags, the order of the tags does matter. The tags should be a mirror image of themselves. For example, it would be incorrect to write code as follows:

```
<strong><em>Wizard of Oz</strong></em>
```

Setting Up File Storage and Preparing a Text Editor

Recall that you can use a text editor such as Notepad or WordPad to create an HTML document. When you do, you should store all your files in the same storage location, such as a folder on your hard drive. If your Web page uses image files or other types of files, the browser looks for those files in the same folder as where you store the HTML document, unless you specify otherwise. If you store the image file in a different folder and do not specify the path to that folder in your HTML code, the browser displays a placeholder icon instead of the image. For now, it's best to store all the files for a Web page in the same file folder.

You're ready to show Andy how to create a basic Web page for Less Sodas and Beverages. Because you plan to use Notepad as your text editor, you can start by creating a shortcut to Notepad on your desktop so you can open it easily. After opening Notepad, you'll make sure the Word Wrap option is selected so that lines of text wrap instead of continuing until you press the Enter key.

To create a desktop shortcut to Notepad:

▶ **1.** Click the **Start** button 🏁 on the taskbar, point to **All Programs**, and then click **Accessories**. The Accessories folder opens.

▶ **2.** Right-click **Notepad**, point to **Send To** on the shortcut menu, and then click **Desktop (create shortcut)**. A shortcut icon for Notepad appears on the Windows desktop.

▶ **3.** Double-click the **Notepad** shortcut icon on the desktop. The Notepad window opens. Maximize the Notepad window.

▶ **4.** Click **Format** on the menu bar. If the Word Wrap command is not checked, click **Word Wrap**.

▶ **5.** Click in the Notepad document area.

With Notepad open and Word Wrap turned on, you're ready to start creating the HTML document. Before you do, you want to review the tags that appear at the beginning of every HTML document.

Inserting the Beginning HTML Tags

Every HTML document must contain the following tags:

* **<html> tag**: Indicates the HTML language to the browser
* **<head> tag**: Indicates the document's header area
* **<title> tag**: Displays the page's name in the browser's title bar
* **<body> tag**: Contains the page content

Each HTML document begins with the start <html> tag. This tag marks the beginning of an HTML document and is required. It is vital that you code this tag. HTML documents can be converted to other file formats, and the <html> tag acts as a signal that an HTML file should be converted into a different file format. You usually place the start <html> tag alone on the first line of the HTML document.

The start <head> tag follows the start <html> tag, typically on its own line. An HTML document's head area contains code and text that does not appear in the browser. Think of the head area as a container for information about the document. The head area usually contains **metadata**—information about the document itself such as its keywords, the author, and a description of its content. Search engines scan this metadata to determine the content of the page. The head area can also contain JavaScript code.

The <head> tag and its metadata are followed by title tags, which contain the title for the Web page. The title tags are:

```
<title></title>
```

The text between the title tags appears in the title bar of the browser window, so it should be short and accurately describe the content of the page. Although the length of the page title is not limited, it should generally not exceed 70 characters, including spaces; otherwise, some Web search engines might ignore the page. After entering the title, you need to enter the end </title> tag. If you fail to close the title text with a </title> tag, or if you incorrectly code the end title tag, the Web page appears blank. If no other code is entered after the title, then an end </head> tag follows the </title> tag.

The start <body> tag comes next. The start <body> and end </body> tags serve as a container for all of the remaining code, text, and images for your document. Leave a blank line before the start <body> tag to make the code easier to read. This blank line is a form of white space, which is the part of the page that doesn't contain text or other content. You create white space by pressing the Spacebar, the Tab key, or the Enter key to improve the visual appearance of the code and to make it easier to read. However, when you are entering white space in Notepad, you are not creating white space in the resulting Web page. This spacing in Notepad is for readability purposes only. In general, you write most of your code at the left edge of the screen, establishing what is known as an "eye line," which makes it easier to find the HTML code in your document by focusing on only one part of the screen.

The last two tags you must code at the end of every HTML document are the end </body> and the end </html> tags. In summary, every HTML file should include the following tags:

```
<html>
<head>
<title> </title>
</head>

<body>

</body>
</html>
```

As you create an HTML document, you should save it periodically. Save your file with the filename extension of either .htm or html. It's usually a good idea to follow the "eight dot three" filenaming convention, which is to have a filename of up to eight characters followed by the .htm or .html extension. The computers that store the files you see on the Web are called **file servers**. Many file servers use an operating system called UNIX. Unlike Windows, some versions of UNIX limit the size of filenames. As such, it's a good coding practice to limit your filenames to no more than eight characters. Furthermore, do not include spaces or punctuation marks in your filenames, and use only letters and numbers in your filenames. Files stored on a UNIX server should also have the filename extension of *.html*, not .htm. Never save your Notepad files with the filename extension of *.txt*. If you do, you are saving the file as an ASCII text file. Files that have the filename extension of .txt will *not* appear in the browser.

You'll show Andy how to begin creating the Less Sodas and Beverages Web page by entering the required HTML tags in a Notepad document, and then saving the file with an .htm filename extension.

To begin creating an HTML document and then save it:

▶ 1. Make sure you have created your copy of the Data Files and that your computer can access them.

Trouble? If you don't have the starting Data Files, you need to get them before you can proceed. Your instructor will either give you the Data Files or ask you to obtain them from a specified location (such as a network drive). In either case, make a backup copy of the Data Files before you start so that you will have the original files available in case you need to start over. If you have any questions about the Data Files, see your instructor or technical support person for assistance.

▶ 2. In the Notepad window, type the following code, pressing the **Enter** key at the end of each line:

```
<html>
<head>
<title></title>
</head>

<body>

</body>
</html>
```

▶ 3. Click between the start and end title tags, and then type Less Sodas and Beverages as the text to appear in the title bar of the browser window. Proofread your code and correct any errors you find. Your code should look like Figure 1-5.

Initial HTML code ◀ Figure 1-5

```
<html>                          <html> tag indicates that
<head>                          this is an HTML document
<title>Less Sodas and Beverages</title>
</head>
                                                          Web page title
<body>

</body>
</html>

</html> tag indicates
the end of the HTML
document
```

▶ 4. Click **File** on the menu bar, and then click **Save As**. The Save As dialog box opens.

▶ 5. Navigate to the **Tutorial.01\Tutorial** folder. This is the folder in which you will store the HTML document.

Trouble? If you do not know where your Data Files are located, consult with your instructor about where to save your Data Files.

▶ 6. Click the **Save as type** button arrow, and then click **All Files**.

Trouble? If you are using a text editor other than Notepad, use its tools to make sure you are saving the file as an .htm file, not as a .txt file.

▶ 7. Select the text in the File name text box, if necessary, and then type **Less.htm** as the name of the file.

▶ **8.** Click the **Save** button to save the file.

As you create an HTML document, you should save it frequently so you don't lose your work. Now that you have specified a name and location for the file, you can save the document by clicking File on the menu bar and then clicking Save instead of Save As.

Besides saving as you work, you should also add comments to your code as you develop an HTML document. You'll show Andy how to do that next.

Including Comments

Comments provide documentation for your code, explain how the code was written, indicate an unusual or particular circumstance, or otherwise include information to help you or other Web developers understand the code better. You can include comments anywhere in a document, including within the <head> </head> tags or within the <body> </body> tags. Comments do not appear in the browser.

| Reference Window | **Including Comments in an HTML Document** |

- On a new blank line in an HTML document, type the start code for a comment:

  `<!--`
- Type the comment.
- Type the end code for a comment:

  `-->`
- Press the Enter key.

HTML comments use the following syntax:

```
<!-- comment -->
```

The comment itself should explain the purpose of the code and other information. The following comment indicates the placement of an image within an HTML document:

```
<!-- image of bottles appears below -->
```

If you fail to close a comment with the end comment code (--> two hyphens followed by an angle bracket), then it's possible that none of your document will be displayed beyond that comment.

You want Andy to establish the habit of including comments in his code, so you'll show him how to add a comment to the Less.htm document.

To add a comment to the HTML document:

▶ **1.** Click directly after the </title> tag (on the same line) and then press the **Enter** key to insert a new blank line in the document.

▶ **2.** Type the following text, pressing the **Enter** key at the end of each line. Substitute your name and today's date where noted.

```
<!-- Less Sodas and Beverages Company Web Page
     Created by: Your First and Last Name
     Date: today's date
-->
```

▶ **3.** Click **File** on the menu bar, and then click **Save** to save your changes.

▶ **4.** If you are continuing to the next session, keep Notepad open. Otherwise, close Notepad.

So far, the Less.htm file you created can serve as a template for an HTML document, meaning you can use it as the basis for all your Web pages. You only need to change the comment and title text that identifies Less Sodas and Beverages Company to text that fits your current HTML project.

Session 1.1 Quick Check | Review

1. What tag always begins an HTML document?
2. What tags are used to contain data that will not display on the page?
3. Where will text you type between the <title> </title> tags be displayed in a browser?
4. What would happen if you did not code the end </title> tag properly?
5. What two tags serve as a container for all of the text and images on the Web page?
6. What two tags are always coded at the end of an HTML document?
7. What would you code to make the following text into a comment: this is a comment.

Session 1.2

Formatting Text on a Web Page

Although you use HTML to format text for your Web page, HTML is not similar to word processing software. Word processing programs offer many more formatting features than HTML. Don't despair—CSS provides most of the features for your Web pages that you have come to expect from a word processing program. You will begin learning about those features of CSS in the next tutorial. A preliminary overview of the HTML **formatting tags** helps you understand what HTML can achieve in terms of Web page formatting. Now that you have shown Andy how to create an HTML file, you will show him the basic formatting features of HTML.

Using the Heading Tags

Use the **heading tags** to increase the size of text. Text size is measured in points. In typography, 72 points is equal to one vertical inch, and the word *point* is abbreviated as *pt*. HTML has six heading tags: <h1>, <h2>, <h3>, <h4>, <h5>, and <h6>, each of which specifies a certain point size. Each heading tag has a start tag and an end tag, as in the following examples:

```
<h1>Less Sodas and Beverages</h1>
<h2>Tired of More? Drink Less</h2>
```

The heading tags are one of the best means of illustrating the differences between HTML and word processing programs. In a word processing program, you have extensive control over the point size of text. If you like, you can change the point size to 22 pt, 48 pt, 72 pt, or many other point sizes. Unlike a word processing program, however, HTML offers limited flexibility in changing the size of text. In HTML, you only have six sizes of type.

Figure 1-6 shows the six HTML heading tags. Heading size <h1> produces the largest text (24 pt); heading size <h6> produces the smallest text (8 pt), as shown in Figure 1-7. You do not have to use heading sizes in order, and you can repeat the same size heading tags as often as you like.

Figure 1-6	HTML headings as code

```
<html>
<head>
<title>Less Sodas and Beverages</title>
</head>

<body>

<h1>A heading 1 is 24pt</h1>
<h2>A heading 2 is 18pt</h2>
<h3>A heading 3 is 14pt</h3>
<h4>A heading 4 is 12pt</h4>
<h5>A heading 5 is 10pt</h5>
<h6>A heading 6 is 8pt</h6>

</body>
</html>
```

headings decrease in size depending on their level

Figure 1-7	How headings appear in the browser

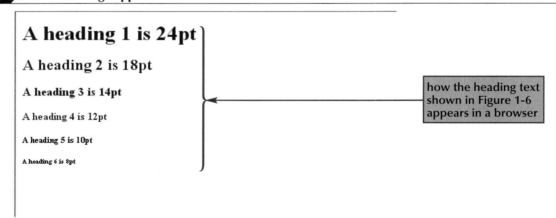

A heading 1 is 24pt

A heading 2 is 18pt

A heading 3 is 14pt

A heading 4 is 12pt

A heading 5 is 10pt

A heading 6 is 8pt

how the heading text shown in Figure 1-6 appears in a browser

Heading tags make text bold, so you don't need to code additional tags that make heading text bold. Headings also create a blank line above and below the heading, so you don't need to code paragraph or break tags either before or after a heading.

Now you can begin adding formatting characteristics to the Web page you are creating for Less Sodas and Beverages. Recall that your plan calls for placing an image at the beginning of the page, so you'll code a comment to remind yourself of where to position the image. You'll show Andy how to perform these tasks in the Less.htm document.

Note that in the remaining figures in this tutorial, the text shown in red is text you should enter into your HTML documents.

To enter the heading tags:

▶ **1.** If necessary, open the **Less.htm** file in Notepad.

▶ **2.** Position the insertion point below the start <body> tag.

▶ **3.** Press the **Enter** key, and then type the following HTML code between the <body> and </body> tags, as shown in red in Figure 1-8.

```
<h1>Less Sodas and Beverages</h1>
<h2>Tired of More? Drink Less</h2>

<!--image of bottles is below-->

<h3>What Makes Us Different?</h3>
```

Code for headings and a comment   ◀   **Figure 1-8**

```
<html>
<head>
<title>Less Sodas and Beverages</title>

<!-- Less Sodas and Beverages Company Web Page
     Created by: Your First and Last Name
     Date: today's date
-->

</head>
<body>

<h1>Less Sodas and Beverages</h1>
<h2>Tired of More? Drink Less</h2>

<!--image of bottles is below-->

<h3>What Makes Us Different?</h3>

</body>
</html>
```

enter the text shown in red

▶ **4.** Save your document.

Now that you've entered some basic content in the Web page for Less Sodas and Beverages, you're ready to view the page in a browser.

Displaying a Web Page in a Browser

As mentioned earlier, you should test your Web pages in more than one browser as you develop the HTML code. Doing so ensures that most or all of your audience can view the page. As you make changes to the HTML document in your text editor, you can open the document in your Web browser to see how it is displayed. Each time you open the document in a browser, you should refresh the page to make sure the browser displays the current version of the file. Each browser provides a Refresh command or Refresh button. In Internet Explorer 7.0, for example, you can press the F5 key or click the Refresh button 🔄 to refresh the page.

Reference Window | **Displaying a Web Page in a Browser**

- Create and save an HTML document.
- Start your Web browser, and then use the browser's tools to open the HTML document.
- After changing the HTML document, open it in the browser again or refresh the page in the browser.

The following steps use Internet Explorer to display the Less.htm Web page, but you can use any other browser as well. You do not need to be connected to the Internet to view the page. Besides saving an HTML document as you work, you should also display it in a Web browser periodically to make sure the code is free of errors such as missing end tags. You'll show Andy how to use a Web browser to display the Web page you created.

To view the Less Sodas and Beverages Company Web page:

▶ **1.** Start Internet Explorer and wait for the home page to appear. Maximize the browser window.

Trouble? If you are using a different Web browser, start that program instead of Internet Explorer.

Trouble? If a dialog box opens explaining you are not connected to the Internet, close the dialog box. You do not need to be connected to the Internet to display an HTML document.

▶ **2.** Open the **Less.htm** file from the Tutorial.01\Tutorial folder containing your Data Files. Your browser displays the Web page, shown in Figure 1-9.

Figure 1-9 ▶ **Headings displayed in the browser**

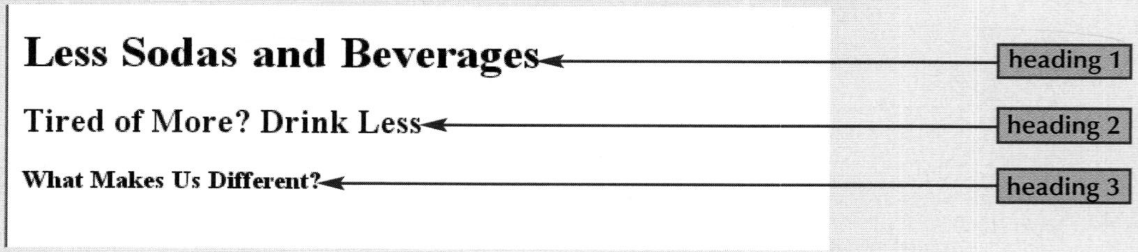

Less Sodas and Beverages ◀———————————————— heading 1

Tired of More? Drink Less ◀———————————————— heading 2

What Makes Us Different? ◀———————————————— heading 3

▶ **3.** Minimize the browser window.

So far, you've created an HTML document that contains the required HTML codes, and then inserted and formatted some content and comments. Next, you'll continue creating the Web page by adding body text, an image, and a list.

Creating Body Text

Now that you have developed an HTML template document and started a Web page by inserting headings, you can customize the Web page by using tags to control the appearance of text. You can do so using paragraph and line break tags.

The paragraph tag is one of two tags that control line endings in an HTML document:

```
<p></p>
```

The start <p> tag precedes each paragraph; the end </p> tag ends each paragraph. Together, the start and end paragraph tags create a blank line between paragraphs when the document is displayed in the browser. As such, the paragraph tags are equivalent to pressing the Enter key twice to create a blank line in a word processing document. You type your paragraph text in Notepad the same way you would if you were typing a word processing document, by letting the text wrap as you type the paragraph. You do not need to press the Enter key at the end of each line unless you intend to end the line before the right margin, as you do when you type the inside address in a letter.

A paragraph typed in Notepad would look like this:

```
<p>Our Orange Nut Cream is a blend of natural orange flavors and real
coconut milk. The resulting combination gives our Orange Nut Cream an
incredibly smooth and rich taste.</p>
```

The line break tag is equivalent to pressing the Enter key once to end a line. Recall that the break tag is an empty element, meaning it has no corresponding end tag and no content. Instead, the break tag ends with the combination of a space and a slash. The break tag looks like this:

```
<br />
```

Code the <br /> tag at the beginning of a line of code, rather than at the end of a line of code. Doing so makes it easier to find where you have coded <br /> tags. Use the <br /> tag when you want to end a line before the right margin without wrapping, such as in a mailing address:

```
<p>Mr. Andy Chanos
<br />4708 N. Washington
<br />Sheffield Ridge, IL 61361</p>
```

At this point, you'll show Andy how to enter text for the body of the document using the paragraph tags.

To enter the body text using paragraph tags:

1. In the Less document, click below the <h3> heading and then press the **Enter** key twice to insert a new blank line.

2. Type the text following text, but do *not* press the **Enter** key until after you type the end </p> tag.

   ```
   <p>Our products do not contain sugar or artificial colors and
   sweeteners. If it's not all natural, it's not in the bottle. Less
   sodas have almost as many calories as good old H2O, and they
   have only half the carbonation of regular soft drinks like Coke or
   other national brands.</p>
   ```

3. Press the **Enter** key to insert a blank line, and then type another paragraph of text, again letting the text wrap just as you would if you were typing a paragraph in a word processing document. Press the **Enter** key after you type the end </p> tag. Figure 1-10 shows all the inserted text in red.

   ```
   <p>Our Orange Nut Cream is a blend of natural orange flavors and
   real coconut milk. The resulting combination gives our Orange
   Nut Cream an incredibly smooth and rich taste.</p>
   ```

Tip

Be sure to save your HTML document before you open the file in your browser.

| Figure 1-10 | Entering body text with paragraph tags |

```
<html>
<head>
<title>Less Sodas and Beverages</title>

<!-- Less Sodas and Beverages Company Web Page
     Created by: Your First and Last Name
     Date: today's date
-->

</head>
<body>

<h1>Less Sodas and Beverages</h1>
<h2>Tired of More? Drink Less</h2>

<!--image of bottles is below-->

<h3>What Makes Us Different?</h3>

<p>Our products do not contain sugar or artificial colors and sweeteners. If it's not all natural,
it's not in the bottle. Less sodas have almost as many calories as good old H2O, and they have only
half the carbonation of regular soft drinks like Coke or other national brands.</p>

<p>Our Orange Nut Cream is a blend of natural orange flavors and real coconut milk. The resulting
combination gives our Orange Nut Cream an incredibly smooth and rich taste.</p>

</body>
</html>
```

body text entered using paragraph tags

▶ **4.** Click **File** on the menu bar, and then click **Save** to save your changes.

▶ **5.** Restore the browser window and then refresh the page. Your document should look as it does in Figure 1-11.

| Figure 1-11 | Web page with paragraph added |

Less Sodas and Beverages

Tired of More? Drink Less

What Makes Us Different?

block-level tags insert space before and after a paragraph

Our products do not contain sugar or artificial colors and sweeteners. If it's not all natural, it's not in the bottle. Less sodas have almost as many calories as good old H2O, and they have only half the carbonation of regular soft drinks like Coke or other national brands.

Our Orange Nut Cream is a blend of natural orange flavors and real coconut milk. The resulting combination gives our Orange Nut Cream an incredibly smooth and rich taste.

| InSight | **Avoiding Redundant Code** |

You can press the Enter key as many times as you like to enter white space in a word processing document. HTML, however, ignores redundant code. Enter a space once after a colon or any mark of terminal punctuation—which is any punctuation mark that ends a sentence—such as the period, the exclamation point, and the question mark. Extra spaces are deleted in the browser, so you don't need to waste effort by typing more than one space after a mark of terminal punctuation. If you enter two spaces after a period in your code, only one space is displayed in the browser.

Paragraph and heading tags are **block-level elements**, which means they automatically create a blank line above and below the text. Block-level elements also provide internal padding (spacing), a border, and an external margin. Later, when you learn about Cascading Style Sheets (CSS), you will use paddings, borders, and margins to improve the appearance of your Web pages.

Inserting Logical and Physical Formatting Tags

Logical tags let the browser determine how to display the text in an HTML document. For example, two of the most common logical tags are <strong> and <em>. The <strong> tag makes text bold; the <em> tag makes text italic. The logical tags are as follows:

```
<strong>do not contain sugar</strong>
<em>Less</em>
```

You can also make text bold using the <b> tag or make text italic using the <i> tag. These are two of the most common physical formatting tags. **Physical tags** emphatically state how text should be displayed; in this instance as either bold or italic text. The following lines show the same text coded with physical tags:

```
<b>do not contain sugar</b>
<i>Less</i>
```

Both the <b> </b> tags and the <strong> </strong> tags make text bold. Similarly, both the <i> </i> tags and the <em> </em> tags make text italic. Which should you use? Most HTML editing programs use the <strong> and the <em> tags. Therefore, because of the widespread preference for these logical tags over the physical tags, use the logical tags <strong> and <em> in all your code, rather than the physical tags <b> and <i>.

Recall that block-level elements automatically create a blank line above and below the tag. Tags that create formatting within a block of text, such as a paragraph, are said to format text *inline*. The <strong> and the <em> tags are examples of inline elements.

Andy wants to emphasize some text in the Less Sodas and Beverages Web page. He'd like to display "do not contain sugar" in bold so people viewing the Web page notice that text immediately. He'd also like to display "Less" in "Less Sodas" so that viewers understand the play on words. You'll show him how to use the <strong> and <em> tags to format this text according to his preferences.

To format text as bold and as italic:

1. In the first paragraph of the Less document, type **<strong>** before the phrase "do not contain sugar." Do not insert a space after the right angle bracket (>).

2. Type **</strong>** after the phrase "do not contain sugar." Do not insert a space before the left angle bracket (<).

3. At the beginning of the third sentence, type **<em>** before "Less" and type **</em>** after "Less." Again, do not insert spaces between the code and content. Figure 1-12 shows the inserted text in red.

   Trouble? If your lines of code do not wrap as shown in Figure 1-12, click Format on the Notepad menu bar, click Word Wrap if that command is not checked. If the Word Wrap command is already checked, click to remove the check mark. Then click Format on the Notepad menu bar, and click Word Wrap again to select it.

Figure 1-12	Entering <strong> and <em> tags

```
<html>
<head>
<title>Less Sodas and Beverages</title>

<!-- Less Sodas and Beverages Company Web Page
     Created by: Your First and Last Name
     Date: today's date
-->

</head>
<body>

<h1>Less Sodas and Beverages</h1>
<h2>Tired of More? Drink Less</h2>

<!--image of bottles is below-->

<h3>What Makes Us Different?</h3>

<p>Our products <strong>do not contain sugar</strong> or artificial colors and sweeteners. If it's
not all natural, it's not in the bottle. <em>Less</em> sodas have almost as many calories as good
old H2O, and they have only half the carbonation of regular soft drinks like Coke or other
national brands.</p>

<p>Our Orange Nut Cream is a blend of natural orange flavors and real coconut milk. The resulting
combination gives our Orange Nut Cream an incredibly smooth and rich taste.</p>

</body>
</html>
```

> text between <strong> tags appears bold in the browser

> text between <em> tags appears italic in the browser

▶ **4.** Check your work, making sure your document matches Figure 1-12, and then save the Less document in your text editor.

▶ **5.** Refresh the Less Sodas and Beverages page in your browser, and then compare it to Figure 1-13.

Figure 1-13	Web page with bold and italic text

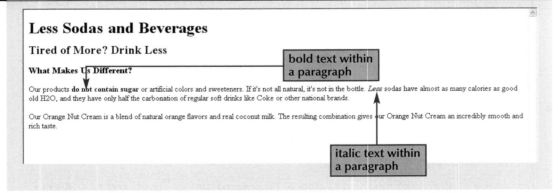

Less Sodas and Beverages

Tired of More? Drink Less

What Makes Us Different?

> bold text within a paragraph

Our products **do not contain sugar** or artificial colors and sweeteners. If it's not all natural, it's not in the bottle. *Less* sodas have almost as many calories as good old H2O, and they have only half the carbonation of regular soft drinks like Coke or other national brands.

Our Orange Nut Cream is a blend of natural orange flavors and real coconut milk. The resulting combination gives our Orange Nut Cream an incredibly smooth and rich taste.

> italic text within a paragraph

The blockquote tags are another type of physical tag. You use the `<blockquote> </blockquote>` tags to establish an indent of about one inch on both the left and the right sides of the page.

Although the tag is named "blockquote," you can use the <blockquote> tag to indent any text—it doesn't have to be quoted text. Also, the <blockquote> tags are block-level elements, so the browser displays a blank line both before and after the blockquote. Another set of tags, the <q> </q> (the quote) tags, are used for inline quotes. However, the quote tags are not yet widely supported by most browsers.

Andy reviews the Less Sodas and Beverages Web page, and decides that he wants to insert another paragraph describing how Less' sodas can be good for you, and he'd like that paragraph to stand out from the rest of the text. To do so, you will show him how to create a blockquote.

To create blockquoted text:

▶ **1.** In the Less document, insert a blank line after the second paragraph you just added. Then type the following HTML code.

```
<blockquote>Think a soft drink can't be good for you? Think again!
<em>Less</em> sodas are enhanced with vitamins and minerals to
fortify you through your busy day. Not only do our sodas and
beverages taste great, they also are a good source of
nutrition.</blockquote>
```

▶ **2.** Press the **Enter** key to end the paragraph. Figure 1-14 shows the inserted text in red.

Code for <blockquote> text   Figure 1-14

```
<h3>What Makes Us Different?</h3>

<p>Our products <strong>do not contain sugar</strong> or artificial colors and sweeteners. If it's
not all natural, it's not in the bottle. <em>Less</em> sodas have almost as many calories as good
old H2O, and they have only half the carbonation of regular soft drinks like Coke or other
national brands.</p>

<p>Our Orange Nut Cream is a blend of natural orange flavors and real coconut milk. The resulting
combination gives our Orange Nut Cream an incredibly smooth and rich taste.</p>

<blockquote>Think a soft drink can't be good for you? Think again! <em>Less</em> sodas are
enhanced with vitamins and minerals to fortify you through your busy day. Not only do our sodas
and beverages taste great, they also are a good source of nutrition.</blockquote>

</body>
</html>
```

<blockquote> tag
to indent the text
in the browser

▶ **3.** Make changes as necessary to match Figure 1-14, and then save the document in your text editor.

▶ **4.** Refresh the Less Sodas and Beverages page in your browser, and then compare it to Figure 1-15.

Figure 1-15 **Block quote displayed in the browser**

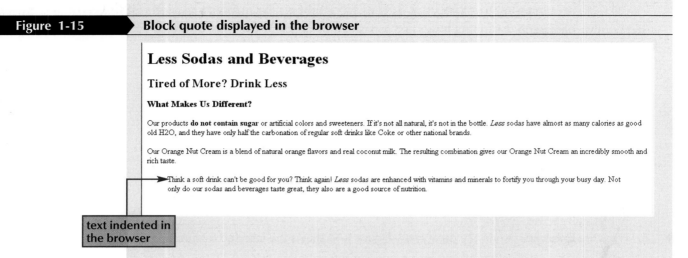

You and Andy examine the Less Sodas and Beverages Web page so far, looking for text that needs to be revised or refined. You notice that "H2O" in the first paragraph should be formatted to display the "2" as a subscript. You also want to insert a registered trademark symbol after "Coke" as well. You'll show Andy how to use special formatting codes to make these types of changes.

Using Special Formatting Codes

As HTML and XHTML evolve from one version to another, they stop using or supporting tags that have proved to be problematic in browsers. They also add codes for special elements such as acronyms, abbreviations, special characters, superscripts, and subscripts. This section describes these formatting codes and explains how to use them.

Identifying Deprecated and Seldom-Used Tags

HTML 4.01/XHTML 1.1 eliminates some of the tags that were used in earlier versions of HTML. A tag that should no longer be used is called a **deprecated tag**. Some of the deprecated tags are <center>, which was used to center text, and <font>, which was used to change the appearance, size, and color of text.

The <u> </u> tags are the underline tags, which underline text. The underline tags are also deprecated—and for good reason. Underlining could be confused with links to a Web site, which are customarily underlined. *Never use the underline tags.* When you want to emphasize text in your Web page, you should substitute italics (emphasized text) for underlining. If you receive a handwritten draft of a Web page from an author who does not know HTML, it might include underlined text. Be sure you substitute that underlining with emphasized text when you code the Web page.

A number of logical formatting tags used to format text in the Courier typeface or to make text italic have been part of HTML since HTML1.0. Although they are seldom used today, you might still encounter them. The <tt> </tt> tags are used to produce text in teletype (a Courier typeface). The teletype tags are deprecated. The tags shown below produce the text shown in Figure 1-16.

```
<code>Code</code>
<dfn>Definition</dfn>
<kbd>Keyboard</kbd>
<samp>Sample</samp>
<var>Variable</var>
```

Seldom-Used HTML logical formatting tags displayed in the browser ◄ Figure 1-16

Code *Definition* Keyboard Sample *Variable*

Using the Acronym and the Abbreviation Tags

An **acronym** is a group of letters that stands for several words. An **abbreviation** is a shortened form of a noun. For example, if you encounter the acronym *CGI* or the abbreviation *pt* in printed text, you might not know the meaning of that acronym or abbreviation. Both the <acronym> </acronym> and the <abbr> </abbr> tags are designed to produce a **ScreenTip** in the browser window. When you use the mouse pointer to point to (or mouse over) the acronym or abbreviated text, a small box containing text on a shaded background (a ScreenTip) is displayed. The ScreenTip text serves to either define or explain the acronym or the abbreviation. In addition, the <acronym> tag displays the acronym on the screen with a dotted line (called a tracer) under the acronym, which helps to draw attention to the acronym. In Internet Explorer versions 6 and earlier, the tracer does not appear. Firefox does display the tracer for both abbreviations and acronyms, shows ScreenTips as black text on a white background, and casts a shadow under the ScreenTip. See the following code examples:

```
<acronym title="Graphical User Interface">GUI</acronym>
<abbr title="The shorthand notation for point">pt</abbr>
```

In the browser, you can point to "GUI" to view "Graphical User Interface" in the ScreenTip. Similarly, you can point to "pt" to view "The shorthand notation for point" in the ScreenTip.

Using the Acronym and Abbreviation Tags | Reference Window

- To display a ScreenTip defining an acronym, use the <acronym> tag with a title attribute, as follows:
    ```
    <acronym title="acronym definition">ACRONYM</acronym>
    ```
- To display a ScreenTip showing the complete form of an abbreviation, use the <abbr> tag with a title attribute, as follows:
    ```
    <abbr title="complete word or phrase">Abbreviation</abbr>
    ```

The <acronym> and <abbr> tags do not format text; however, these tags often appear nested within <em> or <strong> tags. Because the tags serve the same purpose (producing a ScreenTip), the forthcoming XHTML version 2.0 has eliminated the <acronym> tag and kept the <abbr> tag. However, Internet Explorer 6.0 (and earlier versions) do not support the <abbr> tag, but they do support the <acronym> tag.

The text for the <acronym> or the <abbr> tag ScreenTip is coded by using the *title* attribute. An **attribute** defines a change to a tag. Each attribute has (takes) a **value** that describes to what extent or in what manner the tag will be changed. Think of attributes as nouns and values as adjectives.

All values must be enclosed in quotation marks. You code the attribute, an equals sign, and then the value. The following example shows the code for the acronym ASAP and resulting ScreenTip. The attribute is "title" and the attribute's *value* is "As Soon As Possible." Do not insert a space before or after the equals sign, as in the following code:

```
Do you know what <em><acronym title="As Soon As Possible">
ASAP</acronym></em> means?
```

Figure 1-17 shows how the ScreenTip looks in a browser.

Figure 1-17	Acronym and ScreenTip

When you type quotation marks in your HTML code, it's a good coding practice to type both quotation marks first. By doing so, you avoid the mistake of omitting the closing quotation mark.

Now you are ready to show Andy how to insert special characters such as trademark symbols.

Inserting Special Characters

Some characters in HTML cannot be created by using the keyboard. Those characters are called **special characters**. Other characters, such as < > (angle brackets) and the & (ampersand), are reserved for writing code. How do you display these characters in the browser when necessary? You can do so in two ways: by **named entity reference** or by **character reference**. The named entity reference is a combination of symbols, including a suggestion of the name of the character that when typed together, represent a specific character. The named entity reference is preceded by an ampersand and followed by a semicolon. For example, to produce the registered trademark symbol, you enter the following code:

```
&reg;
```

In the browser screen, the registered trademark symbol appears: ®

The character reference refers to the code's position in the ISO (the International Standards Organization) character set. The character number is preceded by the ampersand symbol and the pound symbol, and the reference is followed by a semicolon. To produce the registered trademark symbol using a character reference, you use the following code:

```
&#174;
```

Not all special characters can be coded by using named entity references, but all special characters can be inserted by using character references. For example, the dagger character (†) and the double dagger character (‡) can only be coded by using a character reference.

Figure 1-18 illustrates common named entity references and character references.

Named entity and character references | Figure 1-18

Named Entity Reference	Character Reference	Symbol Displayed in a Browser	Description
&lt;	&#60;	<	Less than or left angle bracket
&gt;	&#62;	>	Greater than or right angle bracket
n/a	&#134;	†	Dagger
n/a	&#135;	‡	Double dagger
&mdash;	&#151;	—	Em dash
&ndash;	&#150;	–	En dash
		(a space)	Space
&copy;	&#169;	©	Copyright
&reg;	&#174;	®	Registered trademark
&middot;	&#183;	•	Round bullet

Andy notices that the word "Coke" should be followed by the registered trademark symbol. In the Less Sodas and Beverages Web page, you'll show him how to insert a special character, the registered trademark symbol, after the word "Coke" in the first paragraph of the page.

To create special characters:

▶ **1.** In the first paragraph of the Less document, position the insertion point directly after the word "Coke," and then type **®** as shown in Figure 1-19.

Code for the registered trademark special character | Figure 1-19

```
<p>Our products <strong>do not contain sugar</strong> or artificial colors and sweeteners. If it's
not all natural, it's not in the bottle. <em>Less</em> sodas have almost as many calories as good
old H2O, and they have only half the carbonation of regular soft drinks like Coke&reg; or other
national brands.</p>
```

registered trademark symbol code

▶ **2.** Save the document in your text editor.

▶ **3.** Refresh the Less Sodas and Beverages Web page in your browser. Figure 1-20 shows the registered trademark symbol as it appears in the browser.

Figure 1-20 **The registered trademark symbol displayed in the browser**

Less Sodas and Beverages

Tired of More? Drink Less

What Makes Us Different?

Our products **do not contain sugar** or artificial colors and sweeteners. If it's not all natural, it's not in the bottle. *Less* sodas have almost as many calories as good old H2O, and they have only half the carbonation of regular soft drinks like Coke® or other national brands.

Our Orange Nut Cream is a blend of natural orange flavors and real coconut milk. The resulting combination gives our Orange Nut Cream an incredibly smooth and rich taste.

Think a soft drink can't be good for you? Think again! *Less* sodas are enhanced with vitamins and minerals to fortify you through your busy day. Not only do our sodas and beverages taste great, they also are a good source of nutrition.

registered trademark
symbol

Creating Superscripts and Subscripts

You use the tags to create a superscript, which raises a character one-half the line of type. Similarly, you use the tags to create a subscript, which lowers a character by one-half the line of type. Superscript and subscript characters are useful when you need to include footnotes, endnotes, and other notations in your Web pages.

Andy wants to create a footnote to follow the word "drinks" in the first paragraph on the Less Sodas and Beverages Web page to qualify his claim that Less' sodas have half the carbonation of regular soft drinks. You code the superscripted number 1 using the codes, then enter the footnote text below the paragraph containing the superscript. You can code the footnote text as a paragraph that includes codes to superscript the number 1 so that people viewing the Web page can find the footnote easily. In addition, you will show Andy how to create a subscript so that the chemical formula for water appears as H_2O.

To create superscripts and subscripts in the Less Sodas and Beverages Web page:

1. In the Less document, click directly before the "2" in H20, type **_{**, click directly after the "2," and then type **}** to subscript the 2.

2. Directly after "drinks" in "regular soft drinks," type **¹** to superscript the 1.

3. Insert a blank link after the first paragraph, and then type the following code:

```
<p><sup>1</sup>When compared to the leading cola-flavored
beverages.</p>
```

Figure 1-21 shows the inserted text in red.

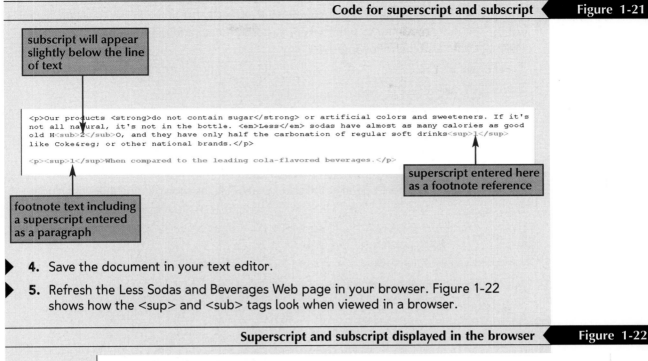

Code for superscript and subscript ◄ Figure 1-21

subscript will appear slightly below the line of text

footnote text including a superscript entered as a paragraph

superscript entered here as a footnote reference

4. Save the document in your text editor.

5. Refresh the Less Sodas and Beverages Web page in your browser. Figure 1-22 shows how the <sup> and <sub> tags look when viewed in a browser.

Superscript and subscript displayed in the browser ◄ Figure 1-22

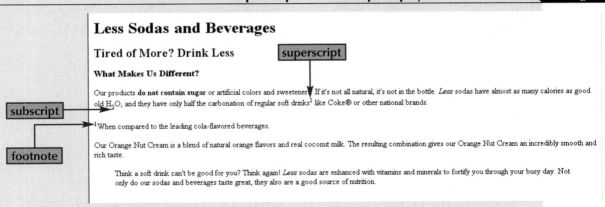

superscript

subscript

footnote

6. If you are continuing to the next session, keep Notepad and your Web browser open. Otherwise, close all open windows.

Tips for Typing HTML Code in a Text Editor

At this point, you have entered much of the code that makes up the basic Web page for Less Sodas and Beverages. The following list contains tips and hints for making your HTML coding error-free.

• **Type all code in lowercase.**

Type your HTML/XHTML code in lowercase. Continue to capitalize the first letter of proper nouns. Filenames may be typed with an initial capital to call attention to a file-name in the code.

• **List codes separately as much as possible.**

With the exception of the <title> </title> tags, don't wrap the tags for an HTML document. You are trying to create an eye line where most of the HTML tags are coded at the left margin. Doing so will make it easier to locate and debug (correct) your HTML code. Use the following style:

```
<html>
<head>
<title>Your Title Goes Here</title>
<head>
```

The following example is poor coding practice:

```
<html><head><title>Your Title Goes Here</title></head>
```

- **Use white space.**

Leave a blank line before and after the start <body> tag, as shown in the following code:

```
</head>

<body>

<p>Here is the first paragraph of the document.</p>
```

Code the paragraph tags as follows, letting the text wrap:

```
<p>Here is the first sentence of the first paragraph. You want to
leave some "breathing room" so that you can easily debug your code.
</p>

<p>Here is another paragraph. Because a blank line was entered
between these paragraphs, it's much easier to see where one paragraph
ends and another begins. In general, your Web page code should
look similar to a typed business letter.</p>
```

When you type a block-level element in a text editor, leave a blank line before and after the block-level element, just as you would if you were typing paragraphs in a letter:

```
<body>

<h1>This Is the Heading</h1>

<p>Here is the first paragraph of text. Note that there is only
one space at the end of each sentence. HTML eliminates extra
space.</p>

<p>Here is the second paragraph of text. Do you notice how this
code includes a blank line between the paragraphs in my code?
Doing so gives the code some "breathing room" and makes the code
much more readable.</p>

<blockquote>Here is the text for the blockquote. Text that has
been blockquoted will be indented about one inch on both the left and
the right.</blockquote>

</body>
</html>
```

At the end of each document, leave a blank line before the </body> and </html> tags, as follows:

```
... the end of the document.</p>

</body>
</html>
```

- **Insert a break code at the beginning of a line, not after it.**

Code your <br /> tags at the start of a line of code, not at the end of a line; code like this:

```
<p>John Doe
<br />28 Smith Street
<br />Santa Fe, CA 30039</p>
```

Rather than this:

```
<p>John Doe<br />
28 Smith Street<br />
Santa Fe, CA 30039</p>
```

- **Enter code between start and end tags.**

Always type your code in a container tag, such as the <p></p> tags or any other of the HTML formatting tags, as follows:

```
<p>This is some paragraph text. This paragraph uses the container
tags for paragraph text, which are the start and end paragraph
tags.</p>
```

The following is an example of poor coding, without tags to contain the paragraph text:

```
This is some paragraph text. This paragraph is not enclosed within
paragraph tags or any other formatting tags.
```

- **Don't use deprecated tags.**

For example, don't use underline tags. If you need to emphasize text or call attention to it, use italics instead and code <em> </em> tags, not <u> </u> tags.

- **Format terminal punctuation properly.**

Insert one space, rather than two, after a colon and space once after any mark of terminal punctuation (the period, the exclamation point, and the question mark). Extra spaces are deleted in the browser.

- **Beware of quotation marks from pasted text.**

If you are cutting/copying and pasting text from a word processing document or another program into Notepad, look to see if any of the copied or pasted text has quotation marks. Notepad only uses straight quotes ("like this") and not curly quotes ("like this"). If your file is still not displayed properly, delete all the quotes from the pasted text and type in straight quotes.

Session 1.2 Quick Check | Review

1. What set of tags display text in the largest size of type?
2. In addition to making text larger or smaller, what else do heading tags do to the appearance of text?
3. What set of logical tags makes text bold?
4. What set of logical tags makes text italic?
5. What set of tags indents text on the left and right by approximately one inch?
6. What does it mean if a tag is deprecated?
7. What is a special character?

Session 1.3

Using Images on a Web Page

In the early days of the Web, many, if not most, Web pages were text only. Even with text-only pages, transmission speeds were very slow. Because pages took a long time to download, Web page authors used very few images. With the greater use of high-speed broadband transmission, today it is quite common to display many images on a Web page. Images are a great way to add variety and interest to your Web pages; however, using too many images can be distracting and even make the page look amateurish. In a later tutorial, you will learn how to use thumbnail images, which are small images that link to a page that displays a larger version of the same image

Understanding Image Files and File Types

Most images used on the Web today are either drawings, such as clip art, and photos. Clip art and photos are typically stored in two different types of files. Clip-art drawings are in a **GIF** (**Graphics Image Format**) file format—in other words, files with a .gif extension. *GIF* is pronounced (most often) with a hard *g* sound, although some people do pronounce it as *jiff*. GIF was originally devised by AOL/CompuServe. A GIF file renders (displays) line drawings and other images on your Web page. The images are generally simple and not as clear and sharp as a photograph because their file size is **compressed**, which means that the image file is reduced to a much smaller file size. Although the image loses some detail and clarity, the image is faster to download.

Photos are usually stored in a **JPG**—or **JPEG**—(**Joint Photographic Experts Group)** file format—in other words, files with a .jpg extension. JPG is pronounced *jay peg*.

A newer image file format is PNG (pronounced *ping*), which is the Portable Network Graphics format, a file format the W3C chose for its superior compression to replace .gif files. Bitmap files, which have the .bmp filename extension, are standard Windows graphics files. In general, avoid using bitmap files because they tend to be much larger than other file formats and therefore take a longer time to download.

Acquiring Images

Because using images affects the overall file size and download time, you need to be judicious in your use of images. If the image will enhance the appearance of the page or convey useful information, then include the image. Displaying a page that is composed mostly of images and very little text is considered amateurish and should be avoided. On the other hand, a page that has text only also is not desirable because it doesn't have very much visual interest.

There are plenty of places to obtain images for use on your Web pages. Many Web sites offer free clip art and photographs in .gif and .jpg file formats. You can also buy images and clip art on CDs or DVDs, or obtain images as part of an Office suite, such as Microsoft Office or image-editing software such as Adobe Photoshop. You can also use your digital camera or your cell phone as sources to capture images.

If you find an image on a Web page that you want to use, make sure you have permission to use the image yourself—you might otherwise be violating United States copyright law. If you purchase an image and the rights to duplicate it, or if an image is specifically marked "free of copyright" or "in the public domain," you can copy an image from the Web directly from a Web page.

| Reference Window

Copying an Image from a Web Page

- On a Web page, right-click the image you want to copy, and then click Save Picture As (or a similar command) on the shortcut menu.
- Change the filename—but not the extension—if necessary.
- Navigate to where you want to save the image file, and then click the Save button.

Using the Image Tag

You use the **image tag** <img> to insert an image on a Web page. Like the <br /> tag, which was discussed earlier, the <img> tag is an empty tag, not a paired tag, so it must end with the "space slash" combination, as in <img />.

For now, you should precede and follow the <img /> tag with a set of paragraph tags, which aligns the image at the left margin in the browser window. In a later tutorial, you will learn how to position an image anywhere on the Web page.

The <img> tag uses several attributes. It always includes the *src attribute*, the source attribute. The value of the source attribute is the name of the image file that should appear in the Web page. Values must always be preceded by an opening quote and followed by a closing quote. For example, the following code displays the image contained in the Bottles.jpg file:

```
<p><img src="Bottles.jpg"
```

The order of the attributes and values does not matter; however, it's a good coding practice to always list the src attribute and its value first.

Another attribute used with images is the *alt* attribute, which gives a brief description of the image. The words associated with the alt attribute appear before the image downloads. Also, when you point to the image, the alternative text appears. It is a good idea to always use the alt attribute with an image, even though doing so is not required. Vision-impaired users who surf the Web using site reader software hear the alternative text that describes the image. In addition, some users do not have a GUI browser, and others with slow Web connections might disable the display of images in order to speed up download times. The alternative text should be brief, but descriptive, as in the following example:

```
<p><img src="Bottles.jpg" alt="image of soda bottles"
```

If the browser can't load the image file specified in the image tag, the **placeholder icon** appears in place of the image. The placeholder icon indicates that an image should appear in its place. The alternative text also appears next to the placeholder icon. See Figure 1-23.

Tip

Be sure to include the end quote after the alt text. If you do not, the browser considers all text that follows as part of the alt text and does not display your document past that point.

Placeholder icon and alternative text in the browser   **Figure 1-23**

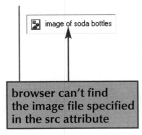

browser can't find
the image file specified
in the src attribute

If you see the placeholder icon instead of an image when viewing your Web page in a browser, check your source code to make sure you typed the tag and the associated HTML code correctly. Be particularly mindful of images that have the numbers 0 and 1 in their filenames—they might be the letters *O* and *I*. Also check the image tag code; a common error is to type <img *scr*> instead of <img src>. Additionally, check to make sure that the file type is correct. If you coded <img src="Bottles.jpg"> and the file actually is a .gif file, the placeholder icon appears because even though you have the correct filename, the file type is incorrect. Finally, confirm that the image file and the HTML file are in the same storage location.

Creating a Folder for Images

If your Web site involves fewer than 10 pages, you should store the .htm files and image files in the same folder. For sites greater than 10 pages, it's a good idea to create a separate folder (usually named "images") in which to store your images. If you have saved the image file in a different storage location than the HTML file, you must specify the path to the image, as follows:

```
<p><img src="/images/beverages/containers/
Bottles.jpg" alt="image of soda bottles" />
```

Using the Width and the Height Attributes

You use the **width** and **height attributes** to scale an image—to change either the width or the height of the image as it appears on a Web page. You can increase or decrease the height or the width of the image in pixels.

Generally, the width of the entire screen is about 640 pixels and the height of the entire screen is 480 pixels. However, most users have their browser window set to display a screen size (a resolution) of at least 800 x 600 pixels and perhaps as many as 1024 x 768 pixels. You can determine the width and the height of an image by using Microsoft Paint or any other image-editing software.

You must use caution in scaling an image because if you enlarge the image too much, it might look grainy and distorted on the screen. To be safe, always scale an image to be smaller, not larger. Also be aware of an image's **aspect ratio**, which is the relationship between the width and the height. If you scale the image by reducing the height *only* or the width *only*, the image becomes distorted. If the original image is 400 x 200 pixels for example, you could scale the image to be 200 x 100 pixels (half its original height and half its original width). Specifying a width and height for the image makes the image download faster. If you omit the width and height attributes, the image generally scales to its original size, which may not be desirable, especially if the image is quite large. You could code the width and height attributes as in the following example:

```
<p><img src="Bottles.jpg" alt="image of soda bottles" width="225"
height="160"
```

Finally, close the image with the space slash combination and follow the image with an end </p> tag, as in the following example:

```
<p><img src="Bottles.jpg" alt="image of soda bottles" width="225"
height="160" /></p>
```

You are now ready to insert an image into the Less Sodas and Beverages Web page. Confirm that the image file Bottles.jpg is stored in the same folder in which you have saved the Less.htm file.

Tip

Although Windows and other operating systems use the backslash (\) to specify the path to a file, HTML code uses only forward slashes (/).

To add a scaled image with alternative text to your Web page:

▶ **1.** If necessary, open the Less.htm file in Notepad or another text editor.

▶ **2.** In the Less document, insert a blank line after the <--image of bottles is below--> comment, and then type the following code, which is also shown in red in Figure 1-24.

```
<p><img src="Bottles.jpg" alt="image of soda bottles" width="225"
height="160" /></p>
```

Code for inserting the Bottles.jpg image ◀ **Figure 1-24**

```
<!--image of bottles is below-->

<p><img src="Bottles.jpg" alt="image of soda bottles" width="225" height="160" /></p>

<h3>What Makes Us Different?</h3>
```

| complete filename | alt text | width and height attributes | space and slash to end the tag |

▶ **3.** Save the document in your text editor.

▶ **4.** If necessary, open the Less document in the browser or refresh the Web page. The page should look like Figure 1-25.

Document with a scaled image ◀ **Figure 1-25**

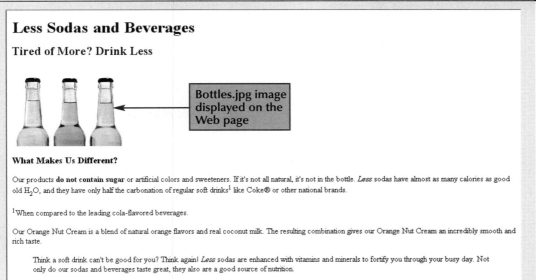

Less Sodas and Beverages

Tired of More? Drink Less

Bottles.jpg image displayed on the Web page

What Makes Us Different?

Our products **do not contain sugar** or artificial colors and sweeteners. If it's not all natural, it's not in the bottle. *Less* sodas have almost as many calories as good old H_2O, and they have only half the carbonation of regular soft drinks[1] like Coke® or other national brands.

[1]When compared to the leading cola-flavored beverages.

Our Orange Nut Cream is a blend of natural orange flavors and real coconut milk. The resulting combination gives our Orange Nut Cream an incredibly smooth and rich taste.

Think a soft drink can't be good for you? Think again! *Less* sodas are enhanced with vitamins and minerals to fortify you through your busy day. Not only do our sodas and beverages taste great, they also are a good source of nutrition.

Looking over the Web page, Andy decides he'd like to include a horizontal line below the image of the bottles to divide the page into two parts. You'll show him how to insert a line, or rule, next.

Creating Horizontal Rules

Horizontal rules are lines that are used to visually divide a page into sections. The tag to create a horizontal rule is:

```
<hr />
```

The <hr /> tag is the only tag needed to display a horizontal rule. The <hr /> tag is an empty element, so it is followed by the space slash combination. By default, horizontal rules are displayed from the left edge to the right edge of the window, are centered, are 2 pixels in height, and are gray or silver, depending on your browser.

Horizontal rules help organize a Web page, dividing the page into areas with similar content. You'll show Andy how to add a horizontal rule to the Less Sodas and Beverages page in the next set of steps.

To add a horizontal rule to the document:

▶ 1. In the Less document, insert a blank line after the image code you entered in the previous steps.

▶ 2. Type **<hr />** and then press the **Enter** key.

▶ 3. Save the document in your text editor.

▶ 4. Refresh the Web page in the browser to display the updated Less.htm file. The page should look like Figure 1-26.

Figure 1-26 | **Horizontal rule below the image**

Less Sodas and Beverages

Tired of More? Drink Less

horizontal rule displayed on the Web page

What Makes Us Different?

Our products **do not contain sugar** or artificial colors and sweeteners. If it's not all natural, it's not in the bottle. *Less* sodas have almost as many calories as good old H_2O, and they have only half the carbonation of regular soft drinks[1] like Coke® or other national brands.

[1]When compared to the leading cola-flavored beverages.

Our Orange Nut Cream is a blend of natural orange flavors and real coconut milk. The resulting combination gives our Orange Nut Cream an incredibly smooth and rich taste.

Think a soft drink can't be good for you? Think again! *Less* sodas are enhanced with vitamins and minerals to fortify you through your busy day. Not only do our sodas and beverages taste great, they also are a good source of nutrition.

Web page designers also often want to display lists on their pages. You'll explore how to create bulleted and numbered lists next.

Creating Unordered and Ordered Lists

You can use HTML to create **unordered lists** (a bulleted list) and **ordered lists** (lists with numbers or letters). A third type of HTML list, the definition list, isn't really a type of list; you usually use it to create a hanging indent. You will learn about definition lists in a later tutorial.

Inserting Unordered (Bulleted) Lists

Use an unordered list when the items in a list have no order of importance and do not need to appear in sequence. For example:

- Banana
- Orange

You begin the unordered list with the start <ul> tag. On separate lines, you include each list item, which is preceded by the <li> start tag and followed by the </li> end tag, as in the following example:

```
<ul>
 <li>Mango Mint</li>
 <li>Orange Nut Cream</li>
 <li>Passion Fruit Cola</li>
```

At the end of the list, you code the </ul> end tag:

```
<ul>
 <li>Mango Mint</li>
 <li>Orange Nut Cream</li>
 <li>Passion Fruit Cola</li>
</ul>
```

Note the list items are indented in the code. Indenting your HTML code has no effect on its appearance in the browser, but it is a good idea to indent the list items because it makes the code easier to read.

Creating Ordered Lists

Use an ordered list when the items in a list have a particular order of importance or should appear in sequence. An ordered list would look as follows:

1. Preheat oven to 450 degrees.
2. Bake for 30 minutes.

You begin the ordered list with the <ol> start tag. As in an unordered list, each list item in the list is preceded by the <li> start tag and followed by the </li> end tag. At the end of the list, you code the </ol> end tag. The code for an ordered list would look like this:

```
<ol>
 <li>Preheat oven to 450 degrees</li>
 <li>Bake for 30 minutes</li>
</ol>
```

Ordered lists can appear as Arabic numbers (1, 2, 3, etc., which is the default), Roman numerals, or uppercase or lowercase letters. You will learn how to change the list style type in a later tutorial.

Lists are block-level elements. The <ol> and <ul> start tags create a blank line before a list. Their corresponding end tags, </ol> and </ul>, create a blank line after a list.

Andy wants to list the most recent and popular flavors that Less Sodas and Beverages offers. You'll show him how to add a list to the Less document. First, you'll insert an <h3> heading to introduce the list, code the list of soda flavors, and then follow the list with a horizontal rule.

To add an <h3> heading, an unordered list, and another horizontal rule:

▶ **1.** In the Less document, insert a blank line after the <blockquote> code.

▶ **2.** Type the following code, which is also shown in red in Figure 1-27.

```
<h3>Some of Our More Popular Flavors</h3>
<ul>
 <li>Mango Mint</li>
 <li>Orange Nut Cream</li>
 <li>Passion Fruit Cola</li>
</ul>
<hr />
```

Figure 1-27	Code for the unordered list

```
<blockquote>Think a soft drink can't be good for you? Think again! <em>Less</em> sodas are
enhanced with vitamins and minerals to fortify you through your busy day. Not only do our sodas
and beverages taste great, they also are a good source of nutrition.</blockquote>

<h3>Some of Our More Popular Flavors</h3>
<ul>
 <li>Mango Mint</li>
 <li>Orange Nut Cream</li>
 <li>Passion Fruit Cola</li>
</ul>
<hr />
```

items in the bulleted list

▶ **3.** Save the document in your text editor.

▶ **4.** Refresh the Web page in the browser. It should look similar to Figure 1-28.

Figure 1-28	Unordered list in the browser

What Makes Us Different?

Our products **do not contain sugar** or artificial colors and sweeteners. If it's not all natural, it's not in the bottle. *Less* sodas have almost as many calories as good old H_2O, and they have only half the carbonation of regular soft drinks[1] like Coke® or other national brands.

[1]When compared to the leading cola-flavored beverages.

Our Orange Nut Cream is a blend of natural orange flavors and real coconut milk. The resulting combination gives our Orange Nut Cream an incredibly smooth and rich taste.

> Think a soft drink can't be good for you? Think again! *Less* sodas are enhanced with vitamins and minerals to fortify you through your busy day. Not only do our sodas and beverages taste great, they also are a good source of nutrition.

Some of Our More Popular Flavors

- Mango Mint
- Orange Nut Cream
- Passion Fruit Cola

soda flavors appear in a bulleted list

Another special kind of text you can add to a Web page is a mailing or e-mail address. You'll learn how to code an address next.

Using the Address Tags

You use the <address> </address> tags to produce italicized text. Although the <address> tag is a not block-level element, it generates a new line, so you should always code the <address> tag as a separate line. By convention, the <address> </address> tags are used at the bottom of the home page to italicize contact information or the e-mail link used to send comments to the Webmaster, the person in charge of the Web site.

Andy would like to display the mailing address for Less Sodas and Beverages at the bottom of the document. You will show him how to do so now. To create line breaks in the address, you will use the <br /> tag.

To add a mailing address to the document:

▶ **1.** In the Less document, insert a new blank line above the </body> tag at the end of the document.

▶ **2.** Type the following code, which is also shown in red in Figure 1-29.

```
<address>Less Sodas and Beverages
<br />28 The Piedmont
<br />Sheffield Ridge, IL
</address>
```

Code for the address ◀ Figure 1-29

```
<h3>Some of Our More Popular Flavors</h3>
<ul>
  <li>Mango Mint</li>
  <li>Orange Nut Cream</li>
  <li>Passion Fruit Cola</li>
</ul>
<hr />

<address>Less Sodas and Beverages
<br />28 The Piedmont
<br />Sheffield Ridge, IL
</address>

</body>
</html>
```

address inserted at the end of the document

▶ **3.** Save the document in your text editor.

▶ **4.** Refresh the page in the browser. It should look like Figure 1-30.

Address text in the browser ◀ Figure 1-30

Some of Our More Popular Flavors

- Mango Mint
- Orange Nut Cream
- Passion Fruit Cola

Less Sodas and Beverages
28 The Piedmont
Sheffield Ridge, IL

italicized address inserted with <address> and <br /> codes

Figure 1-31 shows the final Web page for Less Sodas and Beverages.

Figure 1-31	Completed Web page for Less Sodas and Beverages

Less Sodas and Beverages

Tired of More? Drink Less

What Makes Us Different?

Our products **do not contain sugar** or artificial colors and sweeteners. If it's not all natural, it's not in the bottle. *Less* sodas have almost as many calories as good old H_2O, and they have only half the carbonation of regular soft drinks[1] like Coke® or other national brands.

[1]When compared to the leading cola-flavored beverages.

Our Orange Nut Cream is a blend of natural orange flavors and real coconut milk. The resulting combination gives our Orange Nut Cream an incredibly smooth and rich taste.

Think a soft drink can't be good for you? Think again! *Less* sodas are enhanced with vitamins and minerals to fortify you through your busy day. Not only do our sodas and beverages taste great, they also are a good source of nutrition.

Some of Our More Popular Flavors

- Mango Mint
- Orange Nut Cream
- Passion Fruit Cola

Less Sodas and Beverages
28 The Piedmont
Sheffield Ridge, IL

5. Close all open windows.

As mentioned earlier, the text you include in the head section of an HTML document is used by search engines. You'll learn how to help search engines include your Web page in their search results next.

Working with Search Engines

One of the most useful aspects of the Web is the ability to find Web pages on any topic. By entering one or more keywords, you can find Web pages that contain or are otherwise associated with those keywords. Tags embedded within HTML documents help search engines find the data you are seeking.

Coding Meta Tags

When you view the source code for an HTML page, you often see one or more <meta> tags within the <head> </head> tags. One use of <meta> tags is that they can help **search engines**, such as Google, find your site on the Web based on the keywords you have coded within the <meta> tags on the home page. The <meta> tag is an empty tag, and as such, needs to end with the space slash combination.

The <meta> tag uses several attributes and values. The *name* attribute is used with the *content* attribute. The name attribute uses several values, such as *keywords*. The keywords are those words that best identify the content of your site, so choose words that are most commonly found on your Web pages. Also include common misspellings and a variety of capitalization options to anticipate how users might enter the keywords. You can list the keywords on one line or on several lines, as shown in the following example:

```
<meta name="keywords" content="soda, beverages, refreshments, drinks, fruit,
Less, Lesss, Les" />
```

Other values for the name attribute that you might see are *generator*, which identifies the program used to generate the HTML code, and *author*, which identifies who authored the Web page. The following code uses the generator and author values for the name attribute:

```
<meta name="generator" content="Notepad" />
<meta name="author" content="John Smith" />
```

The *description* and its content value are what appears when a browser generates the list of hits for a particular search topic. The description content is coded as follows:

```
<meta name="description" content="This is the home page for Less Sodas and
Beverages, the maker of refreshing, more healthful drinks for the whole family." />
```

Just as you should know what to include in your HTML documents, it is equally important to know what to avoid when writing HTML code. The following list helps you avoid some programming pitfalls.

- Save your file in Notepad and preview the file in the browser frequently. Don't wait until you've coded an entire Web page before you view the page in the browser. If you save your file and preview it in the browser often, you will catch errors where they occur, and you won't have to debug an entire page of code at a time.
- Make sure that you save your file with the file extension of .htm or .html. If you save your file with the file name extension of .txt, the file will not be displayed in the browser.
- Proofread your code and content carefully. Check for typographical errors and misspellings. A Web page should be error free.
- Check for syntax errors. Are any angle brackets missing? Are any quotation marks missing? Are any end tags missing?
- If your document does not appear in the browser at all, check to see that you have included important end tags such as </title> and </head>. Also check those end tags for syntax and typographical errors. For example, <title /> and </hhead> are typical errors.
- If part of your document does not appear in the browser, check to see if you are missing the end comment code: - -> at the point where the text or images stop displaying in the browser.
- If some text appears unusually large, check to see whether you have failed to code end heading tags or have coded an end heading tag incorrectly. Make sure the headings match. For example, if you coded a start <h2> tag, the line must end with the end </h2> tag, not a different heading tag (e.g., </h3>).
- If your Web page does not appear as you intended in the browser, convert a line of code in the document to a comment (a technique known as "commenting out" the code) to see what effect hiding that code has on the document when viewed in the browser. Insert a start comment tag before the code you are trying to debug and insert an end comment tag after that code. Commenting out code is a good way to isolate an area where there might be an error in the code.

Receiving an HTML File as an E-Mail Attachment

If you receive an HTML file as an e-mail attachment, save the attached file locally to your hard drive, desktop, or flash drive, then open the file in Notepad and view the source code. If you open an attached HTML file in the browser and then save the file by choosing File/Save As *in the browser,* the source code will become corrupt. Compare the original code below with the corrupted code:

Original code:

```
<html>
<head>
<title>What Happened Here?</title>
</head>

<body>

<p>This is an example of a document that was opened as an e-mail
attachment. The reader opened the file, and saved the file by
choosing File/Save in the browser, rather than saving the file locally.
As such, the code has become corrupt.</p>

</body>
</html>
```

Corrupted code:

```
<!DOCTYPE HTML PUBLIC "-//W3C//DTD HTML 4.0 Transitional//EN">

<!-- saved from url=(0141)https://mail3.it.farmingdale.edu/exchange/
inbox/attachment.EML/corrupt.htm/C58EA28C-18C0-4a97-9AF2-036E93DDAFB3/
corrupt.htm?attach=1 -->

<HTML><HEAD><TITLE>What Happened Here?</TITLE>

<META http-equiv=Content-Type content="text/html; charset=iso-8859-1">

<META content="MSHTML 6.00.2900.2180" name=GENERATOR></HEAD>

<BODY>

<P>This is an example of a document that was opened as an
e-mail attachment. The reader opened the file, and saved the file by
choosing File/Save in the browser, rather than saving the file locally.
As such, the code has become
corrupt.</P></BODY></HTML>
```

Session 1.3 Quick Check | Review

1. What attribute must always be used with the image tag?
2. What does it mean to scale an image?
3. What attributes are used to scale an image?
4. What code is used to create a horizontal rule?
5. What are the two types of lists discussed in this chapter?
6. What tags are used to create an area identifying an address?

Tutorial Summary | Review

In this tutorial, you learned about how the Internet and Web work. You were introduced to the concept of tags and how they work in pairs. You learned about the basic HTML tags included in every Web page, along with tags used to format the appearance of text in Web pages. You also learned about tag attributes that can further customize a page's appearance. You learned how to include images on Web pages using the <img> tags. Finally, you learned how to use tags to include horizontal rules, ordered lists, unordered lists, and metadata in your HTML documents.

Key Terms

abbreviation
acronym
aspect ratio
attribute
block-level element
character reference
compressed
deprecated tag
element
element type declaration
empty element
Extensible Hypertext Markup
   Language (XHTML)
file server
formatting tag

Graphics Interchange
   Format (GIF)
heading tag
height attribute
horizontal rule
hypertext
Hypertext Markup
   Language (HTML)
image tag
Internet
Joint Photographic Experts
   Group (JPG or JPEG)
logical tag
markup
metadata

named entity reference
ordered list
physical tag
placeholder icon
scaling
ScreenTip
search engine
special character
unordered list
value
Web browser
width attribute
World Wide Web (Web)
World Wide Web
   Consortium (W3C)

Practice | **Review Assignments**

Take time to practice the skills you learned in the tutorial using the same case scenario.

Data File needed for the Review Assignments: Listing.htm

Warren Metzger, Andy's partner at Less Sodas and Beverages, reviewed the basic Web page you helped Andy create and asks you to revise a different Web page at the Less Sodas and Beverages site. He wants you to add metadata to the head section so that search engines can index this page. In the body of the text, he'd like you to add an acronym and its accompanying ScreenTip. He also thinks the ordered list should be changed to a numbered list. Finally, Warren wants to display a copyright notice at the bottom of the page. Complete the following steps:

1. Use Notepad (or another text editor) to open the file named **Listing.htm** provided in your Tutorial.01\Review folder.
2. Save the file in the same location with the name **ListingNew.htm**.
3. In the <head> </head> section, type the following metadata for the document:

   ```
   <meta name="keywords" content="soda, beverages, soft drinks, cola,
   mango, coconut" />

   <meta name="author" content="Your First Name Your Last Name" />

   <meta name="description" content="This is the home page for Less
   Sodas and Beverages, the healthy alternative to other soft
   drinks." />
   ```
4. Change the unordered list to an ordered list by deleting the <ul> </ul> tags and replacing them with <ol> </ol> tags.
5. Leave a blank line after the last paragraph, and then type the following code to add a line with an acronym:

   ```
   <p>All our products are packaged with our <acronym
   title="Nutritional Information Label">NIL</acronym> easy-to-
   read label.</p>
   ```
6. On a blank line before the </body> tag, type the following code to add an <h5> heading and a special character:

   ```
   <h5>&copy;2010</h5>
   ```
7. Save your HTML document, and then open **ListingNew** in your browser. The document should be similar to the one shown in Figure 1-32.

Figure 1-32

Why People Choose Less Over Other Soft Drinks and Beverages

It's a fact; in blind taste tests, people choose *Less* by a margin of 3:1 over other soft drinks. Here are the top 10 reasons (in order) why people want *Less* in their lives.

1. *Less* just tastes better.
2. *Less* has fewer calories than other soft drinks.
3. *Less* uses ingredients that are all natural; nothing artificial is ever used.
4. People enjoy the light, refreshing carbonation of *Less* products.
5. *Less* has such a variety of flavors that are not available with most other brands.
6. *Less* costs a little more, but people feel it's worth it.
7. Parents like *Less* because it's a more healthful drink than the national brand soft drinks.
8. Everyone loves *Less*!
9. *Less* comes in a four-pack as well as an eight-pack.
10. People love our commercials.

People didn't often mention our bottle design or our easy-to-read informational bottle labels, but we love our consumer-friendly bottle, too. *Less* has NIL.

All our products are packaged with our NIL easy-to-read label.

©2010

8. Point to the acronym. The ScreenTip should show the acronym's definition.
9. Close all open windows.

10. Submit the results of the preceding steps to your instructor, either in printed or electronic form, as requested.

Apply | **Case Problem 1**

Use the skills you learned in the tutorial to update a basic Web page for an insurance company.

Data File needed for this Case Problem: Gwynn.htm

Gwynn & Gwynn Insurance Company John and Mary Gwynn recently decided to embark on a business of their own. John has devoted most of his professional life to insurance, while Mary has been working for the last 10 years as a financial planner. Together, they hope to offer a range of financial services that will appeal to many people in the Santa Ruis Valley in California, where they live. John and Mary have asked you to set up a Web site for them highlighting the services they offer. Complete the following:

1. Use Notepad or another text editor to open the file named **Gwynn.htm** provided with your Data Files in the Tutorial.01\Case1 folder.

2. Save the file in the same location with the name **GwynnNew.htm**.

3. Within the <title> </title> tags, type the following code:

   `Gwynn & Gwynn Insurance`

4. In the <body> section, format "The Gwynn & Gwynn Insurance Company" as an <h1> heading.

5. Below the <h1> heading, insert a horizontal rule.

6. Format the words "Let Us Insure You" and "Let Us Reassure You" as <h3> headings.

7. Insert <p> and </p> tags to format the text after the <h3> heading from "Need your taxes done?" to "not years from now." as paragraph text. Also format the text starting with "No one else" and ending with "financial means." as paragraph text.

8. Format the words "We Offer" as an <h4> heading.

9. Format the next three lines as an unordered list.

10. Format the line that begins "Remember our motto" as an <h4> heading.

11. Format the last four lines of text as an address. Make sure that each line of the address will be displayed in the browser on its own line.

12. Save your HTML document, and then open **GwynnNew** in your browser. The document should be similar to the one shown in Figure 1-33.

Figure 1-33

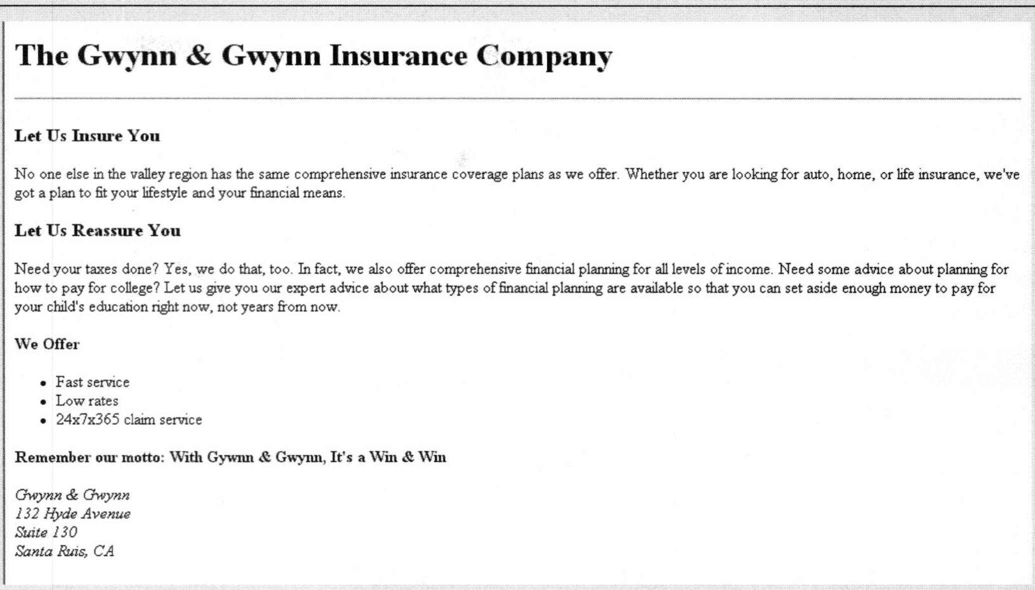

The Gwynn & Gwynn Insurance Company

Let Us Insure You

No one else in the valley region has the same comprehensive insurance coverage plans as we offer. Whether you are looking for auto, home, or life insurance, we've got a plan to fit your lifestyle and your financial means.

Let Us Reassure You

Need your taxes done? Yes, we do that, too. In fact, we also offer comprehensive financial planning for all levels of income. Need some advice about planning for how to pay for college? Let us give you our expert advice about what types of financial planning are available so that you can set aside enough money to pay for your child's education right now, not years from now.

We Offer

- Fast service
- Low rates
- 24x7x365 claim service

Remember our motto: With Gywnn & Gwynn, It's a Win & Win

Gwynn & Gwynn
132 Hyde Avenue
Suite 130
Santa Ruis, CA

13. Close all open windows.
14. Submit the results of the preceding steps to your instructor, either in printed or electronic form, as requested.

Apply | **Case Problem 2**

Use the skills you learned in the tutorial to create a Web page for an umbrella manufacturer.

Data Files needed for this Case Problem: Brella.htm, Married.jpg

Umbrella Universe Umbrella Universe is small start-up company in Duluth, Minnesota, that manufactures and sells specialty umbrellas. Umbrella Universe distinguishes itself in the marketplace by creating custom umbrellas in a variety of shapes, colors, and sizes. The company also imprints custom logos and messages on its umbrellas. Juan Ramos, the marketing manager, has asked you to create a Web site that details the company's products and the customizing services they offer. Complete the following:

1. Use Notepad to open the file **Brella.htm** provided with your Data Files in the Tutorial.01\Case 2 folder.
2. Save the file in the same location with the name **BrellaNew.htm**.
3. Within the title tags, enter **Umbrella Universe** as the title.
4. Format the first line of text so that the words "Umbrella Universe" appear as an <h1> heading.
5. Below the <h1> heading, create a comment that reads **code for image is below**.
6. Below the comment, and between the <p> </p> tags, insert the image **Married.jpg**. Include the phrase **image of just married umbrella** as alternative text for the image. The original height of the image is 300 pixels and the original width is 400 pixels. Scale the image to be 90 percent of the original height and width. (Remember to keep the aspect ratio.)
7. Format the second line of text with the words "Our Bestsellers" as an <h3> heading.
8. In the first paragraph, format the text "Slogans and messages are no problem for us." as both bold and italic.
9. Format each type of umbrella to be an <h4> heading. The umbrella types are, Logobrella, Stormbrella, and so on.

✛ **EXPLORE**

10. In the last paragraph, insert an em dash (a long dash) after the word "pattern." Use a named character reference to do so. (*Hint*: Refer to Figure 1-18 for the correct code for an em dash.)

11. Insert a horizontal rule following the Logobrella paragraph.

12. Format the contact information for the e-mail address using the <address> </address> tags.

✛ **EXPLORE**

13. Format the phone number so that it appears in code font. Use the <code> </code> logical tags to do so.

14. Save your HTML document, and then open **BrellaNew** in your browser. The document should be similar to the one shown in Figure 1-34.

Figure 1-34

Umbrella Universe

Our Bestsellers

Logobrella

Put your company's logo on a custom designed umbrella. ***Slogans and messages are no problem for us.*** If you need a logo, we'll design one for you for a very reasonable price.

Stormbrella

This umbrella is guaranteed to withstand winds of up to 100 miles per hour. Made with a reinforced steel carriage and solid oak handle, this umbrella will get you through the fiercest storms without breaking.

Santabrella

Order this festive umbrella that comes in either red or green. A picture of Santa on his sled will give you season's greetings throughout the holiday weeks.

Jumbobrella

Our largest umbrella. Two people can comfortably be sheltered from harsh weather by this oversized umbrella, more than twice the size of the standard umbrella.

Lovebrella

This umbrella comes in pink or white and has hearts and cupids displayed in an alternating pattern — a perfect give for the special someone in your life.

Contact us at umbrellauniverse@brellamail.com

Or call us at: `(631) 555-0011`

15. Close all open windows.

16. Submit the results of the preceding steps to your instructor, either in printed or electronic form, as requested.

Challenge | **Case Problem 3**

Use what you've learned, and expand your skills, to create a Web page for an ice cream shop.

Data Files needed for this Case Problem: Icecream.jpg, Shep.htm

Shep's Ice Cream Parlour   Shep's Ice Cream Parlour, located in Hefferton, Vermont, is famous for its ice cream confections. Located at the same site for more than 100 years, Shep's Ice Cream is celebrated across the entire New England area. Shep Connor has always prided himself on being very inventive when it comes to ice cream flavors and asks you to build a Web site that is equally inventive to promote his new product line. He provides you with a handwritten outline of the Web page, and asks you to create a page according to this design. Complete the following:

1. Use Notepad to open the file named **Shep.htm** provided with your Data Files in the Tutorial.01\Case3 folder.
2. Save the file in the same location with the name **ShepNew.htm**.
3. Enter **Shep's Ice Cream** as the title.

⊕ EXPLORE

4. In the <head> area, enter a <meta> tag to describe the Web page. For the content, use the text **Shep's is New England's finest ice cream parlour**.
5. Format the first line of text that contains "Shep's Old-Fashioned Ice Cream Parlour" to appear as an <h1> heading.
6. Between the <p> </p> tags, insert the image **Icecream.jpg**. Specify the alternative text for the image as **picture of Shep's sign**. The dimensions of the image are a height of 320 pixels and a width of 450 pixels.
7. Insert a horizontal rule below the image.
8. Format the subheadings including "What We Do," "You Haven't Tried These," "Toppings Include," and "Visit us at:" as <h3> headings.
9. Shep's notes indicate that you should underline the words "dream supreme ice cream" in the first paragraph. Format this text appropriately.
10. In the second paragraph, insert the code to make "IST" into an acronym. The title for the acronym is **Incredibly Scrumptious Toppings**.
11. Insert the registered trademark symbol after the end </acronym> tag following the letters IST. Use a named entity reference to do so.
12. Format the list of toppings as an unordered list.

⊕ EXPLORE

13. Insert the dagger symbol as a superscript after James Dunn's name. Insert another dagger symbol as a superscript after the start <p> tag and before the letter F in the words "Food critic for the Lancaster Gazette" text. (*Hint*: Refer to Figure 1-18 for the correct code for a dagger symbol.)

⊕ EXPLORE

14. Format the quoted text as a blockquote.
15. At the bottom of the page, use the <address></address> tags to format the address. Insert break tags as necessary to display the address on three separate lines.
16. Save your HTML document, and then open **ShepNew** in your browser. The document should be similar to the one shown in Figure 1-35.

Figure 1-35

Shep's Old-Fashioned Ice Cream Parlour

What We Do

Shep's Ice Cream has been at the same site for more than one hundred years. Located in the small town of Hefferton, Vermont, people from all over New England come to Shep's Ice Cream Parlour. You must drop by and try our *dream supreme ice cream*.

You Haven't Tried These

Shep's Ice Cream is noted for making ice cream from very unusual flavors. Some of our new flavors include cheesecake, banana mint, and white chocolate brownie. Try all of our flavors with IST®, our Incredibly Scrumptious Toppings. See the list below:

Toppings Include

- cherries and berries
- shaved fudge
- twice whipped cream
- sprinkles and showers

James Dunn[†] says:

"This is certainly one of the finer Ice Cream Parlours in all of New England. I am always amazed at the freshness of the ingredients. Many people travel to Hefferton just to visit Shep's. It's definitely worth the trip."

[†]Food critic for the Lancaster Gazette

Visit us at:

Shep's Ice Cream
123 Benson Street
Hefferton, VT

17. Close all open windows.
18. Submit the results of the preceding steps to your instructor, either in printed or electronic form, as requested.

Research | Case Problem 4

Work with the skills you've learned and use the Internet to research global warming and create an informational Web page.

Data File needed for this Case Problem: Global.jpg

Hemispheric Research Tony Alovese founded Hemispheric Research in Jacksonville, Florida, to study global warming and its effects on weather, sea levels, and species habitat. He recently hired you to assist him in his research and to produce Web pages that educate and inform interested users. Use the Web or other resources to research the topic of global warming and create an informational Web page for Hemispheric Research. In this case problem, you will be creating a new file. Complete the following:

1. Use your favorite search engine to find and read at least three Web sites or online articles about global warming.

2. Prepare for creating the Hemispheric Research Web page by developing the following material:

a. Write at least four paragraphs about global warming and its effects on the Earth.

b. Compose headings that will precede each paragraph.

c. Find a quote from your research that you can use on the Web page.

d. Create a list of the four of the effects of global warming.

3. Open your browser and Notepad.

4. Create an HTML document with all of the HTML tags required for a basic HTML document.

5. Within the <title></title> tags, give your page a descriptive page title.

6. In the <body> section, include examples of the following:

- Comment
- Global.jpg image file (include the alt attribute as well)
- Horizontal rule
- Four paragraphs of text
- Blockquote
- At least two examples of h2, h3, or h4 headings
- Special character
- Bold text
- Italic text
- Superscript or a subscript
- Ordered or unordered list
- Acronym
- Break tag
- Address tag

7. Save your file with the filename **Warming.htm**.

8. Open Warming.htm in your browser, review the Web page, and make any changes as necessary.

9. Close all open windows.

10. Submit the results of the preceding steps to your instructor, either in printed or electronic form, as requested.

Review | **Quick Check Answers**

Session 1.1

1. <html>
2. <head> </head>
3. in the title bar at the top of the screen
4. nothing would display on the Web page
5. <body> </body>
6. </body> </html>
7. <! -- this is a comment -- >

Session 1.2

1. <h1> </h1>
2. They add a blank line above and below the heading and they make text bold.
3. <strong> </strong>

4. <em> </em>
5. <blockquote> </blockquote>
6. It should no longer be used.
7. a character that cannot be typed from the keyboard

Session 1.3

1. src attribute
2. to specify the size of an image
3. height and width
4. <hr />
5. ordered and unordered
6. <address> </address>

Ending Data Files

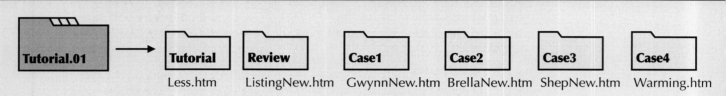

Tutorial.01 → Tutorial | Review | Case1 | Case2 | Case3 | Case4

Less.htm   ListingNew.htm   GwynnNew.htm   BrellaNew.htm   ShepNew.htm   Warming.htm

Objectives

Session 2.1
- Identify the differences between HTML and CSS
- Write CSS styles
- Choose the correct style to format a Web page
- Create an embedded style

Session 2.2
- Specify fonts with font properties
- Control line spacing and white space
- Change text and background color on a Web page
- Create and apply inline styles

Using Styles to Format Web Pages

Creating a Celebrity Web Site

Case | 360 Music

After working as a music producer for major music studios, Justin Carroll started an independent label in Austin, Texas, to promote singers, bands, and other musicians who perform in a variety of genres, including country, pop, hip-hop, indie pop, cabaret, and folk. Because the types of music Justin strives to promote represent the full range of popular styles, he named his company 360 Music.

Justin recently signed Tia Velazquez, an up-and-coming recording artist who began her career as a country and western singer. Recently, however, she recorded several commercially successful pop and hip-hop songs for 360 Music. She's even been asked to record some tracks for rap artist N70. To promote Tia's popularity, Justin wants to create a Web site for Tia's fans. He envisions a Web site that has more visual appeal than a basic informational Web page. He also wants to develop a signature design for Tia's Web site, one that maintains a consistent look for all her Web pages.

In this tutorial, you will use Cascading Style Sheets (CSS) to develop Web pages with visual appeal and a consistent look and feel. You'll use font properties to control the appearance of text, and you'll specify colors to create an identifiable design for your Web pages. Besides learning how to format entire pages and sections, you'll also learn how to apply styles to text within the body of a Web page.

Starting Data Files

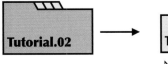

Tutorial.02 →

Tutorial	Review	Case1	Case2	Case3	Case4
N70.gif	Bio.htm	Meyer.gif	Dance.gif	Optical.gif	Slake.htm
Tia.gif	Talk.gif	Meyer.htm	Dance.htm	Optical.htm	Slake.jpg
Tia.htm					
Tialogo.gif					

Session 2.1

Introducing Cascading Style Sheets

In Tutorial 1, you practiced coding individual Web pages. You worked under a principle called *direct formatting*, whereby you changed the appearance of text by inserting HTML tags directly into the document for each Web page, just as you would if you were using word processing software to format a text document. Web sites, however, consist of hundreds, thousands, or even tens of thousands of pages. If you use direct formatting in your HTML pages and want to change the appearance of some or all of the pages at your Web site, you have to open, revise, save, and debug each one of those pages. That's quite a challenge in itself. What if your business required you to change the site's appearance every season or every month or even every day? To revise so many pages so often would be a very time-consuming, if not impossible, task.

Cascading Style Sheets (**CSS**) is a language that eliminates all of that tedious effort. With CSS, you can create one or more documents that control the appearance of some or all the pages at your Web site. You can also format and revise an unlimited number of Web pages easily and efficiently. Just as there have been different versions of HTML, there have been different versions of CSS. Today, most browsers support CSS version 2.1.

CSS offers many advantages over HTML, including the following:

- **Greater consistency in your Web site**: You can apply styles you create in one document to some or all of the other pages in your Web site.
- **Easily modified code**: When you modify code to change the style of one page, all of the pages in your Web site can change, which helps you maintain a consistent design.
- **More flexible formatting**: When you use CSS, you can format and position text in ways that you cannot when you use HTML alone. Many of the features of a word processing program, such as tab indents, line spacing, and margins—none of which are available in HTML—are available in CSS.

You meet with Justin to discuss the Web site for Tia Velazquez. He wants to create a single main page with visual appeal, including vibrant colors. He'd also like to link the main page to a single Web page that provides facts about Tia that fans often request. After reviewing other celebrity Web pages, you and Justin develop the design shown in Figure 2-1.

Design for Tia's Web page ◄ **Figure 2-1**

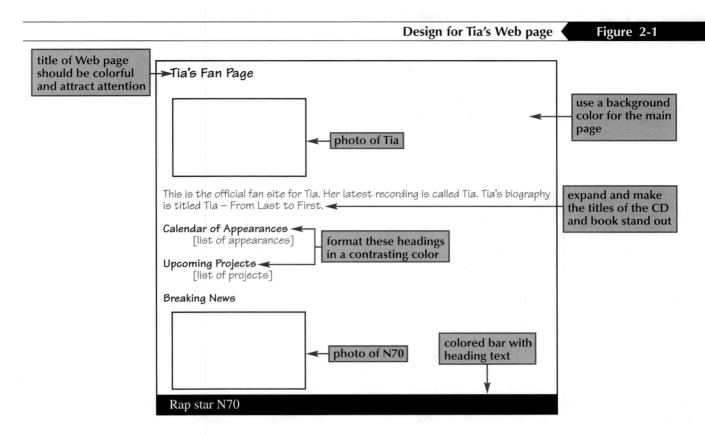

According to your sketch of the Web pages, you need to display a photo of Tia Velazquez on her main Web page, which you already know how to do using the <img> tag. You also need to include headings that use a color other than black, add a block of text with a colored background, and use a colored background for the main page. You also need to emphasize some of the colored text so that it stands out. You can accomplish all of this formatting using CSS styles.

Cross-Browser Support for CSS

Ideally, all browsers would display all of the CSS properties and values, and they would display them all in the same way. Across-the-board compatibility with all browsers is called **cross-browser support**. However, none of the major browsers, including Mozilla Firefox, Safari, Opera, and Microsoft Internet Explorer, supports all the features of CSS, and these browsers do not support the features in a consistent manner. The most recent versions of these browsers do the best job of displaying the most CSS code. For example, Internet Explorer 7 has much better support for CSS than its predecessor, Internet Explorer 6. Because your Web pages will be viewed in several browsers and different versions of each browser, it's a good idea to test and display your pages in each browser and in at least the current and prior version of each browser. Firefox, for example, displays a vertical scroll bar only if the Web page occupies more than one screen. Internet Explorer, however, always displays a vertical scroll bar, which takes up about 1 to 2 percent of the screen width. As such, Web pages that only occupy one screen will be displayed differently in Internet Explorer than they would in Firefox.

Comparing HTML Code to CSS Code

Although CSS is considered a language, it is not HTML. Instead, it is a style language. For example, the HTML <em> tag merely italicizes text. Using CSS, you can create a style for the <em> tag so that whenever you include the <em> tag in your code, the text within the <em> tags is formatted not just as italicized text, but also as 14pt, Arial, and red, or whatever way you want <em> tags to display text.

For example, suppose you are creating an HTML document and want to display each h2 heading as italic, centered, 20pt, orange text in the Arial typeface with a dark background color. Unfortunately, HTML does not provide tags or other tools to format 20pt text or to include a background color, so you have to use the standard 18pt text for h2 headings and use a white background for the text. In addition, using HTML code, you have to enter the following code for each h2 heading on your Web page, as in the following example:

```
<h2 align="center"><font face="arial,helvetica,sans-serif"
color="orange"><em>Here's My Level Two Heading Text</em></font></h2>
```

If you have three h2 headings, you must enter this code three times, which doesn't seem difficult. However, it becomes tedious and hard to manage when your Web site has many h2 headings. If you decide to change the color of h2 headings from orange to blue, for example, you need to find and change each heading, which might involve locating and editing dozens of lines of code. You also have to be cautious in making those editing changes because in doing so, you might inadvertently introduce errors in your code.

In contrast, using CSS, you can enter the following code only once to specify that h2 headings are displayed as italic, 20pt, Arial text that is centered and orange with a background color of black. Note that "h2," the code for level-two headings, does not appear between angle brackets:

```
h2 {
font-style: italic;
font-size: 20pt;
font-family: arial,helvetica,sans-serif;
text-align: center;
color: orange;
background-color: black; }
```

Note the choices in the CSS code for the font-size and background-color properties. As mentioned earlier, a major advantage of using CSS is that it has formatting features that HTML doesn't have. In this instance, instead of being limited to HTML's six heading sizes, you can format the text for the h2 heading as any point size. In addition, the text for all h2 headings appears as orange text on a black background. Background color is one example of the many formatting features that are available in CSS that are not available in HTML. Taken together, the CSS code you enter to define a heading or other element is called a **style**. After you define the style for an h2 heading, all h2 headings follow that format.

Examining CSS Styles and Rules

You are already familiar with a style of dress or a style of music. A style is a consistent, recognizable pattern. A CSS style is a pattern for consistently formatting HTML elements. A CSS style consists of one or more **rules**, which are statements that most often declare how an HTML element will appear in the browser. A collection of styles is called a **style sheet**.

- In a text document, type the selector followed by a left brace, as in the following code, and then press the Enter key.
  ```
  selector {
  ```
- Type the declarations, separating a property from a value with a colon, and then type a semicolon, as in the following code.
  ```
  property:value;
  ```
- Type a right brace to end the declaration list. The following code shows the syntax for a complete rule.
  ```
  selector {
  property1:value;
  property2:value; }
  ```

Creating Rules

A CSS rule has three parts: a selector, a property, and a value. There are four types of selectors: HTML element selectors, class selectors, ID selectors, and the universal selector. You cannot use three HTML elements as selectors: <br />, <frame>, and <frameset>.

The **selector** is the HTML element, class, or ID whose appearance you will change. For now, we will only discuss HTML element selectors, such as the h2 heading. To create a CSS rule, first, you declare the selector, such as h2.

Starting to create a CSS rule ◀ Figure 2-2

selector
h2

The **property** is how you will change the appearance of the selector. CSS has more than 100 properties. To organize them, CSS arranges properties into 15 groups according to their function. For example, you use the text properties to format text, and you use the border properties to create and format borders. Some of the other group names do not reveal their function so clearly. For example, you use the classification properties to position objects (such as an image) or control whether an object will be displayed. The dimension properties are used to control the size of an object. Figure 2-3 shows how the CSS rule is continued to specify font-size as the property. After declaring the selector, you include the property, such as the font-size property. So far, this CSS rule contains two parts—the selector and the property. You would start writing this rule by specifying *h2 font-size*.

Specifying the property ◀ Figure 2-3

selector	*property*
h2	**font-size**

Next, you specify the value. The **value** is the extent—expressed in words, numbers, or as a percent or measurement—to which you will change the property. Figure 2-4 shows "14pt" as the value. Now the CSS rule declares *h2 font-size 14pt*, which you can interpret as "set h2 headings with a font size of 14pt."

Figure 2-4   **Specifying the value for the property**

selector	property	*value*
h2	font-size	**14pt**

Together, the property and the value are known as a **declaration** (also called a definition), as shown in Figure 2-5.

Figure 2-5   **Declaration part of the CSS rule**

selector	*property*	*value*
h2	font-size	14pt
	Declaration	

Together, the selector, the property, and the value are known as a rule. See Figure 2-6.

Figure 2-6   **Parts of a CSS rule**

selector	*property*	*value*
h2	font-size	14pt
	Rule	

A rule can have more than one declaration. When it does, it is called a declaration list. See Figure 2-7.

Figure 2-7   **Creating a declaration list**

selector	*property*	*value*
h2	font-size	14pt
	font-weight	bold
	Rule	

A style is a collection of rules, as shown in Figure 2-8.

Style is a collection of rules ◀ Figure 2-8

selector	property	value
h2	font-size	14pt
	font-weight	bold
em	color	green

Style

Using the Universal Selector | InSight

CSS also has the universal selector, which serves as a wild card to style all of the elements in the document at once. For example, if you wanted all of the elements in the document to be displayed in bold, you would code this:

```
* { font-weight: bold; }
```

The universal selector is not supported by older browsers, so be judicious in your use of the universal selector. Test your pages in the current and prior versions of Internet Explorer, Firefox, and Safari to see if the universal selector works in your browser. If you go on to learn Extensible Markup Language (XML), you will also learn about attribute selectors. Attribute selectors are not, as yet, widely supported by HTML browsers, but are an important part of XML.

Creating Rules

Every programming language has syntax, a specific way in which code has to be written. If you write a program without following the correct syntax, the program won't run or won't run as you had intended. CSS also has syntax. CSS code has to be written a certain way and include certain punctuation. You create a rule by typing code in the following sequence:

1. Type the selector.

   ```
   h3
   ```

2. Type a left brace ({) before the declarations.

   ```
   h3 {
   ```

3. Type the declarations (the properties and values). Separate a property from its value with a colon.

   ```
   h3 {
   color: red
   ```

4. End each declaration with a semicolon. This example includes two declarations.

   ```
   h3 {
   color: red;
   background-color: black;
   ```

5. Type a right brace (}) after the list of declarations (the *declaration list*).

   ```
   h3 {
   color: red;
   background-color: black; }
   ```

InSight | **Guidelines for Writing CSS Rules**

When writing CSS rules, make sure you include the following parts of the code:
- Left brace before the declaration list
- Colon between each property and its value
- Semicolon at the end of each declaration
- Right brace at the end of the declaration list
- Spacing, indentation, line returns, or the position of the braces are irrelevant. Writing code using the following format:

```
    h3        {        color: red    ;
background-color:        black;
}
```

has the same result as writing code using this format:

```
h3 {color:red;background-color:black;}
```

If you are creating Web pages for personal use, pick a format for your CSS code and stick to it. At work, it is common for more than one Web developer to compose or edit code for the same Web pages. If everyone followed their own method for entering code, it would be very confusing. When creating and editing Web pages at work, your code should match your company's best practices for writing HTML and CSS code.

Many Web developers write each rule on a separate line. However, to save screen space, some Web developers will write all their declarations on one line or as wrapping text, similar to the following code:

```
p { color: black; background-color: red; font-size: 14pt; font-style:
  italic; text-align: center; text-indent: 2em; }
```

Writing your rules on one line or as wrapping text does not make your Web page load faster. There's nothing wrong with coding all your rules in this manner, but many Web developers feel that writing code that way makes it harder to read (and debug) CSS code.

When styles are written in the <head> section, they are referred to as an embedded style. Shortly, you will use the Web page Justin has been working on to create an embedded style.

Using the Three Types of CSS Styles

CSS styles fall into three categories: external, embedded, and inline. You apply each of these style types to HTML code in different ways.

An **external** style is one in which you write the CSS code in a document separate from the HTML for the Web page. External style sheets can format some or all of the pages at your Web site. As such, external style sheets are the preferred method for writing CSS code.

An **embedded** style is one in which you write the CSS code in the <head> section of an HTML document. Embedded styles apply only to the one document in which they are embedded.

An **inline** style is one that is written in the <body> section of an HTML document. Inline styles format just a section of text within the <body> text. Figure 2-9 summarizes the three types of CSS styles and how you use them.

Types of CSS styles ◄ **Figure 2-9**

Type of CSS Style	Where You Write the CSS Code	Text the Style Formats
External	In a document separate from the HTML document	Some or all of the pages in a Web site
Embedded	In the <head> section of an HTML document	Only the document in which the styles are embedded
Inline	In the <body> section of an HTML document	Section of text within the <body> text

In this tutorial, you will work with embedded and inline styles. In the next tutorial, you will work with external styles.

Creating an Embedded Style

Embedded styles apply styles locally to a single Web page. For example, you might use an embedded style to design the original version of a Web page. After you have completed testing the page, you could then move the code to an external style sheet. You will learn how to do so in a later tutorial. Although a Web page loads faster if it has an embedded style sheet, you should beware of using too many embedded styles on your Web pages. Using embedded styles limits the ability to apply formatting changes globally to your Web site through the use of external style sheets. You use embedded styles in this text, but in a limited fashion to help you understand how the different styles work.

To create and apply an embedded style, you place the style code within <style> tags in the <head> section of the document. Several attributes and values must be included in the <style> tag, as in the following syntax:

```
<style type="text/css">
declaration
</style>
```

You begin the embedded style code by typing the start **<style>** tag. You enter the <style> tag into the <head> section, right after the <title> </title> tags, as in the last line of the following example.

```
<html>
<head>
<title>Tia's Web Page</title>
<style
```

This sample code doesn't end the style tag yet because you need to include the type attribute and its value first. The type attribute is always used with the value *text/css* to identify this section of code as defining a CSS style. After entering the type attribute and text/css value, you can also enter the end angle bracket for the style tag as follows:

```
<html>
<head>
<title>Tia's Web Page</title>
<style type="text/css">
```

The style rule code (or declaration) follows the style tag to specify what element in the text you are formatting and how it will be formatted. In the following example, the style rule sets the h3 headings to appear in green text.

```
<html>
<head>
<title>Tia's Web Page</title>
<style type="text/css">

h3 {
color: green; }
```

Finally, you code the end </style> tag before the </head> tag. It is critical that you code the </style> tag. If you fail to code the </style> tag, nothing will appear on the page or, if your page does load, your styles will not take effect. Be sure to include the end </head> tag as well.

```
<html>
<head>
<title> Tia's Web Page</title>
<style type="text/css">

h3 {
color: green; }

<style>
</head>
```

When you create an embedded style, it's always a good coding practice to code the start <style> tag, the type attribute and its value, and the end </style> tag. Then, press the Enter key a few times to insert some blank lines to type the code. If you follow this practice, you will be sure to include the all-important </style> tag.

Justin has started creating a Web page for Tia that includes promotional text, a photo of Tia, and a list of her upcoming scheduled appearances. See Figure 2-10.

Tia's Official Fan Page

The Latest Word on the New CD

The excitement keeps building. We are now just days away from the release of Tia's new CD, the self-titled *Tia*, which will be released on **January 25**. Look for it in stores or order copies online. Available in stores right now is Tia's autobiography, *Tia — From Last to First.* Tia is embarking on an extensive promotional tour. She will make several television appearances to talk about herself, the new CD, and her autobiography.

This spring, Tia will go on a cross-country concert tour in the United States. Dates and concert venues have not as yet been finalized, but they will be announced right here at Tia's Official Web site. Tia plans to tour every part of the country and perform in everything from small theatres to large arenas. ***Don't worry — you will get to see Tia!***

Below is a list of Tia's calendar of appearances and upcoming projects.

Calendar of Appearances

1. January 5 – Interview and performance on Ellen
2. January 11 – Interview and performance on The Today Show
3. January 20 – Interview on the Letterman Show
4. January 25 – CD and book signing at the Virgin Music Store in Times Square
5. January 25 – Performance on MTV's TRL

Upcoming Projects

- CD and Book Promotion Tour in the **United States, Mexico, and Europe**
- Concert tour (U.S. only – dates and concert venues to be announced on March 23)
- Co-starring role in a major Hollywood movie!

Breaking News –

Tia will sing a duet with rap star N70 on his upcoming new album, *Givin' Something Back.* The royalties from this album will be donated to more than a dozen inner-city charities. *More details to follow . . .*

Rap Star N70

Justin is eager to get an idea of how styles work. You are ready to show him how to create a style rule for Tia's Web page. You'll open the Web page Justin has been working on and then show him how to create a rule that will format all of the h2 headings to be displayed in green.

To open the initial Web page file:

▶ 1. Use your text editor (such as Notepad) to open **Tia.htm** from the Tutorial.02\ Tutorial folder provided with your Data Files.

▶ 2. Save the file as **TiaNew.htm**.

▶ 3. At the beginning of the file in the <head> section, enter the following comment line to include your name and date in the document. Make sure there is a blank line above and below the comment.

```
<!-- your name, today's date -->
```

▶ 4. Save the file.

Next, you will start creating an embedded style to change the color of the h2 headings on the page. Because embedded styles affect one page only, this style will change the text only on the main page in Tia's Web site.

To begin creating an embedded style:

▶ 1. Position the insertion point below the comment you just typed. Type the following code:

```
<style type="text/css">

h2 {
color: green; }

</style>
```

▶ 2. Your code should look like the code shown in red in Figure 2-11.

Figure 2-11	Start and end style tags

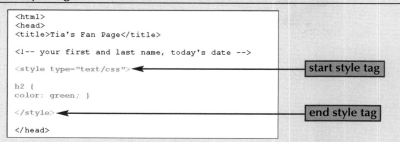

▶ 3. Save your document.

▶ 4. Open **TiaNew** in your browser. Scroll through the document to ensure that all h2 headings now appear in green. Your document should look similar to the one shown in Figure 2-12.

Tia's Official Fan Page

The Latest Word on the New CD

The excitement keeps building. We are now just days away from the release of Tia's new CD, the self-titled *Tia*, which will be released on **January 25**. Look for it in stores or order copies online. Available in stores right now is Tia's autobiography, *Tia — From Last to First*. Tia is embarking on an extensive promotional tour. She will make several television appearances to talk about herself, the new CD, and her autobiography.

This spring, Tia will go on a cross-country concert tour in the United States. Dates and concert venues have not as yet been finalized, but they will be announced right here at Tia's Official Web site. Tia plans to tour every part of the country and perform in everything from small theatres to large arenas. ***Don't worry — you will get to see Tia!***

Below is a list of Tia's calendar of appearances and upcoming projects.

Calendar of Appearances

1. January 5 – Interview and performance on Ellen
2. January 11 – Interview and performance on The Today Show
3. January 20 – Interview on the Letterman Show
4. January 25 – CD and book signing at the Virgin Music Store in Times Square
5. January 25 – Performance on MTV's TRL

Upcoming Projects

- CD and Book Promotion Tour in the **United States, Mexico, and Europe**
- Concert tour (U.S. only – dates and concert venues to be announced on March 23)
- Co-starring role in a major Hollywood movie!

Breaking News –

Tia will sing a duet with rap star N70 on his upcoming new album, *Givin' Something Back*. The royalties from this album will be donated to more than a dozen inner-city charities. *More details to follow . . .*

Rap Star N70

5. If you are continuing on to Session 2.2, leave the document open. Otherwise, close Notepad.

So far, you have been working with style syntax. Now you need to start using some properties and values that change the appearance of the Web page. Perhaps the most common properties are those that affect the appearance of type—the font properties. In the next session, you will work with Justin to show him how to use the font properties to change the appearance of type.

Review | **Session 2.1 Quick Check**

1. What is a style?
2. What is a selector?
3. Name the three components of a CSS rule.
4. Which two components of a CSS rule make up the declaration?
5. What precedes the first declaration in a declaration list?
6. What follows the last declaration in a declaration list?
7. What punctuation mark separates a property from its value? What punctuation mark follows each rule?
8. What is an embedded style? Where (specifically) must the style code be written for an embedded style?

Session 2.2

Changing the Font

In CSS, styles are grouped according to their function. One of the most commonly used groups is the **font properties**. The styles governed by the font properties include changing the size of the type and changing the appearance of the font face, such as Arial or Times New Roman. The font properties also are used to make text appear in italics, as bold text, or in all capitals. In this session, you will also learn about several other properties that are often used with the font properties. For example, the color property determines the (foreground) color of text. The background-color property determines the color that will appear behind text or for the entire Web page.

Using the Font Properties

You use the CSS font properties to change the appearance of text, similar to the way tags such as <em>, <strong>, and <h2> do in HTML. Figure 2-13 describes the font properties.

Figure 2-13 | **CSS font properties**

Font Property	Description
font-style	Sets the appearance of text as italic, oblique, or normal
font-weight	Sets the weight of text as lighter, bold, bolder, or normal
font-size	Sets the size of text
font-family	Sets the typeface, such as serif or sans-serif
font-variant	Displays text in small caps or normal
font	A shortcut property that sets the values for several font properties all at once

The **font-style property** can make text appear slanted or normal. The font-style property has three values: italic, oblique, and normal. Both italic and oblique styles slant text, though oblique text does so to a greater degree than italic text. However, not all browsers display oblique text. Depending on the browser, text you specify as oblique might appear as italic text. Normal text is text that is not italic; you use the normal value to remove italics from text that normally would appear in italics, such as the text between <em> </em> tags or the <address> </address> tags. An example of the font-style property is as follows:

```
h2 {
color: green;
font-style: italic; }
```

You use the **font-weight property** to make text bold. A *keyword* is a value that has a specific meaning for a property in CSS. You can use any one of these keywords as values for the font-weight: lighter, bold, bolder, or normal.

The value of lighter makes bold text slightly less bold than the normal value. The value of bold displays text as regular bold text; the value of bolder displays text as bold as possible. The value of normal displays text as regular text, not as bold text.

You can also use numeric values ranging from 100 to 900 in increments of 100. A value of 100 displays text bold, but in a lighter bold. A value of 900 displays text as bold as possible. A value of 400 displays bold text as it normally would. You specify keyword and numeric font-weight values as shown in the following examples:

```
strong {
font-weight: bolder; }
em {
font-weight: 700; }
```

Because each browser displays the font-weight properties differently, some increments might not display text lighter or darker when viewed in your browser. For example, the values between 100 and 300 might display text in the same weight. The same is true for the values 400 and 500 and the values 600 through 900—or you might not notice any difference in using any of the keyword or numeric values.

Justin would like to change the appearance of all the h2 headings so that in addition to being displayed in green, they also are displayed as italic text. You will show him how to add another rule to the h2 style to do so.

To style the h2 headings as italic:

1. If necessary, use your text editor to reopen the **TiaNew** file.

2. Position the insertion point before the curly brace (}) in the h2 style.

3. Press the **Enter** key.

4. Type the following code shown in bold, which is also shown in red in Figure 2-14:

```
h2 {
color: green;
font-style: italic; }
```

Figure 2-14 ▶ **Styling the h2 headings as italic**

```
<html>
<head>
<title>Tia's Fan Page</title>

<!-- your first and last name, today's date -->

<style type="text/css">

h2 {
color: green;
font-style: italic; }

</style>


</head>
```

font-style property ➞

italic value ↑

▶ **5.** Save the file.

▶ **6.** Start your browser, and then maximize the browser window.

▶ **7.** Open the **TiaNew** file located in the Tutorial.02\Tutorial folder included with your Data Files. Your browser displays Tia's Web page, shown in Figure 2-15, with all of the h2 headings now displayed in green and italic text.

Figure 2-15 ▶ **h2 headings displayed in green italic text**

Tia's Official Fan Page

The Latest Word on the New CD ◀━ h2 heading

The excitement keeps building. We are now just days away from the release of Tia's new CD, the self-titled *Tia*, which will be released on **January 25**. Look for it in stores or order copies online. Available in stores right now is Tia's autobiography, *Tia — From Last to First*. Tia is embarking on an extensive promotional tour. She will make several television appearances to talk about herself, the new CD, and her autobiography.

This spring, Tia will go on a cross-country concert tour in the United States. Dates and concert venues have not as yet been finalized, but they will be announced right here at Tia's Official Web site. Tia plans to tour every part of the country and perform in everything from small theatres to large arenas. ***Don't worry — you will get to see Tia!***

Below is a list of Tia's calendar of appearances and upcoming projects.

Recall that one of the advantages of using CSS is that it allows you to format text in ways that HTML cannot. A good example of that is the **font-size property**, which you use to change the size of type. CSS font sizes offer much greater precision than HTML's six heading sizes. In CSS, you can specify any point size you want. Sizes are expressed in points (pt), pixels (px), and em values. One em is equal to the size of the default point size used by the browser, which is usually 12pt. For example, a value of 1.5em is twice the size of normal browser text, which would be 18pt. Avoid using pixel values because the size of the text could vary depending on the screen resolution the user has set. Font sizes can also be expressed as a percentage, such as 150%, which is 1.5 times the size of the default font size.

In addition, you can express font sizes as absolute values using CSS keywords. Figure 2-16 shows the relationship among HTML headings, point sizes, and CSS keywords for the font-size property.

Setting font size in HTML and CSS **Figure 2-16**

HTML Heading Size	Point Size	CSS Keyword
n/a	36	xx-large
1	24	x-large
2	18	large
3	14	medium
4	12	small
5	10	x-small
6	8	xx-small

HTML also uses the <big> tag, which increases the font size by one size (in other words, from heading 6 to heading 5, for example), and the <small> tag, which does the opposite—it decreases the font size by one size. In CSS, these tags are represented by using the relative keywords *bigger* and *smaller*. Avoid using the <big> and the <small> tags and the absolute and relative keywords because they make it difficult to know what size is actually being specified. Examples of the font-size property and its values are as follows:

```
h2 {
font-size: 18pt; }
h3 {
font-size: 2em; }
h4 {
font-size: 125%; }
```

Be sure you do not insert a space between the number and the type of measurement. For example, typing *18 pt* (with a space between *18* and *pt*), is invalid—the font size will remain unchanged.

You use the **font-variant property** to display lowercase text in small caps, which is smaller than regular capitals. In addition, the first letter of each word will appear slightly larger than the other letters in the word. However, you may have to make the text bold or increase the font size significantly in order to see the first letter slightly larger than the other letters in the same word. The font-variant property has only two values: normal and small-caps. You specify small caps as shown in the following example:

```
address {
font-variant: small-caps; }
```

HTML does not have a tag equivalent to the font-variant property, underscoring the major benefit of CSS—you can format text in CSS in ways that you cannot by using HTML.

Another font property you can use to style text is the **font-family property**, which changes the typeface. Sometimes people confuse a font face with a font family. A font face is a particular type of font, such as Arial. A font family is a group of the same font faces, such as Arial, Arial Narrow, and Arial Black. If you have used a program such as Microsoft Word, you know it provides many font faces for you to use in your written work. HTML does not have such an extensive variety of fonts. HTML fonts are grouped into five major categories: serif, sans-serif, monospace, fantasy, and cursive. Figure 2-17 illustrates the differences among these five groups. You can specify the font-family property using a generic name for a type of font, such as serif or sans-serif, or you can specify a particular font family, such as Arial, Times New Roman, or Courier. You can also use the five generic names for font families shown in Figure 2-17.

Figure 2-17   **Generic names for font families**

Generic Name	Description	Example
serif	Letters have strokes (or serifs) that finish the top or bottom of the letter form	Times New Roman
sans-serif	Letters do not have finishing strokes	Arial or Helvetica
monospace	Fixed-width letters	Courier or Courier New
fantasy	Decorative letters	**Bodoni MT Black**
cursive	Letters designed to look like handwriting	*Monotype Corsiva*

Besides using generic font families, you can declare a named font family, such as Optima, Bookman, or Helvetica. The drawback is that users must have the specified font installed on their computer. If they don't, the browser displays its default font. Another drawback is that although serif, sans-serif, and monospace fonts are common on most computers, cursive and fantasy fonts are not. What one computer interprets as a fantasy font might not be interpreted the same way on another computer. In general, then, you should try to avoid using cursive or fantasy fonts on your Web pages. A common solution for this problem is to compose cursive or fantasy text in software such as Photoshop and then save that text as an image. The Tia logo text has been composed in this manner.

Using Fonts on Various Platforms

Sometimes PC and Apple platforms refer to the same font by different names. For example, the primary sans-serif font on a Windows computer is Arial. A Macintosh computer refers to the same font as Helvetica. These variations can lead to trouble when you try to make your Web pages work across computer platforms. You can best handle this problem by listing several font faces as values for the font-family property, including at least one that is likely to be installed on the user's computer. This list of fonts is called the **font list**. Always include the generic "serif," "sans-serif," or "monospace" at the end of the font list, depending on which font family you are using. For example:

```
font-family: arial,helvetica,sans-serif;
font-family: "times new roman",serif;
```

Note that if the font-family value is more than one word, such as "Times New Roman," you must enclose the value in quotation marks. You can use either single or double quotes.

Justin would like the Web page to have a more modern font. He prefers the Arial font. He also would like the body text to appear bigger. You will show Justin how to style the <body> tag so that all the text on the page is displayed in the font face and size that Justin wants.

To style the body tag:

►   **1.** If necessary, use your text editor to reopen the **TiaNew** file.

►   **2.** Position the insertion point after the code for the h2 style.

►   **3.** Press the **Enter** key twice.

4. Type the following code, which is also shown in red in Figure 2-18 and then press **Enter**:

```
body {
font-size: 14pt;
font-family: arial,helvetica,sans-serif; }
```

Styling the body as 14pt Arial text ◀ Figure 2-18

```
<html>
<head>
<title>Tia's Fan Page</title>

<!-- your first and last name, today's date -->

<style type="text/css">

h2 {
color: green;
font-style: italic; }          font-size property
                                and value
body {
font-size: 14pt;               font-family property
font-family: arial,helvetica,sans-serif; }      and values

</style>

</head>

<body>
```

5. Save the file.

6. Start your browser, and then maximize the browser window.

7. Use the browser to open the **TiaNew** file. Your browser displays Tia's Web page, shown in Figure 2-19, with all of the body text now coded to use the Arial 14pt font.

Text formatted after coding for 14pt Arial font ◀ Figure 2-19

Tia's Official Fan Page

The Latest Word on the New CD

The excitement keeps building. We are now just days away from the release of Tia's new CD, the self-titled *Tia*, which will be released on **January 25.** Look for it in stores or order copies online. Available in stores right now is Tia's autobiography, *Tia — From Last to First.* Tia is embarking on an extensive promotional tour. She will make several television appearances to talk about herself, the new CD, and her autobiography.

This spring, Tia will go on a cross-country concert tour in the United States. Dates and concert venues have not as yet been finalized, but they will be announced right here at Tia's Official Web site. Tia plans to tour every part of the country and perform in everything from small theatres to large arenas. ***Don't worry — you will get to see Tia!***

text coded as 14pt Arial

Next, you'll examine other properties to control the appearance of text.

Setting Other Properties to Style Text

While you use font properties to control the appearance of each letter, you can use properties in other groups to set other text characteristics, such as the spacing of the text. For example, line-height is a text property, rather than a font property. The CSS **line-height property** changes vertical spacing between lines of text, a feature not available in HTML. To set the line height, you specify a value just as you would in a word processing program, such as 1.5, 2.0 (for double spacing), 2.5, or 3.0 (triple spacing).

You can also use em values to indicate how to change the text in relation to the current spacing. For example, 1.5em is one and a half times the normal browser spacing, which is single spacing. A value of 2.0em is twice the normal browser spacing, which is double spacing. In the line-height value, CSS syntax prefers you always include at least one decimal to the right of the decimal point. For example:

```
p {
line-height: 2.0;
line-height: 1.5em; }
```

You can also specify the line-height in points. For example, if you want to double-space 10pt text, specify the line-spacing value as 20pt (2 × 10). If you want 1.5 line spacing for 14pt text, specify 21pt (1.5 x 14) as the line-height. Example:

```
p {
line-height: 21pt; }
```

Related to the line-height property is the **margin property**, which is, not surprisingly, one of the margin properties. You will learn about the margin properties in detail in a later tutorial. The margin property adds white space around an element and is used with block-level elements, such as the <p> tag. If you change the line-height to double spacing, for example, extra white space is inserted between the paragraphs. The lines of text are double spaced, but the spacing between the paragraphs might be equivalent to four blank lines, which is probably not what you had in mind.

To eliminate the extra white space between paragraphs that results when you change the line-height to a choice other than single spacing, use the margin property and change the value to zero, as in the following code:

```
p {
line-height: 2.0;
margin: 0; }
```

You and Justin decide that Tia's Web page will have 1.5 line spacing. To reduce any extra white space between the paragraphs, you'll also use the margin property.

To change the line spacing for a paragraph and eliminate extra white space:

▶ 1. In the TiaNew document in your text editor, insert a new blank line after the body style.

▶ 2. On the next line, type the following code, which is also shown in red in Figure 2-20:

```
p {
line-height: 1.5;
margin: 0; }
```

Changing the line spacing and eliminating extra white space ◄ Figure 2-20

```
<html>
<head>
<title>Tia's Fan Page</title>

<!-- your first and last name, today's date -->

<style type="text/css">

h2 {
color: green;
font-style: italic; }

body {
font-size: 14pt;
font-family: arial,helvetica,sans-serif; }

p {
line-height: 1.5;
margin: 0; }

</style>

</head>

<body>
```

specifies 1.5 line spacing

sets extra white space between paragraphs to 0

▸ **3.** Save TiaNew in your text editor.

▸ **4.** Refresh Tia's Web page in your browser, and then compare it to Figure 2-21 to verify that the line height has been changed to 1.5.

Revised Web page ◄ Figure 2-21

Tia's Official Fan Page

The Latest Word on the New CD

The excitement keeps building. We are now just days away from the release of Tia's new CD, the self-titled *Tia*, which will be released on **January 25.** Look for it in stores or order copies online. Available in stores right now is Tia's autobiography, *Tia — From Last to First.* Tia is embarking on an extensive promotional tour. She will make several television appearances to talk about herself, the new CD, and her autobiography.
This spring, Tia will go on a cross-country concert tour in the United States. Dates and concert venues have not as yet been finalized, but they will be announced right here at Tia's Official Web site. Tia plans to tour every part of the country and perform in everything from small theatres to large arenas. *Don't worry — you will get to see Tia!*

line-height changed to 1.5 and extra white space eliminated

Using the font Shortcut Property

The **font property** is a shortcut property, which means you can use it to specify more than one declaration at a time. For example, all of the following code specifies the style, weight, size, and family for fonts:

```
h3 {
font-style: italic;
font-weight: normal;
font-size: 14pt;
font-family: arial,helvetica,sans-serif; }
```

Using the font shortcut property, you can write a single statement to specify the same properties and values, but using substantially less code to do so.

```
h3  {
font: italic normal 14pt arial,helvetica,sans-serif; }
```

When you use the font shortcut property, you can specify as many of the font properties as necessary. Except in the font list, use spaces, not commas or semicolons, to separate the values, as in the following example:

```
h3 {
font: italic 16pt arial,helvetica,sans-serif; }
```

You can also combine the font-size and the line-height values by first specifying the font size, typing a forward slash, and then specifying the line-height. The following example creates 14pt double-spaced text in the Times New Roman font:

```
p {
font: 14pt/28pt "times new roman",serif; }
```

If you use the font shortcut property, you must specify font-size and font-family properties as well. Although you do not have to use each font property, you must state the properties in the following order:

- font-style
- font-weight
- font-variant
- font-size
- line-height
- margin
- font-family

Justin is pleased with the way the font properties have changed the appearance of his Web page; however, he wants to use more color than just having the h2 headings appear in green. You will now explain to Justin how colors are used on a Web page.

Using Color on a Web Page

If you've ever shopped for a television set, you probably noticed that the TVs on display vary in their picture quality. Some TVs have a bright picture, some are dark. Some have pictures with a greenish tinge, while others have a reddish tinge. When you work with color on the Web, the same is true; with so many different kinds of monitors on the market, don't expect consistency in how these monitors display color. The color you see on a computer monitor is actually a combination of three colors—red, green, and blue. Mixing these three colors and varying their strength (their intensity) produces the palette of colors you see in the world around you. Computer monitors do just that—they vary the intensity (in voltage) of red, green, and blue to display different colors.

In HTML code, you can refer to colors in several ways—by name, RGB value, hexadecimal value, or "short hex" value. HTML uses 216 colors; however, of the 216, only 16 colors are considered to be "Web safe," which means that they are designed to be displayed the same, irrespective of the monitor. The names of the Web-safe colors are: aqua, black, blue, fuchsia, gray, green, lime, maroon, navy, olive, purple, red, silver, teal, white, and yellow. Each of these colors also has an RGB and hexadecimal equivalent value.

Referring to a color by its name is easy if the name is familiar. You won't have too much trouble figuring out what color white or tan is. Other Web color names, such as old lace, peru, and moccasin probably are not familiar to you and could leave you wondering how that color will be displayed.

RGB values are based on the intensity of red, green, and blue. Each RGB letter is represented by a value from 0–255, with 0 at the low end of the color spectrum. If a color's value is 0, it means that very little of that color is used in composing the onscreen hue. The three RGB values are often referred to as **RGB triplets**. For example, the RGB triplet for the color navy is (0,0,128). This means that the color navy has no red, no green, and some blue. Another example shows how yellow is composed. If you mix red and green pixels, you get yellow. The color yellow is made up of the brightest intensity of red and green, but no blue. Therefore, the RGB triplet for yellow is (255,255,0).

The third method for displaying color values is to use the hexadecimal system. The decimal system is based on the number 10. The decimal system uses the numbers 0–9, and then starts repeating those numbers. Computers use the hexadecimal system, which is based on the number 16. After the number 9, the hexadecimal system uses the letters A, B, C, D, E, and F to represent the numbers 10, 11, 12, 13, 14, and 15. See Figure 2-22.

Decimal and hexadecimal numbers | Figure 2-22

Decimal	Hexadecimal
0–9	(Same)
10	A
11	B
12	C
13	D
14	E
15	F

Similar to RGB triplets, the **hexadecimal values** for colors represent the intensity of red, green, and blue. In hexadecimal representation, 00 is the lowest intensity and FF is the highest. The hexadecimal number itself is preceded by a **flag character** (#). A flag character is one that has special significance in CSS code. In this instance, the numbers that follow the # flag character are treated as code, not a number. To specify a color, the flag character is followed by three groups of hexadecimal numbers representing the intensity of red, green, and blue. For example, the hexadecimal notation for the color navy is #000080. The hexadecimal notation for the color yellow is #FFFF00.

For some of the colors, you can also use a shorthand system called "short hex," where only three characters or numbers are used. You can only use short hex if the letters or numbers for each color value are *repeating pairs*. For example, yellow, which is represented in hexadecimal as #FFFF00, would be represented in short hex as #FF0. White, which is #FFFFFF in hexadecimal, would be represented as #FFF in short hex. Black is #000000 in hexadecimal, but #000 in short hex.

Hexadecimal values display colors most reliably, so most Web developers prefer to use hexadecimal values. Also, hexadecimal values are used as color values by most commercial Web page-authoring software. You will use named color values in this text only because doing so helps you understand what you are coding. At work, code your Web pages using hexadecimal values.

Figure 2-23 shows the four ways you can describe Web colors in HTML or CSS code: (1) by name, (2) by their RGB triplet, (3) by a hexadecimal value, and (4) a short hex value if the hexadecimal values are repeating pairs:

Figure 2-23 ▶ **Browser-safe colors**

Tip

CSS 2.1 also adds a seven-teenth safe color: orange.

Name	RGB Triplet	Hexadecimal Value	Short Hex Value
Aqua	(0,255,255)	#00FFFF	#0FF
Black	(0,0,0)	#000000	#000
Blue	(0,0,255)	#0000FF	#00F
Fuchsia	(255,0,255)	#FF00FF	#F0F
Gray	(128,128,128)	#808080	
Green	(0,128,0)	#008000	
Lime	(0,255,0)	#00FF00	#0F0
Maroon	(128,0,0)	#800000	
Navy	(0,0,128)	#000080	
Olive	(128,128,0)	#808000	
Purple	(128,0,128)	#800080	
Red	(255,0,0)	#FF0000	#F00
Silver	(192,192,192)	#C0C0C0	
Teal	(0,128,128)	#008080	
White	(255,255,255)	#FFFFFF	#FFF
Yellow	(255,255,0)	#FFFF00	#FF0

Using the color Property

The CSS **color property** changes the foreground color, which determines the color of text. To change the text color, use the color property and assign a value either as a named color, an RGB value, or a hexadecimal value.

The following examples show three ways to set the color of three levels of headings:

```
h1 {
color: navy; }


h3 {
color: rgb(0,0,128); }


h2 {
color: #000080; }
```

You and Justin decide to display all em elements in navy and to display all strong elements in brown. You will now show Justin how to set the color property for these elements.

To change the colors for the emphasized and strong text:

1. In the TiaNew document in your text editor, insert a new blank line after the paragraph style you created earlier.

2. On the next line, type the following code, which is also shown in red in Figure 2-24.

```
em {
color: navy; }


strong {
color: brown; }
```

Changing the colors for the emphasized and strong text   **Figure 2-24**

```
<html>
<head>
<title>Tia's Fan Page</title>

<!-- your first and last name, today's date -->

<style type="text/css">

h2 {
color: green;
font-style: italic; }

body {
font-size: 14pt;
font-family: arial,helvetica,sans-serif; }

p {
line-height: 1.5;
margin: 0; }

em {
color: navy; }          ← emphasized text
                          will appear as navy

strong {
color: brown; }         ← strong text will
                          appear as brown

</style>

</head>

<body>
```

3. Save TiaNew in your text editor.

4. Refresh Tia's Web page in your browser, scroll through the document, and then compare it to Figure 2-25 to verify that the emphasized text appears in navy and strong text appears as brown.

Figure 2-25	New colors for text on the Web page

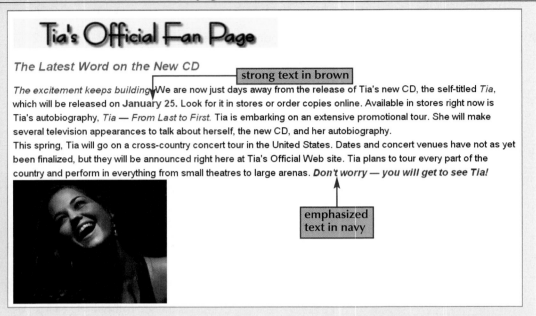

Besides specifying the color of the foreground, which sets the text color, you can also specify the background color of text or other elements.

Setting the background-color Property

As its name implies, you use the **background-color property** to change the background color of an element. The values for the background-color property are the same as those for the color property—use one of the named colors, an RGB triplet, a hexadecimal, or short hex value. The following example sets the color of h2 headings to yellow and the background of those headings to blue:

```
h2 {
color: yellow;
background-color: blue; }
```

Setting the Style of the Body Selector

In addition to headings, you can style the <body> element selector. Enter declarations into the <body> selector to control the appearance of all the text on the page. You can also give the <body> selector a background color to change the color of the Web page itself.

To change the text color or the background color of the entire page, style the <body> selector. If you style any other elements inline to have a different color, those styles override the colors chosen in the body selector. In the following example, the color of all text on the page is navy and the background color of the entire page is wheat:

```
body {
color: navy;
background-color: wheat; }
```

Be judicious in choosing the color and background color for the entire Web page. Your goal is to contrast the text color (the foreground color) with the background color. For example, dark green text on a dark blue background is not a good choice. The most readable text is black text on a white background.

Tip

Some graphical editors refer to instances of styling the <body> tag as the *page properties*. However, this is not technically correct because CSS does not have page properties.

Justin wants to use a more contemporary font on Tia's Web page. He also wants to use a neutral color for the page background, but not white. You decide to change the value of the background-color property to wheat. You'll show Justin how to style the body selector to do so.

To change the style for the body:

▶ **1.** In the TiaNew document in your text editor, position the insertion point to the left of the right brace at the end of the body style you created earlier.

▶ **2.** Press the **Enter** key to insert a new line.

▶ **3.** Type the following code shown in bold, which is also shown in red in Figure 2-26.

```
body {
font-size: 14pt;
font-family: arial,helvetica,sans-serif;
background-color: wheat; }
```

Changing the background-color property to wheat ◀ Figure 2-26

```
body {
font-size: 14pt;
font-family: arial,helvetica,sans-serif;
background-color: wheat; }

p {
line-height: 1.5;
margin: 0; }

em {
color: navy; }

strong {
color: brown; }

</style>
</head>

<body>
```

background-color property sets the background color of the body text

▶ **4.** Save TiaNew in your text editor.

▶ **5.** Refresh Tia's Web page in your browser, and then compare it to Figure 2-27 to verify that the entire page now has the background color wheat.

Figure 2-27 | **Background color displayed on the Web page**

Tia's Official Fan Page

The Latest Word on the New CD

The excitement keeps building. We are now just days away from the release of Tia's new CD, the self-titled *Tia*, which will be released on **January 25.** Look for it in stores or order copies online. Available in stores right now is Tia's autobiography, *Tia — From Last to First.* Tia is embarking on an extensive promotional tour. She will make several television appearances to talk about herself, the new CD, and her autobiography.

This spring, Tia will go on a cross-country concert tour in the United States. Dates and concert venues have not as yet been finalized, but they will be announced right here at Tia's Official Web site. Tia plans to tour every part of the country and perform in everything from small theatres to large arenas. *Don't worry — you will get to see Tia!*

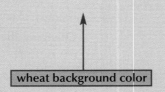

wheat background color

Grouping Selectors

If you want more than one HTML selector to have similar declarations, you do not have to create a separate rule for each selector. For example, if you wanted both ordered lists and unordered lists to have the same appearance, you can group the selectors. Instead of using the following code:

```
ul {
color: teal; }
ol {
color: teal; }
```

Code this:

```
ul, ol {
color: teal; }
```

It doesn't matter if you insert a space between the commas; it's the commas that matter, not the spaces.

Any properties and values you do not specify are displayed in the browser's default value for that selector. Justin would like to have the ordered and unordered lists made more identifiable by having the lists be displayed in a different color from the body text. You will show Justin how to do so.

To create a style for the ordered and unordered lists:

▶ **1.** In the TiaNew document in your text editor, position the insertion point below the style for the strong element, if necessary.

▶ **2.** Press the **Enter** key to insert a new line.

Creating a style for a contextual selector ◀ Figure 2-30

```
p {
line-height: 1.5;
margin: 0; }

em {
color: navy; }

strong {
color: brown; }

ul, ol {
color: teal; }

strong em {
color: orange;
background-color: navy; }

</style>
</head>

<body>
```

when emphasized text appears within strong text, the text appears orange with a navy background color

▶ **4.** Save TiaNew in your text editor.

▶ **5.** Refresh Tia's Web page in your browser, and then compare it to Figure 2-31 to verify that the last sentence in the second paragraph is now orange text on a navy background.

Last sentence displayed in orange on a navy background ◀ Figure 2-31

Tia's Official Fan Page

The Latest Word on the New CD

The excitement keeps building. We are now just days away from the release of Tia's new CD, the self-titled *Tia*, which will be released on January 25. Look for it in stores or order copies online. Available in stores right now is Tia's autobiography, *Tia — From Last to First.* Tia is embarking on an extensive promotional tour. She will make several television appearances to talk about herself, the new CD, and her autobiography.

This spring, Tia will go on a cross-country concert tour in the United States. Dates and concert venues have not as yet been finalized, but they will be announced right here at Tia's Official Web site. Tia plans to tour every part of the country and perform in everything from small theatres to large arenas. *Don't worry — you will get to see Tia!*

emphasized text within a strong tag

Applying Selector Style Inheritance

You don't have to style every aspect of a selector because if a selector already has style characteristics, those characteristics will appear by default. For example, the strong element makes text bold. You do not need to style the strong element to make the contents of the element display text in bold. It will do so automatically.

Recall also that HTML has block-level elements. Block-level elements automatically create a blank line above and below the contents of the element. All the other HTML tags format text *inline*, which means those tags are always contained within the content of another tag. For example, suppose you style the <p> selector to display text in red. If an <em> tag appears in the same paragraph, the contents of the <em> tag are also displayed in red. The inline element inherits the characteristics of the block-level element. This relationship is called selector style inheritance.

Using the display Property

The **display property** is one of the CSS classification properties. The classification properties are a group of properties that affect the positioning of elements. The display property determines how and if an element is displayed. There are many values for the display property, but the two that you will concern yourself with here are inline and block. By using the display property with a value of inline, you can apply a background color to only the text for block-level elements. (Recall that block-level elements include headings and paragraphs.) By using the display property with a value of block, you can have a background color that will extend the entire width of the screen, from one edge of the screen to the other, irrespective of how much text there is in the block-level element, such as a heading. The following example sets h3 headings to appear in white text with a cadet blue background. Because the display property has a value of block, the entire line—from one edge of the screen to the other—will have a background color, not just the text.

```
h3 {
color: white;
background-color: cadetblue;
display: block; }
```

Figure 2-32 shows two h1 headings. One has been formatted to be displayed inline; the other to be displayed block.

Figure 2-32	Inline and block h1 headings

You and Justin want to make sure that the caption for the photo of N70 doesn't go unnoticed. To make the heading eye-catching, you will style the h3 heading to be white text with a background color of blue. Because this heading is at the bottom of the page, you will use the display property with a value of block so that the heading is sure to be seen even though it is at the bottom of the page.

To style the h3 heading to change the color and the background color:

▶ **1.** In the TiaNew document in your text editor, insert a new blank line after the contextual selector for the <strong> and <em> tag styles you created in the previous set of steps.

▶ **2.** Type the following code, which is also shown in red in Figure 2-33, and then press **Enter**.

```
h3 {
color: white;
background-color: blue;
display: block; }
```

Styling the h3 heading to change the text and background color ◄ **Figure 2-33**

```
strong {
color: brown; }

ul, ol {
color: teal; }

strong em {
color: orange;
background-color: navy; }

h3 {
color: white;
background-color: blue;
display: block; }
```

sets the text color to white

sets the background color to blue

displays the text in a block

▶ **3.** Save TiaNew in your text editor.

▶ **4.** Refresh Tia's Web page in your browser, and then compare it to Figure 2-34 to verify that the h3 heading text at the bottom of the page now appears in white, on a cadetblue background, and has a background color that extends the entire width of the window.

Web page with revised heading ◄ **Figure 2-34**

Breaking News –

Tia will sing a duet with rap star N70 on his upcoming new album, *Givin' Something Back.* The royalties from this album will be donated to more than a dozen inner-city charities. *More details to follow . . .*

Rap Star N70

h3 heading appears in white on a blue background and spans the window

Up to now, you have been using an embedded style sheet. All of the styles have been written in the <head> section of the document. You can also write styles in the <body> section of the document. For example, if the Web page had promotional copy about a special one-day sale, you'd want that text about the special sale to stand out. Inline styles are useful to apply styles locally on a Web page within the body section.

Creating and Applying an Inline Style

Although inline styles apply styles locally to a word or a section of text, you should avoid using too many inline styles on your Web pages. Inline styles override both external styles and embedded styles. As such, inline styles should be used sparingly; otherwise, you will lose the ability to apply formatting changes globally to your Web site through the use of external style sheets.

To create and apply an inline style, you place the style code within the tag in the HTML document where you wish the style to take effect. Within the tag selector, type the word *style* followed by the equal sign. There is no space either before or after the equal sign. The code looks like this:

```
<em style=
```

You must place quotation marks both before and after the style code. A semicolon separates each declaration, and a semicolon should follow the last declaration, as in the following example:

```
<em style="font-size: 14pt; font-style: normal; color: white;
  background-color: gray;">More details to follow . . .</em></p>
```

InSight		**Inserting Quotation Marks**

When you need to type quotation marks, it's good coding practice to type the quotation marks first, as follows:
```
<p style=""
```
Then position the insertion point between the quotation marks and type the code or text that should be placed between them.

By typing both of the quotation marks first, you don't have to remind yourself to type the closing quotation mark later. The quotation marks are important! If you omit either one of the quotation marks, the style will not take effect.

Justin wants the words "More details to follow..." to stand out. The text is now styled as emphasized text. One option is to style the <strong> tag instead, but the <strong> tag has also been used in the document, and you do not want to change that tag's appearance. You have decided, therefore, to use an inline style to override this particular instance of the em selector. This is also an ideal place to use an inline style because those words will be deleted after updated information is posted on the Web site. After the new information is posted, you can then delete the inline style as well.

To create the inline style for the em selector:

▶ **1.** In the TiaNew document in your text editor, position the insertion point after the letter "m" in the <em> selector that appears before the word "More," which is located in the last sentence under the "Breaking News" heading.

▶ **2.** Press the **Spacebar** to insert a space, and then type the following code shown in bold, which is also shown in red in Figure 2-35.

```
<em style="font-size: 14pt; font-style: normal; color: white;
background-color: gray;">More details to follow . . .</em>
```

Creating an inline style ◀ Figure 2-35

```
<h2>Breaking News &ndash;</h2>
<p>Tia will sing a duet with rap star N70 on his upcoming new album, <em>Givin' Something Back.
</em> The royalties from this  album will be donated to more than a dozen inner-city charities.
<em style="font-size: 14pt; font-style: normal; color: white; background-color: gray;">More
details to follow . . .</em></p>

<p><img src="n70.gif" alt="picture of rap star N70" height="382" width="261" />
<h3>Rap Star N70</h3>
</body>
</html>
```

inline style code

▶ **3.** Save TiaNew in your text editor.

▶ **4.** Refresh Tia's Web page in your browser. Figure 2-36 shows the final appearance of Tia's Web page.

Figure 2-36 | **Completed Web page**

Tia's Official Fan Page

The Latest Word on the New CD

The excitement keeps building. We are now just days away from the release of Tia's new CD, the self-titled *Tia*, which will be released on **January 25**. Look for it in stores or order copies online. Available in stores right now is Tia's autobiography, *Tia — From Last to First.* Tia is embarking on an extensive promotional tour. She will make several television appearances to talk about herself, the new CD, and her autobiography.

This spring, Tia will go on a cross-country concert tour in the United States. Dates and concert venues have not as yet been finalized, but they will be announced right here at Tia's Official Web site. Tia plans to tour every part of the country and perform in everything from small theatres to large arenas. *Don't worry — you will get to see Tia!*

Below is a list of Tia's calendar of appearances and upcoming projects.

Calendar of Appearances

1. January 5 – Interview and performance on Ellen
2. January 11 – Interview and performance on The Today Show
3. January 20 – Interview on the Letterman Show
4. January 25 – CD and book signing at the Virgin Music Store in Times Square
5. January 25 – Performance on MTV's TRL

Upcoming Projects

- CD and Book Promotion Tour in the **United States, Mexico, and Europe**
- Concert tour (U.S. only – dates and concert venues to be announced on March 23)
- Co-starring role in a major Hollywood movie!

Breaking News –

Tia will sing a duet with rap star N70 on his upcoming new album, *Givin' Something Back.* The royalties from this album will be donated to more than a dozen inner-city charities. More details to follow . . .

inline style

Rap Star N70

▶ **5.** Close your browser and your text editor.

Using Deprecated HTML Tags and CSS | InSight

As you learned in Tutorial 1, deprecated tags are those tags that the W3C has stated should no longer be used. The following HTML tags and their attributes are deprecated tags: <font> and <basefont>. You should use the font-size property instead of the deprecated <font> tag and its size attribute. You should use the font-family property instead of the deprecated <font> tag and its face attribute. Finally, use the CSS color property instead of the HTML <font> tag and its color attribute.

When the background-color property is used to style the <body> tag, it will color the entire page background. As such, the background-color property replaces the HTML bgcolor attribute in the <body> tag and table cells as well. The color property replaces the HTML text attribute in the <body> tag.

Session 2.2 Quick Check | Review

1. Name the six font properties.
2. What would happen if this font size were specified: 18 pt?
3. If a font name was more than one word, such as *comic sans ms*, what must you do to the name of the font when writing the declaration?
4. What line spacing would this code produce: 12pt/24pt?
5. What property is used to change the foreground color of text?
6. What property is used to change the color that appears behind text?
7. What property and value will assign a background color to just the text in a block-level element?
8. Which should you use sparingly—inline styles or embedded styles?

Tutorial Summary | Review

In this tutorial, you learned that HTML works together with CSS to create Web pages. In the first session, you learned that CSS allows for easier coding, greater consistency in your code, and more flexible formatting than is permitted in HTML. You learned about styles, rules, and declarations. You also learned that styles can be written within the <body> of an HTML document, an inline style. Styles can be written within the <head> section of an HTML document, an embedded style. Styles can also be written in a separate document, an external style. In session 2, you learned about the font properties. You also learned what other properties work with the font properties. You also learned about the color and background properties. You learned how one of the classification properties works together with the background-color property. Finally, you learned how to create inline styles.

Key Terms

<style> tag	flag character	line-height property
background-color property	font list	margin property
Cascading Style Sheets (CSS)	font property	property
color property	font-family property	RGB triplet
contextual selector	font-size property	RGB value
cross-browser support	font-style property	rule
declaration	font-variant property	selector
display property	font-weight property	style
embedded style	hexadecimal value	style sheet
external style	inline style	value

| Practice | **Review Assignments** |

Data Files needed for the Review Assignments: Bio.htm and Talk.gif

Tia has asked you to make another page for her Web site. You will create the Tia Facts page that lists some of her personal interests. She has given you the personal information you need to create the Web page, and you have entered the information into a new file. She would like this page to have a background color and font different from those used on her home page. You will create an embedded style sheet to style the tags you have used in the document. Complete the following steps:

1. Use Notepad to open the **Bio.htm** file located in the Tutorial.02\Review folder included with your Data Files, and then save the file as **BioNew.htm**.
2. Within the title tags, type **Tia Facts Page**.
3. In the head section, type the start style tag, and then type the end style tag.
4. Between the start style tag and the end style tag, press the Enter key three times to create white space between the tags.
5. Format the body to display text in the Verdana font, which is a sans-serif font. Also, format the body to have a background color of peachpuff.
6. Format horizontal rules to appear in brown.
7. Using grouped selectors, format h2 and h3 headings to appear as green text.
8. Using either keywords or a numeric value, format bold text to appear as dark as possible and in the color navy.
9. Format the address tag so that text is not italicized, appears in small caps, and in 14pt text. The color of the text should be white with a background color of brown.
10. Save your HTML document, and then open **BioNew** in your browser. The document should be similar to the one shown in Figure 2-37.

Figure 2-37

Facts About Tia

Full Name: Tia Yolanda Velazquez
Date of Birth: April 9, 1989
Place of Birth: San Jose, California
Astrological Sign: Aries
Height: 5'6"
Weight: 120 pounds – I lose about 5 pounds during a concert performance, but I gain it all back after the show!
(Real) Color of Hair: brunette with red highlights; my hair is absolutely straight – not a wave in sight
Color of Eyes: brown
Parents: Juan and Matilda
Siblings: one brother, Carlos, and one sister, Maria
Pets: one dog (Buster)
Favorite Singers: Pretty much everyone: pop, rock, country, R&B, Latin, and rap. I would love to record an album of love songs in Spanish some day.
Boyfriend: Still looking!
Last Dated: About a month ago, but it didn't go too well.
Hobby/Interests: My music. I would be nothing without my music and the people I have met in the music industry. Music is my whole life, but I hope to find someone to share it with.
Favorite Color: Black. Hey, it goes with everything and it makes me look slimmer, especially after I binge on burgers and fries after a concert performance.
Fame: I think it's incredible that people buy my CDs and want to meet me. I can't believe this would ever happen. My fans are awesome!

Write to Tia:

TIA NATIONAL FAN CLUB
22 HIDE AWAY LANE
SKILLINGVILLE, TN 24456

11. Submit the results of the preceding steps to your instructor, either in printed or electronic form, as requested.

Apply | **Case Problem 1**

Use the skills you learned in the tutorial to format a Web page for a wireless communications company.

Data Files needed for this Case Problem: Meyer.gif and Meyer.htm

Meyerbody Wireless Meyerbody Wireless is a small start-up company near the city of Atlanta, Georgia. You will create a Web page that will introduce their new line of personal communication devices. You will create a document with an embedded style sheet so that formatting of the Web page can be simplified. Complete the following steps:

1. Use Notepad to open the **Meyer.htm** file located in the Tutorial.02/Case1 folder included with your Data Files, and then save the file as **MeyerNew.htm**.
2. Within the title tags, type **Meyerbody Wireless**.
3. In the head section, type the start style tag, and then type the end style tag.
4. Between the start style tag and the end style tag, press the Enter key three times to create some white space between the tags.
5. Format the body to display text in 14pt Arial text. Also format the body to have a background color of light blue.
6. Format h3 headings to appear as white text on a navy background. Use the appropriate value for the display property so that only the text itself has a background color.

7. Format the strong element so that the text is displayed in red.

8. Using a contextual selector, create a style where if the <em> tag is nested within the <strong> tag, the text appears in green.

9. Format emphasized text to appear as brown text.

10. Format the address tag so that text is not italicized, but does appear in small caps. Also change the font size to 10pt.

11. Format h4 headings to be in the Verdana font, which is a sans-serif font.

12. In the body section and between the <p></p> tags, type the code needed to insert the logo, which is the image file named **Meyer.gif** located in the Tutorial.02\Case1 folder.

13. Use the words **Meyerbody logo** as the alternative text.

14. Size the image to be 212 pixels high and 600 pixels wide.

15. Save your HTML document, and then open **MeyerNew** in your browser. The document should be similar to the one shown in Figure 2-38.

Figure 2-38

16. Submit the results of the preceding steps to your instructor, either in printed or electronic form, as requested.

Apply | **Case Problem 2**

Use the skills you learned in the tutorial to create a Web page for a dance instruction business.

Data Files needed for this Case Problem: Dance.gif and Dance.htm

MamboSamba Dance Instruction   MamboSamba is a chain of ballroom dance instruction studios located in New York City. With the current popularity of ballroom dancing on reality television shows, MamboSamba has benefited from the resurgence of students seeking dance lessons in all types of ballroom dancing. MamboSamba specializes in Latin dances, but their instruction covers all types of dancing. You are to create a Web site that will illustrate the types of services that MamboSamba offers. You will create a document with an embedded style sheet so that formatting of the Web page can be simplified. Complete the following:

1. Use Notepad to open the **Dance.htm** file located in the Tutorial.02\Case2 folder included with your Data Files, and then save the file as **DanceNew.htm**.
2. Within the title tags, type **MamboSamba Dance Instruction**.
3. In the head section, type the following tags:
   - Start style tag
   - End style tag
4. Between the start style tag and the end style tag, press the Enter key three times to create white space between the tags.

⊕ **EXPLORE**
5. Format the body to appear in 14pt Garamond, which is a serif font. Use a keyword for the font size. Also format the body to have a background color of light green.
6. Format paragraphs to have a line-height of 1.25 and a margin of 0.
7. Format h3 headings to be displayed as navy text.
8. Format h2 headings to be displayed as red text.
9. Format horizontal rules to be displayed in white.
10. Format emphasized text to be 14pt, normal, and navy.

⊕ **EXPLORE**
11. Format blockquote text to be displayed as brown text. Use the font shortcut property to have the blockquote text appear as italic, 18pt text in the Arial font.
12. In the body section and between the <p></p> tags, type the code needed to insert the logo, which is the image file named **Dance.gif** located in the Tutorial.02\Case2 folder. Use the words **MamboSamba Dance Instruction logo** as the alternate text. Size the image to be 74 pixels high and 665 pixels wide.
13. Save your HTML document, and then open **DanceNew** in your browser. The document should be similar to the one shown in Figure 2-39.

Figure 2-39

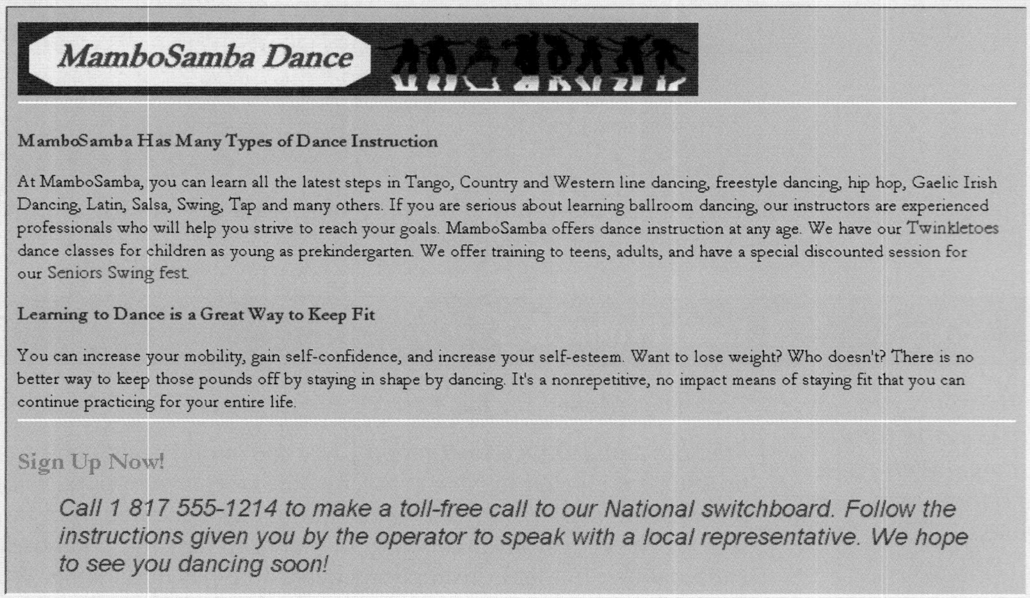

14. Submit the results of the preceding steps to your instructor, either in printed or electronic form, as requested.

Challenge	**Case Problem 3**

Use what you've learned, and expand your skills, to create a Web page for an eye-wear store.

Data Files needed for this Case Problem: Optical.gif and Optical.htm

Otto's Old-Fashioned Optical Store Otto's Old-Fashioned Optical is a small eyewear store located in Rio Lejos, California. Otto Oldman, the owner, has asked you to develop his Web page to call attention to his upcoming specials. Because the specials will be removed from the Web page in not more than a week's time, you have decided to use a mix of embedded styles and inline styles. You are aware that inline styles should be used sparingly. Therefore, you will use the inline styles only in those parts of the Web page where the text and the code will be deleted next week. Complete the following:

1. In Notepad, open the **Optical.htm** file located in the Tutorial.02\Case3 folder included with your Data Files, and then save the file as **OpticalNew.htm**.
2. Within the title tags, type **Otto's Old-Fashioned Optical Store**.
3. In the head section, type the start style and end style tags.
4. Between the start style tag and the end style tag, press the Enter key three times to create some white space between the tags.

⊕ **EXPLORE**
5. Format the body to have a background color of yellow. Use a short hex value, not a named color.

⊕ **EXPLORE**
6. Using the font shortcut property and using as little code as possible, format paragraphs to be bold, 14pt, double spaced, and in the Garamond font (a serif font). Create a style for the margin property to ensure no extra white space appears between paragraphs.
7. Using the font shortcut property, format emphasized text to be bold, 16pt, normal. Also format the text to appear in brown.
8. Using grouped selectors, format h2 and h3 headings to be blue.
9. Format list items to be 14pt and in the Papyrus font, which is a fantasy font.
10. In the body section:
    a. Between the <p></p> tags, type the code needed to insert the logo, which is the image file named **Optical.gif** located in the Tutorial.02\Case3 folder.
    b. Use the words **Otto's Optical logo** as the alternative text. Size the image to be 161 pixels high and 450 pixels wide.
    c. Between the words "Drive" and "Rio Lejos" in the h2 heading, insert the special character ·
    d. Between the words "Optical" and "is for You," insert — as a special character.
    e. Using an inline style to do so, format the word "Special" to be 16pt and navy text.
    f. Format the words "This offer Won't Last" to be 14pt, bold, red text. Use an inline style to do so.
    g. Insert the HTML code to format H20 so that it appears on the Web page as H2O, with the number 2 as a subscript.
11. Save your HTML document, and then open **OpticalNew** in your browser. The document should be similar to the one shown in Figure 2-40.

Figure 2-40

Otto's Old-Fashioned Optical

2020 Mirinda Drive · Rio Lejos, California

Otto's Old-Fashioned Optical — is for You

At Otto's Old-Fashioned Optical, you get treated the old-fashioned way. We're not some 60-minute store trying to get you in and out the door. We take our time to make sure you are getting your prescription filled correctly. You choose the style you want. Take your time doing so.

You don't have to be old to get good old-fashioned service. Mom and Dad — bring in your kids to make sure they are getting the right prescription at the right price. We have styles to fit any budget.

- Sunglasses
- Reading glasses
- Polarized
- Clip Ons
- Designer Closeouts

Special!

Otto's is having a One-Week Special. All frames are discounted up to 50%. This offer Won't Last! **Come in today and see for yourself.** Beat the heat. Get a free bottle of our special H_2O. Our address is easy to remember. We are located at 2020 Mirinda Drive, right here in downtown Rio Lejos.

12. Submit the results of the preceding steps to your instructor, either in printed or electronic form, as requested.

Create | **Case Problem 4**

With the figures provided as guides, create a Web site for a small city.

Data Files needed for this Case Problem: Slake.htm and Slake.jpg

Slake City Town Hall Slake City is a midsized town in Minnesota lake country. The relocation of some major manufacturing facilities from the Detroit, Michigan area has spurred a building boom in the Slake City area. You would like to help people considering moving to Slake City by providing them with some information about Slake City. You have been asked to create a Web site that provides information about the Slake City Town Hall and the types of services that it can provide to those people considering relocating to Slake City. Complete the following:

1. In Notepad, open the file **Slake.htm** located in the Tutorial.02\Case4 folder included with your Data Files, and then save the file as **SlakeNew.htm**.
2. Within the title tags, type **Slake City Town Hall**.
3. In the head section, type the start style and end style tags.
4. Between the start style tag and the end style tag, press the Enter key three times to create some white space between the tags. Figure 2-41 lists the properties and their values that you learned about in this tutorial.

Figure 2-41

Property	Values
font-style	italic, oblique, normal
font-weight	lighter, bold, bolder (also as a number from 100–900 in increments of 100)
font-variant	small-caps, normal
font-size	pts, ems, or as a percentage
font-family	Specify a font list of several fonts; the list must end with the word serif or sans-serif
font	shortcut property
color	Any named color, RGB, or hexadecimal value
background-color	Any named color, RGB, or hexadecimal value
margin	Use a value of zero if you are changing the line-height property to a value greater than 1.0
line-height	Specify a number with a decimal place such as 1.0, 1.5, or 2.0
display	Specify a value of inline if you want to have a background color only for text in a block-level element

5. Using an embedded style sheet, create rules of your choosing for each of the tags below (when you style the paragraph tag, use the font shortcut property to do so):

```
p
h3
em
strong
hr
ul
```

6. In the body section, make sure you code the following:
   - Comment
   - h3 headings
   - Paragraphs
   - Horizontal rule
   - Bold text
   - Italic text
   - Unordered list
   - Slake.jpg image file

7. Include at least two examples of inline styles.

8. Save your HTML document, and then open **SlakeNew** in your browser. Review the Web page and make adjustments in the HTML document until the SlakeNew page appears the way you want it to appear.

9. Submit the results of the preceding steps to your instructor, either in printed or electronic form, as requested.

Review **| Quick Check Answers**

Session 2.1

1. a rule or a collection of rules that change how the contents of an HTML selector will be displayed
2. the HTML selector whose characteristics you want to modify
3. the selector, the property, and the value
4. the property and the value
5. left brace
6. right brace
7. colon; semicolon
8. a style written in an HTML page itself; the style code must be written in the <head> section

Session 2.2

1. font-style, font-weight, font-size, font-family, font-variant, and font
2. The font size would be unchanged because of the space between the font size number and the unit of measurement.
3. enclose it in either single or double quotes
4. double spacing
5. color
6. background-color property
7. display: inline;
8. inline styles

Ending Data Files

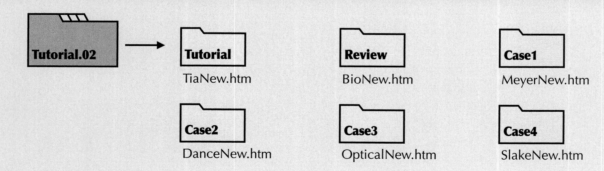

Tutorial.02

Tutorial
TiaNew.htm

Review
BioNew.htm

Case1
MeyerNew.htm

Case2
DanceNew.htm

Case3
OpticalNew.htm

Case4
SlakeNew.htm

Objectives

Session 3.1
- Use classes to style several tags
- Identify the differences between dependent and independent classes
- Apply classes to text
- Use external style sheets to format several Web pages

Session 3.2
- Create a spread heading
- Position text to the left, center, or right
- Identify text attributes to avoid
- Use the CSS pseudo-elements :first-letter and :first-line

Session 3.3
- Identify CSS filters
- Use the <span> tag
- Apply special effects to text using CSS filters
- Create and apply an independent class

Using CSS to Format Multiple Pages

Creating Classes and External Style Sheets

Case | Jupiter Gorge College Career Fair

Jupiter Gorge College, located in San Morillo, Texas, is getting ready to hold its annual Career Fair. The Career Fair is one of the most important events of the year for graduating seniors. More than 100 prospective employers will participate this year, representing a range of employers from the fields of accounting, law, business, information systems, retail, and manufacturing. Prior to the event, the Career Fair organizers will hold seminars for graduating seniors on interviewing techniques, professional etiquette, business ethics, and writing an effective cover letter and resume. Richard Lee, the coordinator of the Career Fair, has asked for your help in creating and formatting Web pages about the Career Fair. Richard would like the Career Fair Web pages to have a consistent look. You will show Richard how to use classes and create external style sheets to simplify and standardize the formatting of his Web pages.

Starting Data Files

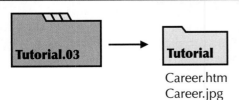

Tutorial.03 →	Tutorial	Review	Case1	Case2	Case3	Case4
	Career.htm	Cover.htm	Beans.htm	Women.htm	Power.htm	Banana.htm
	Career.jpg	Cover.jpg	Beans.jpg	Women.jpg	Power.jpg	Banana.jpg
						Fruit.jpg
						Smoothie.jpg
						Split.jpg

Session 3.1

Creating and Using Classes

Richard has already started work on the Career Fair Web page, but is frustrated in his design efforts because HTML has only a limited number of element selectors. (Recall that HTML element selectors specify what part of an HTML document you want to change, such as h2 headings.) Richard shows you the proposed Web page design. See Figure 3-1.

| Figure 3-1 | Sketch of Career Fair Web page design |

Welcome to the Career Fair

Make Your Contacts at the Career Fair

Image of graduating seniors

photo here

Main body content here

Contact information here

Richard faces a common HTML design problem. What do you do if you want to style an element selector more than one way? For example, what if you want to single-space some paragraphs and double-space other paragraphs? You only have *one* <p> element selector to style. In HTML, you are limited to formatting text based upon the available HTML element selectors. The solution is to use class selectors or ID selectors, both of which allow you to modify the appearance of any HTML element in a virtually unlimited number of ways.

Classes can either be dependent or independent. **Dependent classes** are declarations that let you style the same tag several ways. **Independent classes** are declarations that let you style any tag several ways. You and Richard can use dependent and independent classes to increase your design flexibility on the Career Fair Web page. A few months ago, Richard designed a Web page instructing students how to register for career counseling. In that Web page, he created a style for the <strong> tag for text he wanted to emphasize. The style looked like this:

```
strong {
font-size: 12pt;
font-family: arial,helvetica,sans-serif;
```

```
color: white;
background-color: navy; }
```

However, Richard also wanted to call the reader's attention to important information such as who qualifies for counseling. The document already included the <strong> tag, but he wanted to draw further emphasis to this vital text. The solution was to create a *dependent class*.

To create a dependent class, you start by giving the class a name. Class names must contain only alphabetic or numeric characters, must be one word, and should describe their purpose. Do not start the class name with a number, because not all browsers will recognize it. For example, you could name a class "vital."

In the style sheet, you declare the selector for this dependent class as follows:

```
strong.vital {
```

Note that a period, which serves as a flag character, separates the element selector (strong) from the name of the dependent class (vital). Next, you enter the declarations as you normally do. You can enter as few or as many changes to the original strong class selector as you need. For example, Richard wanted to increase the point size from 12 pt to 14 pt and display the text as a more attention-getting orange text on a black background. Write the selector and its properties as follows:

```
strong.vital {
font-size: 14pt;
font-family: arial,helvetica,sans-serif;
color: orange;
background-color: black; }
```

Richard could use the strong style for text he wanted to emphasize and a customized version of the strong style for text that received special emphasis, such as the date, time, and location information.

Applying the Dependent Class

Using the class in your code is called applying a style. You apply the style by coding the word *class* followed by an equal sign and the name of the class just to the right (and within) the element selector itself, like so:

```
<strong class="vital">Unplug the appliance before making any repairs.
</strong>
```

Enter the code class="vital" in each of the other <strong> tags in which you want to use this particular style. Essentially, you now have two <strong> tags—the HTML <strong> tag and your own version of the <strong> tag.

Creating and Applying Independent Classes

You might want to use a particular style to format several HTML element selectors, such as to center headings, images, and other elements. You can use independent classes to style any HTML element. For example, you could name a class "center." An independent class selector is preceded by the period flag character, like this:

```
.center {
```

You then code the declarations, just as you would for any other style:

```
.center {
color: white;
background-color: navy;
text-align: center; }
```

This code sets text to appear as white on a navy background and centered on the line.

You enter the class name in the element selector, just as you did before, but now you can apply the class to any element selector, like this:

```
<h2 class="center">Jupiter Gorge College</h2>
<h3 class="center">How to Register for Career Counseling</h3>
```

The text would be displayed as shown in Figure 3-2.

Figure 3-2 **Applying the center class**

Jupiter Gorge College

How to Register for Career Counseling

Creating and Applying ID Selectors

ID selectors are the third type of selectors. You use ID selectors for formatting a single particular instance on a Web page where you want to style an element. You can have several different IDs in a document, but each ID name must be unique, and the ID must be applied only once in the document. That is not true with either dependent or independent classes, where you can apply a class repeatedly throughout the document. Similar to classes, you have to give the ID a name. ID names must contain only alphabetic or numeric characters, must be one word, and should be descriptive of their purpose. Do not start the ID name with a number because not all browsers will recognize it. You code an ID in the same way you code an independent class, except that instead of using the period as the flag character, you use the pound symbol (#). An ID looks like this:

> **Tip**
>
> The pound symbol (#) is also known as an *octothorpe* or a *square*.

```
#copyright {
font-variant: small-caps; }
```

You apply the ID the same way as you apply a dependent or independent class, except that you use *id* instead of *class*, as in the following example:

```
<h5 id="copyright">&copy;2008 by Frinlap Publishers, Newark, NJ.
 All rights reserved.</h5>
```

In this example, the h5 heading will display text in all capitals, but in a smaller font size.

Just as you can create dependent classes, you can make an ID selector specific to a particular element. For example, the following code works only with the h2 element to change its color to green. It does not work with any other element:

```
h2#green {
color: green; }
```

InSight | Other Tags to Style

Before you create either dependent or independent classes, don't forget that you can style some of the seldom-used tags such as <code>, <samp>, and <kbd>. You can also style the <b> and <i> physical tags. Recall that the only elements that cannot be styled are <br />, <frame>, and <frameset>.

Creating External Styles

So far, you have created styles using an embedded style sheet in a single Web page. Using embedded style sheets, the formatting of the Web page and the page content are contained in a single document. Most Web sites today consist of hundreds or thousands of pages. If you used embedded styles on all of those pages and later decided to change a style that would affect the design of all of those pages, such as changing the typeface from Arial to Verdana, you would have to open each file, make the revision to the embedded styles code, and save the file. Imagine doing that a thousand or more times! In contrast, external style sheets contain the style codes in a separate file.

Style sheets separate formatting from content. All of the style codes for an external style sheet are written in a separate text file that contains only CSS code. External style sheet documents follow the same naming conventions as any other file, but external style sheet files must end with the filename extension of .css. You do not write any HTML code in an external style sheet document. The external style sheet file consists only of CSS comments and CSS code. The code for an external style sheet would look like this (though it would have many more styles than what you see here):

```
/* Created by Richard Lee, Thompson Hall, Room 114.
 All files for the Career Fair link to this style sheet. */
body {
font-size: 12pt;
font-family: arial,helvetica,sans-serif;
color: #000000;
background-color: #FFFFFF; }
```

The code in the preceding example styles the entire Web page to appear in 12pt Arial text. It also styles the page to display black text on a white background. Not all browsers display Web pages the same way. By styling the body element, you are ensuring that irrespective of the browser, the page will display with *your* choices for point size, font, color, and background color.

Individual Web pages can still have embedded style sheets, though this introduces the possibility of style conflicts, such as styling an h2 selector in the external style sheet and the embedded style sheet. Furthermore, you can still use inline styles to specify the appearance of an h2 heading. To use these three types of styles—external style sheet, embedded style sheet, and inline styles—to your advantage, you need to understand CSS rules for resolving these types of conflicts.

Resolving Style Conflicts

What happens if you style the same selector twice? You might do so in error, but as you will see later in this tutorial, you might also deliberately style the same selector twice to format text. In a later tutorial, you will style the same selector as many as five times. Perhaps you styled the h1 heading in both an external style and an embedded style. Which style will win out? Specificity resolves style conflicts.

Understanding Specificity

Specificity refers to what happens when an element has been assigned a declaration by more than one selector. If you created a style for an h2 heading in an external style sheet, embedded style sheet, and an inline style, how does the h2 heading appear on the Web page? The first factor to consider is location—where was the style written? The specific (and sometimes, the nearer) always overrides the more general. For location, the order of specificity is this:

• **Inline styles**: Override both embedded and external styles

- **Embedded style**s: Override external styles
- **External styles**: Do not override either embedded or inline styles

For example, in an external style sheet, h1 headings have been styled to appear as red. You create an HTML file and link to that style sheet. In that same HTML file, you also created an embedded style, but this time you style all your h1 headings to be green. Which style wins out? Even though you styled your h1 headings to be red in the external style sheet, the embedded style sheet overrides that choice. The h1 headings in the document will be displayed as green. Now suppose that in the same HTML file, you code an inline style in the body of the document that sets an h1 heading as blue. Now which style wins out? This particular h1 heading would appear in blue, not green, text. Inline styles override both external and embedded styles. The h1 heading that was styled using an inline style would appear in blue; however, all other h1 headings in the document would still appear in green. You will also see later that a style declared lower in the style list is more specific than one declared before it in the style list.

The selectors themselves also have specificity. ID selectors are more specific than class selectors (whether dependent or independent). Element selectors (also known as type selectors), are the least specific. The following code styles the <em> selector twice—first as a *class selector* and then as a *type selector*. The class has been applied to the second sentence:

```
<style type="text/css">
em.big {
font-size: 30pt;
color: red; }

em {
font-size: 14pt;
color: green; }
</style>
</head>
<body>
<p>This is some <em>text</em>. This is some <em class="big">text</em>.
 This is some <em>text</em>.</p>
```

Because class selectors are more specific than type selectors, the <em> text in the second sentence will appear in 30pt type and as red text, not in 14pt and green. Figure 3-3 illustrates how the <em> element selector is displayed in this instance.

Figure 3-3 **Class selectors are more specific than type selectors**

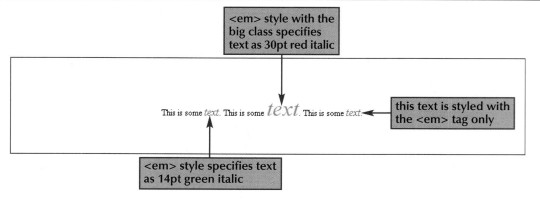

The same result would occur if you used an ID selector. In the following example, the ID selector is coded first, yet it would override the choice for the type selector, even though it is further down on the declaration list. In this style sheet, even though the h2 type selector has been styled to appear in red and is last in the declaration list, the h2 heading would be displayed in green.

```
#green {
color: green; }
h2 {
color: red; }
</style>
</head>
<body>
<h2 id="green">What Color Am I?</h2>
```

Linking an HTML File to an External Style Sheet

The true power of CSS lies in the ability to use an external style sheet to determine the appearance of as many documents as you want. For your HTML documents to use the external style sheet document, the HTML files must be linked to the style sheet document. You can link an unlimited number of HTML documents to one style sheet document. A single style sheet document, therefore, can format thousands of HTML documents. To do so, however, the HTML file and the CSS file must be connected in some way. To make the style available for use by the HTML document, you code a link to the CSS file in the <head> section of the HTML document.

The link tag takes several attributes such as rel, href, and type. **Rel** stands for *relationship*. The rel attribute value is always *stylesheet*. **Href** stands for *hypertext reference*. The href attribute value is the name of the CSS file to which you are linking. The **type** attribute value is always *text/css*.

For example, to use the styles in an external style sheet named Career.css, you use the following code in the <head> section of the HTML document:

```
<head>
<title>Using an External Stylesheet</title>
<link rel="stylesheet" href="Career.css" type="text/css" />
</head>
```

In this tutorial, you will link to only one external style sheet. As you will see in a later tutorial, you can use more than one style sheet document at a time.

Within the <head> tag, repeat the link code for as many external style sheet documents as you want to use. Keep in mind, however, that using more than one external style sheet in a document can lead to conflicts between rules that style the same tags.

Tip

The link tag is an empty element, and must be ended with the space-slash (/) combination.

Tip

You can also create style sheets to print your Web pages.

Coding the Link Tag | Reference Window

To create a link to the CSS file, enter the following code between the start <head> tag and the end </head> tag:

```
<link rel="stylesheet" href="document.css" type="text/css">
```
where the rel attribute and its value specifies this as a link to a stylesheet file, the href attribute and its value identify the CSS file that is the source of the style code, and the type attribute and its value identify that this is a text file.

In this tutorial, you will keep both the CSS style sheet file and the HTML file open in Notepad and frequently switch from one file to the other so that you can see the effect of each style as you create them in the CSS style sheet. Use the program buttons on the Windows taskbar to switch between the two Notepad documents. You are ready to show Richard how to code the link to the external style sheet file. Richard wants to name the external style sheet file Career.css.

To link the HTML file to the Career style sheet file:

▶ **1.** Use Notepad to open the **Career.htm** file located in the Tutorial.03\Tutorial folder included with your Data Files. Save this file as **CareerNew.htm** in the same folder.

▶ **2.** On a blank line after the page title in the <head> section, type the following code, which is also shown in red in Figure 3-4.

```
<link rel="stylesheet" href="Career.css" type="text/css" />
```

Figure 3-4	Code to link to the external style sheet file

```
<html>
<head>
<title>Welcome to the Career Fair</title>

<link rel="stylesheet" href="Career.css" type="text/css" />        code that links the HTML
                                                                   file to the Career style
</head>                                                             sheet file

<body>


<h2>Make Your Contacts at the Career Fair</h2>

<div>
<img src="career.jpg" alt="image of students posing at the career fair" width="500"
height="332" />
</div>

<p>Career fairs present an opportunity for you to showcase yourself before potential employers.
You do not have to be a graduating senior to attend the Fair. You may attend just to see what
opportunities are available for employment after you graduate. There's more to attending a career
fair than just taking notes or bringing a stack of resumes with you.</p>

<p>If you are a graduating senior, let's start by talking about your resume. A good resume alone
won't get you the job, but it should &ndash; in one page &ndash; sum up your accomplishments to
date.</p>

<h3>Your Resume</h3>
<p>Your resume is a reflection of yourself, and like yourself, it should be perfect. There is
absolutely no room in your resume for typographical errors, punctuation errors, spelling errors,
or any other errors. Choose a paper that has substantial weight; don't type your resume on copying
paper. Choose white or beige for both the resume and the cover letter.</p>
```

▶ **3.** Save the file.

Now that the link to the external style sheet has been created, you are ready to show Richard how to create the external style sheet.

Creating the External Style Sheet Code

To create external styles, you write the CSS code in a separate text document in Notepad or another text editor. An external style sheet document does not have any HTML code. You do not even enter the code for the <html>, <head>, or <body> tags—there are no HTML tags at all. After you finish entering the code for the styles, you save the file with a .css extension. If you are using Notepad, you must type *.css* as part of the filename and choose All Files as the file type before saving. *Be sure that you name the file with the .css file extension.* If you do not, the styles will not take affect in the HTML document.

Adding CSS Comments

External style sheets usually begin with a comment that identifies the style sheet, such as its purpose, the author, the date last revised, and so forth. The comment code in CSS is different from the code used to create a comment in HTML. CSS comments look similar to the commenting code found in programming languages. To create a comment in CSS, you use the (/*) and (*/) combination, like this:

```
/* Created by Richard Lee in Thompson Hall, Room 114.
 The file CareerNew.htm links to this stylesheet. */
```

Because Richard is responsible for coding and then maintaining the style sheet, you will show Richard how to create a comment that identifies him as the Web developer who created the style sheet. If other Web developers have any questions about the style sheet, they will know whom to contact.

> **Tip**
>
> Don't use HTML commenting code within a CSS document. Only use CSS comments in a CSS file.

To create the comment:

▶ 1. In Notepad, minimize the CareerNew document.

▶ 2. On your desktop, double-click the **Notepad** program icon to open a second Notepad window.

   Trouble? If you do not have an icon for Notepad on your desktop, click the Start button, point to All Programs, click Accessories, and then click Notepad.

▶ 3. In this new Notepad window, type the following code, which is also shown in red in Figure 3-5.

```
/* Created by Richard Lee in Thompson Hall, Room 114.
 The CareerNew.htm file links to this style sheet. */
```

Example of CSS comment code ◀ **Figure 3-5**

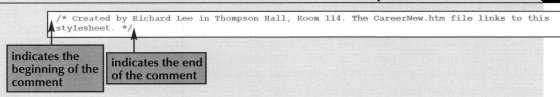

```
/* Created by Richard Lee in Thompson Hall, Room 114. The CareerNew.htm file links to this
stylesheet. */
```

indicates the beginning of the comment   indicates the end of the comment

▶ 4. Save the file as **Career.css** in the Tutorial.03\Tutorial folder included with your Data Files.

The comment ensures that if other Web developers have questions about the file, they know to contact Richard and where he can be reached.

Styling the Body Tag

Styling the body tag in an external style sheet is a great way to design a consistent look and feel for all your Web pages. In addition, each browser has default settings for font, font size, and background color. Setting your own values in the body element overrides any browser default values, which means that your pages are displayed more consistently irrespective of the browser. Following are some of the properties and values that are frequently used when styling the <body> tag.

```
body {
font-size: 12pt;
font-family: arial,helvetica,sans-serif;
color: #000000;
background-color: #FFFFFF;  }
```

The colors chosen here (in hexadecimal values) are black text on a white background. Don't assume that all browsers default to those colors; you can never be sure how an individual user or information technology department within a company has set the browser preferences. Therefore, it's always a good idea to style the body element selector and specify values for the font-size, font-family, color, and background-color properties.

Tip

Some HTML text editors allow you to format the "page properties." These text editors also refer to the Web page itself as "the canvas." The page properties and the canvas do not exist in either HTML or CSS.

InSight | **Designing for Intranets**

An intranet is a private Web site usually designed and maintained by the information technology department of a company or corporation. Only those employees who work for the company have access to the company's intranet. As you know, a company can have many individual departments. External styles sheets are a great way to ensure that each department's Web pages share the same design principles as every other department. If each department designed their Web pages using embedded or inline styles, it would be quite difficult to maintain consistency throughout the company's Web pages.

Many companies standardize the type of computing platforms they use and the software that is used throughout the company. Even so, as a Web developer, don't become lulled into complacency by thinking that the hardware and software platforms used in your company will never change. For example, when coding Web pages for the company's intranet, don't specify the value for the font-family property merely as "Arial Narrow." Always specify a font list for the font-family property, such as arial,helvetica,sans-serif. Each personal computer in the firm might have the Arial Narrow font installed now, but that might not be true tomorrow or next year. Recall that if your computer does not have a particular font installed, it displays pages in the default font, which is probably Times New Roman or a similar serif font. If you are designing pages for an intranet, always specify a complete font list for the font-family property, and always include the generic font name at the end of the list.

You will show Richard how to style the body element selector to style the font size, font family, color, and background color.

To style the body element selector:

1. Make sure the Career CSS file is open in Notepad.

2. On a blank line after the comment code, type the following code to style the body element selector, which is also shown in red in Figure 3-6.

```
body {
font-size: 12pt;
font-family: arial,helvetica,sans-serif;

color: black;
background-color: ivory; }
```

Code to style the body element selector ◄ Figure 3-6

```
/* Created by Richard Lee in Thompson Hall, Room 114. The CareerNew.htm file links to this
stylesheet. */

body {
font-size: 12pt;
font-family: arial,helvetica,sans-serif;
color: black;
background-color: ivory; }
```

code styles the body element in Arial 12pt black text on an ivory background

▶ **3.** Save the Career CSS file.

▶ **4.** Restore the browser window, and then maximize it.

▶ **5.** Refresh the CareerNew Web page and compare it to the page shown in Figure 3-7 to verify that the font has changed to Arial and the background color is ivory.

Body text styled in the CareerNew Web page ◄ Figure 3-7

Make Your Contacts at the Career Fair

12pt Arial black body text on an ivory background

Career fairs present an opportunity for you to showcase yourself before potential employers. You do not have to be a graduating senior to attend the Fair. You may attend just to see what opportunities are available for employment after you graduate. There's more to attending a career fair than just taking notes or bringing a stack of resumes with you.

If you are a graduating senior, let's start by talking about your resume. A good resume alone won't get you the job, but it should – in one page – sum up your accomplishments to date.

Your Resume

Your resume is a reflection of yourself, and like yourself, it should be perfect. There is absolutely no room in your resume for typographical errors, punctuation errors, spelling errors, or any other errors. Choose a paper that has substantial weight; don't type your resume on copying

So far, you have created and used classes to increase your flexibility when designing Web pages. You applied dependent and independent classes, and learned how to create and use ID selectors. You also created external style sheets, explored the differences among external, embedded, and inline styles. Finally, you began creating an external style sheet for Richard's Career Fair Web page, which you'll continue to develop in the next session.

Session 3.1 Quick Check | Review

1. What are the two types of classes?
2. When do you use an ID?
3. Which takes precedence: an external style sheet or an inline style sheet?
4. Which takes precedence: an embedded style sheet or an external style sheet?

5. Which is more specific: an element selector or a class selector?

6. Which is more specific: a style declared at the top of a style list or a style declared at the bottom of a style list?

7. What HTML code is entered into a style sheet document?

8. What should every style sheet document begin with?

9. What filename extension is given to a style sheet document?

Session 3.2

Using the Text Properties

Recall that in the last tutorial, you learned about the font properties, which you used to change the appearance of text. You have already worked with the color property and the line-height property, both of which are text properties. The text properties add several word processing capabilities in your Web documents, which are not available in HTML. The text properties control white space between words and letters, align text, establish tab indents, change the case of text, and add or remove lines above or below text.

Adding White Space between Letters and Words

You use the letter-spacing property to control the amount of white space between letters. You use the word-spacing property to create white space between words. Letter spacing is also known as kerning in typography.

Letter spacing and word spacing are commonly used together to create a spread heading, where the letters of one word or several words are spaced to span a specified area, such as the width of a window. This effect is useful in creating headlines and banners because even a short headline or banner can be spread out to occupy the entire width of the browser window. The values for letter spacing can be em values, percentage, or points. If you want to style a heading for word or letter spacing, choose a heading that is not commonly used, such as the h5 or h6 heading. You could also create a dependent class to style a spread heading. The example below creates a spread heading for the h6 heading:

```
h6 {
font-size: 18pt;
letter-spacing: .2em;
word-spacing: .2em; }
```

This heading specifies 18pt type with 0.2em of space between each letter and between each word.

Richard feels that adding letter spacing and word spacing to the text in an h6 heading would be an ideal place to grab the attention of the visitors to the Web site. You will show him how to add these features now.

Tip

When specifying letter spacing and word spacing, less is more. Keep your text readable—don't place too much white space between letters or words.

To create the spread heading:

▶ **1.** Make sure the Career CSS file is open in Notepad.

▶ **2.** On a blank line after the body element selector code, type the following code to create the spread heading, which is also shown in red in Figure 3-8.

```
h6 {
font-size: 24pt;
letter-spacing: .3em;
word-spacing: .2em; }
```

The h6 heading styled as a spread heading ◀ **Figure 3-8**

```
/* Created by Richard Lee in Thompson Hall, Room 114. The CareerNew.htm file links to this stylesheet.
*/

body {
font-size: 12pt;
font-family: arial,helvetica,sans-serif;
color: black;
background-color: ivory; }

h6 {
font-size: 24pt;
letter-spacing: .3em;
word-spacing: .2em; }
```

⟵ code for creating a spread heading

▶ **3.** Save the Career CSS file.

▶ **4.** Refresh the CareerNew Web page in your browser, and then compare it to Figure 3-9 to verify that the h6 heading text at the top of the page is now a spread heading.

The h6 heading displayed in the browser as a spread heading ◀ **Figure 3-9**

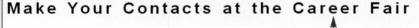

Make Your Contacts at the Career Fair

↑ spread heading

Career fairs present an opportunity for you to showcase yourself before potential employers. You do not have to be a graduating senior to attend the Fair. You may attend just to see what opportunities are available for employment after you graduate. There's more to attending a career fair than just taking notes or bringing a stack of resumes with you.

If you are a graduating senior, let's start by talking about your resume. A good resume alone won't get you the job, but it should – in one page – sum up your accomplishments to date.

Your Resume

You will next show Richard one of the basic formatting features, which is to align text horizontally on a Web page.

Aligning Text

You use the text-align property to align text horizontally. The text-align property takes the following values:

- left (the default)
- center
- right
- justify

The value of *left* is the default and creates an uneven right margin, just as it would if you were creating a word processing document. The value of *center* is used to center text. The value of *right* aligns text at the right edge of the browser window. The value of *justify* aligns text on both the left and the right, filling the entire window width. Justified text is commonly found in columns in a newspaper or magazine. Be careful in using a value of *justify* because it might create more space between letters and words than you want. The <body> element is often used as a selector to justify all the text on the entire page.

Richard has decided that the h6 heading would also look better if it were centered. To do so, you will show him how to add another rule to the h6 style you created earlier.

Tip

Left-justified text is said to have a ragged right margin because the right margin is uneven.

To center the spread heading for the h6 element selector:

1. Make sure the Career CSS file is open in Notepad.

2. In the h6 style, position the insertion point just before the ending brace (}).

3. Press the **Enter** key to create a new line.

4. Type **text-align: center;** to center the spread heading so that the complete h6 code appears as follows (with new text in bold), which is also shown in red in Figure 3-10.

   ```
   h6 {
   font-size: 24pt;
   letter-spacing: .3em;
   word-spacing: .2em;
   text-align: center; }
   ```

Figure 3-10   **Using the text-align property to center the h6 heading**

```
body {
font-size: 12pt;
font-family: arial,helvetica,sans-serif;
color: black;
background-color: ivory; }

h6 {
font-size: 24pt;
letter-spacing: .3em;
word-spacing: .2em;
text-align: center; }
```

add this code to center the h6 heading

5. Save the Career CSS file.

6. Refresh the CareerNew Web page in your browser, and then compare it to Figure 3-11 to verify that the h6 heading text at the top of the page is now a centered spread heading.

Make Your Contacts at the Career Fair

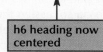
h6 heading now centered

Career fairs present an opportunity for you to showcase yourself before potential employers. You do not have to be a graduating senior to attend the Fair. You may attend just to see what opportunities are available for employment after you graduate. There's more to attending a career fair than just taking notes or bringing a stack of resumes with you.

If you are a graduating senior, let's start by talking about your resume. A good resume alone won't get you the job, but it should – in one page – sum up your accomplishments to date.

Your Resume

One feature missing from HTML is the ability to indent single lines of text, such as to indent the first line of a paragraph. You'll show Richard how CSS can do so using the text-indent property.

Indenting Text

Use the text-indent property to indent the first line of paragraph text, similar to pressing the Tab key on a keyboard. The value for the text-indent property can be stated in em values, as a value in pixels, or as a percentage value, which indents the text as a percentage of the total width of the screen, such as 7%. Following are examples of using the text-indent property:

```
p {
text-indent: 2em; }

blockquote {
text-indent: 7%; }
```

Using the Margin Properties to Control White Space

Recall that you used the margin property in previous tutorials whenever you changed the line height to a value greater than zero. Using the margin property by itself applies a margin to all four sides of an element or the page. You can also use four other margin properties to control white space on the top, right, bottom, or left of a Web page. The value for the margin property can be stated in em values, as a value in pixels, or as a percentage value. The margin properties for the top, right, bottom, and left are as follows:

- margin-top:
- margin-right:
- margin-bottom:
- margin-left:

Tip

Paragraph indents are not all that common on Web pages. They are most useful if you have changed the line spacing to double spacing.

Creating a Hanging Indent

Tip

The values are expressed clockwise as top, right, bottom, and left. Many Web developers use the acronym *TRBL* (trouble) to remember the order for setting values for the margin properties.

You can use the text-indent property and the margin-left property to create a **hanging indent,** where the first line of a paragraph is at the left edge of the window and the remaining lines of the paragraph are indented from the left edge of the window, usually by about one inch. To do so, assign the text-indent property a negative value. For example, you want a particular <p> element selector to display text as a hanging indent. You code a dependent class for the <p> element selector to have a negative value for the text-indent property. You code the margin-left property to have a corresponding (and equal) positive value, as follows:

```
p.hanging {
text-indent: -4em;
margin-left: 4em; }
```

You then apply the dependent class to only those paragraphs where you want a hanging indent.

```
<p class="hanging"><strong>2050</strong>
The year 2050 is the projected date when the Social Security
system faces quite a challenge, as the population of the United States
might actually decline.</p>
```

In the "Dress the Part" section of the Career Web page, Richard notices two paragraphs that would look better if they were styled as a hanging indent—the paragraph that begins with the word "Women," and the paragraph that begins with the word "Men." You will show Richard how to create a dependent style named *hanging* for the <p> element selector.

To create a dependent style named *hanging* for the <p> element selector:

1. Make sure the Career CSS file is open in Notepad.

2. On a blank line after the h6 element style code, type the following code, which is also shown in red in Figure 3-12.

   ```
   p.hanging {
   text-indent: -4em;
   margin-left: 4em; }
   ```

Figure 3-12 ▶ **Code for the dependent paragraph style named hanging**

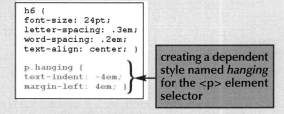

```
h6 {
font-size: 24pt;
letter-spacing: .3em;
word-spacing: .2em;
text-align: center; }

p.hanging {
text-indent: -4em;
margin-left: 4em; }
```

creating a dependent style named *hanging* for the <p> element selector

3. Save the Career CSS file.

Now that the style has been created, you'll show Richard how to apply the style to just those paragraphs where he wants a hanging indent.

To apply the hanging indent style to the <p> element selector for "Women:"

▶ **1.** Click the **CareerNew.htm** program button on the Windows taskbar to switch to the CareerNew HTML file in Notepad.

▶ **2.** Locate the <p> element selector before the word "Women" in the "Dress the Part" section of the HTML document.

▶ **3.** In the paragraph that begins with the word "Women," position the insertion point to the right of the letter "p" in the <p> tag.

▶ **4.** Press the **Spacebar** and then type **class="hanging"** as shown in Figure 3-13.

Code to apply the hanging class to the Women's paragraph ◄ Figure 3-13

applying the hanging indent style to the <p> element selector for "Women:"

```
<h3>Dress the Part</h3>
<p>Make sure your shoes are polished (and don't wear athletic shoes). Hair should be neat and well
groomed. Fingernails should be trimmed. No nail tips, please. Remove any visible body piercing.
Carry only what you'll need for the fair. Don't have pockets jingling with coins or bulging with
other personal belongings. Don't bring a large handbag. Both men and women should choose
conservative clothes and colors &ndash; black, navy or charcoal gray in the colder months; olive
or beige for the warmer months.</p>

<p class="hanging"><strong>Women</strong> should choose a skirted suit or a well-tailored pants
suit. A blouse and skirt is also okay, just as long as the skirt is not too short. The skirt
should not be more than two inches off the knee. Dress shoes with a heel of not more than two
inches would also be appropriate.</p>

<p><strong>Men</strong> should select a classically cut and well-tailored suit. A shirt in lighter
color than the suit, such as white, and a conservative patterned or striped tie is recommended.
Shoes and socks should match and be either black or dark brown.</p>
```

You will now show Richard how to apply the hanging indent style to the paragraph that begins with the word "Men."

To apply the hanging indent style to the <p> element selector for "Men:"

▶ **1.** In the paragraph that begins with the word "Men," position the insertion point to the right of the letter "p."

▶ **2.** Press the **Spacebar** and then type **class="hanging"** as shown in Figure 3-14.

Code to apply the hanging class to the Men's paragraph ◄ Figure 3-14

applying the hanging indent style to the <p> element selector for "Men:"

```
<p class="hanging"><strong>Women</strong> should choose a skirted suit or a well-tailored pants
suit. A blouse and skirt is also okay, just as long as the skirt is not too short. The skirt
should not be more than two inches off the knee. Dress shoes with a heel of not more than two
inches would also be appropriate.</p>

<p class="hanging"><strong>Men</strong> should select a classically cut and well-tailored suit. A
shirt in lighter color than the suit, such as white, and a conservative patterned or striped tie
is recommended. Shoes and socks should match and be either black or dark brown.</p>

<h3>Make the Right First Impression</h3>
<p>Most people make judgments about you in the first five seconds. Give the right non-verbal
signals. Stand up straight, walk confidently, give a firm handshake. Make eye contact, exhibit
good listening skills, and above all, remember the name of the person whom you've been introduced
to. Turn off your cell phone. Carry all your paperwork in a professional-looking briefcase or
attache case.</p>
```

▶ **3.** Save the CareerNew HTML file.

> **4.** Refresh the CareerNew Web page in your browser, and then compare it to Figure 3-15 to verify that the Women's and Men's paragraphs have hanging indents.

Figure 3-15 **Hanging indents displayed in the browser**

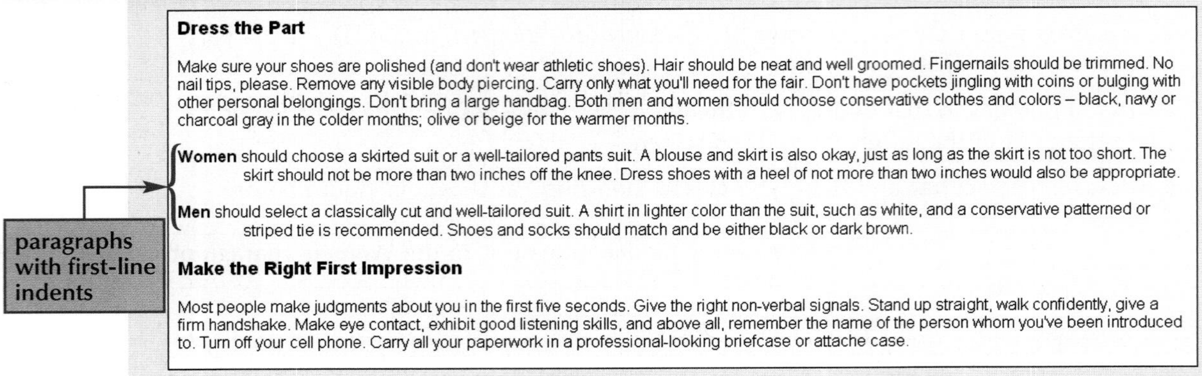

Dress the Part

Make sure your shoes are polished (and don't wear athletic shoes). Hair should be neat and well groomed. Fingernails should be trimmed. No nail tips, please. Remove any visible body piercing. Carry only what you'll need for the fair. Don't have pockets jingling with coins or bulging with other personal belongings. Don't bring a large handbag. Both men and women should choose conservative clothes and colors – black, navy or charcoal gray in the colder months; olive or beige for the warmer months.

Women should choose a skirted suit or a well-tailored pants suit. A blouse and skirt is also okay, just as long as the skirt is not too short. The skirt should not be more than two inches off the knee. Dress shoes with a heel of not more than two inches would also be appropriate.

Men should select a classically cut and well-tailored suit. A shirt in lighter color than the suit, such as white, and a conservative patterned or striped tie is recommended. Shoes and socks should match and be either black or dark brown.

Make the Right First Impression

Most people make judgments about you in the first five seconds. Give the right non-verbal signals. Stand up straight, walk confidently, give a firm handshake. Make eye contact, exhibit good listening skills, and above all, remember the name of the person whom you've been introduced to. Turn off your cell phone. Carry all your paperwork in a professional-looking briefcase or attache case.

paragraphs with first-line indents

Recall that in the last tutorial, you used the font-variant property to have text appear in all capitals. You will now show Richard another property that can be used to change the case of text.

Changing the Case of Text

Recall that the font-variant property formats text in small capitals. In addition, the font-variant property also makes the first letter of each word slightly larger. Both the font-variant property and the text-transform property are used to change the case of text. The text-transform property, however, has several different ways of changing the case of text. The text-transform property takes the following values:

- uppercase (TEXT APPEARS IN ALL CAPS)
- capitalize (Text Appears With The First Letter Of Each Word Capitalized)
- lowercase (text appears in lowercase)
- none (removes any of the preceding choices)

Note that there is no value for sentence case, where the first letter of each sentence is capitalized.

The text-transform property is coded as follows:

```
h3 {
text-transform: capitalize; }
```

Although the text-transform property makes text appear in all uppercase, unlike the font-variant property, it does not reduce the font size from that of the surrounding text or increase the font-size for the first letter of each word. The Career HTML document has several h3 headings. Richard has decided he wants to take advantage of the text-transform property and display all the h3 headings in uppercase. In addition, he wants to change the font size and the color of the text for the h3 headings. You will show him how to style the h3 headings to do so.

To style the h3 headings:

> **1.** Switch to the Career CSS file in Notepad.

2. On a blank line after the code for the hanging indent style, type the following code, which is also shown in red in Figure 3-16.

```
h3 {
font-size: 12pt;
color: navy;
text-transform: uppercase; }
```

The h3 heading styled using the text-transform property ◄ **Figure 3-16**

```
p.hanging {
text-indent: -4em;
margin-left: 4em; }

h3 {
font-size: 12pt;
color: navy;
text-transform: uppercase; }
```

3. Save the Career CSS file.

4. Refresh the CareerNew Web page in your browser, and then compare it to Figure 3-17 to verify that the h3 headings are now in navy and have text displayed in uppercase.

The h3 heading displayed in the browser ◄ **Figure 3-17**

YOUR RESUME

Your resume is a reflection of yourself, and like yourself, it should be perfect. There is absolutely no room in your resume for typographical errors, punctuation errors, spelling errors, or any other errors. Choose a paper that has substantial weight; don't type your resume on copying paper. Choose white or beige for both the resume and the cover letter.

DRESS THE PART

Make sure your shoes are polished (and don't wear athletic shoes). Hair should be neat and well groomed. Fingernails should be trimmed. No nail tips, please. Remove any visible body piercing. Carry only what you'll need for the fair. Don't have pockets jingling with coins or bulging with other personal belongings. Don't bring a large handbag. Both men and women should choose conservative clothes and colors – black, navy or charcoal gray in the colder months; olive or beige for the warmer months.

Women should choose a skirted suit or a well-tailored pants suit. A blouse and skirt is also okay, just as long as the skirt is not too short. The skirt should not be more than two inches off the knee. Dress shoes with a heel of not more than two inches would also be appropriate.

Men should select a classically cut and well-tailored suit. A shirt in lighter color than the suit, such as white, and a conservative patterned or striped tie is recommended. Shoes and socks should match and be either black or dark brown.

MAKE THE RIGHT FIRST IMPRESSION ◄——— h3 heading set in all uppercase 12pt navy text

Most people make judgments about you in the first five seconds. Give the right non-verbal signals. Stand up straight, walk confidently, give a firm handshake. Make eye contact, exhibit good listening skills, and above all, remember the name of the person whom you've been introduced to. Turn off your cell phone. Carry all your paperwork in a professional-looking briefcase or attache case.

ATTRACT, DON'T DISTRACT

Women should use accessories and jewelry sparingly. Don't have bangles and bracelets that make a lot of noise or attract attention. Leave the flashy jewelry at home. Makeup should be understated; don't overdue. Do not use cologne or perfume. Shower before the fair with a mild, fragrant soap. In general, don't be casual and don't be flashy.

SPEAK UP

You'll now show Richard a very useful, if perhaps misnamed, property—the text-decoration property. It doesn't decorate text as you might expect; it formats text to have a line above, through, or under text.

Using the text-decoration Property

As you will see in a later tutorial, the most common use of the text-decoration property is to remove the underline in text in links that the visitor to a Web site has already visited. The text-decoration property takes the following values:

- underline
- overline
- line-through
- blink
- none

The text-decoration value of *underline* does just that—it underlines text. You should not underline text in your Web page. Underlined text might be confused with link text.

The text-decoration value of *overline* displays a line above the text. This value is used primarily in math equations. The value of *line-through* places a horizontal line through the text. Line-through is also referred to as *strikethrough*. Line-through is used as a means of displaying text that has been deleted from one draft version to another, which is commonly done in legal documents. The value of *blink* makes text flash on and off. Do not use the value of blink, as it is considered quite amateurish and distracting. The value of *none* removes any of the preceding values. You'll often see the declaration, *text-decoration: none;* used to eliminate the underline in links. Figure 3-18 illustrates the use of the text-decoration property.

Figure 3-18	Values for text-decoration displayed in the browser

This is a text-decoration of underline.

This is a text-decoration of overline.

~~This is a text-decoration of line-through.~~

This is a text-decoration of none.

Keep in mind that the value of *none* and the value *0* are not the same. If you want to have a text-decoration of *none*, you must use that value, not the number 0. The value of 0 is the only value that does not need a measurement following it.

InSight	Using the text-decoration Property Creatively

Recall that you used the font shortcut property to list more than one property and value. Although it is not a shortcut property, you can use more than one value with the text-decoration property. You can assign the value of underline and overline to create a ruled line above and below text, which can be useful to draw attention to smaller headings, such as h3 and h4. The declaration would be like so:

```
h3 {
text-decoration: underline overline; }
```

Leave a space, not a comma, between the values *underline* and *overline*. In the browser, the underline and overline are displayed in the same color as the text. In a later tutorial, you will learn about a better way to create ruled lines by using the border properties. Using the border properties, you can change the style, the color, and the size of the ruled lines. You cannot do that by using the text-decoration property.

The result of using the values of underline and overline together would be similar to what you see in Figure 3-19.

Overline and underline values for the text-decoration property displayed in the browser | Figure 3-19

> This is a text-decoration of underline.
>
> This is a text-decoration of overline.
>
> **This is a text-decoration of both underline and overline**

Creating Pseudo-Elements

In addition to using the text properties, you can also use pseudo-elements to format a single character or an entire line of text. What is a pseudo-element? The word *pseudo* means "not genuine." You might be familiar with the term *pseudonym*, which is an alias. For example, the famous author Samuel Clemens used the pseudonym of Mark Twain. CSS has several ways of formatting text that do not directly relate to an HTML element selector. For example, no HTML element selector formats only the first letter of a word. Similarly, no HTML element selector formats only the first line of a paragraph. The pseudo-elements create an element selector where none existed before. Although there are several CSS pseudo-elements, you will work with just the **:first-letter** and **:first-line** pseudo-elements in this tutorial. The colon you see before the element names is required and is part of the pseudo-element name. You can use the :first-letter or the :first-line pseudo-elements either separately or together. Both the :first-letter and :first-line pseudo-elements work only with block-level elements. Not all properties can be styled by using the pseudo-elements. Limit your styles to the following properties: the font properties; the color and background-color properties; the margin, padding, and border properties; and the text-transform, font-variant, and line-height properties.

Using the :first-letter Pseudo-Element

The :first-letter pseudo-element formats only the first letter of a word. The :first-letter pseudo-element is used to create a drop cap (also known as an initial cap). In typography, it's common to format the first letter of a chapter in a decorative font and in a larger point size. Styling the :first-letter pseudo-element nearly always occurs as a dependent style, usually with the <p> element selector. It's always a good idea to give the initial cap some white space to the right of the letter; otherwise, the initial cap appears too close to the remaining letters in the word. You can use the margin-right property to create some white space to the right of the drop cap, like so:

```
p.intro :first-letter {
font-size: 36pt;
font-family: arial,helvetica,sans-serif;
margin-right: 4px;
color: orange;
background-color: black; }
```

Note that the colon before :first-letter and :first-line is required. If you omit the colon, the property will not take effect.

Richard would like to use the :first-letter pseudo-element to style the first letter of the first paragraph. You will show him how to do so.

To style the :first-letter pseudo-element:

▶ **1.** Make sure the Career CSS file is open in Notepad.

▶ **2.** On a blank line after the code for the h3 style, type the following code, which is also shown in red in Figure 3-20.

```
p.cap:first-letter {
font-size: 36pt;
font-family: arial,helvetica,sans-serif;
margin-right: 4px;
color: orange;
background-color: black; }
```

Figure 3-20	Code for the :first-letter pseudo-element

```
h3 {
font-size: 12pt;
color: navy;
text-transform: uppercase; }

p.cap:first-letter {
font-size: 36pt;
font-family: arial,helvetica,sans-serif;
margin-right: 4px;
color: orange;
background-color: black; }
```

code for styling the :first-letter pseudo-element

▶ **3.** Save the Career CSS file.

To apply the class, you do not include the property name ":first-line." You use the name of the class, which in this instance is "cap," just as you would when you apply any dependent or independent style, as shown in the following example:

```
<p class="cap">Career fairs present an opportunity for you to showcase
yourself before potential employers. You do not have to be a graduating
senior to attend the Fair. You attend just to see what opportunities
are available for employment after you graduate. There's more to
attending a career fair than just taking notes or bringing a stack of
resumes with you.</p>
```

You will show Richard how to apply the cap class to the first paragraph.

To apply the cap class for the <p> element selector for the first paragraph:

▶ **1.** Switch to the CareerNew HTML file in Notepad.

▶ **2.** Locate the <p> element selector before the word "Career" in the first paragraph of the document.

▶ **3.** Position the insertion point to the right of the letter "p."

▶ **4.** Press the **Spacebar** and type **class="cap"** as shown in red in Figure 3-21.

Code to apply the cap class ◀ Figure 3-21

```
<h6>Make Your Contacts at the Career Fair</h6>

<div>
<img src="career.jpg" alt="image of students posing at the career fair" width="500"
height="332" />
</div>

<p class="cap">Career fairs present an opportunity for you to showcase yourself before potential
employers. You do not have to be a graduating senior to attend the Fair. You may attend just to
see what opportunities are available for employment after you graduate. There's more to attending
a career fair than just taking notes or bringing a stack of resumes with you.</p>
```

applying the cap class for the <p> element selector for the first paragraph

5. Save the CareerNew HTML file.

6. Refresh the CareerNew Web page in your browser, and then compare it to Figure 3-22 to verify that the drop cap has been applied to the first letter of the first paragraph.

Tip

Do not use the following properties, which have been dropped from CSS version 2.1:
font-stretch
font-size-adjust
text-shadow

The cap class displayed in the browser ◀ Figure 3-22

Make Your Contacts at the Career Fair

drop cap → C areer fairs present an opportunity for you to showcase yourself before potential employers. You do not have to be a graduating senior to attend the Fair. You may attend just to see what opportunities are available for employment after you graduate. There's more to attending a career fair than just taking notes or bringing a stack of resumes with you.

If you are a graduating senior, let's start by talking about your resume. A good resume alone won't get you the job, but it should – in one page – sum up your accomplishments to date.

YOUR RESUME

Working with Pseudo-Elements | Reference Window

- To create a style for a pseudo-element, use the syntax:
  selector:pseudo-element: [styles]

- where *selector* is an element, a class, or an ID; *pseudo-element* is the name of the pseudo-element; and [*styles*] are the CSS styles you want to apply to the selector.

You want to pause and discuss an important point with Richard: organizing your declarations by their function.

Grouping Properties

Now that you have worked with several groups of properties, such as the font properties and the text properties, you should try to group these properties together whenever you code your CSS rules. The following code is an example of how code should *not* be written:

```
h2 {
font-family: arial,helvetica,sans-serif;
color: red;
font-weight: bold;
margin-left: 1em;
font-style: italic;
text-transform: uppercase;
font-size: 16pt; }
```

The h2 declaration list, as it is coded, lists declarations for a font property, a text property, a font property, a margin property, a font property, a text property, and a font property. You should list the properties and values by their group so that other Web developers, who may also have to work with your code, will be able to easily understand what you have coded. Also, remember that certain properties, such as the font properties, must be written in a particular order (font style, weight, variant, size, and family). It doesn't matter whether you list one group of properties before or after another, but as you write your CSS code, pick a grouping order for your declarations and be consistent. This declaration list, grouped by function, is understandable (and correct) coded like this:

```
h2 {
font-style: italic;
font-weight: bold;
font-size: 16pt;
font-family: arial,helvetica,sans-serif;
color: red;
text-transform: uppercase;
margin-left: 1em; }
```

Using the :first-line Pseudo-Element

The :first-line pseudo-element formats just the first line of a paragraph. Note the colon that precedes :first-line. The colon is part of the pseudo-element name. Once again, in typography, it's common to format the first line of a paragraph in a chapter in a different font style or font size.

Styling the :first-line pseudo-element nearly always occurs as a dependent style, usually within the <p> element selector, as shown in the following example:

```
p.opening:first-line {
font-size: 16pt;
color: brown;
font-family: arial,helvetica,sans-serif; }
```

Richard would like to use the :first-line pseudo-element in the paragraph that begins with the words, "If you are a graduating senior...." You will show him how to do so.

To style the :first-line pseudo-element:

▶ **1.** Switch to the Career CSS file in Notepad.

▶ **2.** On a blank line after the code for the :first-letter element style, type the following code, which is also shown in red in Figure 3-23.

```
p.opening:first-line {
font-size: 16pt;
font-family: arial,helvetica,sans-serif;
color: brown; }
```

Code for the :first-line pseudo-element ◄ Figure 3-23

```
p.cap:first-letter {
font-size: 36pt;
font-family: arial,helvetica,sans-serif;
margin-right: 4px;
color: orange;
background-color: black; }        using the :first-line
                                  pseudo-element
p.opening:first-line {
font-size: 16pt;
font-family: arial,helvetica,sans-serif;
color: brown; }
```

▶ **3.** Save the Career CSS file.

To apply the style, you do not include the words *:first-line*. You use the name of the style, which in the following example is *opening*, just as you would when you apply any dependent or independent style.

```
<p class="opening">If you are a graduating senior, let's start by talking
about your resume. A good resume alone won't get you the job, but it
should &ndash; in one page &ndash; sum up your accomplishments to
date.</p>
```

You will show Richard how to apply the style *opening* to the first line of the second paragraph.

To apply the style called *opening* for the <p> element selector for the second paragraph:

▶ **1.** In Notepad, switch to the CareerNew HTML file.

▶ **2.** Locate the <p> element selector before the word "If" in the second paragraph of the document.

▶ **3.** Position the insertion point to the right of the letter "p." Press the **Spacebar** and type **class="opening"** as is shown in red in Figure 3-24.

Code to apply the opening class ◄ Figure 3-24

```
<img src="career.jpg" alt="image of students posing at the career fair" width="500"
height="332" />
</div>
```

applying the
"opening"
style to the
<p> element
selector

```
<p class="cap">Career fairs present an opportunity for you to showcase yourself before potential
employers. You do not have to be a graduating senior to attend the Fair. You may attend just to
see what opportunities are available for employment after you graduate. There's more to attending
a career fair than just taking notes or bringing a stack of resumes with you.</p>
<p class="opening">If you are a graduating senior, let's start by talking about your resume. A
good resume alone won't get you the job, but it should &ndash; in one page &ndash; sum up your
accomplishments to date.</p>
```

▶ **4.** Save the Career HTML file.

▶ **5.** Refresh the Career Web page in your browser, and then compare it to Figure 3-25 to verify that the opening class has been applied.

Figure 3-25 **The :first-line text displayed in the browser**

appearance
of the first
line with
opening
style applied

C areer fairs present an opportunity for you to showcase yourself before potential employers. You do not have to be a graduating senior to attend the Fair. You may attend just to see what opportunities are available for employment after you graduate. There's more to attending a career fair than just taking notes or bringing a stack of resumes with you.

If you are a graduating senior, let's start by talking about your resume. A good resume alone won't get you the job, but it should – in one page – sum up your accomplishments to date.

Richard is curious about the meaning of the word *cascade* in Cascading Style Sheets. You will show Richard how the cascade works.

Understanding the Cascade in Cascading Style Sheets

The **cascade** determines which style prevails based upon its source or location. Styles can be written by you (author styles) or created by the reader (user styles). Styles can also be present by default in the browser (user agent styles). This text covers author styles. User styles are set in the browser, usually to improve Web accessibility, such as by increasing the text size to a larger point size to compensate for a visual impairment. Browser styles are those styles that are part of the default choices set in the browser, such as the choices for font size, font family, color, and background color. The rule is that author styles prevail over all other styles; user styles prevail over browser styles.

Author styles come from three locations—inline styles, embedded styles, and external styles. Recall that inline styles prevail over embedded and external styles; embedded styles prevail over external styles.

The cascade also determines which style prevails if you style the same element more than once in the same location. For example, you create an embedded style sheet and style h1 headings to be green at the top of the declaration list, but then style h1 headings to be blue further down the declaration list, such as in the following code:

```
h1 {
color: green; }

strong {
font-size: 14pt; }

h1 {
color: blue; }
```

Which style prevails—the one that styles h1 headings as green or the one that styles h1 headings as blue? The cascade states that when selectors have the same specificity, the selector that is declared further from the top of the style sheet takes effect. In this document, all h1 headings will appear in blue.

In the preceding example, you styled the first h1 heading to be green and the second h1 heading to be blue. The type and the number of the declarations were the same. In both instances, you were trying to style an h1 heading based solely on color. However, what if the first style had other declarations in addition to the color property? For example, what if you had coded the first h1 style to also have a background color in addition to the foreground color, like so:

```
h1 {
color: green;
background-color: yellow; }

h1 {
color: blue; }
```

In the second h1 style, your intent is to style the h1 heading as *only* having the text appear in blue. However, that won't be the result. Because the first style for the h1 heading also has a background color of yellow, all h1 headings will appear as blue text, but they will also have a background color of yellow. Specificity and the cascade resolve only style conflicts. Any other rules that don't conflict still take effect. Because the second style does not specify a background color, the background color from the first style takes effect. The result will be the same as if you had coded this:

```
h1 {
color: blue;
background-color: yellow; }
```

Combining :first-letter and :first-line | InSight

You can combine the :first-letter and the :first-line pseudo-elements by using a class or an ID selector and styling the selector twice—once to style the :first-letter and once to style the :first-line. Use the same number and same types of rules. The example below styles the :first-letter and the :first-line pseudo-elements for their color, font-style, and font-size properties and applies the styles to a paragraph:

```
<html>
<head>
<title>First Line and First Letter</title>
<style type="text/css">

p.opening:first-letter {
font-size: 30pt;
font-family: broadway,fantasy;
color: brown; }

p.opening:first-line {
font-size: 16pt;
font-family: arial,helvetica,sans-serif;
color: navy; }

</style>
</head>

<body>
<p class="opening">This is an example of creating a line that has
both a drop cap and has the first line styled as well. It is common
in typography to bring attention to the first letter and the first
line of a chapter. The second and following lines of the paragraph,
appear in the default style; unless, of course, you have styled the
body text otherwise.</p>
```

Figure 3-26 summarizes the text properties and pseudo-elements.

Figure 3-26	Text properties and pseudo-elements

Property	Values
color	Any named color, RGB, or hexadecimal value
line-height	A number (1.0, 1.5, 2.0, etc.) or in em values
letter-spacing	Specify pts, ems, or as a percentage
word-spacing	Specify pts, ems, or as a percentage
text-align	Specify left, center, right, justify
text-indent	Specify pts, ems, or as a percentage
text-transform	Specify uppercase, capitalize, lowercase, normal
text-decoration	Specify overline or line-through
:first-letter	Use to set the style of the first letter of a word
:first-line	Use to set the style of the first line of a paragraph

You now have learned about the text properties and to use them to change the color and alignment of text. You changed the case of text and used the letter-spacing and word-spacing properties together to create a spread heading. You also worked with two pseudo-elements, :first-line and :first-letter, to change the appearance of a single letter or a single line. You organized your declaration lists so that properties are grouped by their function, and learned about the cascade in cascading style sheets. In the next session, you will use filters to change the appearance of text.

Review	Session 3.2 Quick Check

1. What property would you use to create or remove underlining?
2. What property would you use to indent text for a paragraph?
3. What property would you use to center text?
4. What effect do the letter-spacing and word-spacing properties usually create?
5. How does the text-transform property differ from the font-variant property?
6. How is it possible to establish a hanging indent?
7. What is line-through? What profession in particular uses this feature?
8. What text-decoration value should never be used?
9. What text-decoration value would eliminate underscoring?

Session 3.3

Using Filters

Proprietary code functions on only one hardware or software platform, such as Internet Explorer or Firefox. Both Microsoft and Mozilla Firefox have developed proprietary code that can add special effects to text. These special effects are known as **filters**. The forthcoming CSS version 3 might resolve these differences and create CSS code for filters, not proprietary code. Because you want to be kind to your Web page visitors and not rely on proprietary code, most special text effects that you see on the Web have been created using third-party software such as Adobe PhotoShop. The text is saved as a .gif image file. In the HTML file, you write code to display the image, just as you would with any other image, even though the image is of a block of text. Because of the design limitations of the CSS font and text properties, filters are often used to create text for Web pages. Some popular filter effects are shown in Figure 3-27.

Some popular filter effects shown in the browser ◄ **Figure 3-27**

Alpha Filter   Blur Filter

Glow Filter   *Wave Filter*

DropShadow Filter **Shadow Filter**

Filters are coded within the <span> </span> tags. The <span></span> tags have no formatting of their own; they are used to format text inline similar to the <em></em> or the <strong></strong> tags.

All of the filters must be given a height and a width. Figure 3-28 describes some popular CSS filters.

> **Tip**
> Similar to the <div> tag, you can apply class and ID selectors to the <span> tag.

Some popular CSS filters ◄ **Figure 3-28**

Filter	Description
Alpha	Creates a gradient fill
Blur	Makes text appear out of focus
Drop shadow	Casts a second separate shadow behind text
Glow	Creates an irregular-shaped, colored shadow behind text
Shadow	Casts a single shadow behind text
Wave	Bends text

This tutorial reviews filters generally so that you are aware of how they function, but unless you are developing Web pages for a corporate intranet and Internet Explorer is the default browser, you should avoid using filters on your Web pages.

Working with Filters

The **alpha filter** creates a gradient (a gradually increasing, shading) effect. The term *opacity* means the degree to which something reduces the passage of light. The more opaque an object is, the darker it is. For example, an object with 90 percent opacity is very dark. An object with 10 percent opacity is very light. As its name implies, the **blur filter** creates a blurred effect that makes the text seem out of focus. The **wave filter** causes text to

Tip

Avoid extremes in bending or blurring text. Make sure your text is readable.

bend. The **shadow filter** casts a single shadow behind the text. The **drop shadow filter** casts a second separate shadow behind the text. The **glow filter** creates a shadow behind text, but if you select bright colors for the background, the text has an irregular bright background, which mimics a glowing effect.

The glow filter takes the attributes and values described in Figure 3-29.

Figure 3-29 | **Glow filter attributes and values**

Attribute	Values
Color	The color for the shadow effect, which should be a bright color
Strength	The intensity of the glow effect, which can range from 1 to 255; the higher the number, the less intense the glow effect

Following is an example of how the glow filter would be coded:

```
<span style="width: 400; height: 150; font-size: 40pt; font-family:
arial; color: black; filter: glow(color=orange, strength=20)">Glow
Filter</span>
```

InSight | **Selecting a Filter**

With several filters to choose from, which filter should you use? If you are styling headlines or banners, the glow filter and the alpha filter are good choices for calling attention to a single line of text. For a single word, such as "Sale" or "Wow," the wave filter and the blur filter are ideal. For blocks of text, such as paragraphs, blockquotes, and addresses, the shadow and drop shadow filters are best.

Avoid using too many filters in your document. You want to use filters as a special effect to draw attention to a particular place on the Web page. If you have too many special effects on a Web page, it's difficult for the visitor to determine what's most important. Use filters sparingly. Filters can be fun to experiment with. Just be mindful that you want to use filters to enhance your Web page. At all times, keep the readability of the text in mind. Make sure the text can be easily read. If you use filters sparingly and use the effects in moderation, filters can be a very useful tool to add visual interest to your Web pages.

Richard has decided to create a banner at the top of the Career Fair Web page and wants to use the glow filter to make the banner stand out. You will show Richard how to use the glow filter in the banner.

To create a banner using the glow filter:

1. In Notepad, make sure the CareerNew HTML file is open.

2. Position the insertion point on the blank line below the start <body> tag and then press the **Enter** key.

3. Type the following code, which is also shown in red in Figure 3-30.

```
<p><span style="width: 400; height: 50; font-size: 40pt; font-family:
arial; color: black; filter: glow(color=orange, strength=20)">
The Career Fair</span></p>
```

The glow filter code ◄ Figure 3-30

code for creating a banner using the glow filter

```
<html>
<head>
<title>Welcome to the Career Fair</title>

<link rel="stylesheet" href="career.css" type="text/css" />
</head>

<body>

<p><span style="width: 400; height: 50; font-size: 40pt; font-family: arial; color: black; filter:
glow(color=orange, strength=20)">The Career Fair</span></p>

<h6>Make Your Contacts at the Career Fair</h6>
```

▶ **4.** Save the CareerNew HTML file.

▶ **5.** Refresh the CareerNew Web page in your browser, and then compare it to Figure 3-31 to verify that the glow filter heading is correct.

The glow filter effect in the browser ◄ Figure 3-31

The Career Fair ← glow filter applied

Make Your Contacts at the Career Fair

C areer fairs present an opportunity for you to showcase yourself before potential employers. You do not have to be a graduating senior to attend the Fair. You may attend just to see what opportunities are available for employment after you graduate. There's more to attending a career fair than just taking notes or bringing a stack of resumes with you.

Trouble? If you have coded a CSS filter and your browser displays a message in the Information bar explaining it has restricted the file from showing active content, click the message, click Allow Blocked Content, and then click the Yes button in the Security Warning Alert box.

Richard is also interested in using the shadow filter. The shadow filter takes the attributes and values described in Figure 3-32.

Figure 3-32 ▶ **Shadow filter attributes and values**

Attributes	Values
color	The color of the shadow
direction	The offset of the shadow in 45-degree increments between 0 and 315

Following is an example of how to code the shadow filter:

```
<span style="width: 400; height: 150; font-size: 40pt; font-family:
arial; color: black; filter: shadow(color=gray, direction=45)">Shadow
Filter</span>
```

Richard would like to use the shadow filter to draw attention to the address at the bottom of the page. You will show him how to code the shadow filter effect.

To create the shadow filter effect:

▶ **1.** In Notepad, make sure the CareerNew HTML file is open.

▶ **2.** Leave a blank line after the line that ends with "Contact:</p>."

▶ **3.** Type the following code, which is also shown in red in Figure 3-33.

```
<p><span style="width: 300; height: 30; font-size: 24pt; font-
family: arial; color: black; filter: shadow(color=gray,
direction=45)">
The Career Fair
<br />P. O. Box 35657A
<br />San Morillo, TX 37888
</span></p>
```

Figure 3-33 ▶ **The shadow filter code**

```
<h3>Don't Overstate</h3>
<p>If you are asked if you meet a particular qualification for a job, tell the truth if you don't.
If you don't have training in an area, stress that you have always been a quick learner and look
forward to training in that area. Want More Information? Contact:</p>

<p><span style="width: 300; height: 30; font-size: 24pt; font-family: arial; color: black; filter:
shadow(color=gray, direction=45)">
The Career Fair
<br />P. O. Box 35657A              ←——— code for creating the
<br />San Morillo, TX 37888              shadow filter effect
</span></p>
```

▶ **4.** Save the CareerNew HTML file.

▶ **5.** Refresh the CareerNew Web page in your browser, and then compare it to Figure 3-34 to verify that the shadow filter effect is correct.

The shadow filter in the browser — Figure 3-34

DON'T OVERSTATE

If you are asked if you meet a particular qualification for a job, tell the truth if you don't. If you don't have training in an area, stress that you have always been a quick learner and look forward to training in that area. Want More Information? Contact:

**The Career Fair
P. O. Box 35657A
San Morillo, TX
37888**

Earlier, you showed Richard how to create and apply a dependent class, a class that will style just one selector. You will now show Richard how to create and apply an independent class, a class that will style any selector.

Working with Filters | Reference Window

- To create a style for a filter, enclose the style code within a start <span> and an end </span> tag.
- Use an inline style to set properties and values for the height, the width, and all other properties and values you want to apply to the text. To style the filter, use the following syntax:

  `filter: filtername (attributes/values) Text`

  where *filter* is the property name, *filtername* is the type of filter you are using, such as glow or shadow; *attributes/values* are those attributes and values specific to the filter type, and *text* is the text that will be displayed.

Working with an Independent Class

In reviewing the Career Fair Web page, Richard decides that several elements on the page would look better if they were centered. He'd like to center the glow filter text and the image at the top of the page. You could accomplish these tasks by formatting with inline styles, but doing so would mean having to enter substantially more code in the HTML document. Also, if you changed your mind later and decided to have those elements left-aligned or right-aligned, you would have to edit the HTML document to find each inline style and edit the code.

This is a good opportunity to show Richard how to create and apply an independent class. Recall that an independent class can be applied to any element as many times as you want.

> **Tip**
>
> Choose meaningful names for class and ID selectors; sidebar, main, and banner are much more descriptive than class1, class2, and ID3.

To create the independent style:

▶ 1. Switch to the Career CSS file in Notepad.

▶ 2. On a blank line after the code for the p.opening:first-line element style, type the following code, which also appears in red in Figure 3-35.

```
.center {
text-align: center; }
```

Figure 3-35 ▶ **Code for the center independent class**

```
p.cap:first-letter {
font-size: 36pt;
font-family: arial,helvetica,sans-serif;
margin-right: 4px;
color: orange;
background-color: black; }

p.opening:first-line {
font-size: 16pt;
font-family: arial,helvetica,sans-serif;
color: brown; }

.center {
text-align: center; }
```

> independent style to center the glow filter text and the image at the top of the page

▶ **3.** Save the Career CSS file.

Now that the independent class has been created, you are ready to show Richard how to apply the class.

Applying an Independent Class

Once the independent class has been coded, you need to apply it. To apply the class, you use the class attribute and the value, which in this instance is "center".

```
<p class="center"><span style="width: 400; height: 50; font-size: 40pt;
font-family: Arial; color: black;Filter: Glow(Color=orange, Strength=20)">
The Career Fair</span></p>
```

Recall that Richard wants to center two elements—the glow filter text and the image. First, you will show Richard how to apply the center class to the glow filter text.

To apply the center class to the glow filter text:

▶ **1.** Switch to the CareerNew HTML file in Notepad.

▶ **2.** Locate the <p> element selector before the start <span> tag in the glow filter code, and then position the insertion point to the right of the letter "p."

▶ **3.** Press the **Spacebar** and then type **class="center"** as shown in red in Figure 3-36.

Figure 3-36 ▶ **Code to apply the center class**

```
<html>
<head>
<title>Welcome to the Career Fair</title>

<link rel="stylesheet" href="Career.css" type="text/css" />
</head>

<body>

<p class="center"><span style="width: 400; height: 50; font-size: 40pt; font-family: Arial; color:
black; Filter: Glow(Color=orange, Strength=20)">The Career Fair</span></p>

<h6>Make Your Contacts at the Career Fair</h6>
```

▶ **4.** Save the CareerNew HTML file.

▶ **5.** Refresh the CareerNew Web page in your browser. It should appear with the glow filter text centered as shown in Figure 3-37.

Next, you will show Richard how to apply the center class to the image. To center an image, you must establish a page division using the <div> tags. A start <div> tag precedes the image code and end </div> tag follows the code. The class is applied to the start <div> tag.

To apply the center class to the image:

▶ **1.** In Notepad, make sure the CareerNew HTML file is open.

▶ **2.** Locate the start <div> element selector above the image code, and then position the insertion point to the right of the word "div."

▶ **3.** Press the **Spacebar** and type **class="center"** as is shown in red in Figure 3-38.

Code to apply the center class to the <div> tag ◀ Figure 3-38

```
<html>
<head>
<title>Welcome to the Career Fair</title>

<link rel="stylesheet" href="Career.css" type="text/css" />
</head>

<body>

<p class="center"><span style="width: 400; height: 50; font-size: 40pt; font-family: Arial; color:
black; Filter: Glow(Color=orange, Strength=20)">The Career Fair</span></p>

<h6>Make Your Contacts at the Career Fair</h6>

<div class="center">
<img src="career.jpg" alt="image of students posing at the career fair" width="500"
height="332" />
</div>
```

▶ **4.** Save the CareerNew HTML file.

▶ **5.** Refresh the CareerNew Web page in your browser. It should appear as shown in Figure 3-39 with the image centered.

Figure 3-39 Image centered in the browser

The Career Fair

Make Your Contacts at the Career Fair

Career fairs present an opportunity for you to showcase yourself before potential employers. You do not have to be a graduating senior to attend the Fair. You may attend just to see what opportunities are available for employment after you graduate. There's more to attending a career fair than just taking notes or bringing a stack of resumes with you.

You will now show Richard how to create and apply an ID selector. Unlike independent classes, which can be used repeatedly to style elements on a Web page, ID selectors are used to style only a single instance of an element on a Web page.

Working with an ID Selector

Richard likes the look of the address at the bottom of the page. However, he'd like that address to be offset from the left margin by about an inch. As this will be the only instance in the document that will have such an offset, you will show Richard how to create and style an ID selector named *offset*.

To create the ID selector named offset.

▶ 1. Switch to the Career CSS file in Notepad.

▶ 2. On a blank line after the code for center style, type the following code, which also appears in red in Figure 3-40.

```
#offset {
margin-left: 5%; }
```

Code for the offset ID selector ◄ Figure 3-40

```
p.opening:first-line {
font-size: 16pt;
font-family: arial,helvetica,sans-serif;
color: brown; }

.center {
text-align: center; }

#offset {
margin-left: 5%; }
```

▶ **3.** Save the Career CSS file.

Styling the Same Element in Different Ways | InSight

So far, you have only created ID selectors that were independent of any element selector. You coded the flag character and the ID name, as follows: #borderthick. However, what if you wanted to style the same element several unique ways? For example, if you had a Web page with three images and you wanted each image to have its own unique border—one that had a thin border, another that had a medium border, and a third that had a thick border, it would be helpful to identify the element the ID selector is meant to style. It would be correct to code three independent ID selectors named #borderthin, #bordermedium, and #borderthick, but it would be better if you were to code three dependent ID selectors named thin, medium, and thick, like so:

```
img#thin {
border: navy thin solid; }

img#medium {
border: navy medium solid;}

img#thick {
border: navy thick solid; }
```

You would then apply each of the dependent IDs within the code for each of the three images. By creating dependent IDs, your code becomes self-documenting. You know that these ID selectors are designed to work with the img element selector and no other. You also are restricting the use of the IDs thin, medium, and thick to just the img element selector. If, for example, you erroneously applied the ID selector thin to an h1 element selector, the code would not take effect and the error would not occur.

Now that the ID has been created, you are ready to show Richard how to apply the ID selector.

Applying the ID Selector

Last, you will show Richard how to apply the ID selector to the address text.

To apply the ID selector to the address text:

▶ **1.** Switch to the CareerNew HTML file in Notepad.

▶ **2.** Locate the <p> element selector before the start <span> tag in the shadow filter code for the address, and then position the insertion point to the right of the letter "p."

► **3.** Press the **Spacebar** and then type **id="offset"** as shown in red in Figure 3-41.

Figure 3-41

Code to apply the offset ID selector

```
<p id="offset"><span style="width: 300; height: 30; font-size: 24pt; font-family: arial; color:
black; filter: shadow(color=gray, direction=45)">
The Career Fair
<br />P. O. Box 35657A
<br />San Morillo, TX 37888
</span></p>

</body>
</html>
```

► **4.** Save the CareerNew HTML file.

► **5.** Refresh the CareerNew Web page file in your browser. The completed Web page file should appear as shown in Figure 3-42 with the address indented.

The Career Fair

Make Your Contacts at the Career Fair

Career fairs present an opportunity for you to showcase yourself before potential employers. You do not have to be a graduating senior to attend the Fair. You may attend just to see what opportunities are available for employment after you graduate. There's more to attending a career fair than just taking notes or bringing a stack of resumes with you.

If you are a graduating senior, let's start by talking about your resume. A good resume alone won't get you the job, but it should – in one page – sum up your accomplishments to date.

YOUR RESUME

Your resume is a reflection of yourself, and like yourself, it should be perfect. There is absolutely no room in your resume for typographical errors, punctuation errors, spelling errors, or any other errors. Choose a paper that has substantial weight; don't type your resume on copying paper. Choose white or beige for both the resume and the cover letter.

DRESS THE PART

Make sure your shoes are polished (and don't wear athletic shoes). Hair should be neat and well groomed. Fingernails should be trimmed. No nail tips, please. Remove any visible body piercing. Carry only what you'll need for the fair. Don't have pockets jingling with coins or bulging with other personal belongings. Don't bring a large handbag. Both men and women should choose conservative clothes and colors – black, navy or charcoal gray in the colder months; olive or beige for the warmer months.

Women should choose a skirted suit or a well-tailored pants suit. A blouse and skirt is also okay, just as long as the skirt is not too short. The skirt should not be more than two inches off the knee. Dress shoes with a heel of not more than two inches would also be appropriate.

Men should select a classically cut and well-tailored suit. A shirt in lighter color than the suit, such as white, and a conservative patterned or striped tie is recommended. Shoes and socks should match and be either black or dark brown.

MAKE THE RIGHT FIRST IMPRESSION

Most people make judgments about you in the first five seconds. Give the right non-verbal signals. Stand up straight, walk confidently, give a firm handshake. Make eye contact, exhibit good listening skills, and above all, remember the name of the person whom you've been introduced to. Turn off your cell phone. Carry all your paperwork in a professional-looking briefcase or attache case.

ATTRACT, DON'T DISTRACT

Women should use accessories and jewelry sparingly. Don't have bangles and bracelets that make a lot of noise or attract attention. Leave the flashy jewelry at home. Makeup should be understated; don't overdue. Do not use cologne or perfume. Shower before the fair with a mild, fragrant soap. In general, don't be casual and don't be flashy.

SPEAK UP

In all your dealings at the fair, make sure that the person you are speaking to can hear you. This is not the time to be either shy or pushy either. Strike a balance between the two that will convey self-confidence without being pompous or overbearing

DON'T OVERSTATE

If you are asked if you meet a particular qualification for a job, tell the truth if you don't. If you don't have training in an area, stress that you have always been a quick learner and look forward to training in that area. Want More Information? Contact:

**The Career Fair
P. O. Box 35657A
San Morillo, TX
37888**

▶ **6.** Close Notepad and close your browser.

In this session you worked with filters. You learned that you should be judicious in your use of filters, as they are not standard CSS. When creating filters, bear in mind at all times that the text must still be readable. Use filters sparingly to create special text effects. You also learned how to create and apply an independent class. You did so to format several elements using the same style. You also learned how to create and apply an ID selector. Each ID selector can be used only once in the document.

Review | **Session 3.3 Quick Check**

1. Which filter creates a gradient fill?
2. Which filter causes text to appear as though it were bent?
3. Which filter creates a single shadow behind text?
4. Which filter creates a second shadow behind text?
5. Which filter causes the text to appear out of focus?
6. Which filter can be used to cast an irregular shadow in a brighter color behind text?
7. In using filters, what should you always keep in mind?

Review | **Tutorial Summary**

In Session 3.1, you learned classes are used to extend the number of selectors that are available to style. Classes can be dependent, which means they will only work with a particular HTML element selector. Classes can be independent, which means they will work with any HTML element selector. IDs are used to style a single instance of an HTML element. To apply either an independent or a dependent class, use the word *class* within the HTML element selector you want to style. External style sheet documents contain only CSS code; they do not contain any HTML code. To link an HTML file to a CSS file, use the <link> tag. Specificity and the cascade resolve style conflicts. In Session 3.2, you learned about the following text properties: letter-spacing, word-spacing, text-align, text-indent, text-transform, and text-decoration. Pseudo-elements can be used to style the first letter of a word or the first line of a paragraph. In Session 3.3, you learned about the following CSS filters: alpha, blur, shadow, drop shadow, wave, and glow. You also learned how to create and apply an independent style and how to create and apply an ID selector.

Key Terms

:first-letter	drop shadow filter	media attribute
:first-line	filter	proprietary code
alpha filter	glow filter	rel attribute
blur filter	hanging indent	shadow filter
cascade	href attribute	type attribute
dependent class	independent class	wave filter

Practice | **Review Assignments**

Take time to practice the skills you learned in the tutorial using the same case scenario.

Data Files needed for the Review Assignments: Cover.htm and Cover.jpg

Richard is satisfied with the Career Fair Web page. He now needs your help in creating a Web page that will help students prepare for an interview by writing an effective cover letter. Richard knows that a great cover letter is as important as having an attractive resume. He wants you to create a Web page that offers tips for composing a cover letter. First, you will show Richard how to create an external style sheet. Recall that external style sheets have no HTML code; they only have a comment and CSS code, and must be saved with a .css filename extension. After creating the CSS file, you will show Richard how to link an HTML file to the CSS style sheet. Last, you will apply classes in the HTML file. Richard has already created the HTML file, which he has named Cover. Complete the following steps:

1. In Notepad, open a new document and save it as a CSS file named **Cover.css** in the Tutorial.03\Review folder included with your Data Files.
2. Begin coding a CSS external style sheet by creating a comment that includes separate lines for your first and last name as the author, today's date, and the name of the HTML file that will link to this style sheet, which is CoverNew.htm.
3. Format the <body> element selector to display text in 12pt, Verdana font (a sans-serif font), with a text color of black and a background color of honeydew.
4. Format paragraphs to have a text indent of 3em.
5. Create a dependent style for the <p> element selector named **hanging**. The style creates a hanging indent with a text indent of –3em and a left margin of 3em.
6. Format h1 headings to appear in blue.
7. Format h3 headings to appear in teal.
8. Format the address element selector to display text in all uppercase, bold, but not italicized.
9. Format the <em> element selector to display text in bold and brown.
10. Save the Cover CSS file. In Notepad, open the **Cover** HTML file located in the Tutorial.03\Review folder included with your Data Files. Save this file as **CoverNew.htm** in the same folder.
11. Within the <head> section, type the necessary code to link the CoverNew HTML document to the Cover CSS file.
12. Apply the dependent class named *hanging* to the paragraph that begins with the word "Paper" and to the paragraph that begins with the word "Font."
13. Insert the **Cover** image (located in the Tutorial.03\Review folder included with your Data Files) between the set of <p></p> tags above the h3 heading "Explain Why You Are Writing to This Employer." The alternate text for the image should be **image of young job seekers**. The image is 250 pixels wide and 166 pixels high.
14. Save your CoverNew HTML document, and then open it in your browser. The document should be similar to the one shown in Figure 3-43.

Figure 3-43

The Cover Letter

The Mechanics of the Letter

It may go without saying, but the cover letter must be perfect. The cover letter is not intended to get you the job, it's intended to get your foot in the door. You can eliminate yourself from being considered for a job if your cover letter is nothing less than perfect. Proofread the letter at least three times. Have someone else proofread the letter, too. A second set of eyes can find mistakes that you might miss. Grammar and punctuation must be 100% correct. No typos, please. Don't rely on just the spell check feature of a word processor alone. *Proofread for meaning.*

Paper – The paper must be at least 20lb paper, preferably a 100% cotton fiber. A more substantial paper weight of 24lb would be better. Choose bright white or off-white (beige). Don't choose a color such as red or bright yellow that will actually put off a potential employer. A White or a neutral color works best.

Font – Don't choose a font face that is hard to read, such as a fantasy font or a script font. Choose Arial or Times New Roman. Arial is a more modern typeface. Times New Roman is a more conservative type face. The more conservative the company, the more likely you would be to choose a serif font, like Times New Roman.

Explain Why You are Writing to This Employer

Identify your skills and accomplishments. Don't embellish. State the truth in simple facts. If you started a newsletter, participated in charity events, were the president or an officer of one or more clubs, or was the quarterback of the football team – just state what you did and why it mattered to you. All of these activities give you experience in leadership and working as part of a team.

Tell the Employer Why You Want to Work for the Company

Do some research. What makes this company so special? Is it that they are a start-up company and you have a special talent that will help them get off the ground? Is it an established company whose reputation and stability are the attraction? Tell the employer that you want to be part of that organization and that it really matters to you that you get the job. Don't tell them that you need a job – tell them how *their company* will benefit from hiring you.

Wrap it Up

Thank the reader for his or her time, and invite him or her to contact you. Give them your phone number(s) and email address. Invite the reader to contact you so that you may better explain in greater detail why you are qualified for the position you are seeking. *Your gain is their gain.*

THE CAREER FAIR
P. O. BOX 35657A
SAN MORILLO, TX 37888

15. Close all open windows.
16. Submit the results of the preceding steps to your instructor, either in printed or electronic form, as requested.

Apply | Case Problem 1

Use the skills you learned in the tutorial to create a Web page for a chain of restaurants.

Data Files needed for this Case Problem: Beans.htm and Beans.jpg

Bean's Beans Restaurants   Bean's Beans Restaurants is a small chain of restaurants located in the Boston area and its surrounding suburbs. Bean's Beans specializes in dishes that complement Boston baked beans. The family-friendly restaurants serve their customers simple food at reasonable prices in a relaxed atmosphere. Jackie Jermaine, the owner of Bean's Beans, has asked you to create a Web page that features the restaurant's new line of special dishes, which are:

- Wings over Boston
- Baby back beans
- Bean bombs (flaky pastry stuffed with beef and beans filling)

- Rice and beans
- Bean curd ice cream

You will make use of the glow filter to draw attention to the menu items in the HTML file. You will first create a CSS style sheet, and then link the HTML file to the CSS file. Finally, you will apply classes to the HTML file. Complete the following steps:

1. In Notepad, open a new document and save it as a CSS file named **Beans.css** in the Tutorial.03\Case1 folder included with your Data Files.

2. Begin coding a CSS external style sheet by creating a comment that includes separate lines for your first and last name as the author, today's date, and the name of the HTML file that will link to this style sheet, which is BeansNew.htm.

3. Format the <body> element selector to display text in 14pt Arial font (a sans-serif font), with white text on a black background. Use short hex values for the colors.

4. Create an independent class named **center** that formats text as centered.

5. Format the <p> element selector to center text.

6. Format the <strong> element selector to display text in navy with an orange background.

7. Create a dependent class for the <strong> element selector named **special** that formats text to be 16pt white text on a green background.

8. Save the Beans CSS file. In Notepad, open the **Beans** HTML file located in the Tutorial.03\Case1 folder included with your Data Files. Save this file as **BeansNew. htm** in the same folder.

9. Within the <head> section, type the necessary code to link BeansNew.htm to Beans.css.

10. Apply the dependent class named *special* to the last instance of the <strong> tag at the bottom of the page.

11. Just above the </body> tag, insert the code for the Beans image. The alternate text for the image is **picture of creamy, bean curd ice cream**. The image is 500 pixels wide and 361 pixels high.

12. Just above the image code, insert a start <div> tag and apply the center class. Below the image code, insert an end </div> tag.

13. Save your BeansNew HTML document, and then open it in your browser. The document should be similar to the one shown in Figure 3-44.

Figure 3-44

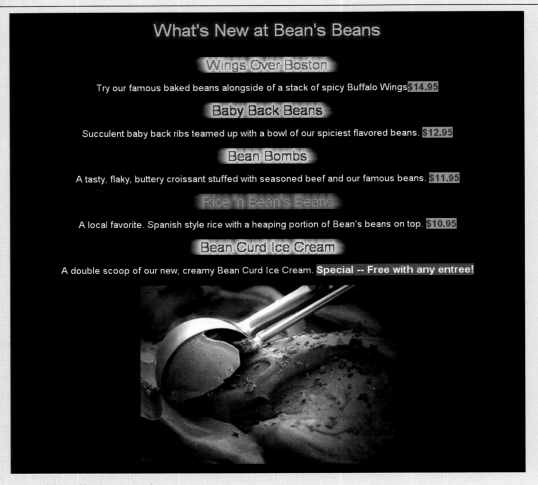

14. Close all open windows.
15. Submit the results of the preceding steps to your instructor, either in printed or electronic form, as requested.

| Apply | **Case Problem 2** |

Use the skills you learned in the tutorial to create and style a Web page for a women's organization.

Data Files needed for this Case Problem: Women.htm and Women.jpg

Women's Web Entrepreneurs Women's Web Entrepreneurs (WWE) is an organization in Wilmington, Delaware, dedicated to helping women start their own businesses on the Web. Lynda Fong, an associate at WWE, has contacted you about creating a Web page that offers some tips for women thinking of creating an online business. She has asked you to tap into your own experience in creating visitor-friendly Web pages. In the WWE Web page, she wants you to highlight important facts to remember when starting up a business online. You will first create a CSS style sheet, and then you will link and apply classes to an HTML file. Complete the following:

1. In Notepad, open a new document and save it as a CSS file named **Women.css** in the Tutorial.03\Case2 folder included with your Data Files.

2. Begin coding a CSS external style sheet by creating a comment that includes separate lines for your first and last name as the author, today's date, and the name of the HTML file that will link to this style sheet, which is WomenNew.htm.

3. Format the <body> element selector to display text in 13pt Verdana (a sans-serif) font, with black text on a light yellow background.

4. Style the <p> element selector so that paragraphs have a text indent of 2em.

5. Create an independent style named **center**. Format the style to center text.

EXPLORE

6. Create a dependent class named **opening** for the <p> element selector using the :first-line pseudo-element. The text should appear in a 16pt Arial font and in brown.

7. Style the h2 element selector to display text as italic and maroon on a wheat background.

8. Style the h3 element selector as navy text on a wheat background. Make sure that the background color does not extend from the left edge of the screen to the right edge of the screen.

9. Style the <address> element selector to display as bold and Arial text. The text should be all uppercase letters as white text on a navy background. Make sure the background color does not extend from the left edge of the screen to the right edge of the screen.

EXPLORE

10. Create an ID selector named **left**. Format the ID so that elements are left-aligned and have a text indent of 0.

11. Save the Women CSS file. In Notepad, open the **Women** HTML file located in the Tutorial.03\Case2 folder included with your Data Files. Save this file as **WomenNew.htm** in the same folder.

12. Within the <head> section of the WomenNew HTML file, type the code to link **WomenNew** to the **Women** CSS file.

13. Apply the independent class named *center* to the h1 heading.

14. Apply the dependent class named *opening* to the first paragraph of the document.

15. Just above the end </body> tag and between the <p></p> tags, insert the code for an image named **Women.jpg**. The alternate text is **picture of businesswomen**. The image is 162 pixels wide and 250 pixels high.

16. Apply the ID selector named *left* to the paragraph tag that precedes the image code.

17. Save your WomenNew HTML document, and then open the **WomenNew** HTML file in your browser. Refresh the screen. The document should be similar to the one shown in Figure 3-45.

Figure 3-45

Women's Web Entrepreneurs

Let Your Web Site Do Your Work

You want to run a business out of your home or a storefront, but you need a sales and marketing plan. The Web can be your most effective, tireless 24x7 salesperson. Here are some tips to turn your Web site into an effective marketing tool:

Looks Matter

If your site looks amateurish, you've lost credibility with your customers. Turn off the blinking, flashing, scrolling, and crawling text. You're running a business Web site, not an amusement park. Choose a readable font in a size that's easy to read. Stick to one font face and not more than three font sizes. It may be interesting to have 10 different font faces on your site, but having too many font faces tends to detract from your site, not enhance it. Your Web site should not look like a ransom note. Use neutral tones or colors that complement each other. Avoid red — 5% of the population is color blind and can't see it; also red is associated with danger and financial loss.

Title Tales

No, I'm not talking about titles such as Ms. or Mrs. and the like. Search engines scan the title bar in their search for "hits." If your company name is "Astro Galaxy Unlimited" and you sell cosmetics, you might do a great job in attracting astrophysicists to your Web site, but you're not going to land at the top of anyone's hit list who's searching for cosmetics. Include meaningful words in the title, not just the company name.

Let Your Page Inform, not Entertain

Flash is a technology that places interesting animations on a Web page. Don't let your site have a Flash "splash page," whereby the visitor to your site has to click to first get past the Flash page in order to view your home page. Put the Flash presentations on your home page so that the user has a choice of whether or not to view the Flash presentation.

Get Their Attention

At the top of your page, state what your company can do for the customer. Why are you the best? Why should the customer use your services? What makes you so special? Why should the customer buy your goods or use your services? Make these reasons clear from the start and at the top.

Let's Make Contact

Don't make the customer have to search for contact information. That's a great way to kill a sale, not create one. Make sure your contact information is easy to find. Have your address, phone number, fax number, email address and link at the top and the bottom of every page.

Get the Picture

Photos should be the right size (not more than 3 inches by 3 inches and not be distorted. Your photos should not look like a fun house mirror. Background graphics should contrast with, not compete with, text. If you have a lot of photos, create thumbnail images (about 1 - 1 1/2 inches square) that link to larger-size images. Having the large images on separate pages means your home page will download faster. Also, pages with several large photos and little text look quite "old school" and amateurish — it looks as if you've got nothing to say, and that's the last thing you want to convey to your readers.

How Will You Compete?

Decide early on how you will differentiate yourself from others — price, selection, expertise, market niche, uniqueness, speed of delivery, unique knowledge of the subject matter — all of these aspects are important in starting a business and staying in business

WOMEN'S COUNCIL ON ENTREPRENEURSHIP IN THE AMERICAS
23 BUTLER BLVD.
SUITE 400B
HAMILTON CREEK, NJ 35688

18. Close all open windows.
19. Submit the results of the preceding steps to your instructor, either in printed or electronic form, as requested.

| Challenge | **Case Problem 3** |

Use what you've learned and expand your skills to create and style a Web page for an alternative power company.

Data Files needed for this Case Problem: Power.htm and Power.jpg

Panama River Power Solutions A new alternative energy company, Panama River Power Solutions serves the customers primarily in the Pacific Northwest. Eventually the company hopes to expand its energy services throughout the entire United States. Panama River Power Solutions specializes in alternative fuel energy. It prides itself that none of the energy it produces comes from fossil or nuclear fuels. Panama River Power Solutions hopes to offer cheap, abundant, nonpolluting sources of renewable energy. You have been asked to create a Web page that highlights the benefits of the new company and the services it offers to its customers. You will create an external CSS style sheet, and then link an HTML file to the style sheet and apply classes in the HTML file. Complete the following:

1. In Notepad, open a new document and save it as a CSS file named **Power.css** in the Tutorial.03\Case3 folder included with your Data Files.
2. Begin coding a CSS external style sheet by creating a comment that includes separate lines for your first and last name as the author, today's date, and the name of the HTML file that will link to this style sheet, which is PowerNew.htm.
3. Format the <body> element selector to display text in 12pt Arial black with a background color of linen.

◆EXPLORE 4. Create an independent class named **spread** that formats text to have letter spacing of 0.3em, word spacing of 0.3em, and a margin of 0.

◆EXPLORE 5. Create a dependent class for the <p> element selector named **dropcap** that will format the drop cap to be 36pt and bold with a right margin of 2px. The drop cap should also have green text and a background color of linen.

◆EXPLORE 6. Create a dependent class for the <p> element selector named **contact** that formats the first line of a paragraph to appear in 13pt bold green text.

7. Format the <ul> element selector to display text as 14pt and brown.
8. Format the <strong> element selector to display text in green.
9. Save the Power CSS file. In Notepad, open the **Power** HTML file located in the Tutorial.03\Case3 folder included with your Data Files. Save this file as **PowerNew.htm** in the same folder.
10. Within the <head> section of the PowerNew HTML document, type the code to link PowerNew.htm to Power.css.
11. Apply the independent class named *spread* to the <p> element selector that begins with the code for the words "Alternative Clean Energy."
12. Apply the dependent class named *dropcap* to the <p> element selector in the paragraph that begins with the word "Here."
13. In the next to last paragraph, apply the dependent class named *contact* to the <p> element selector before the word "Contact."
14. Between the <p></p> tags and below the drop shadow text for "Panama River Power Solutions," insert the code for the Power.jpg image. The alternate text is **image of solar panels**. The image has a width of 250 and a height of 166.

15. In the last line of the document, apply the independent class named *spread* to the <p> element selector before the number "220."

16. Save your PowerNew HTML document, and then open it in your browser. The document should be similar to the one shown in Figure 3-46.

Figure 3-46

Panama River Power Solutions

Alternative Clean Energy

H ere at **Panama River Power Solutions**, we are dedicated to supplying the nation and the world with "green" energy – energy that is clean, reliable, abundant, inexpensive, renewable, and environmentally friendly. It's energy with a "zero-carbon footprint." There is no use of fossil or nuclear fuels. In today's uncertain times, it is imperative that new solutions for today's – and tomorrow's – energy needs be implemented. When you factor in global warming and national security concerns, green energy supplied by **Panama River Power Solutions** is the right choice at the right time. Don't delay in getting started now.

We specialize in the following green energy sources:

- Wind Turbine Power
- Ocean Wave and Tidal Energy
- Hydrogen Fuel Cell
- Solar Energy
- Geothermal Energy

Contact Panama River Power Solutions today for a free evaluation of your alternative energy needs.

220 · The Landing · Mt. Marrone, Washington 67845

17. Close all open windows.

18. Submit the results of the preceding steps to your instructor, either in printed or electronic form, as requested.

| Create | **Case Problem 4** |

With the figure provided as a guide, create a Web page for a frozen fruit producer.

Data Files needed for this Case Problem: Banana.htm, Banana.jpg, Fruit.jpg, Smoothie.jpg, and Split.jpg

BrrrNana The BrrrNana Company is a Plainsfield, North Dakota company that sells frozen fruit desserts. As you can expect, many of the products are made primarily from bananas, but the company also sells a line of smoothie drinks created from a variety of fruits, including its famed BrrrNana Smoothie. You have been asked to create a Web page that markets their products. Complete the following:

1. In Notepad, open a new document and save it as a CSS file named **Banana.css** in the Tutorial.03\Case4 folder included with your Data Files.

2. Begin coding a CSS external style sheet by creating a comment that includes separate lines for your first and last name as the author, today's date, and the name of the HTML file that will link to this style sheet, which is BananaNew.htm.

3. Format the <body> element selector for point size, font, color, and background color of your choice.

4. In the style sheet, create styles that illustrate the use of each of the properties that you learned about in this tutorial. Available tags to be styled are <h1>, <h2>, <h3>, <p>, <strong>, <em>, <blockquote>, <ul>, and <address>. You can also style additional tags in the HTML document if you want.

5. Create one dependent class.

6. Create one independent class.

7. Create one ID selector.

8. Save the Banana CSS file. In Notepad, open the **Banana** HTML file located in the Tutorial.03\Case4 folder included with your Data Files. Save this file as **BananaNew. htm**, and then open it in the browser. The Web page you are creating will be similar to the one shown in Figure 3-47.

Figure 3-47

B r r r N a n a   F r o z e n   D e s s e r t s

Looking for a Refreshing Drink for All Seasons?

BrrrNana is this region's leading maker of frozen desserts. We specialize, of course, in our famous *BrrrNana smoothie*, but we are much more than that! BrrrNana products are available year-round. We even have an entire line of low-calorie frozen desserts. All our products are made from 100% fruits and fruit juice. We use no artificial colors, no artificial flavors, and no preservatives. **We are 100% all natural.**

If you are looking to please a large group, buy one of our fruit plates. We sell them in all sizes, from 1 serving to 100. If you are just pleasing yourself or pleasing an entire crowd, we can satisfy your needs for fresh, wholesome desserts. Skip the cake and the brownies and try one of our fruit plates instead. You will be glad you did, and your friends and family will thank you for it as well. If you are in the mood for ice cream, try one of our frozen yogurt banana splits instead. You will get all the taste of ice cream, but only half the calories.

Here are some of our smoothie flavors

- BrrrNana Kiwi
- Grrrape
- Strrrawberry Pineapple
- Lemon BrrrNana
- Orange Tangerrrine

Here's what *Dessert Maker Magazine* had to say about our products

BrrrNana products continue to amaze. All of their products are highly recommended. Their smoothies have just the right amount of consistency so that they are not too thick nor too thin. I think they are made by Goldilocks – they are always just right!

Want to learn more?

Contact Us At:

BrrrNana Frozen Products
23 Steinway Street
Lansing, ND 45899
1 880-654-4566

BrrrNana Yogurt Split

9. Within the head section of BananaNew.htm, type the code to link BananaNew.htm to Banana.css.
10. Apply the dependent class.
11. Apply the independent class.
12. Apply the ID selector.
13. In your document, use at least one of the images located in the Tutorial.03\Case4 folder included with your Data Files: Banana.jpg, Fruit.jpg, Smoothie.jpg, or Split.jpg. Size the image to your liking, but retain the aspect ratio of the original image. Use <div> </div> tags and apply a class to center the image.
14. Save the BananaNew HTML document, Refresh the BananaNew Web page in your browser, and then compare your screen with the one shown in Figure 3-47.
15. Close all open windows.

16. Submit the results of the preceding steps to your instructor, either in printed or electronic form, as requested.

Review | **Quick Check Answers**

Session 3.1

1. dependent and independent
2. When the selector will only be applied once in the document.
3. an inline style
4. an embedded style
5. a class selector
6. Assuming the selectors have the same specificity, the selector that is declared further from the top of the style sheet will take effect.
7. There should be no HTML code in a style sheet document.
8. a comment
9. .css

Session 3.2

1. text-decoration
2. text-indent
3. text-align
4. a spread effect
5. The text-transform property will display text in all capitals, all lowercase, or in initial capitals. The font-variant property displays text in all capitals in a smaller point size.
6. Use the text-indent property and assign it a negative value. Use the margin-left property and assign it a corresponding and equal positive value.
7. Line-through is a text-decoration property. It creates a line through text that is marked for deletion. The legal profession.
8. Blink. Also, do not underscore text.
9. none

Session 3.3

1. the alpha filter
2. the wave filter
3. the shadow filter
4. the drop shadow filter
5. the blur filter
6. the glow filter
7. the readability of the text

Ending Data Files

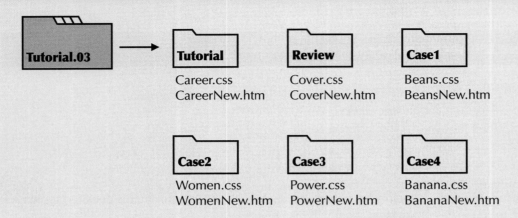

Tutorial 4

Objectives

Session 4.1
• Wrap text around an image
• Use an image as a horizontal rule
• Format the default horizontal rule
• Use the <div> tag

Session 4.2
• Investigate the box model
• Explore the padding, margin, and border properties
• Float an image or text
• Use the clear property

Session 4.3
• Change the list style type and position
• Use an image in a bulleted list
• Format and float headings
• Create definition lists
• Work with background properties

Exploring Graphic Elements and Images

Enhancing a Web Page with Rules, Lists, and Images

Case | Gina and Dina's Cooking Show

Gina Hanson and Dina Miraldi have a weekly cable TV show in St. Paul, Minnesota. During the show, they feature simple home cooking and demonstrate how to make a variety of meals that people can prepare in 45 minutes or less. Their audience ranges from viewers with little or no cooking experience to those who know how to cook, but have little time to prepare meals. Each week, Gina and Dina show how to prepare, cook, and serve dishes that are appealing, nutritious, and popular with children and adults. After each show, Gina and Dina publish a Web page with the week's recipe, a photo of the dish, and shopping tips. Jennifer Broxton, the show's sales and marketing associate, asks for your assistance in creating a Web page for the weekly recipe. This week's theme is Italian-style cooking, and the featured recipe is a simple, inexpensive staple—spaghetti and meatballs. Jennifer has already written some promotional copy and saved it as a Web page, which you will use as the content for the Web page you will design.

In this tutorial, you enhance a Web page by adding rules (lines), lists, and images. You fine-tune the layout by wrapping text around an image and using the <div> tag to position images. You control the white space on the Web page by setting style properties. You also specify the appearance of lists, including using an image as a bullet. Finally, you work with background properties to set the appearance of the Web page background.

Starting Data Files

Tutorial.04 →

Tutorial
Gina.htm
GinaLogo.gif
Meatballs.jpg
Paste.jpg
Spaghetti.jpg
Sunset.gif
Tile.jpg
Tomato.gif
Veggies.gif

Review
Cook.htm
Frying.jpg
Pans.jpg
Parchment.gif
Pot.gif

Case1
Bullet.gif
Galaxy.gif
Planet.htm
Shore.gif

Case2
Block.gif
Dragon.gif
Dragon.htm
Slide.gif
Splash.gif

Case3
Beach.gif
Beach.htm
Collage.gif
Sand.gif

Case4
Fire.htm
Fire.jpg
Stone.gif
Truck.jpg

Session 4.1

Including Images, Borders, and Text on Web Pages

Tip

To create graphic elements such as lines and shapes and to draw or edit images such as drawings, clip art, and photos, use commercially available graphics software.

When you used images in some of the Web pages you have created so far, you might have noticed that the text on the page did not wrap around the image. You have also placed all of the code for images within <p></p> tags. Doing so causes the image to appear at the left edge of the browser window, but it also creates too much white space to the right of the image. You can control the appearance of images and white space on a Web page by positioning images and wrapping text around an image. You can also enhance the appearance of a Web page by working with the box properties to add padding, borders, and margins to HTML elements and by using images with lists. In addition, you will take advantage of a CSS feature that allows you to position an image anywhere on a Web page, not just at the left edge of the browser window.

InSight | **Improving Web Page Design with Graphics**

Following are a few general guidelines for using graphic elements and images on your Web page. Your goal is to enhance the visual appeal and convey information with graphic elements. Be especially careful to avoid cluttering the page.

- Add extra space around images so the text doesn't crowd them.
- Use light, simple backgrounds that don't interfere with the text.
- Add space between text and borders to avoid clutter.
- Put graphics and text side by side to minimize scrolling.

Although you cannot create graphic elements or draw pictures with HTML or CSS, you can use them to place graphics including horizontal rules, borders, and list item entries on a Web page.

To view the original Gina and Dina Web page:

▶ **1.** Use Notepad to open the **Gina.htm** file located in the Tutorial.04\Tutorial folder included with your Data Files. Save the file as **GinaNew.htm** in the same folder.

▶ **2.** Open the file in your browser. The Web page should look similar to the one shown in Figure 4-1.

Original Gina and Dina Web page   Figure 4-1

This Week's Recipe — Spaghetti with Meatballs

Spaghetti and meatballs is an inexpensive dish that everyone seems to enjoy. The trick is to get the spaghetti al dente, which is to cook the pasta so that it is not too firm (uncooked) and yet not too tender so that it becomes a pile of blonde mush.

Getting Started

Don't scrimp on the water. Cook your pasta in plenty of water in a high-rimmed saucepan. Some people like to add oil to the water, but oil and water don't mix, so a better strategy is to put a little extra virgin olive oil on the pasta after it's been cooked and drained. That will add flavor and keep the pasta from sticking.

Water does matter. If you live in an area where the water quality is not up to par, consider boiling the pasta in bottled water or filtered water from a tap if you have a filter installed on the faucet. The pasta can pick up bad odors and taste from water that does not taste good to begin with.

Boil that Water

Get the water to a roiling (that means "really bubbling") temperature. Toss in the pasta and stir with a wooden spoon or fork. Follow the package label for cooking times, but generally cook the pasta in boiling water for about 10-12 minutes. The last 3 minutes are critical. You want the pasta al dente (firm, yet tender). Try tasting some of the pasta every minute for the last three minutes. When you think you've got the right tenderness, strain the pasta in a colander and then pour cold water on the pasta to stop the pasta from cooking any further.

Make Some Sauce

For the sauce, you can use any commercial canned or jar sauce to save time. Most of the sauces sold in the supermarket are quite good. If you want to make your own sauce, chop up a medium-sized onion and 1 or 2 cloves of garlic. Toss the onion and garlic into a large saucepan. Add two 28-ounce cans of whole tomatoes, one 6-ounce can of tomato paste, and 1 tablespoon of extra virgin olive oil.

Heat in a saucepan and stir on very low heat. Some people feel that sauce should be cooked for several hours. Most people don't have such discriminating palettes, so a slow simmer on low heat for about 10-15 minutes is just fine.

Cook the Meatballs

Of course, while the pasta is cooking (set the timer to 10 minutes) you can make the meatballs and the sauce. For the meatballs, in a large mixing bowl, mix one cup of breadcrumbs, 2 large eggs, and 1 pound of lean, ground beef. You can season as you like with salt, pepper, chicken broth, oregano, and basil. For an added touch, you can also mix in 1/4 cup freshly grated Romano or Parmesan cheese. Mix all the ingredients together and spoon into meatballs about 1" round. After you've formed the meatballs, one by one, place the meatballs into a frying pan that has been greased with one or two tablespoons of extra virgin olive oil. Cook on low-to-medium heat until the meatballs are brown.

Pour it On

Put the pasta on a large platter, spoon on the meatballs, and cover with the sauce.

Ingredients

Pasta:

You may use either boxed pasta or refrigerated, fresh pasta.

- 1 pound spaghetti

Meatballs:

Use either 93% lean beef or a mix or ground turkey and ground pork.

- 1 cup of breadcrumbs
- 2 large eggs
- 1 pound lean ground beef
- 1/4 cup grated Romano cheese
- 1 teaspoon fresh oregano
- 1/2 teaspoon salt
- 1/4 teaspoon pepper

Tomato Sauce:

If you wish to have home made, rather than from a jar or can.

- 1 teaspoon vegetable oil
- 1 medium onion, chopped
- 2 cloves garlic, chopped
- 2 28-ounce cans whole tomatoes
- 1 6-ounce can tomato paste
- lightly salt and pepper to taste

You are setting the style for the Gina and Dina Web page using an embedded style sheet. You'll show Jennifer how to insert the style tags.

To insert the style tags for the Web page:

▶ **1.** Make sure the GinaNew file is open in Notepad.

▶ **2.** On a blank line below the page title, type the following code, which is also shown in red in Figure 4-2.

```
<style type="text/css">



</style>
```

Tip

Be sure to set the style for the <body> tag to give the document a consistent look and override any choices users set in their browsers.

Figure 4-2 ▶ **The start and end style tags**

```
<html>
<head>
<title>Gina and Dina's Simple Home Cooking</title>

<style type="text/css">

</style>

</head>

<body>
```

specifies an embedded style sheet

Jennifer wants the page to have a modern look, so she suggests using the Arial font. You will show her how to style the body element now. You'll insert code to specify black, 11pt text on a bisque background.

To insert the code to set the style for the body:

▶ **1.** In the GinaNew document in your text editor, position the insertion point below the start <style> tag.

▶ **2.** On a blank line below the start <style> tag, type the following code, which is also shown in red in Figure 4-3.

```
body {
margin: 20px;
color: black;
background-color: bisque;
font-size: 11pt;
font-family: arial,helvetica,sans-serif; }
```

Code to set the style for the body element ◄ Figure 4-3

```
<html>
<head>
<title>Gina and Dina's Simple Home Cooking</title>

<style type="text/css">

body {
margin: 20px;
color: black;
background-color: bisque;
font-size: 11pt;
font-family: arial,helvetica,sans-serif; }

</style>

</head>

<body>
```

specifies black, 11pt text on a bisque background

▶ **3.** Save GinaNew, and then refresh the file in a browser. Compare the Web page to Figure 4-4 to verify that the font is 11pt Arial and the background color is bisque.

Web page with the formatted body text ◄ Figure 4-4

black, 11pt text on a bisque background

This Week's Recipe — Spaghetti with Meatballs

Spaghetti and meatballs is an inexpensive dish that everyone seems to enjoy. The trick is to get the spaghetti al dente, which is to cook the pasta so that it is not too firm (uncooked) and yet not too tender so that it becomes a pile of blonde mush.

Getting Started

Don't scrimp on the water. Cook your pasta in plenty of water in a high-rimmed saucepan. Some people like to add oil to the water, but oil and water don't mix, so a better strategy is to put a little extra virgin olive oil on the pasta after it's been cooked and drained. That will add flavor and keep the pasta from sticking.

Water does matter. If you live in an area where the water quality is not up to par, consider boiling the pasta in bottled water or filtered water from a tap if you have a filter installed on the faucet. The pasta can pick up bad odors and taste from water that does not taste good to begin with.

The document contains several headings, which you also want to format. To add some variety to the appearance of the headings, you will show Jennifer how to set the style for the h2 and h3 headings.

To insert the code to format the h2 and h3 headings:

▶ **1.** Make sure the GinaNew file is open in Notepad.

▶ **2.** On a blank line below the body style, type the following code, which is also shown in red in Figure 4-5.

```
h2 {
font-size: 14pt;
color: green;
margin-top: .5em; }

h3 {
font-size: 12pt;
color: maroon; }
```

Figure 4-5	Code to set the style for the h2 and h3 headings

```
h2 {
font-size: 14pt;
color: green;
margin-top: .5em; }
```
sets the style of h2 headings as 14pt green text

```
h3 {
font-size: 12pt;
color: maroon; }
```
sets the style of h3 headings as 12pt maroon text

```
</style>

</head>

<body>
```

▶ **3.** Save GinaNew, and then refresh the file in a browser. Compare the Web page to Figure 4-6 to verify that the h2 and h3 headings are now formatted.

Figure 4-6	The h2 and h3 headings on the Web page

This Week's Recipe — Spaghetti with Meatballs ◀— h2 heading

Spaghetti and meatballs is an inexpensive dish that everyone seems to enjoy. The trick is to get the spaghetti al dente, which is to cook the pasta so that it is not too firm (uncooked) and yet not too tender so that it becomes a pile of blonde mush.

Getting Started ◀— h3 heading

Don't scrimp on the water. Cook your pasta in plenty of water in a high-rimmed saucepan. Some people like to add oil to the water, but oil and water don't mix, so a better strategy is to put a little extra virgin olive oil on the pasta after it's been cooked and drained. That will add flavor and keep the pasta from sticking.

Jennifer has provided you with an image file for the Gina and Dina Web site logo, which she wants to display at the top of the page. The logo and the Web page will make extensive use of the colors green, white, and red, which are the colors of the Italian flag. You will show Jennifer how to insert the image file of the logo at the top of the page.

To insert the logo image:

▶ **1.** Make sure the GinaNew file is open in Notepad.

▶ **2.** Position the insertion point below the start <body> tag, and then press the **Enter** key twice to create a new line.

▶ **3.** Type the following code, which is also shown in red in Figure 4-7.

```
<img src="ginalogo.gif" alt="the gina and dina logo" width="650"
height="100" />
```

Tip

Although the filenames of the Data Files used mixed case, as in GinaLogo, use all lowercase text to enter filenames in code to be consistent with CSS specifications.

Image code for the logo ◀ **Figure 4-7**

inserts the logo and specifies the alt text

```
</head>

<body>

<img src="ginalogo.gif" alt="the gina and dina logo" width="650" height="100" />

<hr />
```

▶ **4.** Save GinaNew, and then refresh the file in a browser. Compare the Web page to Figure 4-8 to verify that the image of the Gina and Dina logo is displayed.

Gina and Dina logo displayed on the Web page ◀ **Figure 4-8**

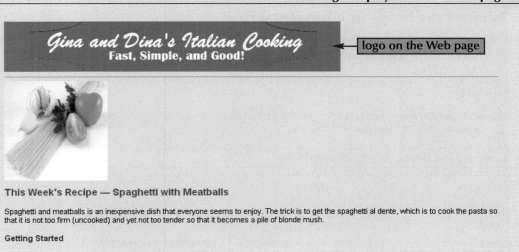

logo on the Web page

This Week's Recipe — Spaghetti with Meatballs

Spaghetti and meatballs is an inexpensive dish that everyone seems to enjoy. The trick is to get the spaghetti al dente, which is to cook the pasta so that it is not too firm (uncooked) and yet not too tender so that it becomes a pile of blonde mush.

Getting Started

Jennifer is pleased with the appearance of the Gina and Dina logo. She would, however, like some separation between the logo and the page content. You will show Jennifer how horizontal rules can act as dividers to organize the page content.

Enhancing the Appearance of Horizontal Rules

In earlier tutorials, you used the <hr /> tag to create a horizontal rule. However, the default rule is a thin gray line, which by itself is a rather plain graphics object. To create more visual interest, you can use an image as a horizontal rule. Many clip-art packages available on CDs, DVDs, or downloaded from the Web have hundreds of images designed for use as horizontal rules. When you use an image as a rule, you do not use the <hr /> tag—you insert the image of the rule as you would any other image, using all the attributes and values for an image. The following example uses an image file named Veggies.gif as a horizontal rule, which is a repeating image of vegetables. The image is shown in Figure 4-9.

```
<img src="veggies.gif" alt="horizontal rule of image of vegetables"
width="650" height="50" />
```

Figure 4-9   **Veggies.gif image as an example of an image as a horizontal rule**

You will add an image as a horizontal rule below the image code for the logo.

To insert the image as a horizontal rule:

▶ **1.** In the GinaNew document in your text editor, position the insertion point after the code for the logo image.

▶ **2.** Press the **Enter** key, and then type the following code, which is also shown in red in Figure 4-10.

```
<imgsrc="veggies.gif" alt="horizontal rule image of vegetables"
width="650" height="50" />
```

Figure 4-10   **Code for the image as a horizontal rule**

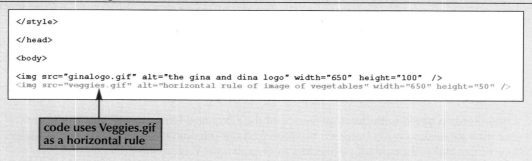

```
</style>
</head>
<body>
<img src="ginalogo.gif" alt="the gina and dina logo" width="650" height="100" />
<img src="veggies.gif" alt="horizontal rule of image of vegetables" width="650" height="50" />
```

code uses Veggies.gif as a horizontal rule

▶ **3.** Save GinaNew, and then refresh the file in a browser. Compare the Web page to Figure 4-11 to verify the image as a horizontal rule is displayed below the logo image.

image used as a horizontal rule

Jennifer wonders if it is possible to add color and thickness to the default horizontal rule. You will show her how to specify properties to enhance the appearance of basic lines you create with the <hr /> element.

Specifying Properties for Horizontal Rules

In addition to replacing a horizontal rule with an image, you can set the style for the <hr /> element to give the horizontal rule more visual appeal. The following properties are often used with the <hr /> element. You can use as many of these properties, and in any order, as necessary:

- width
- text-align
- height
- color

Setting Horizontal Rule Properties | Reference Window

- To specify the format of a horizontal rule, enter the following code where you want the rule to appear:
  ```
  <hr property: value />
  ```
  Use the following properties to set the apperance of the rule:
- width: Use to set the width in pixels or as a percentage value of the screen width. Percentages are preferred.
- text-align: Use to align the rule left, center, or right. Center is the default value.
- height: Use to set the height (the thickness) of the rule in pixels. The default value is 2px.
- color: Use to change the color of the rule. Use named values, RGB values, or hex values.

The following sections provide details about using each of the horizontal rule properties.

The width Property and Horizontal Rules

When used with a horizontal rule, the **width property** controls the width of the rule. By default, a horizontal rule extends the entire width of the screen. You can, however, specify a value in pixels or as a percentage of the screen for the width. Specifying the rule width as a percentage (rather than in pixels) is preferable because doing so means the rule will assume the correct width despite the screen resolution setting. For example:

```
hr {
width: 50%; }
```

The height Property and Horizontal Rules

When used with a horizontal rule, the **height property** affects the thickness of the rule. In other words, you can make the rule thicker by increasing the value for the height property. You specify a height in pixel values. Generally, one pixel is equivalent to 1 point in typography, where 72 points is equal to one vertical inch. The last line in the following code specifies a horizontal rule that has a height of 10 pixels:

```
hr {
width: 50%;
height: 10px; }
```

The text-align Property and Horizontal Rules

You use the text-align property to position text on a line. Rules are centered by default. If you change the width of the rule, you might also want to change the rule alignment so the rule does not seem to be off center. Recall that you can use the text-align property to align the contents of HTML elements horizontally. When setting the style for the <hr /> element, use the text-align property and assign it the value of left, right, or center. The last line in the following code centers a rule:

```
hr {
width: 50%;
height: 10px;
text-align: center; }
```

The color Property and Horizontal Rules

You can also change the color of the rule. Use the color property and assign one of the named colors, an RGB triplet, or a hexadecimal value. The last line in the following code sets the rule to appear in green:

```
hr {
width: 50%;
height: 10px;
text-align: center;
color: green; }
```

Internet Explorer and the Firefox browsers treat the color property differently. If you use only the color property to change the color of the rule, the rule is displayed correctly in Internet Explorer. That's not true of Firefox. If you use only the color property, the rule is not displayed properly. To get the rule to display correctly in Firefox, you must use both the color property and the background-color property. For example, the following rule sets both the color property and the background-color property to have a value of green:

```
hr {
color: green;
background-color: green; }
```

You notice that Jennifer included a horizontal rule in the HTML document. You will show her how to style the rule to give it some color and thickness.

To change the appearance of the default horizontal rule:

▶ **1.** Make sure the GinaNew file is open in Notepad.

▶ **2.** On a blank line after the h3 selector code, type the following code, which is also shown in red in Figure 4-12.

```
hr {
color: green;
background-color: green;
width: 100%;
margin-top: .4em;
height: .5em; }
```

Code to set the style of the horizontal rule ◄ Figure 4-12

```
hr {
color: green;
background-color: green;      sets the style of the
width: 100%;                  horizontal rule to green
margin-top: .4em;             with a height of .5em
height: .5em; }

</style>

</head>
```

▶ **3.** Save GinaNew, and then refresh the file in a browser. Compare the Web page to Figure 4-13 to verify that the horizontal rule is displayed in green.

Horizontal rule displayed on the Web page ◄ Figure 4-13

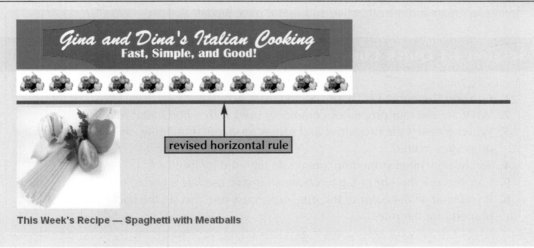

revised horizontal rule

This Week's Recipe — Spaghetti with Meatballs

Figure 4-14 lists the properties that you can use with horizontal rules.

Figure 4-14
Properties to use with horizontal rules

Property	Purpose	Comment
color	Changes the color of the rule	Use named values, RGB values, or hex values
background-color	Changes the background-color of the rule	Must be used together with the color property in order to display properly in the Firefox browser
height	Sets the height (the thickness) of the rule in pixels	The default is 2px
text-align	Use if the width is less than 100%; aligns the rule left, center, or right	Center is the default
width	Sets the width in pixels or as a percentage value of the screen width	Percentages are preferred

In this session, you learned that you cannot use HTML or CSS to create images, though you can use them to create horizontal lines and borders, including repeating images designed to be used as a horizontal rule. It is possible to add some variety to the default HTML horizontal rule by changing its color, background-color, width, and size. In the next session you will learn how to position images so that text can wrap around the image to create a more attractive and useful page layout.

Review | **Session 4.1 Quick Check**

1. Can you use either HTML or CSS to create images?
2. What are the four properties commonly used with a horizontal rule?
3. When entering the properties and values for a horizontal rule, does the order of the properties matter?
4. Today, how often is the horizontal rule tag used by itself?
5. Can you use the <hr /> tag to create an image used as a horizontal rule?
6. If you change the color of the rule, why must you also set the background-color property for the rule?

Session 4.2

Using the Box Model

Tip

White space between columns of text is called a gutter.

Recall that a block-level element is any element that automatically generates a blank line above and below the element, such as the <p></p> tags or the <h1></h1> tags. The box properties are used to control the internal padding, the borders, and the external margins of block-level elements. The internal padding is the white space that surrounds the contents of an element. You can draw a decorative border around the padding. The external margin is the white space outside of the border.

Figure 4-15 illustrates an example of an element's internal padding, border, and external margin.

An element's internal padding, border, and external margin ◄ Figure 4-15

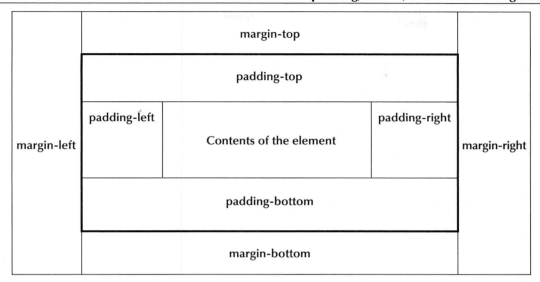

By default, the border around a block-level element is not visible, and so far you have always accepted the default amount of white space surrounding an element. When you view an HTML document in the browser, you don't see the rectangular area that surrounds each element, but an HTML document actually consists of rectangular areas, called boxes. If you could see the border around a block-level element, your page content would appear like so:

```
<h1>The Box Properties</h1>
<p>The box properties are used to control the padding, the border,
and the margins of block-level elements.</p>
<blockquote>This area of text is still another example of the hidden
nature of block-level elements.</blockquote>
```

You will show Jennifer how the padding, borders, and margins work together to position text on a Web page. You will start by showing Jennifer how the padding properties work.

Using the Padding Properties

While the **margin property** controls white space outside an element, the **padding property** controls white space inside an element. Padding and margin values can be expressed in a number of ways:

- em (em values)
- px (pixels)
- mm (millimeters)
- cm (centimeters)
- in (inches)
- % (as a percentage of the browser's display width)

When you create an element with a background color, letters that have **ascenders** (such as the letter *d*) or **descenders** (such as the letter *g*) might be clipped. To correct that problem, you can add padding to the top and the bottom of the element. The padding properties are used to set the padding for each side individually or all at once. Following are the padding properties:

- padding-top:
- padding-right:
- padding-bottom:
- padding-left:
- padding:

The padding property is the shortcut that controls the padding on all four sides at once. Next, you will show Jennifer how to control the white space outside an image by using the margin properties.

Using the Margin Properties

You have already used the margin property with the line-height property. The margin property is often used with images to create white space on one or more sides of an image. By default, there's only one pixel of space above, below, and to the left and right of an image—that's very little space. If you do not create a margin around an image, the surrounding text may be too close to the image, crowding the image and making the text difficult to read. Use the following margin properties and a value in pixels, em values, or a percentage to create margin space around one side or all sides of an image.

- margin-top:
- margin-right:
- margin-bottom:
- margin-left:
- margin:

The margin property is the shortcut property that can be used to set the values for all four margins at once.

Setting Values for the Padding and the Margin Properties

Should you want to write your code more concisely, you can take advantage of the two shortcut properties that were mentioned earlier, padding and margin. The following sections explain how to set values for these two shortcut properties.

If one value is listed, the value is used for all four sides, like so:

```
p.box {
padding: 1em;
margin: 2em; }
```

If two values are listed, the first value is applied to the top and bottom sides equally. The second value is applied to the left and the right sides equally.

```
p.box {
padding: 1em 2em;
margin: 2em 1em; }
```

If three values are listed, the first value is applied to the top side. The second value is applied to the left and the right sides equally. The third value is applied to the bottom side.

```
p.box {
padding: 1em 2em 3em;
margin: 2em 1em 2em; }
```

If four values are listed, the values apply to the top, right, bottom, and left sides individually.

```
p.box {
padding: 3em 1em 2em 1em;
margin: 1em 3em 2em 1em; }
```

Figure 4-16 illustrates how to assign values to the margin property.

Values for the margin property ◀ **Figure 4-16**

Margin Property and Value	Result
margin: 0;	No margins; the value affects all four sides
margin: 0 5px;	Top and bottom margins are 0; the left and right margins are 5px
margin: 0 5px 4px;	Top margin is 0, the left and right margins are 5px, and the bottom margin is 4px
margin: 1px 2px 3px 4px;	Top margin is 1px, the right margin is 2px, the bottom margin is 3px, and the left margin is 4px.

Earlier, you showed Jennifer the graphics capabilities of horizontal rules. Now you will show her how to add colorful, decorative borders to HTML elements.

Tip

The margin values are top, right, bottom, and left, which creates the acronym trbl.

Using the Border Properties

You use the **border properties** to draw a border around any block-level element, such as headings, blockquotes, or paragraphs. You can also place a decorative border around an image or inline elements, such as <em> and <strong>, which makes those elements stand out. To customize a border, you can change its color, style, and width.

Working with the Border Shortcut Property | Reference Window

- To create a style using the border shortcut property, use the style:
  ```
  border: color style thickness;
  ```
  where *color* is a named color, RGB triplet, or hexadecimal value, *style* is solid, double, dotted, dashed, groove, ridge, inset, outset, or none, and *thickness* is thin, medium, or thick.

Applying the Border Style

The border style can be any one of these values:

- solid
- double
- dotted
- dashed
- groove
- ridge
- inset
- outset
- none (there is no border)

Figure 4-17 illustrates the border styles.

Figure 4-17 ▶ **Border styles**

```
border style of solid

border style of double

border style of dotted

border style of dashed

border style of groove

border style of ridge

border style of inset

border style of outset

border style of none
```

Following are the border-style properties:

- border-top-style:
- border-right-style:
- border-bottom-style:
- border-left-style:
- border-style:

The **border-style property** is the shortcut property that can be used to set the values for all four borders at once.

Setting the Border Width

The border width values can also be expressed as measurements in points, ems, or as a percentage. You can also express the border width as any of the following relative values:

- thin
- medium
- thick

Following are the border-width properties:

- border-top-width:
- border-right-width:
- border-bottom-width:
- border-left-width:
- border-width:

The **border-width property** is the shortcut property that can be used to set the values for all four borders at once.

Figure 4-18 illustrates the use of the border-width properties.

Border widths ◄ Figure 4-18

border style of solid; border width of thin

border style of solid; border width of medium

border style of solid; border width of thick

Setting the Border Color

The border color can be a named color, RGB triplet or a hex value. These are the border-color properties:

- border-top-color:
- border-right-color:
- border-bottom-color:
- border-left-color:
- border-color:

The **border-color property** is the shortcut property that can be used to set the values for all four borders at once. Figure 4-19 illustrates the border colors.

Border colors ◄ Figure 4-19

border style of solid; border width of thin; border color navy

border style of solid; border width of medium; border color of green

border style of solid; border width of thick; border color of red

Following are the eight border shortcut properties:

- border-color:
- border-style:
- border-width:
- border-top:
- border-right:
- border-bottom:
- border-left:
- border:

Specifying Values for Color, Style, and Width Shortcuts

You specify values for the border-color, style, and width properties in the same manner as you did earlier for the padding and margins.

If one value is listed, the value is used for all four borders, like so:

```
p.box {
border-color: teal; }
```

If two values are listed, the first value is applied to the top and bottom borders. The second value is applied to the left and the right borders.

```
p.box {
border-style: solid double; }
```

If three values are listed, the first value is applied to the top border. The second value is applied to the left and the right borders. The third value is applied to the bottom border.

```
p.box {
border-width: thin medium thick; }
```

If four values are listed, the values apply to the top, right, bottom, and left borders individually.

```
p.box {
border-color: teal navy red orange; }
```

Specifying Values for Border Shortcuts

As with the font properties, the border properties let you specify several different values at once. You can change the color, the style, and width at the same time for each border, or you can use the border property to specify the color, style, and width for all four borders.

The following example specifies a different appearance for each of the four borders.

```
p.box {
border-top: red solid thin;
border-right: black double thick;
border-bottom: red solid thin;
border-left: gray solid medium; }
```

The following example specifies a border (on all four sides) that is red, dotted, and thick:

```
img {
border: red dotted thick; }
```

The order of the values for the border shortcut property does not matter. These three rules have the same result:

```
p.box {
border-top: red solid thin;}
p.box {
border-top: solid red thin;}
p.box {
border-top: solid thin red;}
```

However, you should be consistent when using the border shortcut property. Decide on the order to list values or follow your workplace's best practices guidelines.

Jennifer would like to include a decorative border around all of the images, one that is red, dotted, and thick. You will show her how to apply that style to the images.

To add a border to the images:

▶ **1.** Make sure the GinaNew file is open in Notepad.

▶ **2.** On a blank line after the hr selector code, type the following code, which is also shown in red in Figure 4-20.

```
img {
border: red dotted thick; }
```

Style to apply a border to the images ◀ **Figure 4-20**

```
color: maroon; }

hr {
color: green;
background-color: green;
width: 100%;
margin-top: .4em;
height: .5em; }

img {
border: red dotted thick; }
```

↑

applies a thick red
dotted border
around images

▶ **3.** Save GinaNew, and then refresh the file in a browser. Compare the Web page to Figure 4-21 to verify that the images now have a border that is red, dotted, and thick.

Images with a decorative border in the browser ◀ **Figure 4-21**

image with a dotted
red border

This Week's Recipe — Spaghetti with Meatballs

Now that Jennifer knows that any block-level element can have a border, she also wants to include borders for the h4 headings. To make sure there is some space between the border and the text in the heading, you will show her how to increase the distance between the text and the border by using the padding property.

To add a border to the h4 headings:

▶ **1.** Make sure the GinaNew document is open in Notepad.

▶ **2.** On a blank line after the img selector code, type the following code, which is also shown in red in Figure 4-22.

```
h4 {
font-size: 12pt;
color: navy;
background-color: white;
border: navy thin solid;
padding: 3px;
display: inline;
width: 200px; }
```

Figure 4-22	Code to style the h4 headings

```
margin-top: .4em;
height: .5em; }

img {
border: red dotted thick; }

h4 {
font-size: 12pt;
color: navy;
background-color: white;
border: navy thin solid;
padding: 3px;
display: inline;
width: 200px; }
```

sets h4 headings to be 12pt navy text on a white background with a thin navy border and 3px padding

▶ **3.** Save GinaNew, and then refresh the file in a browser. Compare the Web page to Figure 4-23 to verify that the h4 heading is formatted correctly.

Figure 4-23	The h4 headings have a blue border on the Web page

Pasta: ◀— h4 heading

You may use either boxed pasta or refrigerated, fresh pasta.

- 1 pound spaghetti

Meatballs:

Use either 93% lean beef or a mix or ground turkey and ground pork.

- 1 cup of breadcrumbs
- 2 large eggs
- 1 pound lean ground beef
- 1/4 cup grated Romano cheese
- 1 teaspoon fresh oregano
- 1/2 teaspoon salt
- 1/4 teaspoon pepper

Tomato Sauce:

Including Borders Above and Below Headings | InSight

Recall in an earlier tutorial, that you could use the text-decoration property with the values of underline and overline to create a heading with a line above and below. However, by using this method to create ruled lines with a heading, you did not have the option to change the style, color, or width of the ruled lines. You can use the border properties to create decorative borders for any element, but it is common to create ruled lines above and below a heading. The top border is typically styled to be thinner than the bottom border. For example, the following code sets the style for an h2 heading to have ruled lines above and below the heading.

```
h2 {
border-top: green solid thin;
border-bottom: navy double medium;
display: inline; }
```

When you create ruled lines above and below a heading, they appear as shown in Figure 4-24.

Example of ruled lines above and below a heading ◀ Figure 4-24

An h2 Heading with Ruled Lines Above and Below

Next, you'll learn how to position images on a Web page.

Positioning Images

To balance page content, it is always a good idea to position some images in the center, some on the left edge of the page, and some on the right edge of the page. Jennifer feels that the Gina and Dina Web page would look more balanced if the images at the top of the page were centered. Recall in Tutorial 3, you created an independent class for the text-align property to center elements. You applied that independent class in a start <div> tag. You entered the code for an end </div> tag below the element you wanted to center. You will show Jennifer how to code an independent class named *center* to do so.

To enter the code to center the images:

▶ **1.** Make sure the GinaNew file is open in Notepad.

▶ **2.** On a blank line after the h4 element selector code, type the following code, which is also shown in red in Figure 4-25.

```
.center {
text-align: center; }
```

Figure 4-25 ▶ **Code to center the images**

```
h4 {
font-size: 12pt;
color: navy;
background-color: white;
border: navy thin solid;
padding: 3px;
display: inline;
width: 200px; }

.center {
text-align: center; }
```

independent class
named center

Now that you have created the independent class, you also need to apply the class. You will show Jennifer how to do so.

To apply the independent class:

▶ **1.** In the GinaNew document in your text editor, position the insertion point on the line above the code for the Ginalogo image.

▶ **2.** Type the following code, which is also shown in red in Figure 4-26.

```
<div class="center">
```

Figure 4-26 ▶ **Code for the center independent class applied to the start <div> tag**

center style in
the <div> tag

```
</style>
</head>

<body>
<div class="center">
<img src="ginalogo.gif" alt="the gina and dina logo" width="650" height="100" />
<img src="veggies.gif" alt="horizontal rule image of vegetables" width="650" height="50" />
```

▶ **3.** Position the insertion point on the line below the code for the Veggies.gif image.

▶ **4.** Type the following code, which is also shown in red in Figure 4-27.

```
</div>
```

Figure 4-27 ▶ **Code for the end </div> tag**

```
<body>
<div class="center">
<img src="ginalogo.gif" alt="the gina and dina logo" width="650" height="100" />
<img src="veggies.gif" alt="horizontal rule image of vegetables" width="650" height="50" />
</div>
```

▶ **5.** Save GinaNew, and then refresh the file in your browser. Compare the Web page to Figure 4-28 to verify that the images are centered.

Centered images on the Web page | Figure 4-28

centered logo and rule image

Jennifer likes the appearance of the centered image, but she notices that too much white space surrounds the other images on the page. You will show Jennifer how to wrap the text around the images to create a more attractive and balanced page layout.

Using the float Property

When you inserted images on Web pages in earlier tutorials, the text near an image did not wrap around the image. The first line of text appears at the base of the image, not alongside it, as it should. Because of the default positioning for text near an image, your Web page can have large gaps of white space next to an image. If you want to wrap text around an image, use the **float property** with a value of *left* or *right*. If the float property has a value of left, the image is displayed at the left edge of the browser window, with the text wrapping to the right of the image. If the float property has a value of right, the image is displayed at the right edge of the browser window, with the text wrapping to the left of the image. The float property does not have a value of center, which is why you applied an independent class to style the images at the top of the page.

Keep two important considerations in mind when floating an HTML element. First, to maintain the correct position of the element, you must specify a width for any HTML element that you float. Second, you can float any element, not just images. For example, you can float paragraphs and headings.

Jennifer wants the text to wrap around the images on the Gina and Dina Web page. She wants to position the Spaghetti.jpg and the Meatballs.jpg images at the left edge of the screen, and she wants to position the Paste.jpg image at the right edge of the screen. You have already styled the image tag, so to accomplish these tasks, you will have to create a dependent class for the <img /> element selector to float the images to the left. Later, you will create an ID selector to float only the Paste.jpg image at the right edge of the screen. Jennifer also wants these images to have thick, solid, maroon borders and to eliminate the crowding between the text and the images. To place some white space between the images and the text, you will also show her how to add margin space alongside the images as well.

> **Tip**
>
> When you use the float property, you are floating the image or the element, not the text.

To create the dependent class to float the images to the left:

▶ **1.** Make sure the GinaNew file is open in your browser.

▶ **2.** On a blank line below the center style code, type the following code, which is also shown in red in Figure 4-29.

```
img.left {
float: left;
border: maroon thick solid;
margin-top: .5em;
margin-right: 1em; }
```

Figure 4-29 | **Code to float the images at the left edge of the window**

```
.center {
text-align: center; }

img.left {
float: left;
border: maroon thick solid;
margin-top: .5em;
margin-right: 1em; }

</style>
</head>
```

code sets the images to appear at the left of the window, with text wrapping around the image

code adds a border around the images and white space between the text and the images

Now that you have created the dependent class, you also need to apply the class. You will show Jennifer how to do so next.

To apply the dependent class:

▶ **1.** In the GinaNew document in your text editor, position the insertion point to the right of the alternate text in the code for the Spaghetti.jpg image.

▶ **2.** Press the **Spacebar** and type the following code shown in bold text, which is also shown in red in Figure 4-30.

```
<img src="spaghetti.jpg" alt="image of plate of spaghetti"
class="left" width="200" height="200" />
```

Figure 4-30 | **Code to apply the *left* class to float the top image**

```
<hr />

<img src="spaghetti.jpg" alt="image of plate of spaghetti" class="left" width="200"
height="200" />
```

applies the *left* dependent class to images

▶ **3.** Position the insertion point to the right of the alternate text in the code for the Meatballs.jpg image.

▶ **4.** Press the **Spacebar** and type the following code shown in bold text, which is also shown in red in Figure 4-31.

```
<img src="meatballs.jpg" alt="image of spaghetti with meatballs"
class="left" width="200" height="200" />
```

Figure 4-31 | **Code to apply the *left* class to float the bottom image**

```
<img src="meatballs.jpg" alt="image of spaghetti with meatballs" class="left" width="200"
height="200" />
```

▶ **5.** Save GinaNew, and then refresh the file in your browser. Compare the Web page to Figure 4-32 to verify that the Spaghetti.jpg and the Meatballs.jpg images are now floated left. The Paste image, however, remains the same.

Images aligned left with text wrapping to the right ◄ **Figure 4-32**

This Week's Recipe — Spaghetti with Meatballs

Spaghetti and meatballs is an inexpensive dish that everyone seems to enjoy. The trick is to get the spaghetti al dente, which is to cook the pasta so that it is not too firm (uncooked) and yet not too tender so that it becomes a pile of blonde mush.

text wraps around the image

Getting Started

Don't scrimp on the water. Cook your pasta in plenty of water in a high-rimmed saucepan. Some people like to add oil to the water, but oil and water don't mix, so a better strategy is to put a little extra virgin olive oil on the pasta after it's been cooked and drained. That will add flavor and keep the pasta from sticking.

Water does matter. If you live in an area where the water quality is not up to par, consider boiling the pasta in bottled water or filtered water from a tap if you have a filter installed on the faucet. The pasta can pick up bad odors and taste from water that does not taste good to begin with.

style for the Paste image has not been set

Boil that Water

Now you can turn your attention to floating the Paste image.

Using ID Selectors to Format and Position Individual Images

Jennifer wants to alternate the positioning of the images so that the Paste.jpg image is the only image floated right. To gain pinpoint control over an individual element, you use ID selectors. Because the image will be floated right, you will also want some margin space above, below, and to the left of the image. You will show Jennifer how to use an ID selector to format an individual element in a document.

To create the ID selector to float the image right:

► **1.** Make sure the GinaNew document is open in Notepad.

► **2.** On a blank line after the dependent selector code for the img selector, type the following code, which is also shown in red in Figure 4-33.

```
#right {
float: right;
border: maroon thick solid;
margin-top: .5em;
margin-left: 1em; }
```

Code for the ID selector named *right* ◄ **Figure 4-33**

```
img.left {
float: left;
border: maroon thick solid;
margin-top: .5em;
margin-right: 1em; }

#right {
float: right;          ◄── floats images to the right
border: maroon thick solid;
margin-top: .5em;
margin-left: 1em; }
```

Now that you have created the ID selector, you need to apply it. You will show Jennifer how to do so next.

To apply the ID selector:

1. In the GinaNew document in your text editor, position the insertion point to the right of the alternate text in the code for the Paste image.

2. Press the **Spacebar** and type the following code shown in bold, which is also shown in red in Figure 4-34.

```
<img src="paste.jpg" alt="image of jar of tomato paste"
id="right" width="200" height="200" />
```

| Figure 4-34 | Code to apply the ID selector named *right* |

```
<img src="paste.jpg" alt="image of jar of tomato paste" id="right" width="200" height="200" />

<h3>Boil that Water</h3>
```

3. Save GinaNew, and then refresh the file in your browser. Compare the Web page to Figure 4-35 to verify that the Paste image floats to the right.

| Figure 4-35 | Paste image floated right in the browser |

This Week's Recipe — Spaghetti with Meatballs

Spaghetti and meatballs is an inexpensive dish that everyone seems to enjoy. The trick is to get the spaghetti al dente, which is to cook the pasta so that it is not too firm (uncooked) and yet not too tender so that it becomes a pile of blonde mush.

Getting Started

Don't scrimp on the water. Cook your pasta in plenty of water in a high-rimmed saucepan. Some people like to add oil to the water, but oil and water don't mix, so a better strategy is to put a little extra virgin olive oil on the pasta after it's been cooked and drained. That will add flavor and keep the pasta from sticking.

Water does matter. If you live in an area where the water quality is not up to par, consider boiling the pasta in bottled water or filtered water from a tap if you have a filter installed on the faucet. The pasta can pick up bad odors and taste from water that does not taste good to begin with.

Boil that Water

Get the water to a roiling (that means "really bubbling") temperature. Toss in the pasta and stir with a Wooden spoon or fork. Follow the package label for cooking times, but generally cook the pasta in boiling water for about 10-12 minutes. The last 3 minutes are critical. You want the pasta al dente (firm, yet tender). Try tasting some of the pasta every minute for the last three minutes. When you think you've got the right tenderness, strain the pasta in a colander and then pour cold water on the pasta to stop the pasta from cooking any further.

Make Some Sauce

For the sauce, you can use any commercial canned or jar sauce to save time. Most of the sauces sold in the supermarket are quite good. If you want to make your own sauce, chop up a medium-sized onion and 1 or 2 cloves of garlic. Toss the onion and garlic into a large saucepan. Add two 28-ounce cans of whole tomatoes, one 6-ounce can of tomato paste, and 1 tablespoon of extra virgin olive oil.

After setting a float property, you usually need to clear the property so the text is aligned at the left margin again.

Clearing Float Settings

Jennifer notices that the "Pour It On" heading is separated from the body text that follows the heading. She wants to know how to place that heading on its own line at the left edge of the window. To have an element clear settings after an image, use the clear property.

Using the Clear Property | Reference Window

- To create a style to clear an element, use the property:
  ```
  clear: value;
  ```
  where *value* is left, right, or both.

The clear property takes these values:

- **left** (text begins below an element floated left)
- **right** (text begins below an element floated right)
- **both** (text begins below an element floated either left or right)

Because you want to clear settings in several instances in the document, you decide to create an independent class named *clear*. You will now show Jennifer how to code the clear property.

Tip

If you are not sure which clear property value to use, use the value of *both*.

To insert the code to clear settings after an image:

▶ **1.** Make sure the GinaNew document is open in Notepad.

▶ **2.** On a blank line after the code for the ID selector named *right*, type the following code, which is also shown in red in Figure 4-36.

```
#clear {
clear: both; }
```

Code for clearing the image ◀ Figure 4-36

```
#right {
float: right;
border: maroon thick solid;
margin-top: .5em;
margin-left: 1em; }

#clear {
clear: both; }
```
← clears the setting and stops wrapping text after a floated element

Now that you have created the ID selector, you also need to apply the selector. You will show Jennifer how to do so next.

To apply the ID selector:

▶ **1.** In the GinaNew document in your text editor, position the insertion point to the right of the number "3" in the h3 heading for "Pour It On."

▶ **2.** Press the **Spacebar** and type the following code shown in bold, which is also shown in red in Figure 4-37.

```
<h3 id="clear">Pour it On</h3>
```

Applying the ID named *clear* ◀ Figure 4-37

```
<h3 id="clear">Pour it On</h3>
<p>Put the pasta on a large platter, spoon on the meatballs, and cover with the sauce.</p>
```
include the *clear* ID in the h3 heading tag

▶ **3.** Save GinaNew, and then refresh the file in a browser. Compare the Web page to Figure 4-38 to verify that the heading is now clear of the image.

Figure 4-38 ▶ **The h3 heading clears the image**

Cook the Meatballs

Of course, while the pasta is cooking (set the timer to 10 minutes) you can make the meatballs and the sauce. For the meatballs, in a large mixing bowl, mix one cup of breadcrumbs, 2 large eggs, and 1 pound of lean, ground beef. You can season as you like with salt, pepper, chicken broth, oregano, and basil. For an added touch, you can also mix in 1/4 cup freshly grated Romano or Parmesan cheese. Mix all the ingredients together and spoon into meatballs about 1" round. After you've formed the meatballs, one by one, place the meatballs into a frying pan that has been greased with one or two tablespoons of extra virgin olive oil. Cook on low-to-medium heat until the meatballs are brown.

Pour it On ◄──────────────────────────── clear ID returns this h3 heading to the original left margin after the Paste image

Put the pasta on a large platter, spoon on the meatballs, and cover with the sauce.

InSight | **Styling and Floating Other Elements**

You can float block-level elements in the same manner that you can float images. In the following example, changes have been made to the border-width, the border-style, and the border-color properties. The h2 heading has been floated right.

```
<head>
<style type="text/css">
h2 {
border-width: 1em;
border-style: inset;
border-color: yellow;
padding: 4px;
color: orange;
background-color: black;
font-family: arial,helvetica,sans-serif;
float: right;
width: 50%;
display: inline; }
</style>
</head>
```

Figure 4-39 shows how the heading would appear when displayed in the browser.

Figure 4-39 ▶ **Example of a heading floated right**

This is an h2 Heading Floated Right

In this session, you learned about the box model. You learned that all block-level elements have an internal padding, a border, and an external margin. You can use settings to make borders visible and to have a color, a style, and a width. Images can be centered, but they can also be floated left or right. Floating an image left or right allows text that is adjacent to the image to wrap around the image. When you want to display content after an image, you can use the clear property. Finally, you learned that in addition to images, you can set the style for and float other elements to achieve interesting text effects and layout.

Session 4.2 Quick Check | Review

1. What is the box model?
2. What is the internal padding?
3. What is the external margin?
4. What are the values for the float property?
5. When using the shortcut for the border property, what is the order of the values?
6. What property is used to continue text after an image?

Session 4.3

Enhancing the Appearance of Lists

Lists can also be enhanced by graphics and images. To do so, you can use several properties in the classification category of properties: list-style-type, list-style-position, and list-style-image.

Setting List Properties | Reference Window

- To specify the format of a list, enter the following code where you want the list to appear:
  ```
  ul {  or ol {
   list-style-property: value;
  ```
  Use the following properties to set the appearance of the list:
  - list-style-type: Use this to change the bullet type, the numbering, or the lettering for a list. Values are disc, circle, square, decimal, lower-roman, upper-roman, lower-alpha, upper-alpha, and none.
  - list-style-image: Use this to insert an image instead of one of the list style types. Specify a value in the format *url(imagename)*.
  - list-style-position: Use this to position the bullet either inside or outside the indented text for the list item. Values are inside or outside (the default).
  - list-style: This is the shortcut property that specifies the type, the image, and the position; list the values for each property in that order.
  - vertical-align (for images): If necessary, use the vertical-align property to align a list-style-image with the list item text. Values are top, middle, and bottom.

The Gina and Dina Web page makes extensive use of lists at the bottom of the page, where the recipe ingredients and steps are provided. You will show Jennifer how to style bullet items to give them greater visual appeal by changing the list style type and the list style position. Last, you will show her how to use an image as a bullet.

Using the list-style-type Property

You use the **list-style-type property** to change the appearance of the default solid bullet for unordered lists. Unordered lists can use only one of the following three values for list-style-type:

- disc (the default)
- circle (a hollow circle)
- square (a square)

To create a style that generates a square bullet rather than a disc, you would use the list-style-type property in the following code:

```
ul {
list-style-type: square; }
```

For ordered lists, you can set the style of the <ol> selector to create the following list-style types:

- **decimal** (the default Arabic numbers)
- **lower-roman** (i, ii, iii and so forth)
- **upper-roman** (I, II, III and so forth)
- **lower-alpha** (a, b, c, and so forth)
- **upper-alpha** (A, B, C, and so forth)

For example, to create a style that numbers a list using lowercase Roman numerals, use code similar to the following:

```
ol {
list-style-type: lower-roman; }
```

Figure 4-40 illustrates the use of the list-style-type property.

Figure 4-40 **Example of list styles**

Unordered Lists

- list-style-type disc
- list-style-type circle
- list-style-type square

Ordered Lists

1. list-style-type: decimal
ii. list-style-type: lower-roman
III. list-style-type: upper-roman
d. list-style-type: lower-alpha
E. list-style-type: upper-alpha

Creating Nested Lists InSight

You can place an ordered list within another ordered list, which is called a nested list. Nested lists are used to construct outlines with a combination of Roman numerals and upper- and lowercase alphabetic letters. You restart the numbering or use a different value other than 1 or A by using the start attribute. The start attribute works with both letters and numbers. If you want to start a list with the number 3, for example, you would code `start="3"` inside the `<ol>` tag. If you want to start a list with the letter C, you would use the same attribute and value. The following code illustrates the use of the start attribute.

```
ol.roman {
list-style-type: upper-roman; }
</style>
</head>
<body>
<p>Largest Cities</p>
<ol start="3">
  <li>New York</li>
  <li>Chicago</li>
  <li>Los Angeles</li>
</ol>
<p>Largest Cities</p>
<ol class="roman" start="3">
  <li>New York</li>
  <li>Chicago</li>
  <li>Los Angeles</li>
</ol>
```

Recall that the blockquote element selector creates an indent on the left and the right. You can use the list-style-type property to create an indent on the left only. First, create a dependent style for the ul element selector. This dependent class named *indent* changes the list-style-type to none, as shown in the following code:

```
ul.indent {
list-style-type: none; }
```

In the body of the document, apply the dependent class *indent* to the `<ul>` selector. In the body text, instead of using `<p></p>` tags, use a single pair of `<li></li>` tags for the text, as shown in the following code:

```
li {
font-size: 14pt;
font-family: arial; }
</style>
</head>
<body>
<ul class="indent">
<li>This is an indent on the left without a bullet. This text will be
indented on the left only. The blockquote element indents text on both
the left and the right. This indent will occur on just the left only.
</li>
</ul>
```

The result looks similar to Figure 4-41.

Figure 4-41 **Example of a left indent using a list style type of** *none*

> This is an indent on the left without a bullet. This text will be indented on the left only. The blockquote element indents text on both the left and the right. This indent will occur on just the left only.
>
> This is text that is in a blockquote. Note that the margins are indented on both the left and the right. In the example above, the text is indented on the left only.

Using the list-style-position Property

You use the **list-style-position property** to change the position of the bullet included with a list. You can have unordered lists with bullets either inside the element, such as a paragraph indent, or outside the element, which is the default. The following example changes the list-style-type to square and the list-style-position to inside:

```
ul {
list-style-type: square;
list-style-position: inside; }
```

Each bullet in the list would display like so:

■ This is some text for the bulleted items. As you can see, this bulleted item has the appearance of a paragraph indent.

Applying the list-style-image Property

You use the **list-style-image property** to change the bullet to a graphic image. For the value for the list-style-image property, you include the letters *url* and the name of the image file in parentheses. For example, to use an image named redarrow.gif as the bullets, write the following code:

```
ul {
list-style-image: url(redarrow.gif;) }
```

Depending on the image, the bullets would be displayed something similar to this:

Applying the list-style Property Shortcut

The **list-style property** is the shortcut property for list styles. You use this to set the list-style-type, the list-style-image (if you are using one), and the list-style-position. You only need to specify the position if you want to position bullets inside (outside is the default value). Examples include:

```
ul {
list-style: square inside; }
ul {
list-style: url(bubbles.gif); }
ol {
list-style: upper-roman inside; }
```

You would also use the list-style property if you do not want to have bullets. To do so, change the list-style value to none:

```
ul {
list-style: none; }
```

When using the images as bullets, you must sometimes adjust the position of the image with the surrounding text. You can use the vertical-align property to do so.

Using the vertical-align Property

When you have an image with one line of text alongside it, it is often necessary to align the image with the text. The vertical-align property can be used to position an element, such as an image, vertically with text. There are several values for the vertical-align property, but these are the most common values and their function:

- **top** (the top of the image is aligned with the text)
- **middle** (the image is aligned to be vertically centered with the text)
- **bottom** (the bottom of the image is aligned with the text)

The following code is used with the Paste.jpg image. Dependent classes have been created to align the image top, middle, and bottom. The classes have been applied to the images.

```
<style type="text/css">
p {
font-size: 18pt;
font-family: arial; }
img {
border: navy thick solid;
margin-right: 1em; }
img.top {
vertical-align: top; }
img.middle {
vertical-align: middle; }
</style>
</head>
<body>
<p><img src="paste.jpg" width="100 height="100" class="top">This is
vertical-align top.</p>
<p><img src="paste.jpg" width="100 height="100" class="middle">This is
vertical-align middle.</p>
<p><img src="paste.jpg" width="100 height="100" class="bottom">This is
vertical-align bottom.</p>
```

Figure 4-42 illustrates the use of the vertical-align property with a single line of text.

Examples of vertical align **Figure 4-42**

 This is vertical-align top.

 This is vertical-align middle.

 This is vertical-align bottom.

Jennifer wants to use an image as a bullet. You suggest an image of a small tomato as a bullet for the items in the ingredients list in the GinaNew Web page. You will also make the list items themselves appear in bold text.

To use an image as a bullet and align the images:

▶ **1.** Make sure the GinaNew file is open in Notepad.

▶ **2.** On a blank line after the clear independent style code, type the following code, which is also shown in red in Figure 4-43.

```
ul {
list-style-image: url(tomato.gif);
vertical-align: bottom; }

li {
font-weight: bold;
vertical-align: bottom; }
```

Figure 4-43 ▶ **Code for the list-style-image**

```
#clear {
clear: both; }        code specifies using tomato.gif
                      as the bullet image

ul {
list-style-image: url(tomato.gif);
vertical-align: bottom;   }

li {
font-weight: bold;
vertical-align: bottom; }
```

▶ **3.** Save GinaNew, and then refresh the file in a browser. Compare the Web page to Figure 4-44 to verify that the bullets are now represented as images.

List item bullets displayed as a graphic with bold list items ◄ Figure 4-44

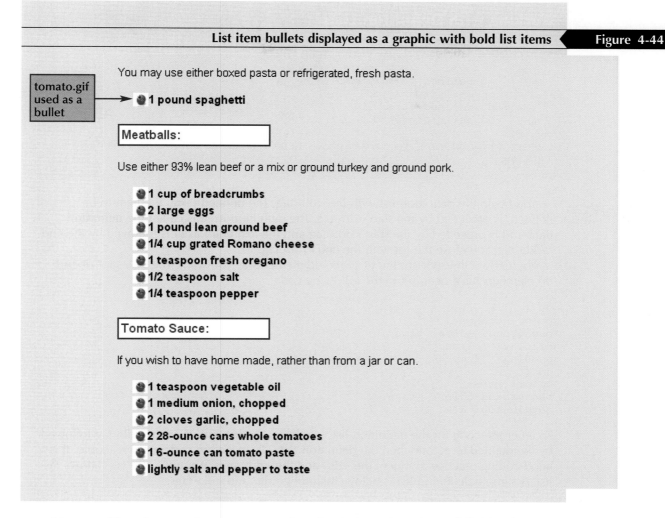

Next, you'll explore another way to set a hanging indent—by using a definition list.

Using Definition Lists

A definition list is another means of establishing a hanging indent. Definition lists are often used for glossaries, which list terms, followed by their definitions. You can, however, use definition list code whenever you need to establish a hanging indent. The disadvantage to using a definition list is that it does add quite a bit of code to a document. The advantage of using definition lists is that you can style the list to create some interesting visual effects.

Reference Window | **Working with Definition Lists**

- To create a definition list, use the following syntax:

```
<dl>
    <dt>defined term1</dt>
    <dd>definition1</dd>
    <dt>defined term2</dt>
    <dd>definition2</dd>
</dl>
```

where *defined term* is the word or phrase to be defined and *definition* is the definition of the term.

You begin the definition list with the <dl> tag. The **defined term**, the item to be defined, is preceded by the start <dt> tag. The definition itself is called the **definition data** and is preceded by the start <dd> tag and the text entry itself is followed by the end </dd> tag. You close the list with the end </dl> tag.

You can set the style for the dt or the dd elements as you want. The styles for dt and dd elements have been set in the following code:

```
dt {
color: orange;
background-color: black;
display: inline;
padding: .5em; }
dd {
color: navy;
background-color: white;
margin-top: 1em; }
```

To enter the code for the definition list, you begin the list with the start <dl> tag followed by the defined term, and then the definition data. To make the code more readable, it is good coding practice to indent the <dt> and the <dd> tags. An end </dl> tag follows the list. A sample definition list is below, including <dt> and <dl> tags:

```
<dl>
  <dt>Central Processing Unit</dt>
  <dd>The CPU, the Central Processing Unit, is often referred to as
  the "brains" of the computer. The CPU, however, does not think for
  itself; it merely processes data at a very rapid speed.</dd>
</dl>
```

The preceding code appears in the browser as shown in Figure 4-45.

Figure 4-45 **Example of a styled definition list**

Central Processing Unit

The CPU, the Central Processing Unit, is often referred to as the "brains" of the computer. The CPU does not think for itself; it merely processes data at an amazing speed.

You can also create a hanging indent using different techniques. For example, you can use the text-indent and margin properties to do so, as shown in an earlier tutorial. Which one of these several methods you choose is your preference as a Web page developer. On the job, follow the company's best practices for formatting hanging indents.

Including White Space with Lists

All of the list tags (<ol>, <ul>, and <dl>) are block-level elements. As such, they auto-matically create a blank line before the list. Their corresponding closing tags (</ol>, </ul>, and </dl>) automatically create a blank line after the list. You can also precisely change the line spacing for lists by using the margin-top or the margin-bottom property. For example, in the following code, the dependent class ul.*less* reduces the white space between list item entries by using the margin-bottom property and assigning a negative value; in this instance, -.2em. The dependent class ul.*more* increases the white space between list item entries by using the margin-bottom property and assigning a positive value; in this instance, 1em.

```
ul.less li {
margin-bottom: -.2em;}

ul.more li {
margin-bottom: 1em; }
</style>
</head>
<body>
<p>The Normal List Item Spacing</p>
<ul>
    <li>Chicago</li>
    <li>New York</li>
    <li>Dallas</li>
    <li>Los Angeles</li>
</ul>
<p>Bottom Margin Spacing of -.2em</p>
<ul class="less">
    <li>Chicago</li>
    <li>New York</li>
    <li>Dallas</li>
    <li>Los Angeles</li>
</ul>
<p>Bottom Margin Spacing of 1em</p>
<ul class="more">
    <li>Chicago</li>
    <li>New York</li>
    <li>Dallas</li>
    <li>Los Angeles</li>
</ul>
```

The preceding code appears in the browser as shown in Figure 4-46.

Figure 4-46 — **Example of line spacing for list items**

The Normal List Item Spacing

- Chicago
- New York
- Dallas
- Los Angeles

Bottom Margin Spacing of -.2em

- Chicago
- New York
- Dallas
- Los Angeles

Bottom Margin Spacing of 1em

- Chicago

- New York

- Dallas

- Los Angeles

Figure 4-47 summarizes the list-style properties.

Figure 4-47 — **List-style properties**

Property	What it Does	Values
list-style-type:	Changes the bullet type, the numbering, or the lettering for a list	disc circle square decimal lower-roman upper-roman lower-alpha upper-alpha none
list-style-image:	Inserts an image instead of a list style type	url(imagename);
list-style-position:	Positions the bullet inside or outside the indented text for the list item	inside outside (the default)
list-style:	Shortcut property that specifies the type, the image, and the position; list the values for each property in that order	

Using the Background Properties

You use the background properties to set the appearance of a Web page background. You can set the following background properties:

- background-image
- background-color
- background-position
- background-repeat
- background-attachment
- background (shortcut)

Setting Background Properties

- To specify the appearance of a background, enter the following code:
  ```
  body {
  background-property: value; }
  ```
  Use the following properties to set the appearance of the background:
  - background-image: Use this to place an image behind the contents of an element. The image can be any .gif or jpg image, but the syntax must be similar to this: *url(imagename.gif)*.
  - background-position: Use this to position an image on the page without the need for tables or frames. Use keywords or percentage values.
  - background-repeat: Use this to repeat an image horizontally, vertically, or to fill the entire screen. When using the default value, repeat, (the image is repeated to the right and down the page to fill the entire window with copies of the same image). Other values are repeat-x (the image is repeated horizontally across the window), repeat-y (the image is repeated vertically down the window), no-repeat (the image is not repeated), and background-attachment (determines whether an image scrolls with the insertion point).
  - background: This is the shortcut property used to change all of the background properties. Properties and values must be listed in a set order.

The following sections provide details about using each of the background properties.

Using the background-image Property

You use the **background-image property** to fill the contents of an element with an image. First, you select an appropriate image for the background. Choose an image that provides the right color and contrast so that the text does not become unreadable against the background of the image. As such, the image should contrast with the text, rather than compete with it. The value for the background-image property begins with the letters *url*. The name of the image file is then specified in parentheses, like so:

```
body {
background-image: url(tile.jpg;) }
```

If the background-image property is used with the <body> tag as a selector, the background image will occupy the entire screen.

Applying the background-color Property

You should always use the background-color property when you use the background-image property. Ordinarily, when a browser has a problem displaying an image, it shows a placeholder icon instead. However, if the background-image code contains an error, the image placeholder icon is not displayed. By specifying a background color, even if there is an error in the image code, the element's contents still appear against a background color. Also, specifying a background-color property overrides any default setting in the browser for background color, which is usually white. If you are using a background image in the body, make sure your body text has a contrasting, not a competing, color. Recall that when you set the style for the body tag earlier, you set a background-color for the Web page.

Tip

The url is the name and location of the image file. Store the image and the HTML file in the same folder or specify the path to the image.

Setting the background-position Property

The **background-position property** allows you to position an image in nine different locations on the page. The values for the background-position property can be expressed several ways. You can either use keywords or percents. The keywords are used together to divide the screen into nine regions that describe the location of where the image will be positioned, as shown in Figure 4-48.

Figure 4-48 ▶ **Keywords that describe the position of an image**

Left	Center	Right
top left	top center	top right
center left	center center	center right
bottom left	bottom center	bottom right

Tip

If only one keyword is given, "center" is presumed to be the other keyword.

You can be even more precise by using percentage pairs. The first percentage describes the horizontal position across the screen; the second percentage describes the vertical position down the screen, as shown in Figure 4-49.

Figure 4-49 ▶ **Describing the position of an image using percentage pairs**

Left	Center	Right
0% 0%	50% 0%	100% 0%
0% 50%	50% 50%	100% 50%
0% 100%	50% 100%	100% 100%

Tip

If only one percentage is given, it is assumed to be the horizontal position; the other percentage is assigned the vertical position of 50%.

You don't have to use the percentages of 0, 50, and 100%. You can specify any percentage from 0–100 for the horizontal position and any percentage from 0–100 for the vertical position. If only one percentage is given, the percentage is assumed to be the horizontal position; the other percentage is assumed to be the vertical position of 50%, which has the result of centering the image vertically on the page.

Using the background-repeat Property

You use the **background-repeat property** to display copies of an image across the page, down the page, or both. The background-repeat property takes the four values shown in Figure 4-50.

Figure 4-50 ▶ **Values for the background-repeat property**

Property	What it Does
repeat	The image is repeated (tiled) to the right and down the page to fill the entire screen with copies of the same image
repeat-x	The image is repeated horizontally across the screen
repeat-y	The image is repeated vertically down the screen
no-repeat	The image is displayed once in the upper-left corner of the screen and is not repeated

The following code illustrates the use of the background properties used to style the body element selector to repeat an image horizontally across the page:

```
body {
background-image: url(face.gif);
background-position: 0% 0%;
background-repeat: repeat-x; }
```

Tip

Repeating an image is also known as tiling an image. An image can be tiled horizontally, vertically, or both.

The document would appear as shown in Figure 4-51.

Example of repeat-x | **Figure 4-51**

The following code illustrates the use of the background properties used to style the body element selector to repeat an image vertically across the page:

```
body {
background-image: url(face.gif);
background-position: 0% 0%;
background-repeat: repeat-y; }
```

The document would appear as shown in Figure 4-52.

Figure 4-52 | **Example of repeat-y**

Applying the background-attachment Property

The **background-attachment property** allows an image to scroll down the page along with the insertion point. The background-attachment property takes two values: scroll, where the image will scroll down the page along with the insertion point, and fixed, whereby the image stays in place and text would overlay the image as the user scrolls down the page. This value would be useful, for example, to ensure that an image of a corporate logo at the top of the page is always seen on the page, even though the user scrolls down the page. However, some visitors to your Web site might find this effect to be distracting, and even annoying. The following code sets the background–attachment property to have a value of fixed.

```
img {
background-image: url(logo.gif);
background-position: center;
background-attachment: fixed; }
```

Using the background Shortcut Property

The background property is used as the shortcut to specify any or all of the background properties. Note that in the background shortcut property, you use spaces, not commas, to separate the values. You can use as few or as many of the properties as you like, but you must specify the properties and their values in this order:

- background-image
- background-color
- background-position
- background-repeat
- background-attachment

For example:

```
body{
background: url(flowers.jpg) yellow center center repeat-y fixed; }
```

Jennifer has decided the Gina and Dina Web page would look better with a textured background, rather than just a color. You have a background image that will do just that. You will now show Jennifer how to add a background image to the page. You will edit the style for the body element selector to do so.

To add the background image to the page:

▶ **1.** Make sure the GinaNew file is open in Notepad.

▶ **2.** Position the insertion point to the left of the } brace for the body style, and then press the **Enter** key to create a new line.

▶ **3.** Type the following code shown in bold, which is also shown in red in Figure 4-53.

```
body {
margin: 20px;
color: black;
background-color: bisque;
font-size: 11pt;
font-family: arial,helvetica,sans-serif;
background-image: url(tile.jpg); }
```

Code for the background image ◀ **Figure 4-53**

```
body {
margin: 20px;
color: black;
background-color: bisque;
font-size: 11pt;
font-family: arial,helvetica,sans-serif;
background-image: url(tile.jpg); }
```

image used for the background

▶ **4.** Save GinaNew, and then refresh the file in the browser. Compare the Web page to Figure 4-54 to verify that the background image is displayed in the page background.

Figure 4-54 ▶ **Background image displayed on the Web page**

This Week's Recipe — Spaghetti with Meatballs

Spaghetti and meatballs is an inexpensive dish that everyone seems to enjoy. The trick is to get the spaghetti al dente, which is to cook the pasta so that it is not too firm (uncooked) and yet not too tender so that it becomes a pile of blonde mush.

Getting Started

Don't scrimp on the water. Cook your pasta in plenty of water in a high-rimmed saucepan. Some people like to add oil to the water, but oil and water don't mix, so a better strategy is to put a little extra virgin olive oil on the pasta after it's been cooked and drained. That will add flavor and keep the pasta from sticking.

Water does matter. If you live in an area where the water quality is not up to par, consider boiling the pasta in bottled water or filtered water from a tap if you have a filter installed on the faucet. The pasta can pick up bad odors and taste from water that does not taste good to begin with.

Boil that Water

Get the water to a roiling (that means "really bubbling") temperature. Toss in the pasta and stir with a Wooden spoon or fork. Follow the package label for cooking times, but generally cook the pasta in boiling water for about 10-12 minutes. The last 3 minutes are critical. You want the pasta al dente (firm, yet tender). Try tasting some of

Next, you'll add a background image to elements other than the Web page.

Adding a Background Image or Background Color to Other Elements

Although you have seen examples of adding a background image to an entire page by setting the style for the <body> element selector, you can also add a background image to block-level and inline elements. Any element, such as headings, can be given a height and width, which will apply a background image (or a background color) to any size area you want. You can then fill that area with a background image. Once again, be sure that the image contrasts, and does not compete with, the text. In the following example, the h1 heading is used as the selector, which is the heading size most commonly used with a background image. By applying the background image to the h1 selector, the text seems to display on top of the image, as shown in Figure 4-55.

```
h1{
font-size: 18pt;
height: 200px;
width: 500px;
color: gold;
padding: 15 15 0 0;
background-image: url(globe.jpg);
background-color: wheat;
float: left;
text-align: center; }
</style>
</head>
<body>
<h1>The World is Within Your Reach</h1>
```

Example of a heading with a background image ◀ Figure 4-55

However, if you have other h1 tags in the Web page, you could create an ID and apply the class using the <div> </div> tags, as shown in the following code:

```
#globe h1 {
font-size: 18pt;
height: 200px;
width: 500px;
color: gold;
padding: 15 15 0 0;
background-image: url(globe.jpg);
background-color: wheat;
float: left;
text-align: center; }
</style>
</head>
<body>
<div id="globe">
<h1>The World is Within Your Reach</h1>
</div>
```

Jennifer wants to use a background image with the h4 headings. She also wants you to expand the width of the headings to draw attention to the h4 headings. You will show her how to do so now.

To use a background image with the h4 headings:

▶ **1.** In the GinaNew document in your text editor, position the insertion point to the left of the closing } in the h4 heading style.

▶ **2.** Press the **Enter** key to create a new line.

▶ **3.** Type the following code shown in bold, which is also shown in red in Figure 4-56.

```
h4 {
font-size: 12pt;
color: navy;
background-color: white;
border: navy thin solid;
padding: 3px;
display: inline;
width: 200px;
background-image: url(sunset.gif);}
```

Figure 4-56   **Code for the background image applied to the h4 headings**

```
h4 {
font-size: 12pt;
color: navy;
background-color: white;
border: navy thin solid;
padding: 3px;
display: inline;
width: 200px;
background-image: url(sunset.gif);}


.center {
text-align: center; }
```

sunset picture used as the background image

4. Save GinaNew, and then refresh the file in your browser. Compare the Web page to Figure 4-57 to verify that the background image is displayed in the h4 headings.

Figure 4-57   **The h4 headings in the browser**

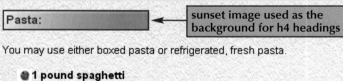

Pasta:

sunset image used as the background for h4 headings

You may use either boxed pasta or refrigerated, fresh pasta.

- 1 pound spaghetti

Meatballs:

Use either 93% lean beef or a mix or ground turkey and ground pork.

- 1 cup of breadcrumbs
- 2 large eggs
- 1 pound lean ground beef
- 1/4 cup grated Romano cheese
- 1 teaspoon fresh oregano
- 1/2 teaspoon salt
- 1/4 teaspoon pepper

Tomato Sauce:

If you wish to have home made, rather than from a jar or can.

- 1 teaspoon vegetable oil
- 1 medium onion, chopped
- 2 cloves garlic, chopped
- 2 28-ounce cans whole tomatoes

Figure 4-58 summarizes the background properties.

Property	What it Does	Values
background-image:	Places an image behind the contents of an element	Any .gif or .jpg image, but the syntax must be similar to url(*imagename*.gif)
background-position:	Positions an image on the page	Use keywords or percentage values
background-repeat:	Repeats an image horizontally, vertically, or to fill the entire screen	*repeat* (the default) The image is repeated to the right and down the page to fill the entire screen with copies of the same image *no-repeat* The image is displayed once in the upper-left corner of the screen *repeat-x* The image is repeated horizontally across the screen *repeat-y* The image is repeated vertically down the screen
background-attachment:	Determines whether an image scrolls with the insertion point	fixed scroll
background:	The shortcut property used to change all of the background properties	Properties and values must be listed in a set order

Resizing the Browser Window

Most of the time, visitors to a Web page have their screen maximized. However, visitors occasionally resize the browser window to less than the full height and width of the screen. The Web page should have the same appearance no matter how large or small the browser window. You want to show Jennifer how text and images can be repositioned if the user resizes the window.

To resize the browser window:

► 1. If necessary, switch to the GinaNew document in your browser.

► 2. If the browser window is maximized, restore the window by clicking the **Restore Down** button in the upper-right corner of the browser window.

► 3. Point to the upper-right corner of the window; when the pointer changes to the resize pointer, drag down and to the left to narrow the window.

When you resize the browser window, the text should reposition itself so that visitors can still see all of the text.

Preventing Elements from Repositioning

To keep the elements on the page from repositioning, you need to place the contents of the document into a container. You can use the <div></div> tags to do so. You will use the width property with a value expressed in pixels. Because most visitors to Web pages set their screen size to 800 x 600, a pixel value of 750-775 pixels for the width is a good choice. You will also set the left and right margin values to have a value of auto. Doing so will center the page horizontally when the page is viewed in the Firefox browser, irrespective of the screen resolution. These margin values, however, will not change the horizontal alignment of the page when viewed with the Internet Explorer browser.

You will use an ID selector and show Jennifer how to create a style that will prevent elements from repositioning.

To create the ID selector:

▶ **1.** Make sure the GinaNew file is open.

▶ **2.** On a blank line after the <li> element code, type the following code, which is also shown in red in Figure 4-59.

```
#main {
width: 750px;
margin-left: auto;
margin-right: auto;  }
```

Figure 4-59 ▶ **Code for the ID selector named** *main*

```
#main {
width:  750px;◄────── code sets the width and margins
margin-left:  auto;          for the main ID selector
margin-right:  auto;  }

</style>
</head>
```

Now that you have created the ID selector, you also need to apply it. You will show Jennifer how to do so next.

To apply the ID selector:

▶ **1.** In the GinaNew document in your text editor, position the insertion point on a blank line below the start <body> tag.

▶ **2.** Type the following code, which is also shown in red in Figure 4-60.

```
<div id="main">
```

Code to apply the ID selector named main to the start <div> tag | Figure 4-60

```
#main {
width: 750px;
margin-left: auto;
margin-right: auto; }

</style>
</head>

<body>
<div id="main">
<div class="center">
```

▶ **3.** Position the insertion point above the </body> tag at the bottom of the page, and then type the following code, which is also shown in red in Figure 4-61.

```
</div>
```

Code for the end </div> tag | Figure 4-61

```
<ul>
    <li>1 teaspoon vegetable oil</li>
    <li>1 medium onion, chopped</li>
    <li>2 cloves garlic, chopped</li>
    <li>2 28-ounce cans whole tomatoes</li>
    <li>1 6-ounce can tomato paste</li>
    <li>lightly salt and pepper to taste</li>
</ul>
</div>
</body>
</html>
```

▶ **4.** Save GinaNew, and then refresh the file in your browser.

▶ **5.** Resize the window. The elements on the screen should show little or no movement. The completed Web page is shown in Figure 4-62.

Figure 4-62 | **Completed Gina and Dina Web page in the browser**

Gina and Dina's Italian Cooking
Fast, Simple, and Good!

This Week's Recipe — Spaghetti with Meatballs

Spaghetti and meatballs is an inexpensive dish that everyone seems to enjoy. The trick is to get the spaghetti al dente, which is to cook the pasta so that it is not too firm (uncooked) and yet not too tender so that it becomes a pile of blonde mush.

Getting Started

Don't scrimp on the water. Cook your pasta in plenty of water in a high-rimmed saucepan. Some people like to add oil to the water, but oil and water don't mix, so a better strategy is to put a little extra virgin olive oil on the pasta after it's been cooked and drained. That will add flavor and keep the pasta from sticking.

Water does matter. If you live in an area where the water quality is not up to par, consider boiling the pasta in bottled water or filtered water from a tap if you have a filter installed on the faucet. The pasta can pick up bad odors and taste from water that does not taste good to begin with.

Boil that Water

Get the water to a roiling (that means "really bubbling") temperature. Toss in the pasta and stir with a Wooden spoon or fork. Follow the package label for cooking times, but generally cook the pasta in boiling water for about 10-12 minutes. The last 3 minutes are critical. You want the pasta al dente (firm, yet tender). Try tasting some of the pasta every minute for the last three minutes. When you think you've got the right tenderness, strain the pasta in a colander and then pour cold water on the pasta to stop the pasta from cooking any further.

Make Some Sauce

For the sauce, you can use any commercial canned or jar sauce to save time. Most of the sauces sold in the supermarket are quite good. If you want to make your own sauce, chop up a medium-sized onion and 1 or 2 cloves of garlic. Toss the onion and garlic into a large saucepan. Add two 28-ounce cans of whole tomatoes, one 6-ounce can of tomato paste, and 1 tablespoon of extra virgin olive oil.

Heat in a saucepan and stir on very low heat. Some people feel that sauce should be cooked for several hours. Most people don't have such discriminating palettes, so a slow simmer on low heat for about 10-15 minutes is just fine.

Cook the Meatballs

Of course, while the pasta is cooking (set the timer to 10 minutes) you can make the meatballs and the sauce. For the meatballs, in a large mixing bowl, mix one cup of breadcrumbs, 2 large eggs, and 1 pound of lean, ground beef. You can season as you like with salt, pepper, chicken broth, oregano, and basil. For an added touch, you can also mix in 1/4 cup freshly grated Romano or Parmesan cheese. Mix all the ingredients together and spoon into meatballs about 1" round. After you've formed the meatballs, one by one, place the meatballs into a frying pan that has been greased with one or two tablespoons of extra virgin olive oil. Cook on low-to-medium heat until the meatballs are brown.

Pour it On

Put the pasta on a large platter, spoon on the meatballs, and cover with the sauce.

Ingredients

Pasta:

You may use either boxed pasta or refrigerated, fresh pasta.

- 1 pound spaghetti

Meatballs:

Use either 93% lean beef or a mix or ground turkey and ground pork.

- 1 cup of breadcrumbs
- 2 large eggs
- 1 pound lean ground beef
- 1/4 cup grated Romano cheese
- 1 teaspoon fresh oregano
- 1/2 teaspoon salt
- 1/4 teaspoon pepper

Tomato Sauce:

If you wish to have home made, rather than from a jar or can.

- 1 teaspoon vegetable oil
- 1 medium onion, chopped
- 2 cloves garlic, chopped
- 2 28-ounce cans whole tomatoes
- 1 6-ounce can tomato paste
- lightly salt and pepper to taste

▶ **6.** Close Notepad and close your browser.

You have completed the Web page for Gina and Dina's Cooking Show.

Session 4.3 Quick Check | Review

1. What property is used to change the style of a bullet?
2. What property is used to change the position of a bullet?
3. What are the possible values to change the position of a bullet?
4. What property is used to have an image used as a bullet?
5. What type of list is used to create a hanging indent?
6. What tag is used for the defined term?
7. What property is used to change the color of an element's background?

Tutorial Summary | Review

In this tutorial, you worked with creating horizontal rules and using an image as a horizontal rule. In Session 4.2 you learned about the box model and how the padding, margin, and border are used with elements. In Session 4.3 you learned about how to enhance the appearance of lists and how to use an image as a bullet. You also learned that the background-image property displays an image behind the contents of an element. You should always use the background-color property when you use the background-image property. The background-repeat property is used to tile an image horizontally and vertically, horizontally, vertically, or not at all. Values used with the background-repeat property are repeat, repeat-x, repeat-y, and no-repeat.

Key Terms

ascender
background-attachment
   property
background-image
   property
background-position
   property
background-repeat
   property

border property
border-color property
border-style property
border-width property
defined term
definition data
descender
float property
height property

list-style property
list-style-image property
list-style-position property
list-style-type property
margin property
padding property
width property

| Practice | | **Review Assignments** |

Take time to practice the skills you learned in the tutorial using the same case scenario.

Data Files needed for the Review Assignments: Cook.htm, Frying.jpg, Pans.jpg, Parchment.gif, and Pot.gif

In addition to having their Web site for recipes, Gina and Dina also market a complete line of cookware. Each week, either Gina or Dina have a brief segment in their show in which they emphasize that using the proper cookware to cook a meal is just as important as choosing the right ingredients for the meal. The Gina and Dina pots and pans have gained a reputation for being fairly inexpensive, yet long-lasting, pots and pans. Jennifer has asked you to compose a Web page that promotes the Gina and Dina line of pots, pans, and other cooking utensils. You'll start by creating a CSS style sheet for the Web page. Complete the following steps:

1. Open Notepad and create a document named **Cook.css** and save it in the Tutorial. 04\Review folder included with your Data Files.

2. Begin the CSS style sheet by including a comment that includes your first and last name as the author, today's date, and the name of the file that links to this style sheet (CookNew.htm).

3. Enter code for the body selector to display text as 12pt Verdana (a sans-serif font). In addition, set the body selector to have a background-image named **Parchment.gif** and a background color of white.

4. Set the style for the hr element selector to have a height of 1em. In addition, the hr element should be navy with a background color of navy and a border that is green, thick, and outset.

5. Set the style of the h2 headings to display text in white with a background color of teal. The h2 headings should also have a border that is navy, thick, and outset. The border should be .5em wide on all sides with a padding of 4px on all sides.

6. Set the style for the address element selector to display text in bold and in all upper-case letters. There should be .5em space between the words in the address.

7. For the img element selector, create a dependent ID named **pans**. Set the style for this selector to have a border that is navy, thick, and solid. The image should float right and have a margin on the left of 1em.

8. For the img element selector, create a dependent ID selector named **frying**. Set the style for this selector to have a border that is black, thick, and solid. The image should float left and have a margin on the right of 1em.

9. For the img element selector, create a dependent ID selector named **pot**. Set the style for this selector to have a border that is green, thick, and solid. The image should float right and have a margin on the left of 1em.

10. Create an independent class named **newline**. Set the style for the newline class to clear after all images are floated left or right. Set the class to have a top margin of 2em.

11. Save the Cook CSS file.

12. Use Notepad to open **Cook.htm** from the Tutorial.04\Review folder included with your Data Files, and then save the file as **CookNew.htm** in the same folder.

13. In the <head> section of the CookNew HTML document, and above the code for the embedded style sheet code, type the necessary code to link CookNew to the Cook CSS file.

14. In the <img> tag for Pans.jpg, apply the ID selector *pans* after the alternate text.

15. In the <img> tag for Frying.jpg, apply the ID selector *frying* after the alternate text.

16. In the <img> tag code for Pot.jpg, apply the ID selector *pot* after the alternate text.

17. Above the code for the h3 heading "Put a Lid on It," insert a start <div> tag and apply the *newline* class. Below the h3 heading "Put a Lid on It," insert an end </div> tag.

18. Save the CookNew HTML document, and then open it in your browser. The document should be similar to the one shown in Figure 4-63.

Figure 4-63

Collect the Full Line of Gina and Dina Cookware

With Our Pots You Don't Need Luck

What good is cooking if you don't have the right cookware to go along with it? You can collect the full line of Gina and Dina Cookware right in your home. We have several packages to offer that will satisfy the needs of the most basic cooking needs right up to the practice gourmet cook. What's special about Gina and Dina Cookware? We're glad you asked. All of our cookware is stainless steel that is designed to last for many years to come. It's sturdy, yet remarkably lightweight for cookware that's so durable. Best of all, all Gina and Dina Cookware is available at the lowest price possible. Because of the incredible demand, you should make sure you don't delay; especially if you are thinking of ordering for the holidays.

Be a Smash in the Pan

We have a full line of frying pans to match your every need. With our pans, you'll get a nice, even, and well-distributed heat that disperses heat to the entire cooking surface, not just the center or the edges. With our pans, it's tough to make a mistake. Whether you are cooking on low heat, high heat, or anything in between, our stick-resistant surface will make you a pro in the kitchen.

You'll draw raves for your cooking; you don't have to tell anyone that Gina and Dina are there to help you please your friends and family with your cooking. It will be our secret.

Put a Lid on It

Got a lot to cook? If you've got a big family or if you are just cooking for a lot of people or even if you are just cooking for yourself, we have pots in every size from smallest to largest.

Need to cook 3 pounds of pasta in a hurry? Need to cook just one hard-boiled egg? Don't worry, we've got your pot! All of the Gina and Dina's pots are guaranteed to last for 10 years from the date of purchase. With Gina and Dina pots, we do all the worrying; you get the compliments.

Gina And Dina Cooking · Santa Monica, California

19. Close all open windows.

20. Submit the results of the preceding steps to your instructor, either in printed or electronic form, as requested.

Apply | **Case Problem 1**

Use the skills you learned in the tutorial to create a Web page for a planetarium and space museum.

Data Files needed for this Case Problem: Bullet.gif, Galaxy.gif, Planet.htm, and Shore.gif

Shore River Planetarium When it is completed next month, the Shore River Planetarium will be one of the largest planetariums in the South. Located in the city of East Landing, which is about 20 miles northeast of the city of Charleston, South Carolina, this state-of-the-art facility will house a planetarium and a space museum. Edward Ortiz, the director of the planetarium, asks you to create a Web page that describes the attractions at Shore River Planetarium. You'll start by creating a CSS style sheet for the Web page. Complete the following steps:

1. Open Notepad, create a document named **Planet.css**, and save it in the Tutorial. 04\Case1 folder included with your Data Files.
2. Begin the CSS style sheet by inserting a comment that includes your first and last name as the author, today's date, and the name of the file that links to this style sheet (PlanetNew.htm).
3. Set the style for the <body> element selector to display text as white, 12pt, bold, and Arial. The background color should be black.
4. Create an ID selector named **floatright**. Set the style of the ID to float an element right and have a left margin of 1em.
5. Set the style of the h3 headings to display text in gold.
6. Set the style of the <hr /> element selector to be gold, with a background color of black, a height of 20px, a width of 100%, and a border that is gold, thick, and outset.
7. Set the style of the paragraphs to have a text indent of 2em.
8. Set the style of the <ul> element selector to have a list-style image named Bullet.gif.
9. Set the style of the <li> element selector to have a margin on all four sides of 1em.
10. Set the style of the h4 headings to be 12pt. The text should appear in small capitals, with a height of 18pt. The color should be white with a background color of brown. Set the style of the text as centered.
11. Save the Planet CSS file.
12. Use Notepad to open the file **Planet.htm** from the Tutorial.04\Case1 folder included with your Data Files, and then save the file as **PlanetNew.htm** in the same folder.
13. Within the <head> section and above the embedded styles code, insert the necessary code to link PlanetNew.htm to the Planet CSS file.
14. To the right of the alternate text, apply the floatright ID to the <img> tag code for the Galaxy image.
15. Save the PlanetNew HTML document, and then open it in your browser. The Web page should be similar to the one shown in Figure 4-64.

Figure 4-64

SHORE RIVER PLANETARIUM

What is a Planetarium?

A planetarium is a building with a domed ceiling that uses special projection equipment to reproduce images of the night sky. A planetarium offers the visitor a theatre-like experience in that the room itself is dark, and the "show" is narrated usually by a famous actor or actress. Each season, the planetarium offers different shows based upon the night sky of that particular season.

Shows run for a period of about three months and are not repeated after that. If you've been to the planetarium more than three months ago, there's a new, never-been-seen show waiting for you. Of course, there's no harm in seeing the same show more than once, as many people do. Most shows are about 42 minutes long, which allows time for exit and entry between shows. Shows start on the hour every hour the planetarium is open. The planetarium is not only a place to enjoy a show about the stars, but it's also a place to experience what the stars are about. A visit to the planetarium is interesting, educational, and fun.

Group Rates and Admission

Regular admission is $10 for adults and $7 for children under 12. There are discounted admission plans for public and private schools and colleges. Discounted admission is for groups of 20 or more for shows Monday through Thursday. Reservations must be made at least 60 days in advance. Group rates do not apply on weekends. In addition, there are some dates when group rates do not apply, such as all Federal and State holidays. There is separate admission charge for both the IMAX theatre, and for the StarTours virtual reality ride. Admission to those events is discounted for students only and only for shows during the hours of 9 a.m. to 3 p.m. You must be 12 or older to take the StarTours virtual reality ride.

Chaperone Policy

The planetarium requires a chaperone rate of 1:5 for grades 1-8; 1:10 for grades 9-12. Chaperones (including teachers) receive free museum admission. Chaperones must accompany students at all times. We have separate bathroom facilities for school groups. We also have separate dining facilities for school groups. Educators may visit the planetarium Monday through Thursday and speak with a planning representative, who will give you detailed information about how to plan your trip to the planetarium. There is no admission charge or fees of any kind for these planning visits.

Special Note for School Field Trips

Teachers and chaperones should follow these rules for field trips:

- Disembark in the designated arrival area.

- Conduct a head count on arrival.

- Wait for the guide to greet you and escort you into the facility.

The Planetarium for Adults

The planetarium is not just a learning, fun experience for children. Adults will enjoy many of the other features we have at the Shore River Planetarium. Our Moonbeam Restaurant is open from 6 p.m. till 12 midnight. The Moonbeam offers the best of fine dining. The Galaxy Coffee Bar is located above the Moonbeam Restaurant. The Galaxy serves coffee, tea, juice, salads, and our universally-famous desserts. The Comet's Tail Food Court is open at all times while the Planetarium is open.

The StarStruck nightclub is open for dancing from 9:30 p.m. till 2 a.m. on Friday and Saturday nights. There is a separate admission to the StarStruck night club. The IMAX theatre shows first-run movies on a 3-story tall movie screen. There is a separate admission charge for the IMAX theatre. Adults can purchase a Night on the Stars package, which includes a one-price discounted admission to all ticketed events: the planetarium show, the StarTours reality ride, the StarStruck night club, and the IMAX theatre.

SHORE RIVER PLANETARIUM · 45 RIVER DRIVE · EAST LANDING, SC

16. Close all open windows.

17. Submit the results of the preceding steps to your instructor, either in printed or electronic form, as requested.

| Apply | | Case Problem 2 |

Use the skills you learned in the tutorial to create a Web page for a water amusement park.

Data Files needed for this Case Problem: Block.gif, Dragon.gif, Dragon.htm, Slide.gif, and Splash.gif

Dragon's Dare Water Park Dragon's Dare Water Park, located in Sea Cove, Florida, is a major attraction in northwest Florida. Dragon's Dare is known for its thrill rides and their ability to soak riders to the bone. Dragon's Dare has rides for all ages, including a Lazy River, but it prides itself on being a thrill ride spectacular. Libby Showalter is the director of outreach at the park, and asks you to create a Web page for Dragon's Dare that emphasizes its friendly atmosphere. You'll start by creating a CSS style sheet for the Web page. Complete the following steps:

1. Open Notepad, create a document named **Dragon.css**, and save it in the Tutorial. 04\Case2 folder included with your Data Files.

2. Begin the CSS style sheet by inserting a comment that includes your first and last name as the author, today's date, and the name of the file that links to this style sheet (DragonNew.htm).

⊕ EXPLORE   3. Set the style of the <body> element selector to display text as white, 12pt, bold, and Verdana. Also set the style of the body to have a background-image named **Block. gif**. The background image should repeat vertically, and the background color should be blue.

4. Set the style of the <dl> element selector to have a margin of 0.

5. Set the style of the <dt> element selector to display text as orange italic text, with a top margin of .5em, a bottom margin of .5em, and left margin of 1em.

6. Set the style of the <dd> element selector to display text in yellow and set the left margin to 235px.

7. Set the style of the <hr /> element selector as light green with a background color of light green and a height of 5px.

8. Set the style of the <h3> element selector to display text in yellow.

⊕ EXPLORE   9. For the <img> element selector, create a dependent class named **right**. Set the style of the class to have a border that is green, thick, and solid. Also, set the style of the class to have a top margin of .5em, a left margin of 1em, and to float right.

10. For the <div> element selector, create a dependent class named **center**. Set the style of the class to center text.

11. Create an independent class named **main**. Set the style of this class to have a left margin of 235px.

12. Save the Dragon CSS file.

13. Use Notepad to open the file **Dragon.htm** from the Tutorial.04\Case2 folder included with your Data Files, and then save the file as **DragonNew.htm** in the same folder.

14. Within the <head> section, type the necessary code to link the DragonNew HTML document to the Dragon CSS file.

15. Above the code for the <img> tag for the Dragon image, include the code for a start <div> tag, and apply the class named *center*.

16. Just below the code for the <img> tag for the Dragon image, include the code for an end </div> tag.
17. Apply the dependent class named *right* to the <img> tag for the Splash image and to the <img> tag for the Slide image.
18. Just above the code for the Splash image, insert a <div> tag and apply the class named *main*.
19. Just above the end </body> tag, include the code for an end </div> tag.
20. Save the **DragonNew** HTML document, and then open it in your browser. The document should be similar to the one shown in Figure 4-65.

Figure 4-65

21. Close all open windows.
22. Submit the results of the preceding steps to your instructor, either in printed or electronic form, as requested.

Challenge | **Case Problem 3**

Use what you've learned, and expand your skills, to create a Web page for a new coastal housing community.

Data Files needed for this Case Problem: Beach.gif, Beach.htm, Collage.gif, and Sand.gif

Sol Mer Sol Mer means "sun and sea," and is the name of a new community of luxury homes along the Atlantic coast in Carlisle, Virginia. Marilee Atkinson is in charge of public relations for Sol Mer, and is helping to manage a major expansion that is adding several new homes. In order to attract new home buyers, Marilee asks you to create a new Web site for Sol Mer, highlighting the attractions of purchasing a residence in Sol Mer. You'll start by creating a CSS style sheet for the Web page. Complete the following steps:

1. Open Notepad, create a document named **Beach.css**, and then save it in the Tutorial.04\Case3 folder included with your Data Files.
2. Begin the CSS style sheet by inserting a comment that includes your first and last name as the author, today's date, and the name of the file that links to this style sheet (BeachNew.htm).
3. Set the style of the <body> selector to display text as 12pt, bold, and Arial. The text should be navy on a wheat background. Also set the style of the <body> tag to have a background-image named **Sand.gif**.
4. Set the style of the <h3> selector to display text in cadet blue.
5. Set the style of the <hr /> selector to have a height of 5px, a width of 100%, a color of navy, and a background color of navy.

⊕ **EXPLORE**
6. Set the style of the <ul> selector to have a list-style-type of square and a list-style-position of inside.
7. Set the style of the h4 selector to have a height of 20px, a width of 100%, and to center text. The text should also be white on a navy background.
8. Create an ID selector named **left** that has a background position of 0% 0%. Float the element left, and use a right margin of 2em.
9. Create an ID selector named **main** that has a left margin of 225px.

⊕ **EXPLORE**
10. Create an ID selector named **content**. Set the style of the content ID selector to have a width of 750px, a left margin with a value of auto, and a right margin with a value of auto.
11. Save the Beach CSS file.
12. Use Notepad to open the file **Beach.htm** from the Tutorial.04\Case3 folder included with your Data Files, and then save the file as **BeachNew.htm** in the same folder.
13. Within the <head> section, type the necessary code to link BeachNew HTML document to the Beach CSS file.
14. Just below the start <body> tag, insert a start <div> tag and apply the *content* ID selector.
15. Just above the end </body> tag, insert an end </div> tag.
16. Apply the ID selector named *left* to the <img> element for Collage.gif.
17. Just above the h2 heading "We've Got a Village to Fit Your Lifestyle," include the code for a start <div> tag and apply the *main* ID selector.
18. Near the bottom of the page, just above the start <h4> tag, include the code for an end </div> tag.
19. Save the BeachNew HTML document, and then open it in your browser. The document should be similar to the one shown in Figure 4-66.

Figure 4-66

20. Close all open windows.
21. Submit the results of the preceding steps to your instructor, either in printed or electronic form, as requested.

| Create | **Case Problem 4** |

With the steps provided as a guide, create a Web page for a fire department.

Data Files needed for this Case Problem: Fire.htm, Fire.jpg, Stone.gif, and Truck.jpg

Ramona Hills Fire Department The Ramona Hills Fire Department is a nonprofit, volunteer fire department serving over 200,000 people in Ramona Hills, Ohio. Ben Amin, the fire chief, is trying to point out the dangers of carbon monoxide poisoning. Ben asks you to create a Web page that focuses on making the public aware of the dangers of carbon monoxide and how to avoid exposure to carbon monoxide. You'll begin by creating an embedded style sheet. Complete the following:

1. Open Notepad, open the **Fire.htm** file from the Tutorial.04\Case4 folder included with your Data Files, and then save it as **FireNew.htm**.
2. In the <head> area, enter the code for the start <style> tag and the end </style> tag.

3. Below the start <style> tag, create a comment that includes your first and last name as the author and today's date.

4. In the embedded style sheet, set the style of the <body> element selector for font size, font, color, and background color of your choice. Also in the <body> tag, use the Stone.gif image file as the background image for the page. Repeat the image vertically down the left edge of the page.

5. Set the style for the <hr /> element to have a width less than 100%. Set the style for the rule to have a height, a color, and a background color. Align the rule left, center, or right.

6. Use examples of creating white space with padding and margins.

7. Use examples of styling borders.

8. Create one dependent class and apply that class in the body of the HTML document.

9. Create one independent class and apply that class in the body of the HTML document.

10. Create one ID selector and apply that selector in the body of the HTML document.

11. Use either of the images Truck.jpg or Fire.jpg on your Web page. Scale the Truck image to be 250px wide and 200px high; scale the Fire image to be 500px wide and 100px high.

12. Float the image either left or right.

13. Use the clear property to clear after the image.

14. Save your FireNew HTML document, and then open it in your browser.

15. Close all open windows.

16. Submit the results of the preceding steps to your instructor, either in printed or electronic form, as requested.

Review | **Quick Check Answers**

Session 4.1

1. No. HTML and CSS will only insert and position an already existing image.
2. Width, height, text-align, and color.
3. No. You can use as few or as many properties in any order.
4. Not very. Most rules today are actually images.
5. No; use the <img /> tag.
6. You must also use the background-color property so that the rule displays correctly in Firefox.

Session 4.2

1. Block-level elements have an invisible padding, border, and external margin.
2. The internal padding is the white space that surrounds the contents of an element.
3. The external margin is the white space outside of the border.
4. left, right, and both.
5. The order does not matter, but specify a color, a style, and a thickness.
6. the clear property

Session 4.3

1. list-style-type
2. list-style-position
3. inside and outside
4. list-style-image
5. definition list
6. <dt>
7. background-color

Ending Data Files

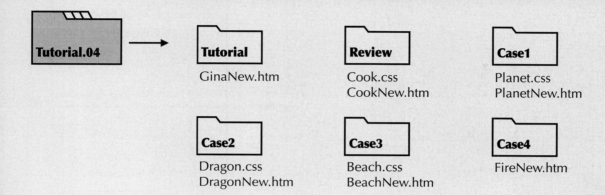

Tutorial.04 →

Tutorial
GinaNew.htm

Review
Cook.css
CookNew.htm

Case1
Planet.css
PlanetNew.htm

Case2
Dragon.css
DragonNew.htm

Case3
Beach.css
BeachNew.htm

Case4
FireNew.htm

Tutorial 5

Using CSS for Layout and Printing

Designing a Web Page Using CSS

Case | America, America—The Musical

America, America is a new Broadway musical that has recently opened to rave reviews. Audiences are responding enthusiastically to its unique mix of comedy, suspense, dance, and lively music, indicating that *America, America* will be the biggest hit musical on Broadway this year. The play takes place in 1777, just as the Revolutionary War begins to affect New York City. The story centers on a love affair between an American patriot, Nathaniel, and his British loyalist girlfriend, Linda. Despite their political differences, they overcome significant obstacles and triumph together. Danny D'Angelo, the play's producer, asks you to create several Web pages about this new musical. He wants you to strike a patriotic theme to be consistent with the play's title and subject. You will be working with Wendy Klein, who is in charge of marketing and promoting the play. Wendy knows HTML and some CSS, but she has no experience using CSS to create layouts for Web pages. Wendy has already begun creating a Web page for the site. Her Web page includes details about the play, the cast, and the great reviews the play has received. Now she needs your help in using CSS to create an eye-catching, attractive layout for the page.

Starting Data Files

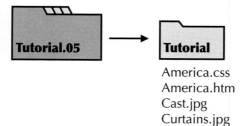

Tutorial.05 →	Tutorial	Review	Case1	Case2	Case3	Case4
	America.css	Actor.gif	Global.gif	Bio.jpg	Haircut.jpg	Check.jpg
	America.htm	Actress.gif	Group.htm	Book.htm	Harpers.css	Client.jpg
	Cast.jpg	Leading.htm	House.gif	Science.jpg	Harpers.htm	Couple.jpg
	Curtains.jpg		Money.gif	Travel.jpg		Movie.jpg
	Flag.gif					Pool.jpg
						Skyscraper.jpg
						Tower.htm
						Walkway.jpg

Session 5.1

Sizing and Positioning Boxes

As you know, neither HTML nor CSS has all the features of a word processing program. In particular, they do not include a feature that creates or formats columns automatically. In Microsoft Word, for example, you can create columns with a few mouse clicks. Unfortunately, that ease of use and design consistency does not exist in CSS. The World Wide Web Consortium (W3C) does not have an approved method for page layout. Web developers have devised their own, often different, approaches to page layout. Some methods Web developers use to create page layout include absolute positioning, relative positioning, setting extreme left and right margins, floating elements, and using padding and negative margins. Each of these methods has its advantages and disadvantages.

Similarly, CSS does not provide a standard terminology to describe the areas of the page layout. A text document you create or format using a word processor has a **header** area, which is the top part of the document; a main document area, and a **footer** area, which is the bottom part of the page. Web page developers refer to the header area as the masthead, banner, or header. They call the main window the main, content, body, container, box, or frame area. Web developers often refer to the bottom of the page as the footer. However, using the terms *header* or *footer* in Web page design is misleading. In a word processor, a header or footer repeats information at the top or the bottom of each page, but CSS does not repeat this information unless you place it on each page manually.

To further complicate matters, Web developers do not consistently use the same selectors for page layout. Some Web page developers prefer to use independent ID selectors, while some prefer dependent classes for the div element, and others prefer a mix of class and ID selectors. All are correct, but the inconsistency can lead to problems in maintaining Web sites.

In Tutorial 4, you learned about the box properties and how block-level elements have padding, a border, and an external margin. You also learned that you can float an image or text. One advantage of using the box properties is that they let you create a block-level element (a box) and then size and position the box for the browser window. You can float the box left or right and have text wrap to either the right or the left of the box, similar to the way you float an image and wrap text around it. For the America, America Web page layout, you will create several boxes and place an image, text, or both text and images into each box. You will begin by viewing the Web page that Wendy has created so far, and then you will work with her on creating a page layout.

To view the original America, America Web page:

▶ 1. In Notepad, open the **America.htm** file located in the Tutorial.05\Tutorial folder included with your Data Files. Save the file as **AmericaNew.htm** in the same folder.

▶ 2. Open the file in your browser. The file should look similar to the one shown in Figure 5-1.

Original America, America Web page | Figure 5-1

Tickets on Sale Now!

America, America — The Musical

The Cast

Nathaniel · Max Wilton
Linda · Kathy Meade
Prof. Bean · Tony Taylor
Jal · Rasheed Thomas
Shai · Tara Morris
Mr. Hal · Varun Singh
Katie · Antoinette Carter
Tanya · Keisha Kenton
Ross · Harry Williams
Gen. Montback · Tony Fallon
Lt. Rider · Gus Todd

Tickets are going fast!

Please call the box office at:
212 474-4567

AMERICA, AMERICA — The Smash Broadway Hit!

From the writers and directors that gave you the smash musicals, *Crazy Over the Moon*, and *Serendipity* comes their greatest work yet, *America, America —The Musical*. This show takes you back in time to the American Revolution and weaves a story that blends comedy, drama, and song, to tell an enchanting tale of the founding of our nation. Set in New York City in 1777, you'll experience a one-of-a-kind, breathtaking experience that will make you laugh and cry.

Tickets for holiday performances are now on sale. Good seats in all sections can be purchased at the box office, by mail order, or by phone. Group rates are not being honored for holiday shows. Please arrive 30 minutes before show times.

The Critics Have Spoken

America, America, is a fun-filled, touching and enchanting experience. The cast is uniformly wonderful, and the sets and the lighting are first-rate. This is a musical for all ages. You will be uplifted and filled with joy by this musical. — *Janet O'Toole, Broadway Gazette*

This play is unlike any other Broadway play I have ever seen. It will leave you breathless. This is a fantastic work of Broadway art. Be ready to be captivated. — *Fred Berrs, Broadway in Review*

The Hanson Theatre · 246 North Broadway, · New York, New York 10019

You will be creating the layout for the America, America Web page using an embedded style sheet. First, you'll show Wendy how to create the code for the style tags. You will also include a comment with your first name, last name, and today's date.

To insert the style tags for the Web page:

▶ **1.** Make sure the AmericaNew file is open in Notepad.

▶ **2.** On a blank line below the page title, type the following code, which is also shown in red in Figure 5-2.

```
<style type="text/css">

/* Your First Name Your Last Name
Today's Date */




</style>
```

Figure 5-2 ▶ **Inserting style tags and the document comment**

```
<html>
<head>
<title>America, America -- The Musical</title>



<style type="text/css">

/* Your First Name Your Last Name
Today's Date */



</style>
</head>
```

InSight | **Troubleshooting Complex Web Pages**

In addition to entering the code for the start <style> and the end </style> tags together in an embedded style sheet, it's a good coding practice to type both the begin brace and the end brace after you type the selector. For example, to set the style for the h1 selector, you first enter the following code:

```
h1 { }
```

Next, position the insertion point between the two braces and type your declarations, like this:

```
h1 {
font-size: 14pt;
font-family: arial,helvetica,sans-serif; }
```

By including both the begin brace and the end brace for your declaration list, you avoid the common error of omitting the end brace. If a particular declaration is not taking effect in the browser, check the code for that selector to make sure you included the end brace. Another common error is to inadvertently type a begin brace ({) at the end of the declaration list, rather than an end brace (}).

Web page designers typically use layouts that include one or more of the following design components: a horizontal **banner**, or bar, at the top of the page that usually includes a corporate logo; a **sidebar**, which is a narrow vertical column commonly used for links; the **main** document window, which is the largest window and contains most of the page content; and a **footer**, which is a row at the bottom of the page, which usually displays the contact information for the Web site, such as the address.

Wendy wants to know how you will design the layout of the page. You explain to her that you will use ID selectors and several <div> sections. Initially, a <div> section has no formatting of its own. Instead, the IDs and classes that you apply to a <div> section give that section its formatting. You plan to use a container <div> that will specify the margins of the page. In addition, four other <div> sections will be formatted by ID selectors, as follows:

- **#container** formats the background and specifies the dimensions of the containing box that will hold the contents of the four other boxes.
- **#banner** formats the banner at the top of the page.

- **#sidebar** formats a narrow column at the left of the page that will contain a list of the cast members and an image.
- **#main** formats the information about the play itself in the main document window.
- **#footer** formats the address at the bottom of the page.

Each section of the Web page will be contained within <div> </div> tags, as shown in Figure 5-3.

Organizing the Web page into four sections | **Figure 5-3**

div Banner	
div Sidebar	div Main
div Footer	

The basic document structure matches the following code outline, with the four divs for the page content being enclosed within the container div.

```
<div id="container">
    <div id="banner"></div>
    <div id="sidebar"></div>
    <div id="main"></div>
    <div id="footer"></div>
</div>
```

For this page layout, you will be floating one box to the left and one box to the right. To align the two boxes vertically, you need to keep both floated boxes in a **container box**, which is an element that contains other elements.

Wendy wants the page to have a modern look, so she suggests using a sans-serif font. You will show her how to set the style for the container ID selector.

Tip

Use a container box when you need to position more than one floating element.

To set the style for the container ID selector:

1. In the AmericaNew document in your text editor, position the insertion point below the start <style> tag.

▶ **2.** On a blank line below the comment, type the following code, which is also shown in red in Figure 5-4.

```
#container {
width: 775px;
color: navy;
background-color: beige;
font-size: 11pt;
font-family: 'lucida sans unicode',helvetica,sans-serif; }
```

Figure 5-4 ▶ Code for the container ID selector

```
<style type="text/css">

/* Your First Name Your Last Name
Today's Date */

#container {
width: 775px;
color: navy;
background-color: beige;
font-size: 11pt;
font-family: 'lucida sans unicode',helvetica,sans-serif; }

</style>
```

the container ID selector specifies navy 11pt Lucida Sans Unicode text on a beige background

Now that you have created the ID selector, you need to apply it. You will show Wendy where to insert the code for the first set of <div> </div> tags that will be used in this document.

To apply the container ID selector:

▶ **1.** In the AmericaNew document in your text editor, position the insertion point below the start <body> tag.

▶ **2.** On a blank line below the start <body> tag, type the following code, which is also shown in red in Figure 5-5.

```
<div id="container">
```

Figure 5-5 ▶ Applying the container ID selector

```
#container {
width: 775px;
color: navy;
background-color: beige;
font-size: 11pt;
font-family: 'lucida sans unicode',helvetica,sans-serif; }

</style>
</head>

<body>
<div id="container">
```

code that applies the ID selector

▶ **3.** On a blank line below the address for the Hanson Theatre, type the following code, which is also shown in red in Figure 5-6.

```
</div>
```

The end </div> tag for the container div ◄ Figure 5-6

```
<p>The Hanson Theatre &middot; 246 North Broadway, &middot; New York, New York 10019</p>

</div>                insert the </div> tag
</body>               after the address
</html>               paragraph
```

▶ **4.** Save the AmericaNew file.

▶ **5.** Refresh the AmericaNew Web page in your browser, and then compare it to Figure 5-7 to verify that the document is displayed in 11pt Lucida Sans Unicode font.

Web page with the container styles ◄ Figure 5-7

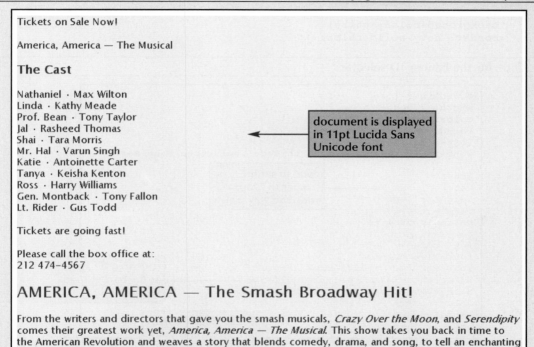

Tickets on Sale Now!

America, America — The Musical

The Cast

Nathaniel · Max Wilton
Linda · Kathy Meade
Prof. Bean · Tony Taylor
Jal · Rasheed Thomas
Shai · Tara Morris
Mr. Hal · Varun Singh
Katie · Antoinette Carter
Tanya · Keisha Kenton
Ross · Harry Williams
Gen. Montback · Tony Fallon
Lt. Rider · Gus Todd

Tickets are going fast!

Please call the box office at:
212 474-4567

AMERICA, AMERICA — The Smash Broadway Hit!

From the writers and directors that gave you the smash musicals, *Crazy Over the Moon*, and *Serendipity* comes their greatest work yet, *America, America — The Musical.* This show takes you back in time to the American Revolution and weaves a story that blends comedy, drama, and song, to tell an enchanting tale of the founding of our nation. Set in New York City in 1777, you'll experience a one-of-a-kind, breathtaking experience that will make you laugh and cry.

document is displayed in 11pt Lucida Sans Unicode font

Wendy likes the appearance of the font. She also wants to include an eye-catching banner at the top of the page. Because the Web page is trying to strike a patriotic theme, she wants to repeat an image of an American flag across the top of the page. You will work with Wendy to create a banner for the Web page.

Creating the Banner

The banner will use a background image flag.gif. You will use the background-repeat property and repeat the image horizontally. The banner will be 775px wide and 100px high. You will also create a border around the banner. You will show Wendy how to create the banner now.

To set the style for the banner ID selector:

▶ **1.** In the AmericaNew document in your text editor, position the insertion point below the container ID selector code.

▶ **2.** On a blank line, type the following code, which is also shown in red in Figure 5-8.

```
#banner {
width: 775px;
height: 100px;
margin-top: 0;
margin-bottom: 10px;
text-align: center;
font-weight: bold;
font-size: 24pt;
font-family: 'lucida sans unicode',sans-serif;
background-image: url(flag.gif);
background-repeat: repeat-x;
color: navy;
background-color: white;
border: navy solid thick; }
```

Figure 5-8 ▶ **Code for the banner ID selector**

```
#container {
width: 775px;
color: navy;
background-color: beige;
font-size: 11pt;
font-family: 'lucida sans unicode',helvetica,sans-serif; }

#banner {
width: 775px;          code to set the
height: 100px;         banner to 775px
margin-top: 0;         wide and 100px high
margin-bottom: 10px;
text-align: center;
font-weight: bold;
font-size: 24pt;
font-family: 'lucida sans unicode',sans-serif;   code to use flag.gif
background-image: url(flag.gif);                  as the background
background-repeat: repeat-x;                      image
color: navy;
background-color: white;       background-repeat
border: navy solid thick; }    property repeats the
                               image horizontally
```

Now that you have created the banner ID selector, you need to apply it.

To apply the banner ID selector:

▶ **1.** In the AmericaNew document in your text editor, position the insertion point above the "America, America — The Musical" paragraph.

▶ **2.** On the blank lines above and below the "America, America—The Musical" paragraph, type the following bold code, which is also shown in red in Figure 5-9.

```
<div id="banner">
<p>America, America &mdash; The Musical</p>
</div>
```

Code to apply the banner ID selector ◄ Figure 5-9

```
</style>
</head>

<body>
<div id="container">


<p>Tickets on Sale Now!</p>


<div id="banner">◄──
<p>America, America &mdash; The Musical</p>
</div>
```

applies the banner ID selector to the title of the play

▶ **3.** Save the AmericaNew file.

▶ **4.** Refresh the AmericaNew Web page in your browser, and then compare it to Figure 5-10 to verify that the banner appears at the top of the page.

Web page with the banner ID selector ◄ Figure 5-10

Tickets on Sale Now!

America, America — The Musical

banner ID selector with flag.gif as the background

The Cast

Nathaniel · Max Wilton
Linda · Kathy Meade
Prof. Bean · Tony Taylor
Jal · Rasheed Thomas
Shai · Tara Morris
Mr. Hal · Varun Singh
Katie · Antoinette Carter
Tanya · Keisha Kenton
Ross · Harry Williams
Gen. Montback · Tony Fallon
Lt. Rider · Gus Todd

Tickets are going fast!

Please call the box office at:
212 474-4567

AMERICA, AMERICA — The Smash Broadway Hit!

Now you are ready to turn your attention to the sidebar box, which will appear on the left side of the page. In the sidebar, Wendy wants to list the cast members in a column and display a photo of several cast members below the list. You will show Wendy how to create the sidebar box. Because she might add content to the sidebar later, you need to show Wendy how to use the overflow property, which determines what will be displayed if the box is not tall or wide enough to display all of its contents.

Using the overflow Property

The **overflow property** is used to determine what happens if there is too much text (or an image is too large) to be displayed in the space for the box. The values for the overflow property are as follows:

- **visible** allows the box to expand as much as possible; as such, a height need not be specified.
- **hidden** does not display overflow text; scroll bars do not display.
- **scroll** displays scroll bars so users can scroll through the box when more text is entered into the box than can be displayed; the size of the box remains the same.
- **auto** displays scroll bars only if necessary; the size of the box remains the same.

If this were a box for a banner or logo at the top of the page, you would not want to display scroll bars. A good choice for the overflow property for a banner or logo is a value of *hidden*. If you do want the scroll bars to appear if needed, a value of *auto* is appropriate.

This sidebar box will contain both text and a background image. If you are using a background image for the box, make sure the size of the image is slightly bigger than the size of the box. If the size of the image is too small, it will not fill the box contents and the background color will be displayed along one or more sides of the image. For this Web page, you will use the width property with the overflow property, which will have the effect of cropping the image to an appropriate size.

> **Tip**
>
> If you specify a height, but not the overflow, the box continues to grow past the height measurement you want.

> **Tip**
>
> If you are uncertain about which value to use for the overflow property, choose the value of *auto*.

InSight | **Creating Boxes**

When you create a box, it is good coding practice to first create the code for the properties and values that are most relevant to the size, appearance, and position of the box. Whenever you create a box, use these properties first:

```
width:
height:
overflow:
float:
border:
padding:
margin:
```

You will now show Wendy how to create the sidebar.

To set the style for the sidebar ID selector:

1. In the AmericaNew document in your text editor, position the insertion point below the banner ID selector code.

2. On a blank line, type the following code, which is also shown in red in Figure 5-11.

```
#sidebar {
width: 300px;
overflow: hidden;
float: left;
border: red thick inset;
padding: .5em;
padding-left: 1em;
font-weight: bold;
color: white;
background-color: black; }
```

Code for the sidebar ID selector | **Figure 5-11**

```
#sidebar {
width: 300px;
overflow: hidden;
float: left;
border: red thick inset;
padding: .5em;
padding-left: 1em;
font-weight: bold;
color: white;
background-color: black; }

</style>
</head>

<body>
<div id="container">


<p>Tickets on Sale Now!</p>
```

overflow property with a value of hidden expands the sidebar box only when necessary to display all of its text

sidebar will appear on the left with a thick red border and use bold white text on a black background

Tip

The two padding declarations in Figure 5-11 can be expressed more concisely as *padding: .5em .5em .5em 1em;*. However, writing a separate declaration isolates the measurement most likely to change.

Now you will show Wendy how to apply the sidebar ID selector.

To apply the sidebar ID selector:

▶ **1.** In the AmericaNew document in your text editor, position the insertion point above the h3 heading "The Cast."

▶ **2.** On a blank line above the h3 heading for "The Cast," type the following code, which is also shown in red in Figure 5-12.

```
<div id="sidebar">
```

Code to apply the sidebar ID selector | **Figure 5-12**

```
<div id="banner">
<p>America, America &mdash; The Musical</p>
</div>

<div id="sidebar">
<h3>The Cast</h3>
<p>Nathaniel &middot; Max Wilton
<br />Linda &middot; Kathy Meade
<br />Prof. Bean &middot; Tony Taylor
<br />Jal &middot; Rasheed Thomas
<br />Shai &middot; Tara Morris
<br />Mr. Hal &middot; Varun Singh
<br />Katie &middot; Antoinette Carter
<br />Tanya &middot; Keisha Kenton
<br />Ross &middot; Harry Williams
<br />Gen. Montback &middot; Tony Fallon
<br />Lt. Rider &middot; Gus Todd
```

applies the sidebar ID selector to the cast list

▶ **3.** On a blank line below the box office phone number, type the following code, which is also shown in red in Figure 5-13.

```
</div>
```

Figure 5-13 | Code for the end </div> tag for the sidebar div

```
<br />Mr. Hal &middot; Varun Singh
<br />Katie &middot; Antoinette Carter
<br />Tanya &middot; Keisha Kenton
<br />Ross &middot; Harry Williams
<br />Gen. Montback &middot; Tony Fallon
<br />Lt. Rider &middot; Gus Todd
</p>


<p>Tickets are going fast!</p>

<p>Please call the box office at:
<br />212 474-4567</p>
</div>
```

insert the </div> tag after the phone number paragraph

4. Save the AmericaNew file.

5. Refresh the AmericaNew Web page in your browser, and then compare it to Figure 5-14 to verify that the sidebar appears on the left side of the page.

Figure 5-14 | Web page with the sidebar

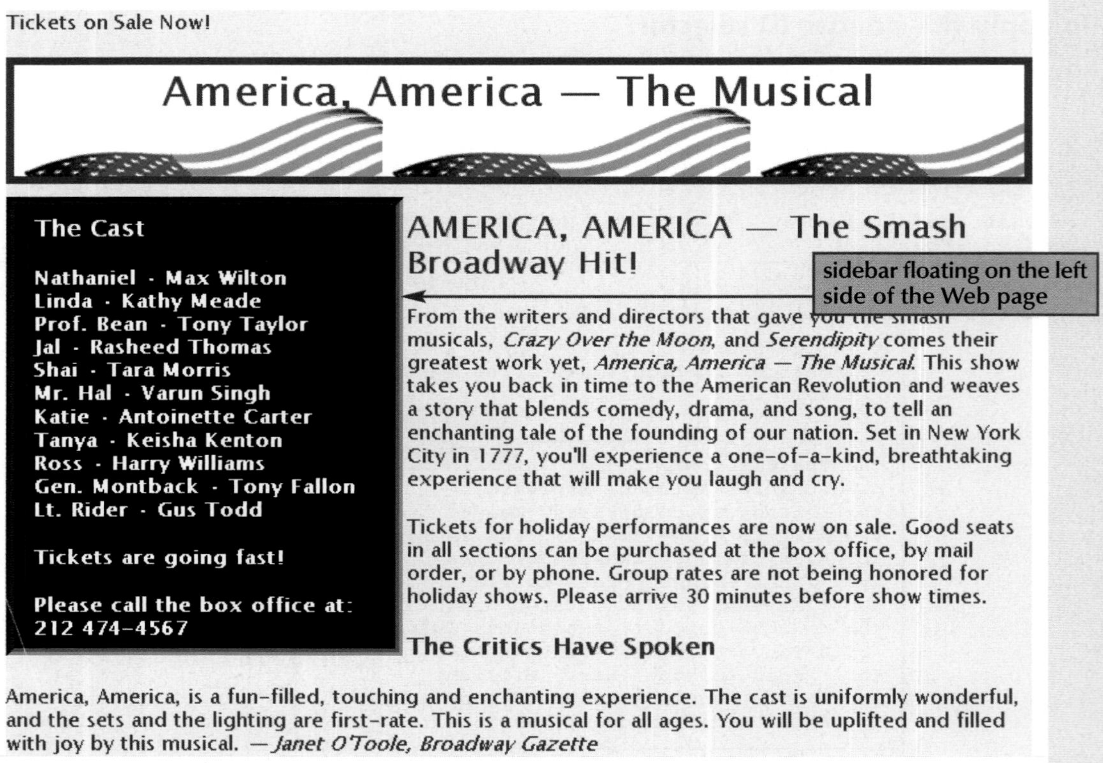

Tickets on Sale Now!

America, America — The Musical

The Cast

Nathaniel · Max Wilton
Linda · Kathy Meade
Prof. Bean · Tony Taylor
Jal · Rasheed Thomas
Shai · Tara Morris
Mr. Hal · Varun Singh
Katie · Antoinette Carter
Tanya · Keisha Kenton
Ross · Harry Williams
Gen. Montback · Tony Fallon
Lt. Rider · Gus Todd

Tickets are going fast!

Please call the box office at:
212 474-4567

AMERICA, AMERICA — The Smash Broadway Hit!

sidebar floating on the left side of the Web page

From the writers and directors that gave you the smash musicals, *Crazy Over the Moon*, and *Serendipity* comes their greatest work yet, *America, America — The Musical.* This show takes you back in time to the American Revolution and weaves a story that blends comedy, drama, and song, to tell an enchanting tale of the founding of our nation. Set in New York City in 1777, you'll experience a one-of-a-kind, breathtaking experience that will make you laugh and cry.

Tickets for holiday performances are now on sale. Good seats in all sections can be purchased at the box office, by mail order, or by phone. Group rates are not being honored for holiday shows. Please arrive 30 minutes before show times.

The Critics Have Spoken

America, America, is a fun-filled, touching and enchanting experience. The cast is uniformly wonderful, and the sets and the lighting are first-rate. This is a musical for all ages. You will be uplifted and filled with joy by this musical. *—Janet O'Toole, Broadway Gazette*

Enhancing the Appearance of the Sidebar

Wendy wants to make the sidebar more visually appealing to capture the attention of visitors to the Web page. You will show Wendy how to add visual interest to the sidebar by including a background image. You will also add an image below the sidebar text.

To add a background image to the sidebar:

▶ **1.** In the AmericaNew document in your text editor, position the insertion point after the semicolon in the padding-left: em; declaration.

▶ **2.** Press the **Enter** key to create a new line.

▶ **3.** Type the following code, which is also shown in red in Figure 5-15.

```
background-image: url(curtains.jpg);
background-repeat: no-repeat;
```

Code for the sidebar background image ◀ **Figure 5-15**

```
#sidebar {
width: 300px;
overflow: hidden;
float: left;
border: red thick inset;
padding: .5em;
padding-left: 1em;
background-image: url(curtains.jpg);
background-repeat: no-repeat;
font-weight: bold;
color: white;
background-color: black; }

</style>
</head>
```

code to display curtains.jpg as the background image for the sidebar

▶ **4.** Save the AmericaNew file.

▶ **5.** Refresh the AmericaNew Web page in your browser, and then compare it to Figure 5-16 to verify that the background image of curtains is displayed behind the cast members list.

Figure 5-16 | **Web page with the sidebar background image**

Tickets on Sale Now!

America, America — The Musical

curtains image displayed in the background

The Cast

Nathaniel · Max Wilton
Linda · Kathy Meade
Prof. Bean · Tony Taylor
Jal · Rasheed Thomas
Shai · Tara Morris
Mr. Hal · Varun Singh
Katie · Antoinette Carter
Tanya · Keisha Kenton
Ross · Harry Williams
Gen. Montback · Tony Fallon
Lt. Rider · Gus Todd

Tickets are going fast!

Please call the box office at:
212 474-4567

AMERICA, AMERICA — The Smash Broadway Hit!

From the writers and directors that gave you the smash musicals, *Crazy Over the Moon*, and *Serendipity* comes their greatest work yet, *America, America — The Musical*. This show takes you back in time to the American Revolution and weaves a story that blends comedy, drama, and song, to tell an enchanting tale of the founding of our nation. Set in New York City in 1777, you'll experience a one-of-a-kind, breathtaking experience that will make you laugh and cry.

Tickets for holiday performances are now on sale. Good seats in all sections can be purchased at the box office, by mail order, or by phone. Group rates are not being honored for holiday shows. Please arrive 30 minutes before show times.

The Critics Have Spoken

America, America, is a fun-filled, touching and enchanting experience. The cast is uniformly wonderful, and the sets and the lighting are first-rate. This is a musical for all ages. You will be uplifted and filled with joy by this musical. — *Janet O'Toole, Broadway Gazette*

To draw more attention to the sidebar, you will show Wendy how to include an image of some of the play's cast members.

To add an image to the sidebar:

▶ **1.** In the AmericaNew document in your text editor, position the insertion point above the paragraph "Tickets are going fast."

▶ **2.** If necessary, press the **Enter** key to create a new line.

▶ **3.** Type the following code, which is also shown in red in Figure 5-17.

```
<img src="cast.jpg" alt="image of leading characters"
width="300" height="200" />
```

Code for the cast image ◄ Figure 5-17

```
<div id="sidebar">
<h3>The Cast</h3>
<p>Nathaniel &middot; Max Wilton
<br />Linda &middot; Kathy Meade
<br />Prof. Bean &middot; Tony Taylor
<br />Jal &middot; Rasheed Thomas
<br />Shai &middot; Tara Morris
<br />Mr. Hal &middot; Varun Singh
<br />Katie &middot; Antoinette Carter
<br />Tanya &middot; Keisha Kenton
<br />Ross &middot; Harry Williams
<br />Gen. Montback &middot; Tony Fallon
<br />Lt. Rider &middot; Gus Todd
</p>

<img src="cast.jpg" alt="image of leading characters" width="300" height="200" />
```

code to display an image of some cast members at the bottom of the sidebar

▶ **4.** Save the AmericaNew file.

▶ **5.** Refresh the AmericaNew Web page in your browser, and then compare it to Figure 5-18 to verify that the image of three cast members is displayed below the cast members list.

Web page displaying the cast image ◄ Figure 5-18

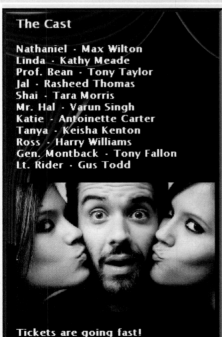

The Cast

Nathaniel · Max Wilton
Linda · Kathy Meade
Prof. Bean · Tony Taylor
Jal · Rasheed Thomas
Shai · Tara Morris
Mr. Hal · Varun Singh
Katie · Antoinette Carter
Tanya · Keisha Kenton
Ross · Harry Williams
Gen. Montback · Tony Fallon
Lt. Rider · Gus Todd

Tickets are going fast!

AMERICA, AMERICA — The Smash Broadway Hit!

From the writers and directors that gave you the smash musicals, *Crazy Over the Moon*, and *Serendipity* comes their greatest work yet, *America, America — The Musical*. This show takes you back in time to the American Revolution and weaves a story that blends comedy, drama, and song, to tell an enchanting tale of the founding of our nation. Set in New York City in 1777, you'll experience a one-of-a-kind, breathtaking experience that will make you laugh and cry.

Tickets for holiday performances are now on sale. Good seats in all sections can be purchased at the box office, by mail order, or by phone. Group rates are not being honored for holiday shows. Please arrive 30 minutes before show times.

The Critics Have Spoken

America, America, is a fun-filled, touching and enchanting experience. The cast is uniformly wonderful, and the sets and the lighting are first-rate. This is a musical for all ages. You will be uplifted and filled with joy by this musical. — *Janet O'Toole, Broadway Gazette*

Now that you've included the basic parts of the sidebar, including images, you'll show Wendy how to fine-tune the sidebar text.

Styling HTML Elements Within a Box

Note that the h3 heading in the sidebar is not centered. When you want to set the style for HTML elements within a box, you must specifically target that individual HTML selector. You do so by using descendant selectors. You cannot, for example, insert the following code to center the h3 heading:

```
h3 {
text-align: center; }
```

This code centers the text in the h3 heading in the box, but it also centers every other h3 heading in the document, which might not be what you intend. You might, for example, want to have all your other h3 headings to appear flush left rather than centered. To format only the h3 selector in the box, create a descendant selector, like so:

```
#sidebar h3 {
text-align: center; }
```

Wendy decided that white text on a navy background in the sidebar would be attractive. You will show Wendy how to set the style for the h3 selector for the sidebar.

To set the style for only the h3 selector in the sidebar:

► **1.** In the AmericaNew document in your text editor, position the insertion point below the sidebar ID selector code.

► **2.** On a blank line, type the following code, which is also shown in red in Figure 5-19.

```
#sidebar h3  {
width: 250px;
text-align: center;
color: white;
background-color: navy;
padding: .2em; }
```

Figure 5-19   Code to set the style for the sidebar h3 heading

```
width: 300px;
overflow: hidden;
float: left;
border: red thick inset;
padding: .5em;
padding-left: 1em;
background-image: url(curtains.jpg);
background-repeat: no-repeat;
font-weight: bold;
color: white;
background-color: black; }

#sidebar h3  {
width: 250px;
text-align: center;          ◄── code displays the sidebar
color: white;                     heading as white text on
background-color: navy;           a navy background
padding: .2em; }

</style>
</head>
```

► **3.** Save the AmericaNew file.

► **4.** Refresh the AmericaNew Web page in your browser, and then compare it to Figure 5-20 to verify that the sidebar h3 heading is now formatted.

If you lay out pages using boxes, create styles for elements by using descendant selectors. If you are styling the same element more than once, make sure that the elements all have the same properties (though they can have different values).

For example, if you use a descendant selector to set the style for an h3 heading in one box to display text in blue, and you use a descendant selector in another box to display text in green, one box will display h3 headings in blue; the other will display h3 headings in green as intended because both h3 selectors have a rule that specifies a color. However, if you create a rule for one h3 selector to display text in a different font size, such as 24pt, and the other h3 selector did not have a rule that specified a font size, then both h3 headings would be displayed in 24pt, which may not be what you intended.

So far, you have shown Wendy how to plan the design for layout using the CSS box properties. You created a banner and used a repeating image behind the text. You created a sidebar, which included both text and an image. You also learned how to format HTML elements within a box without affecting other HTML elements on the page. You will now learn about the CSS positioning properties, which can be used to position an object anywhere on the Web page.

Session 5.1 Quick Check | Review

1. In addition to creating a box, what else can you do to call attention to the box?
2. What properties determine the size of a box?
3. What property determines whether a box will have scroll bars?
4. What are the four values for that property?
5. What property will position a box left or right?
6. If a box is floated right, where will the text wrap?

Session 5.2

Using the Positioning Properties

So far, you have been working with the box model, which specifies that the page layout is made up of boxes. The largest box is the browser window itself (the HTML element). Inside this box is the body box, which in turn contains other smaller boxes, such as headings, paragraphs, and em and strong elements. This is called the **normal flow** of the HTML document. Each element is displayed on the page in the order it was entered. The normal flow is equivalent to a line of people waiting to purchase tickets for a concert.

The **positioning properties** allow you to display an element out of the normal flow. The positioning properties allow you to place any element—images or text—anywhere on the screen irrespective of where it appears in the document. In addition, CSS positioning allows you to create pages with elements with **layering**, which means that you can have text or images overlap each other to create interesting visual effects. If you were waiting in a line to buy concert tickets, the positioning properties allow you to cut the line and disrupt the normal flow.

The position property takes several values, with the two most important values being absolute and relative. When you use **absolute positioning**, the element is displayed in the exact position you specify, no matter what elements surround it. For example, if you want an element to be displayed 400 pixels down from the top edge of the screen and 150 pixels from the left edge of the screen, then that is where the element will be displayed.

If text or an image already appears in that screen location, the positioned text is displayed on top of that object. No matter how you revise the page to add or delete text or images, an absolutely positioned element remains in the same position. Because you are positioning individual elements, you should create an ID selector, like so:

```
<html>
<head>
<style type="text/css">
h1 {
font-family: arial,helvetica,sans-serif; }

#firstline {
position: absolute; }
```

When you use **relative positioning**, you are shifting the element's position from the point where that element normally would be displayed. For example, if an element is usually displayed 382 pixels down from the top of the page, you might position that element and its contents 20 pixels to the right to overlay that text on top of an image or other text. If you add or delete text or images, however, the position of this relatively positioned element changes.

Using the left and top Properties

The **left property** with a positive value positions an element a certain distance from the left edge of the screen, moving the element to the right. The **top property** with a positive value positions an element a certain distance from the top edge of the screen, moving the element down. Although they are not used nearly as often, the **bottom property** and **right property** function in the same way. The bottom property with a positive value will move an element up; the right property with a positive value will move an element to the left.

You can use negative numbers as values for these properties. The left property with a negative value positions an element to the left. The top property with a negative value positions an element above the normal position. You don't have to use both the left and the top properties; you can use either the left property or the right property or you can use both. The values for the left and top properties can be expressed in any of the CSS measurements, such as pixels, points, percentages, or em values. The following code includes two elements—one has been positioned 30 pixels from the top of the screen and 30 pixels from the left edge of the screen. The second element has been positioned 100 pixels from the top and 100 pixels from the left.

```
h1 {
font-family: arial,helvetica,sans-serif;
font-size: 72pt;
margin: 0;
padding: 0; }

#firstline {
position: absolute;
top: 30px;
left: 30px;
color: red; }

#secondline {
position: absolute;
top: 100px;
left: 100px;
color: black; }
```

In Figure 5-21, the two lines are positioned as they normally would be, with the second line following the first line.

Two elements absolutely positioned in the browser   Figure 5-21

Learning About
CSS Positioning

If you change the top and left position for the second line using the following code, the second line is displayed on top of the first line, as shown in Figure 5-22.

```
#secondline {
position: absolute;
top: 30px;
left: 30px;
color: red; }
```

One element taken out of normal flow in the browser   Figure 5-22

Using the z-index Property

One of the primary reasons the positioning properties are so valuable is that you can create layered elements, where one element can be stacked on top of another element. The **z-index property** is used to stack elements in the browser window. There is no limit to the number of elements you can stack, but for purposes of visual clarity, you should not stack more than three elements. The value for the z-index property determines the stacking order. The higher the z-index value, the higher the text or the image is in the stack. Think of the z-index values as floors in a multistory building. The higher up you are (the greater the z-index value), the better the view and the higher the element is in the stack. If you want to always have a particular element displayed on top of the stack, then assign the z-index value to be a very high number, such as 100. If you always want to have an element displayed at the bottom of the stack, then assign that element a z-index value of 0.

Following is an example of how stacking works. The code includes the z-index property and sets its value to 2 for the first line and its value to 1 for the second line. Doing so places the first line on top of the second line, as shown in Figure 5-23.

```
#firstline {
position: absolute;
top: 40px;
left: 30px;
color: red;
z-index: 2; }

#secondline {
position: absolute;
top: 30px;
left: 30px;
color: black;
z-index: 1; }
```

Figure 5-23 ▶ **Effect of the z-index property**

Using the z-Index Property

- To layer one element on top of another using the z-index property, use the following style:
  z-index: *value*;
  where *value* is a number 0 or greater. The higher the number, the higher the element is in the stack. Negative numbers can be used, but negative values are not supported by all browsers.

In the America, America Web page, Wendy wants to position the words "Tickets on Sale Now" in the upper-left corner of the screen. She also wants to display those words in orange. To do so, you will show Wendy how to create a container box named, salebox. You will also show her how to create a style for the paragraph selector that will set the style for paragraphs within the salebox.

To set the style for and apply the salebox ID selector:

▶ **1.** In the AmericaNew document in your text editor, position the insertion point below the sidebar h3 ID selector code.

▶ **2.** On a blank line, type the following code, which is also shown in red in Figure 5-24.

```
#salebox {
position: absolute;
top: 20;
left: 20;
width: 140px;
height: 100px;
z-index: 2;
overflow: auto; }

#salebox p {
color: orange;
font-size: 14pt;
font-weight: bold;
margin: 0; }
```

Code for the salebox ID selector and code to style the heading within it ◀ **Figure 5-24**

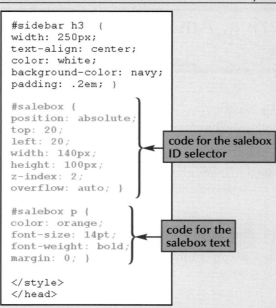

```
#sidebar h3  {
width: 250px;
text-align: center;
color: white;
background-color: navy;
padding: .2em; }

#salebox {
position: absolute;
top: 20;
left: 20;                    code for the salebox
width: 140px;                ID selector
height: 100px;
z-index: 2;
overflow: auto; }

#salebox p {
color: orange;
font-size: 14pt;             code for the
font-weight: bold;           salebox text
margin: 0; }

</style>
</head>
```

▶ **3.** In the AmericaNew document in your text editor, position the insertion point after the line for <div id="container">.

▶ **4.** If necessary, press the **Enter** key to create a new line.

▶ **5.** Type the code shown in bold, which is also shown in red in Figure 5-25.

```
<div id="salebox">
<p>Tickets on Sale Now!</p>
</div>
```

Figure 5-25	Code to apply the salebox ID selectors

```
#salebox p {
color: orange;
font-size: 14pt;
font-weight: bold;
margin: 0; }

</style>
</head>

<body>
<div id="container">

<div id="salebox">          applies the salebox ID
<p>Tickets on Sale Now!</p>  selector to the "Tickets
</div>                        on Sale Now!" paragraph
```

▶ **6.** Save the AmericaNew file.

▶ **7.** Refresh the AmericaNew Web page in your browser, and then compare it to Figure 5-26 to verify that the salebox text is displayed in the upper-left corner of the window.

Figure 5-26	Web page with the salebox

salebox appears in the banner

Now Wendy asks for your help in styling and positioning the main document text. You will float the main window text to the right and assign the box a width of 440px. In addition, Wendy wants the h2 and h3 headings in the main window to really stand out. You'll format the h2 heading to have white text on a navy background. You'll also center h2 heading text, and create a margin on the top with some padding. For the h3 headings, Wendy wants the text be centered and white text on a red background.

To set the style for and apply the main ID selector:

▶ **1.** In the AmericaNew document in your text editor, position the insertion point below the salebox p code.

2. On a blank line, type the following code, which is also shown in red in Figure 5-27.

```
#main {
float: right;
width: 440px; }

#main h2 {
height: 60px;
text-align: center;
font-family: 'arial black',sans-serif;
color: white;
background-color: navy;
margin-top: 0;
padding: .3em; }

#main h3 {
margin-top: 0;
margin: 0;
color: white;
background-color: red;
padding: .5em;
text-align: center; }
```

Code for the main ID selector   **Figure 5-27**

```
overflow: auto; }

#salebox p {
color: orange;
font-size: 14pt;
font-weight: bold;
margin: 0; }

#main {
float: right;          floats the main window
width: 440px; }        text to the right and
                       sets a width of 440px

#main h2 {
height: 60px;
text-align: center;
font-family: 'arial black',sans-serif;
color: white;
background-color: navy;
margin-top: 0;
padding: .3em; }       code to make the h2 and
                       h3 headings stand out
#main h3 {
margin-top: 0;
margin: 0;
color: white;
background-color: red;
padding: .5em;
text-align: center; }
```

3. In the AmericaNew document in your text editor, position the insertion point above the h2 heading, "AMERICA, AMERICA — The Smash Broadway Hit!"

4. On a blank line above the "AMERICA, AMERICA — the Smash Broadway Hit!" h2 heading, type the following code, which is also shown in red in Figure 5-28.

```
<div id="main">
```

Figure 5-28 **Code to apply the main ID selector**

```
<p>Please call the box office at:
<br />212 474-4567</p>
</div>

<div id="main">
<h2>AMERICA, AMERICA &mdash; The Smash Broadway Hit!</h2>
<p>From the writers and directors that gave you the smash musicals, <em>Crazy Over the Moon</em>,
and <em>Serendipity</em> comes their greatest work yet, <em>America, America &mdash; The Musical
</em>. This show takes you back in time to the American Revolution and weaves a story that blends
comedy, drama, and song, to tell an enchanting tale of the founding of our nation. Set in New York
City in 1777, you'll experience a one-of-kind, breathtaking experience that will make you laugh
and cry.</p>
```

insert the start <div> tag before the h2 heading

▶ **5.** On a blank line after the last paragraph for Fred Berrs review, type the following code, which is also shown in red in Figure 5-29.

   </div>

Figure 5-29 **Inserting the end </div> tag for the main div**

```
<p>Tickets for holiday performances are now on sale. Good seats in all sections can be purchased
at the box office, by mail order, or by phone. Group rates are not being honored for holiday
shows. Please arrive 30 minutes before show times.</p>

<h3>The Critics Have Spoken</h3>

<p>America, America, is a fun-filled, touching and enchanting experience. The cast is uniformly
wonderful, and the sets and the lighting are first-rate. This is a musical for all ages. You will
be uplifted and filled with joy by this musical. <em>&mdash; Janet O'Toole, Broadway Gazette</em>
</p>

<p>This play is unlike any other Broadway play I have ever seen. It will leave you breathless.
This is a fantastic work of Broadway art. Be ready to be captivated. <em>&mdash; Fred Berrs,
Broadway in Review</em></p>
</div>
```

insert the end </div> tag after the second paragraph in "The Critics Have Spoken" section

▶ **6.** Save the AmericaNew file.

▶ **7.** Refresh the AmericaNew Web page in your browser, and then compare it to Figure 5-30.

   Trouble? Depending on your browser, the footer text may not be positioned correctly. You will correct the position of the footer text shortly.

AMERICA, AMERICA — The Smash Broadway Hit! `h2 heading`

From the writers and directors that gave you the smash musicals, *Crazy Over the Moon*, and *Serendipity* comes their greatest work yet, *America, America — The Musical*. This show takes you back in time to the American Revolution and weaves a story that blends comedy, drama, and song, to tell an enchanting tale of the founding of our nation. Set in New York City in 1777, you'll experience a one-of-a-kind, breathtaking experience that will make you laugh and cry.

Tickets for holiday performances are now on sale. Good seats in all sections can be purchased at the box office, by mail order, or by phone. Group rates are not being honored for holiday shows. Please arrive 30 minutes before show times.

The Critics Have Spoken `h3 heading`

America, America, is a fun-filled, touching and enchanting

The last box to create is the footer box, which contains the name and address of the theatre. Right now, depending on your browser, the text in the footer might not be positioned correctly on the screen. You want the footer text to clear the main box. You will show Wendy how to set the style for the footer box and correct the problem.

Creating the Footer Box

Address or contact information often appears at the bottom of a home page. Although HTML does not have a headers and footers feature, it is a common convention to set the style for the last line of a Web page and describe that line as being the footer box. You would like to have the name and address of the theatre enclosed in a box at the bottom of the page. To do so, you will show Wendy how to create an ID selector named footer and apply that selector to the last line of text.

To set the style for the footer box and apply the footer ID selector:

▶ **1.** In the AmericaNew document in your text editor, position the insertion point below the main h3 selector code.

▶ **2.** On a blank line, type the following code, which is also shown in red in Figure 5-31.

```
#footer {
height: 50px;
clear: both;
color: black;
margin-top: .5em;
border: navy thin inset;
padding: .5em;
text-align: center;
word-spacing: .2em;
letter-spacing: .1em;
text-transform: uppercase; }
```

Figure 5-31 **Code for the footer ID selector**

```
padding: .3em; }

#main h3 {
margin-top: 0;
margin: 0;
color: white;
background-color: red;
padding: .5em;
text-align: center; }

#footer {
height: 50px;
clear: both;
color: black;
margin-top: .5em;
border: navy thin inset;
padding: .5em;
text-align: center;
word-spacing: .2em;
letter-spacing: .1em;
text-transform: uppercase; }
```

footer ID selector to enclose the name and address of the theatre in a box

▶ **3.** Position the insertion point above the address for the theatre.

▶ **4.** On a blank line, type the code shown in bold, which is also shown in red in Figure 5-32.

```
<div id="footer">
<p>The Hanson Theatre &middot; 246 North Broadway, &middot;
New York, New York 10019</p>
</div>
```

Figure 5-32 **Code to apply the footer ID selector**

```
<h3>The Critics Have Spoken</h3>

<p>America, America, is a fun-filled, touching and enchanting experience. The cast is uniformly
wonderful, and the sets and the lighting are first-rate. This is a musical for all ages. You will
be uplifted and filled with joy by this musical. <em>&mdash; Janet O'Toole, Broadway Gazette</em>
</p>

<p>This play is unlike any other Broadway play I have ever seen. It will leave you breathless.
This is a fantastic work of Broadway art. Be ready to be captivated. <em>&mdash; Fred Berrs,
Broadway in Review</em></p>
</div>

<div id="footer">
<p>The Hanson Theatre &middot; 246 North Broadway, &middot; New York, New York 10019</p>
</div>

</div>
</body>
</html>
```

footer ID selector applies only to the name and address of the theatre

▶ **5.** Save the AmericaNew file.

▶ **6.** Refresh the AmericaNew Web page in your browser, and then compare it to Figure 5-33 to verify that the footer is formatted and the text is positioned correctly.

Web page displaying the footer ◀ **Figure 5-33**

Please call the box office at:
212 474–4567

This play is unlike any other Broadway play I have ever seen. It will leave you breathless. This is a fantastic work of Broadway art. Be ready to be captivated. — *Fred Berrs, Broadway in Review*

THE HANSON THEATRE · 246 NORTH BROADWAY, · NEW YORK, NEW YORK 10019

You have now shown Wendy how to use the positioning properties to position an element anywhere on a page. You learned that in addition to taking an element out of the normal flow, you can also stack one element on top of another. You also learned the z-index property and its value determine the stacking order.

Using Print Styles

Printing a three-column or even a two-column layout Web page can be problematic. To make sure a Web page prints correctly, you need to create a **print style**, which is a style that resembles printed copy; namely, one column of black text on a white background and in a serif font. By default, most browsers do not print background images. If you floated elements on the Web page, however, you have to make sure that these elements do not float over text or off the page on the printed copy. You might also want to hide elements in the printed copy, such as banner ads.

You will be creating a separate, external style sheet for the print styles. The **media attribute** determines where the output will go. The most common values for the media attribute are *screen*, which limits output to the screen, and *print*, which is designed to format your page to print appropriately. There are many other media types, specifically designed for accessibility or for portable computing devices, but they are not all supported by most browsers. Some of these other media types are aural, Braille, embossed, handheld, tty, and tv.

You will now show Wendy how to create a link to the external style sheet file for the print styles. You will also show Wendy how to change the embedded style sheet to one that is limited to a screen style.

To insert the code to link to the external style sheet file:

▶ **1.** In the AmericaNew document in your text editor, position the insertion point below the page title in the head section.

▶ **2.** On a blank line, type the following code, which is also shown in red in Figure 5-34.

```
<link rel="stylesheet" href="AmericaPrint.css" type="text/
css" media="print" />
```

Tip

The default value for the media attribute is *all*. To limit a style sheet's use to a browser, use the value of *screen*. To limit it to a printer, use the value of *print*.

Figure 5-34 | Code for the link to the print styles external style sheet

```
<html>
<head>
<title>America, America -- The Musical</title>

<link rel="stylesheet" href="AmericaPrint.css" type="text/css" media="print" />

<style type="text/css">

/* Your First Name Your Last Name
Today's Date */
```

▶ **3.** Save the AmericaNew file.

Tip

If you are using more than one style sheet, make sure the style sheet with the media attribute and value of *screen* comes last. If you don't, the document might not be displayed properly in the browser.

The link to the external print style sheet is now entered in the code. You must now change the media type for the embedded style sheet to have the media attribute with a value of screen.

To insert the code to change the media type for the embedded style sheet:

▶ **1.** In the AmericaNew document in your text editor, position the insertion point before the end angle bracket (>) in the <style type="text/css"> code.

▶ **2.** Press the **Spacebar**, and then type the following bold code, which is also shown in red in Figure 5-35.

```
<style type="text/css" media="screen">
```

Figure 5-35 | Code to change the embedded style to screen style

```
<html>
<head>
<title>America, America -- The Musical</title>

<link rel="stylesheet" href="AmericaPrint.css" type="text/css" media="print" />

<style type="text/css" media="screen">

/* Your First Name Your Last Name
Today's Date */
```

▶ **3.** Save the AmericaNew file.

Reference Window | **Creating Media Styles**

- To create a style sheet for different media, enter the following code in either the link code to an external style sheet or within the start <style> tag of an embedded style sheet:
  `media="type"`
  where *type* is one of the following values: print, screen, or all.
- Because of the rules governing specificity, if you are using more than one media type within the same Web page, make sure that the last media type declared on the page is *screen*.

Now you will show Wendy how to set the style for the external print style sheet. Although sans-serif fonts such as Arial look fine on the screen, most people agree that serif fonts such as Times New Roman are easier to read. You need to specify a font size—the default 12pt is fine. You also want to make sure the text color is black and the background is set to white. For this Web page, you don't want the salebox to be displayed, so you'll set the display property for that ID selector to none. To make sure that the Web page prints within the page margins, you'll add white space on all four sides of the document. First, you will create a comment to identify the author and document the date the CSS file was created. You will also show Wendy how to enter the code for the print style sheet, making extensive use of grouped selectors.

To insert the code for the comment and for the print styles:

▶ **1.** Use Notepad to open the **America.css** file located in the Tutorial.05\Tutorial folder included with your Data Files. Save the file as **AmericaPrint.css** in the same folder.

▶ **2.** Below the existing comment, type the following code to create a comment for your first and last name and today's date, which is also shown in red in Figure 5-36.

```
/* Your First Name Your Last Name
Today's Date */
```

Code for the comment in the external style sheet ◀ Figure 5-36

```
/* This is a print style sheet. The AmericaNew HTML file links to this stylesheet. */

/* Your First Name Your Last Name
Today's Date */
```

▶ **3.** Press the **Enter** key to position the insertion point below the comment you just created.

▶ **4.** On a blank line, type the following code, which is also shown in red in Figure 5-37.

```
body, #sidebar, #main, #footer, #banner, p, h1, h2, h3 {
font-size: 12pt;
font-family: 'times new roman', times, serif;
color: black;
background-color: white; }

#salebox {
display: none; }

#sidebar {
float: none; width: auto; }

img {
display: none; }

body {
margin: 3em; }
```

Figure 5-37 **Code for the print styles**

```
/* This is a print style sheet. The AmericaNew HTML file links to this stylesheet. */

/* Your First Name Your Last Name
Today's Date */

body, #sidebar, #main, #footer, #banner, p, h1, h2, h3 {
font-size: 12pt;
font-family: 'times new roman', times, serif;
color: black;
background-color: white; }

#salebox {
display: none; }

#sidebar {
float: none; width: auto; }

img {
display: none; }

body {
margin: 3em; }
```

grouped selectors for the print style sheet

▶ **5.** Save the AmericaPrint CSS file.

▶ **6.** Refresh the AmericaNew Web page in your browser, and then compare it to Figure 5-38 to view the completed America, America Web page.

Figure 5-38 **Completed America, America Web page**

▶ **7.** In your browser, choose Print Preview, and then compare the image to Figure 5-39 to view the AmericaPrint style sheet.

The print style sheet displayed in the browser using Print Preview | Figure 5-39

America, America – The Musical   Page 1 of 2

America, America — The Musical

The Cast

Nathaniel · Max Wilton
Linda · Kathy Meade
Prof. Bean · Tony Taylor
Jal · Rasheed Thomas
Shai · Tara Morris
Mr. Hal · Varun Singh
Katie · Antoinette Carter
Tanya · Keisha Kenton
Ross · Harry Williams
Gen. Montback · Tony Fallon
Lt. Rider · Gus Todd

Tickets are going fast!

Please call the box office at:
212 474-4567

AMERICA, AMERICA — The Smash Broadway Hit!

From the writers and directors that gave you the smash musicals, *Crazy Over the Moon*, and *Serendipity* comes their greatest work yet, *America, America — The Musical*. This show takes you back in time to the American Revolution and weaves a story that blends comedy, drama, and song, to tell an enchanting tale of the founding of our nation. Set in New York City in 1777, you'll experience a one-of-kind, breathtaking experience that will make you laugh and cry.

Tickets for holiday performances are now on sale. Good seats in all sections can be purchased at the box office, by mail order, or by phone. Group rates are not being honored for holiday shows. Please arrive 30 minutes before show times.

The Critics Have Spoken

America, America, is a fun-filled, touching and enchanting experience. The cast is uniformly wonderful, and the sets and the lighting are first-rate. This is a musical for all ages. You will be uplifted and filled with joy by this musical. —*Janet O'Toole, Broadway Gazette*

This play is unlike any other Broadway play I have ever seen. It will leave you breathless. This is a fantastic work of Broadway art. Be ready to be captivated. — *Fred Berrs, Broadway in Review*

file://E:\tutorial 5\AmericaNew.htm

▶ **8.** Close all open files and windows.

In this session you worked with the positioning properties to position elements to the left or right of where they would be displayed in the normal flow. You also learned how to create a print style sheet so that a visitor to the Web site could print just the text and not any of the other elements on the page.

Session 5.2 Quick Check | Review

1. What property will position text from the left edge of the screen?
2. What property will position text down from the top edge of the screen?
3. Do you always have to use both the left and the top properties together?
4. What is the function of the z-index property?
5. If there are three elements layered on top of each other, where in the stack will the element be with the z-index of 100?

6. If there are four elements layered on top of each other, where in the stack will the element be with the z-index of 0?
7. Should elements be floated in a print style?
8. What property and value can be used to hide an element for a print style?
9. How can you display the document for print?

| Review | **Tutorial Summary** |

IDs are used to control one specific instance of a selector. The # is the flag character used when creating IDs. IDs are applied in the same way that classes are applied to HTML elements. There are two primary ways to position an element: absolute and relative. Absolute positioning positions an element a certain distance from the left edge of the screen and down from the top edge of the screen. Relative positioning positions an element a certain distance from its normal text flow and down from its normal text flow. The left and the top properties are the ones most commonly used with the positioning properties. The z-index property is used to stack elements on the screen; the higher the number of the z-index, the higher that element is in the stack. Print styles are used to facilitate the printing of a page. It is important that any elements that were floated on the screen are not floated for the print style. Objects that do not relate to the body text should be hidden.

Key Terms

absolute positioning	layering	relative positioning
banner	left property	right property
bottom property	main	scroll
container box	media attribute	sidebar
footer	normal flow	top property
header	overflow property	visible
height property	positioning properties	z-index property
hidden	print style	

| Practice | **Review Assignments** |

Take time to practice the skills you learned in the tutorial using the same case scenario.

Data Files needed for the Review Assignments: Actor.gif, Actress.gif, and Leading.htm

The America, America cast has asked you to create a Web page that will highlight the two leading characters of the play. The leading actor, Max Wilton, plays the role of Nathaniel. Kathy Meade plays the role of Linda. You have decided to use the box properties to contain text and images about the two leading characters. You will use the positioning properties to position the boxes. You will be creating an embedded style sheet. Complete the following steps:

1. Use Notepad to open the **Leading.htm** file located in your Tutorial.05\Review folder included with your Data Files. Save this file as **LeadingNew.htm** in the same folder.
2. In the head area below the page title, enter the code for the start <style> and the end </style> tags.
3. Below the start <style> tag, insert a comment that includes your first and last name as the author and today's date.
4. Set the style for the <p> element selector to have a line height of 2.0, a margin of 0, and 14pt Arial text.
5. Create an ID selector named **banner**. Set the style for the ID selector as follows:
   - For the font, use Bernhardfashion BT, a sans-serif font. The text should be white with a background color of navy.
   - The margin should be 0.5em; padding should be 1%, and text should be centered.
   - The four border colors should be red, black, black, and red. The border style should be groove. The four border widths should be medium, thick, thick, and medium.
   - The width of the banner box should be 100%; the height should be 12%. Overflow should be hidden.
6. Create an ID selector named **rightbox**. Set the style for the ID selector as follows:
   - The text should be white on a navy background.
   - Padding should be 4%. The left margin should be 0.5em.
   - The border colors should be red, black, black, and red. The border style should be groove. The border widths should be medium, thick, thick, and medium, respectively.
   - The width of the box should be 30%; the height should be 75%. Overflow should be auto. The box should float to the right.
7. Create an ID selector named **leftbox**. Set the style for the leftbox ID selector exactly as you did the rightbox ID selector, except that the box should float left instead of float right. Also, use the margin-right property instead of the margin-left property. Assign the margin-right property a value of 0.5em.
8. Create an ID selector named **footer**. Set the style for the ID selector as follows:
   - The footer should have white text on a red background.
   - The margin on the top should be 0.5em.
   - The box should clear both margins. The height of the box should be 10%; the width of the box should be 100%. Text in the box should be centered.
9. Set the style for the <h3> element selector to have Arial text and padding on the top of 0.5em.
10. In the body of the document, insert the <div></div> tags and apply the ID selector banner to the <h1> text.

11. Insert the <div></div> tags and apply the ID selector named, rightbox to the following block of code:

```
<p><img src="actor.gif" alt="image of Max Wilton"
width="300" height="470" /></p>
<p>Nathaniel
<br />played by Max Wilton</p>
```

12. Insert <div></div> tags and apply the ID selector named, leftbox to the following block
of code:

```
<p><img src="actress.gif" alt="image of Kathy Meade"
width="450" height="380" /></p>
<p>Linda
<br />played by Kathy Meade</p>
```

13. Insert <div></div> tags and apply the ID selector footer to the following block
of code:

```
<h3>Write to both Max and Kathy in care of
<br />The Hanson Theatre &middot;
 246 North Broadway, New York, New York10019</h3>
```

14. Save the LeadingNew HTML document, and then open it in your browser. The document should be similar to the one shown in Figure 5-40.

Figure 5-40

15. Close all open windows.
16. Submit the results of the preceding steps to your instructor, either in printed or electronic form, as requested.

Apply | **Case Problem 1**

Use the skills you learned in the tutorial to create a Web page for a financial newsletter.

Data Files needed for this Case Problem: Global.gif, Group.htm, House.gif, and Money.gif

The Zeider Financial Group The Zeider Financial Group is an investment firm located in Strasbourg, Pennsylvania. In the past, they have relied upon a printed publication to address its audience, which is a savvy group of financial investors. The Zeider Group now wishes to establish a Web presence. You have been asked to create a Web page that closely matches the format of their printed version. To do so, you will create a banner box, a left box, and a right box, which will create a two-column layout with a banner. To create the illusion of a vertical rule between the columns, you will set the style for the left border of the right box. You will be creating an embedded style sheet. Complete the following steps:

1. Use Notepad to open the **Group.htm** file located in your Tutorial.05\Case1 folder included with your Data Files. Save this file as **GroupNew.htm** in the same folder.
2. In the head area below the page title, enter the start <style> and end </style> tags.
3. In the head area below the start <style> tag, insert a comment that includes your first and last name as the author and today's date.
4. Set the style for the <body> element selector to display text that is a 10pt Georgia font (a serif font).
5. For the banner box, create an ID selector named **banner** and set its style as follows:
   - This selector should have a background image named money.gif. Repeat this background image.
   - The box position should be absolute: top 0% and left 0%.
   - The box should have a width of 775 px and a height of 15%.
6. For the column on the left, create an ID selector named **leftbox** and set its style as follows:
   - The box position should be absolute: top 15%, left 2%.
   - The width of the box should be 350 px.
   - There should be a padding of 0.25em and a top margin of 0.5em.
7. For the column on the right, create an ID selector named **rightbox** and set its style as follows:
   - The box position should be absolute: top 15% and left 400 px.
   - The box should be 375 px wide with a padding on the left of 2em.
   - The left border should be navy, solid, and thick. The top margin should be 0.5em.
8. Set the style for the h1 element selector to have white text with a background color of brown. The text should be centered and appear in all caps.
9. Set the style for the h2 element selector to have white text with a background color of navy. Padding should be 0.25em.
10. Set the style for the <p> element selector to have a text indent of 1em.
11. Create an independent class named **center**. Set the style for the class to center elements.
12. In the body section and above the h1 heading, insert a start <div> tag and apply the ID selector named, banner. Insert an end </div> tag below the h1 heading.
13. Above the h2 heading, "The Fallacy of Median Home Prices," insert a start <div> tag and apply the ID selector named, leftbox.
14. Insert an end </div> tag above the comment <!--the right column -->.
15. Insert a start <div> tag and apply the ID selector named, rightbox, before the <h3> heading, "Divest, Divest, and Divest."

16. Insert an end </div> tag after the last paragraph of the document.

17. Insert a start <div> tag and apply the center class before the code for House.gif and before the code for Global.gif. Insert an end </div> tag below the code for each of those two images.

18. Save your GroupNew HTML document, and then open it in your browser. The document should be similar to the one shown in Figure 5-41.

Figure 5-41

THE ZEIDER GROUP FINANCIAL JOURNAL

The Fallacy of Median Home Prices

With the real estate market continuing to retreat from its 2005 records, let's take a look at what's ahead – or likely – for the next five years. Of course, everyone wants to know if the housing market is just in a brief, contraction period, or is it headed for a more prolonged period of depressed home values, similar to what last occurred in the period from 1988 through 1997.

At present, home prices have for the most part remained stable in many areas of the country, but those figures might be deceptive. Builders are luring buyers with add-ons and incentives to entice buyers into signing on the dotted line. For example if a builder tosses in another garage, a solarium, a finished basement or if the builder agrees to pay the first year's property taxes – those incentives are not reflected in the average home price that the government keeps track of.

Therefore, there is no way at present to record, and therefore reflect, how those builder incentives are holding up. You can't therefore, just look at median home price sales and say that the market is firm or steady. Because of that "builder bias," the median home values, which actually might be or are falling – are not reflected in regional or national statistics.

What Should You Do?

At this point, there's no clear direction you should take, unless you want to stay in this for the long haul. Some markets will do better than others, but if you have invested in a second or third or fourth home purely on speculation, you might want to consider limiting your exposure to risk.

Divest, Divest, and Divest

It used to be that the three tenets of real estate were location, location, and location. That no longer is true. By divest, we mean divesting your interest in those areas that are at greatest risk for contraction, such as certain areas in the West.

It's Always Hot Somewhere

Of course, areas with limited land are going to be the ones to ride out this storm the best. There will always be markets, particularly those such as Hawaii and San Francisco, which can ride out a downward ripple – or even a wave – in the housing market.

The Global Outlook

Oil prices continue their roller coaster ride. The past six months saw a steep decline in the price of light sweet crude, but recent tensions in Africa and South America in particular, have roiled the markets once again.

Still, today with most of the world's infrastructure tied into fossil fuels, it has been difficult to dislodge the nation's dependence on fossil fuels. Biofuels, such as ethanol, continue to gain greater market share, but there is a flip side to those gains. As the demand for corn increases, so does the price of corn to feed not only the buying public, but also for that of the cattle rancher, too. Expect to see increases in the price of beef. The same is true for any product that relies on corn syrup as an ingredient – and there are many in that category. Expect to see price increases on a regular basis.

19. Close all open windows.

20. Submit the results of the preceding steps to your instructor, either in printed or electronic form, as requested.

| Apply | | **Case Problem 2** |

Use the skills you learned in the tutorial to create and format a Web page for a book retailer.

Data Files needed for this Case Problem: Bio.jpg, Book.htm, Science.jpg, and Travel.jpg

Wordpendium Books   Wordpendium Books, a regional book retailer located in Kaniliho, Hawaii, has always relied on print media to promote its new book listings. Wordpendium would like to open an online store so that it can market its books in other states. You have been asked to create a Web page that will highlight some of Wordpendium's books. To do so, you will create a series of horizontal boxes; each of which will feature a new book from a different category. You will be creating an embedded style sheet. Complete the following steps:

1. Use Notepad to open the **Book.htm** file located in your Tutorial.05\Case2 folder included with your Data Files. Save this file as **BookNew.htm** in the same folder.
2. In the head area below the page title, enter the code for the start <style> and the end </style> tags.
3. In the head area below the start <style> tag, insert a comment that includes your first and last name as the author and today's date.
4. Set the style for the body tag to have 11pt text in the Arial font. The body should also have a background color of wheat. The width should be 775 px.
5. Create an ID selector named **top**. Position should be absolute: top 10%; left 2%; with a border on the bottom that is gray, solid, and thin. The width should be 775 px.
6. Create an ID selector named **middle**. Position should be absolute: top 43%; left 2%; with a border on the bottom that is gray, solid, and thin. The width should be 775 px.
7. Create an ID selector named **bottom**. Position should be absolute: top 77%; left 2%; with a border on the bottom that is gray, solid, and thin. The width should be 775 px.

⊕ **EXPLORE**
8. Set the style for the h1 element selector as follows:
   - The position should be absolute: left 2%.
   - The font should be Lucida Calligraphy, a serif font. The text should be orange with a background color of black. Text should be centered.
   - There should be a border on the bottom of 0. The width should be 775 px.
9. Set the style for the h2 element selector as black text with a background color of orange.
10. Set the style for the <img> element selector to float right, have a margin on the left of 0.5em, and have a margin on the bottom of 0.5em.
11. Set the style for the <strong> element selector to display text in navy.
12. Set the style for the <address> element selector to have bold, uppercase text. The text should not be italic. The text should be brown.
13. In the body section, insert a start <div> tag and apply the ID selector named, top, above the h2 code for "The Herds of Nebula."
14. Insert an end </div> tag above the comment code for "middle section starts here."
15. Insert a start <div> tag and apply the ID selector named, middle, above the h2 code for "Forget, Forgive, Follow."
16. Insert an end </div> tag above the comment for "bottom section starts here."
17. Insert a start <div> tag and apply the ID selector bottom to the h2 section for "My Years at Remsentown."
18. Insert an end </div> tag above the </body> tag.
19. Save the BookNew HTML document, and then open it in your browser. The document should be similar to the one shown in Figure 5-42.

Figure 5-42

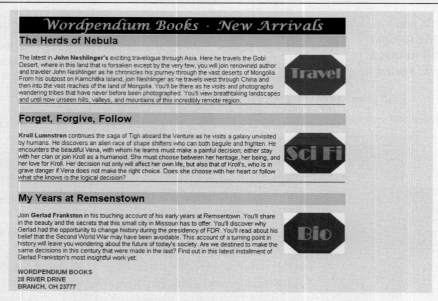

20. Close all open windows.
21. Submit the results of the preceding steps to your instructor, either in printed or electronic form, as requested.

Challenge | Case Problem 3

Use what you've learned, and expand your skills, to create and format a Web page for a hair salon.

Data Files needed for this Case Problem: Haircut.jpg, Harpers.css, and Harpers.htm

Harper's Hair for There Harper's is a new hair salon that has just opened in the Hamilton, Iowa, township. As an incentive to draw in new customers, Harper's is offering substantial discounts through the use of coupons. Customers can go to the Web page, print out the Web page, and use the coupons in the store. You have been asked to create a promotional Web page for Harper's. You will create boxes for each of the coupons so that they align evenly at the left edge of the page. Because the visitors to this Web page will very likely want to print the page, you will also create a print style sheet as an external style sheet file. You will also create an embedded style sheet that will use two boxes; one for the coupon text and one for the main body text. Complete the following steps:

1. Use Notepad to open the **Harpers.htm** file located in your Tutorial.05\Case3 folder included with your Data Files. Save this file as **HarpersNew.htm** in the same folder.

⊕ **EXPLORE**
2. In the head area, below the page title, insert a link to an external style sheet named HarpersPrint.css. Use the media attribute with a value of print.

3. In the <head> area and below the link to the external style sheet, enter the code for the start <style> and the end </style> tags.

4. In the head area below the start <style> tag, insert a comment that includes your first and last name as the author and today's date.

⊕ **EXPLORE**
5. In the start <style> tag, insert the media attribute with a value of screen.

6. Set the style for the body element selector to display text as 14pt and in the Arial font. The background color for the page should be ivory.

7. For the coupon content box, create an ID selector named **coupon**. Format this selector as follows:
   - Text should be bold, 14pt, Arial, and centered. The text also should be green with a background color of wheat.
   - There should be a border on all four sides that is green, thin, and dashed.
   - The height should be 18% and the width should be 175 px.

8. For the main content box, create an ID selector named **main**. Set the style for the ID selector to be positioned as absolute: top 0%; left 220 px. The box should be 600 px wide.

9. Set the style for the <h1> element selector to display text in 40pt, gold, and in the Bradley Hand ITC sans-serif font. Text should be centered. The margin on the top should be 0.

10. Set the style for the <h2> element selector to have brown text. The text should also be centered.

11. Set the style for the <li> element selector to have a list-style-type property value of square and a letter-spacing property value of 0.3em.

12. Set the style for the <img> element selector to float right and have a margin on the left of 1em.

13. In the body section, insert a start <div> tag, and apply the ID selector named, coupon, above the code for *each* of the five coupons. Insert an end </div> tag below the code for each of the five coupons.

14. Above the h1 heading "Harper's Hair for There," insert a start <div> tag and apply the ID selector named, main.

15. Insert an end </div> tag just above the </body> tag.

16. Save the HarpersNew HTML document, and then open it in your browser. The document should be similar to the one shown in Figure 5-43.

Figure 5-43

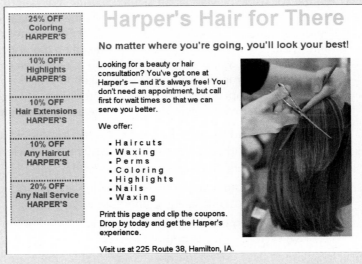

17. Use Notepad to open the **Harpers.css** file located in your Tutorial.05\Case3 folder included with your Data Files. Save this file as **HarpersPrint.css** in the same folder.

18. Create a comment with your first and last name and today's date.

◆ EXPLORE   19. Group the body, #main, h1, and h2 selectors, and then set their style as follows:
- Text should appear in 12pt Times New Roman, a serif font. The text color should be black with a background color of white.
- The float property should have a value of none.
- The width should be set to auto.

20. Set the style for the coupon ID selector as follows:
- Text should appear in 16pt Comic Sans MS, a sans-serif font. The text color should be black with a background color of white.
- The selector should not float.
- The width is 40%.
- The border is navy, dashed, and thick. The text is centered.

21. Set the style for the <img> element selector so that the display property has a value of none. (*Hint*: You won't see any difference when you refresh your Web page, but when you view the document in Print Preview, the Haircut image is no longer displayed.)

22. Save the HarpersPrint CSS file.

◆ EXPLORE   23. In your browser, display the HarpersNew HTML document, and refresh the screen. Display the document in Print Preview. Close Print Preview.

24. Close all open windows.

25. Submit the results of the preceding steps to your instructor, either in printed or electronic form, as requested.

Create		Case Problem 4

Using the files provided, create a Web page for a real estate firm.

Data Files needed for this Case Problem: Check.jpg, Client.jpg, Couple.jpg, Movie.jpg, Pool.jpg, Skyscraper.jpg, Tower.htm, and Walkway.jpg

Pendulum Towers on the Hudson   Pendulum Towers is a planned high-rise construction on the west side of Manhattan Island. Soaring to a height of 70 stories, Pendulum Towers will be the tallest building on midtown Manhattan's west side. The construction will boast 20 floors of commercial space and 50 floors of residential condominium apartment units. Planned links to mass transit will heighten the appeal of the new towers. Its location in midtown Manhattan near the Jacob J. Javits Center will make Pendulum Towers a very attractive property. You have been asked to create a Web page for Pendulum Towers to promote the upcoming launch of the Pendulum Towers sales campaign. You will be creating an embedded style sheet. Complete the following steps:

1. Use Notepad to open the **Tower.htm** file located in your Tutorial.05\Case4 folder included with your Data Files. Save this file as **TowerNew.htm** in the same folder.
2. Enter the code for the <start> style and the end </style> tags.
3. In the head area below the start <style> tag, insert a comment that includes your first and last name as the author and today's date.
4. Using the properties and values you learned about in this tutorial, design an attractive Web page for Pendulum towers.
5. Use at least one of the images supplied for this Case Problem in your Tutorial.05\Case4 folder.
6. Scale the images as you want, but maintain the aspect ratio.
7. Insert <div></div> tags and apply classes as needed.
8. Save the TowerNew HTML document, and then open it in your browser.

9. Close all open windows.
10. Submit the results of the preceding steps to your instructor, either in printed or electronic form, as requested.

Review | **Session 5.1 Quick Check Answers**

1. Place a decorative border around it.
2. height and width
3. overflow
4. visible, hidden, scroll, and auto
5. float
6. to the left of the box

Review | **Session 5.2 Quick Check Answers**

1. left
2. top
3. No. You can use them alone or together.
4. When elements are displayed on top of each other, the z-index determines the stacking order.
5. It should be on the top.
6. It should be on the bottom.
7. no
8. display: none
9. In the browser, choose Print Preview.

Ending Data Files

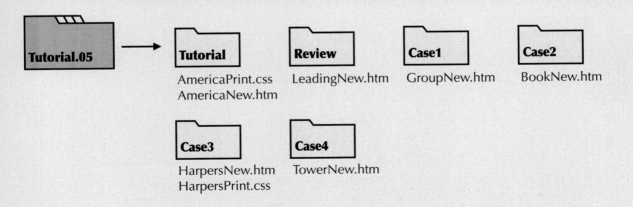

Tutorial.05 →

Tutorial
AmericaPrint.css
AmericaNew.htm

Review
LeadingNew.htm

Case1
GroupNew.htm

Case2
BookNew.htm

Case3
HarpersNew.htm
HarpersPrint.css

Case4
TowerNew.htm

Using Links on a Web Page

Creating and Styling Links

Case | Success Airlines

Success Airlines is a charter jet service based in Dover, Delaware. Success Airlines flies executives of large corporations to cities in the middle Atlantic states, primarily Washington, D.C., Pittsburgh, and Philadelphia. The airline flies small passenger jets that seat as few as six and as many as 16 passengers. Executives who fly Success Airlines are pleased that they can avoid the delays that are common when flying on large, commercial passenger jets. Because Success Airlines has mostly on-demand charter flights, executives enjoy the prestige of boarding a private jet for business travel. Success Airlines has embarked on an aggressive expansion and has opened a newly expanded and modernized terminal in New York City. The company plans to serve most of the major cities along the east coast of the United States, eastern Canada, and parts of the Caribbean. To advertise and promote its expansion efforts, Success Airlines would like to create a new home page. Marketing expert Michael Brown is working on developing the new home page for Success Airlines. Michael has both a background in HTML and CSS, but he has not had much experience in coding links on a Web page. To date, he has focused primarily on Web page design. As his assistant, you will be working with Michael to show him the different types of links that are available and how these links are put into code.

Starting Data Files

Tutorial.06 →

Tutorial	Review	Case1	Case2	Case3	Case4
About.htm	Copter.jpg	Bath1.jpg	Cap.gif	Clothing.jpg	Bios.htm
Cargo.htm	Copters.htm	Bath2.jpg	Cloth.jpg	Food.htm	Forest.jpg
Flight.htm	Hanger.jpg	Bed1.jpg	Glove.jpg	Food.jpg	Greenlogo.gif
Info.htm	Pad.jpg	Bed2.jpg	Hotdog.jpg	General.htm	Lawbooks.gif
Nyphotos.htm	Taxi.htm	Brad.gif	Kids.gif	General.jpg	Lawyers.htm
Reserve.htm		Bradford.htm	News.htm	Linens.htm	Team.gif
Taxi.htm		Ken.gif	Pitcher.jpg	Linens.jpg	
+ 15 image files		Kensington.htm	Roster.htm	Mall.gif	
		Kit1.jpg	Stadium.gif	Shoes.htm	
		Kit2.jpg	Team.htm	Shoes.jpg	
		Real.gif	Teamlogo.gif	Shopping.gif	
		Real.htm	Tickets.htm	Victor.gif	
				Victor.htm	

Creating Links

The popularity that the World Wide Web enjoys today is largely the result of the ability to locate and view information at a Web site in a nonlinear manner, which means that a visitor to a Web site does not have to read one page after another in a specific order. To let visitors view information on a Web site in a nonlinear manner, Web pages use links. A **link** is a reference to another place on the same Web page, another Web page, or another Web site. By convention, links are generally indicated by underlined text. By clicking a link, visitors can choose the pages and topics that are of greatest interest to them and visit those pages in any order. Before you create links, you should understand their underlying technology.

Using Protocols

A **protocol** is a standard for sending and receiving data over phone lines, cable, or by satellite. These standards are important. If every company who made transmission media had their own proprietary, incompatible standard for communicating data, it would be much more difficult to send and receive data, video, and voice over transmission media. Using a protocol sets just one standard and everyone follows the rules for that standard.

The protocol used to access the Web is **hypertext transfer protocol**, or **HTTP**. HTTP establishes standards for communications between **file servers**—the computers that contain or direct information—and **client computers (clients)**, the computer on your desktop or your laptop computer. Another protocol, **TCP/IP**, is used to send small bursts of information, called **packets**, across communication lines. TCP/IP is actually a pair of protocols, Transmission Control Protocol and Internet Protocol, which work in tandem. TCP is responsible for ensuring that data is correctly delivered from the client computer to the server. IP moves packets of information from one computer to another.

Understanding Web Site Addresses

Internet addresses are composed of a series of four numbers (from 0 to 255) separated by periods, such as 12.34.222.111. These numbers represent IP addresses. Unfortunately, it is not easy to remember Web sites based on IP addresses. To make the Web more user friendly, the domain name system was introduced. The **domain name system** refers to Web sites by a server name, rather than an IP address. Initially, there was only one company that was granted permission to create and register domain names. Now, many companies have been granted this right. The domain name is generally a registered trademark or corporate name, such as Ford or CNN. The domain name is followed by a **suffix**, a two- to four-letter abbreviation that groups domain names based on their category, such as .com, .net, .org, .edu, .mil, and .info. Suffixes are also referred to as top-level domain names.

A **URL** is the **Uniform Resource Locator**, which is the complete address of the Web site and page you are viewing, such as *http://www.cnn.com*. When entering a URL in a browser's Address text box, you type forward slashes (/), not backslashes.

Tip

For Web sites that originate in foreign countries, the domain name also includes a two-letter country code, such as *uk,* which stands for United Kingdom.

A URL for a Web page has this structure:

protocol//service.domainname.suffix/path/filename

For example, in this URL *http://www.generousdonations.org/charities/index.htm*

- **http** is the protocol
- **www** is the service
- **generousdonations** is the domain name—the registered name of the file server on which the Web pages for this site are located
- **.org** is the suffix (the .org suffix is used for nonprofit organizations)
- **charities** is the path (a file folder—or folders—on the server)
- **index.htm** is the name of the Web page you are viewing (the home page for a Web site typically has the name index.htm)

Not all URLs contain a service. For example, to transfer a file to or from a server, you could use FTP (File Transfer Protocol). Depending on the FTP software you use, the URL for an FTP site would contain only the protocol, the server name, and the suffix, with a period between the letters *ftp* and the domain name, as in *ftp.generousdonations.org*. More commonly, the URL to an FTP site appears with ftp followed by a colon, two slashes, and then the domain name, as in *ftp://generousdonations.org*.

You can also use a URL to connect to an e-mail client, such as Microsoft Outlook. Such a URL uses the mailto protocol and the e-mail address, as in *mailto:johndoe@generousdonations.org*.

Creating Links

Recall that one of the greatest factors that led to the explosive popularity of the Web is being able to view topics in a nonlinear manner. Allowing readers to quickly find topics of interest is therefore critical to the success of any Web site. Your goal as a Web designer is to get the reader to those places, pages, and sites of interest efficiently. Using links, your visitors can go to four different destinations:

- A specific place on the same Web page
- A different Web page at your Web site
- A specific place on a different Web page at your Web site
- A different Web site

To visit these destinations, users click a link. The text that users click for the link is called the **link text**. In addition to using text as a link, you can also use an image as a link. You can also use a single image as a source for several links.

For the Success Airlines Web page, you will create several boxes and place an image, text, or both text and images into the box. You will be creating an embedded style sheet for this Web page, so you will start by opening the file and then showing Michael how to put the start and end style tags in code. You will also include a comment to document the file's author and file creation date.

To include the style tags and create the comment:

▶ **1.** Use Notepad to open the **Flight.htm** file located in the Tutorial.06\Tutorial folder included with your Data Files. Save this file as **FlightNew.htm** in the same folder.

2. On a blank line after the page title in the <head> section, type the following code, which is also shown in red in Figure 6-1.

```
<style type="text/css" media="screen">

/* Your First Name Your Last Name
Today's Date */

</style>
```

Figure 6-1 ▶ **Style codes and comment**

```
<html>
<head>
<title>Success Airlines</title>

<style type="text/css" media="screen">

/* Your First Name Your Last Name
Today's Date */

</style>
</head>

<body>
```

3. Save the file.

Next, you will set the style for the body element selector. Michael would like the Web page to have text displayed in the Arial font. You will show Michael how to style the body element.

To style the body element selector:

1. Make sure the FlightNew HTML file is open in Notepad.

2. On a blank line after the comment code, type the following code to style the body element selector, which is also shown in red in Figure 6-2.

```
body {
font-family: arial,helvetica,sans-serif; }
```

Figure 6-2 ▶ **Code to style the body element**

```
<html>
<head>
<title>Success Airlines</title>

<style type="text/css" media="screen">

/* Your First Name Your Last Name
Today's Date */

body {
font-family: arial,helvetica,sans-serif; }

</style>
</head>
```

▶ **3.** Save the FlightNew HTML file.

▶ **4.** Open the FlightNew Web page in your browser, refresh the screen, and then compare it to Figure 6-3 to verify that the font is set to Arial.

The body element style in the browser ◀ Figure 6-3

Are You Successful?

You know you are when you fly *Success Airlines*. We offer the finest on-demand service for the busiest and most successful executives in the country along the East Coast corridor, from Canada to Florida and the Caribbean. Pass your mouse over the map of our renovated New York terminal to see its new features.

Service

We have unparalleled in-flight service. Our jets seat from 6 to 16 passengers. Our flight attendants will cater to your every need. First-class dining is all we offer. Your meals are prepared either just prior to flight or on board. We will arrange to follow any special dietary principles or restrictions you may have.

Safety

Success Airlines flies the newest fleet of small jet aircraft of any airline. All of our planes are TechJSX jet aircraft manufactured within the last five years. Equipment is fully state-of-the-art. Our pilots have been hand-picked from among the best of commercial and private air carriers. Each pilot has more than 15 years of full-time flying experience with the airline industry, and all our pilots are recertified at least once a year.

Productivity

Think it's not cost-effective to fly Success Airlines? Think about all the lost time wasted in traveling to a busy airport and dealing with lengthy security delays. As a frequent flyer with *Success Airlines*, you are security-vetted once a year. You arrive at our terminal, get on the plane, and take off. We have our own private terminals. Your baggage travels on board with you or on the flight itself. Your baggage never gets lost or misrouted. All of our seats fully recline, so you can sleep comfortably on longer flights. Whether you choose to do paperwork, read, or get some

Now you are ready to plan the links and insert anchors on the FlightNew Web page.

Creating a Link to a Specific Place on the Same Web Page

Most visitors to a Web page like to find what they are looking for right away. Forcing your visitors to scroll several screens down the page to find the information they want is one sure way to lose a visitor's interest. Anchors and links help your readers locate a topic or a specific place on a Web page. An **anchor** is HTML code that identifies a particular location on a Web page. Using anchors and links, your visitors can find what they are looking for quickly.

Creating an Anchor | Reference Window

• To create an anchor, use the following code:
  ```
  <a id="anchorname"></a>
  ```
  where *a* is the start anchor tag, `id` is the id attribute, *anchorname* is the name of the anchor, and `</a>` is the end anchor tag.

If your home page is several screens long, you should insert code for your anchors so that readers do not have to scroll down the page to locate what they are looking for. Also, if the page is several screens long, make sure you don't strand the reader at the bottom of a Web page—include links back to the top of the page, the next page (if there is one), the previous page (if there was one), and the home page (if the user is not currently viewing the home page).

Using the Start Anchor Tag

Ideally, you should catch the reader's attention on the first screen of text on a Web page. If your Web page is longer than one screen, you need to assist your readers to view the remainder of the page quickly and easily. Anchors are the way to do that.

Because you determine where to insert the code for anchors, you need to plan where this code will appear. To do so, you insert start and end anchor tags. The <a> tag is the start anchor tag. The anchor tag is a paired tag—you will examine the end anchor tag shortly. It is very common to include an anchor at the top of every Web page so that the visitor can click a link at the bottom of the page and quickly return back to the top. As a suggestion, code the anchor tag at the top of the page just above the start <body> tag, like so:

```
<html>
<head>
<title>Success Airlines</title>
</head>
<a>
<body>
```

Tip

The bottom of the first screen at a home page is called the fold.

Using the id Attribute

You have already used ID selectors to style documents. There is also an **id attribute**, which assigns a unique identifier to an element. You give the anchor a name by using the id attribute and assigning the id a value. You should give an anchor a descriptive name based on its location, its purpose, or the surrounding text. Don't, for example, name your anchors as anchor1, anchor2, and so forth.

It is common to have an anchor at the top of the page named *top* or *pagetop*. Pick a name for this purpose and be consistent throughout your Web site. Values for the id attribute must be preceded and followed by quotes, as shown in the following code:

```
</head>
<a id="top">
<body>
```

Tip

You can also use the name attribute instead of the id attribute, though the name attribute is deprecated.

Using the End Anchor Tag

The end </a> anchor tag follows the value for the id attribute, as shown in the following code:

```
</head>
<a id="top"></a>
<body>
```

Note that you do not enter any text between the code for the start anchor tag and the end anchor tag. You will show Michael how to code an anchor at the top of the page. You will name the anchor *top*.

Tip

Links to anchors on the same page or links to other pages at the same Web site are also called *navigational links*.

To code the anchor named top:

1. Make sure the FlightNew HTML file is open in Notepad.

2. On a blank line between the end </head> tag and the start <body> tag, type the following code, which is also shown in red in Figure 6-4.

```
<a id="top"></a>
```

Code for the anchor named top ◄ **Figure 6-4**

```
body {
font-family:  arial,helvetica,sans-serif; }

</style>
</head>
<a id="top"></a>
```
anchor code for the top of the page

After creating an anchor, you are ready to insert a link to that anchor.

Linking to an Anchor on the Same Page

After you have created all the anchors, you need links—text or images—that when clicked, display another screen location, page, or Web site.

Creating a Link to an Anchor on a Different Page | Reference Window

- To create a link to an anchor on another page, enter the following code:
    `<a id="filename.htm#anchorname">linktext</a>`
    where `filename` is the name of the file on which the anchor resides, `#anchorname` is the name of the anchor you are linking to preceded by the flag character, and `linktext` is the text that the user will click to activate the link.

To create the link, you again code the start anchor tag, but this time you use the **hypertext reference attribute**, which is shortened to href in HTML code. The value of the hypertext reference attribute is the destination for the link. In this instance, the value of the hypertext reference attribute is the name of the anchor. The link code begins like so:

`<a href=`

Every Web page that goes past the fold (is longer than one screen) should have a link at the bottom of the page that will serve as a link (a jump) back to the top of the page. In that way, you won't strand the reader at the bottom of the page and force him or her to scroll back to the top of the page. To link to an anchor, use the anchor's name as the value of the hypertext reference attribute. In addition, however, before the anchor name, you also include a flag character; in this instance, the flag character is the pound symbol (#), as shown in the following code:

`<a href="#top">`

To complete the link, you need something, such as text, to click. Because this is a link to the top of the page, the words "Back to Top" will be used as the link text.

`<a href="#top">Back to Top`

The end anchor tag comes last and completes the code for the link:

`<a href="#top">Back to Top</a>`

Tip

In the link text, avoid expressions such as "click here," and use text that describes what readers see when they click the link text.

Tip

If your page has a top margin, the insertion point does not return to the exact top of the page when users click a Back to Top link. To avoid this, eliminate (or adjust) the top margin.

When the page appears in the browser, the words "Back to Top" will be underlined, which identifies those words as a link. In addition, when the mouse pointer passes over the words "Back to Top," it changes to an icon of the hand cursor 🖑, the icon that indicates that this text is a hypertext reference.

You will now show Michael how to code the link to the anchor named top.

To code the link to the anchor named top:

1. Make sure the FlightNew HTML file is open in Notepad.

2. On a blank line above the end </body> tag at the bottom of the page, type the following code, which is also shown in red in Figure 6-5.

   ```
   <p><a href="#top">Back to Top</a></p>
   ```

Figure 6-5	Code for the link to the anchor named top

```
<p>Contact us today so you can join our Air Taxi Club for even better service. We'll fly you from
your heliport to ours.</p>

<p><a href="#top">Back to Top</a></p>

</body>
</html>
```

code for the
Back to Top link

3. Save the FlightNew HTML file.

4. Refresh the FlightNew Web page in your browser, and then compare it to Figure 6-6 to verify that the link to the anchor called top is now displayed.

Figure 6-6	Link to the anchor named top in the browser

terminal to see its new features.

Service

We have unparalleled in-flight service. Our jets seat from 6 to 16 passengers. Our flight attendants will cater to your every need. First-class dining is all we offer. Your meals are prepared either just prior to flight or on board. We will arrange to follow any special dietary principles or restrictions you may have.

Safety

Success Airlines flies the newest fleet of small jet aircraft of any airline. All of our planes are TechJSX jet aircraft manufactured within the last five years. Equipment is fully state-of-the-art. Our pilots have been hand-picked from among the best of commercial and private air carriers. Each pilot has more than 15 years of full-time flying experience with the airline industry, and all our pilots are recertified at least once a year.

Productivity

Think it's not cost-effective to fly Success Airlines? Think about all the lost time wasted in traveling to a busy airport and dealing with lengthy security delays. As a frequent flyer with Success Airlines, you are security-vetted once a year. You arrive at our terminal, get on the plane, and take off. We have our own private terminals. Your baggage travels on board with you or on the flight itself. Your baggage never gets lost or misrouted. All of our seats fully recline, so you can sleep comfortably on longer flights. Whether you choose to do paperwork, read, or get some sleep, you'll be ready to go for that upcoming executive meeting. You'll be at your peak performance because you traveled with Success Airlines.

Convenience

We can arrange for limousine service to bring you to the airport and take you back to your office or residence. Ride in comfort for your entire trip, from door to door. Now that's the way to do business!

Contact us today so you can join our Air Taxi Club for even better service. We'll fly you from your heliport to ours.

Back to Top ← Back to Top link appears at the bottom of the Web page

5. Click the **Back to Top** link text. Verify that the top of the page is now displayed on your screen.

Now that you have created a link to a place on the same page, you will show Michael how to create a link to a different Web page.

Linking to a Different Page

The code to link to a different page at the same Web site is similar to the link you just created to link to an anchor on the same page. To link to a different page, the value of the hypertext reference attribute is the name of the page you want to link to. The page where the link is included is called the **referring page**. The page that will be displayed when the user clicks the link is called the **target page**. To link to a different page, you do not precede the name of the link with the # symbol as you did when you used a link to an anchor.

Creating a Link to a Different Web Page | Reference Window

- To create a link to a different Web page, use the following code:
  ```
  <a href="filename.htm">linktext</a>
  ```
  where a is the start anchor tag, `filename`.htm is the name of the file you are linking to, `linktext` is the text that the user will click to activate the link, and `</a>` is the end anchor tag.

The code to link to a different page would be similar to the following code example:

```
<a href="Taxi.htm">Air Taxi Club</a>
```

Using Placeholders

During the early part of the Web site development process, the pages you want to link to typically have not yet been created. Early on in a project, it is often common to dispense with the actual filenames and instead use the pound symbol (#) as a **placeholder character** in a link, like so:

```
<a href="#">Air Taxi Club</a>
```

Here, the placeholder character serves as a reminder to insert the filename after the page has been created. The link will not work until an actual filename has been provided, but the links can be created as an aid in planning the overall design of the page.

The placeholder character is replaced by the name of the actual target page once the page has been created. **Placeholder pages** are those pages that are still in the early stages of the development process. These are pages with little content, but they can be used as the target pages for links. Later, the placeholder pages will be further developed and given more content. A page about the Success Airlines Air Taxi service has been developed, but the other pages you will now link to are just placeholder pages. You will show Michael how to code links to other pages at the same Web site.

To code the links to other pages at the same Web site:

1. Make sure the FlightNew HTML file is open in Notepad.

2. On a blank line below the start <body> tag, type the following code, which is also shown in red in Figure 6-7.

```
<a href="about.htm">About Us</a>
<a href="taxi.htm">Air Taxi</a>
<a href="cargo.htm">Cargo</a>
<a href="info.htm">Information</a>
<a href="reserve.htm">Reservations</a>
```

Figure 6-7 ▸ Code for links to documents at the same Web site

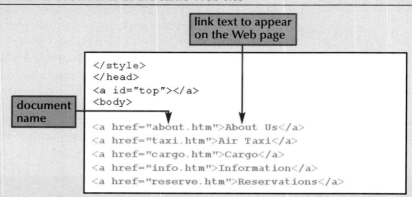

link text to appear
on the Web page

document
name

```
</style>
</head>
<a id="top"></a>
<body>

<a href="about.htm">About Us</a>
<a href="taxi.htm">Air Taxi</a>
<a href="cargo.htm">Cargo</a>
<a href="info.htm">Information</a>
<a href="reserve.htm">Reservations</a>
```

▸ **3.** Save the FlightNew HTML file.

▸ **4.** Refresh the FlightNew Web page in your browser, and then compare it to Figure 6-8 to verify that the list of links to other Web pages is now displayed at the top of the page.

Figure 6-8 ▸ Links to documents at the same Web site in the browser

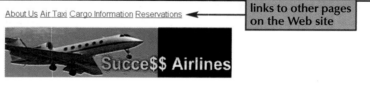

About Us Air Taxi Cargo Information Reservations ◂—— links to other pages
on the Web site

Succe$$ Airlines

Are You Successful?

You know you are when you fly *Success Airlines*. We offer the finest on-demand service for the busiest and most successful executives in the country along the East Coast corridor, from Canada to Florida and the Caribbean. Pass your mouse over the map of our renovated New York terminal to see its new features.

Service

We have unparalleled in-flight service. Our jets seat from 6 to 16 passengers. Our flight attendants will cater to your every need. First-class dining is all we offer. Your meals are prepared either just prior to flight or on board. We will arrange to follow any special dietary principles or restrictions you may have.

Safety

Success Airlines flies the newest fleet of small jet aircraft of any airline. All of our planes are TechJSX jet aircraft manufactured within the last five years. Equipment is fully state-of-the-art. Our pilots have been hand-picked from among the best of commercial and private air carriers. Each pilot has more than 15 years of full-time flying experience with the airline industry, and all our pilots are recertified at least once a year.

Productivity

Think it's not cost-effective to fly Success Airlines? Think about all the lost time wasted in traveling to a busy airport and dealing with lengthy security delays. As a frequent flyer with *Success Airlines*, you are security-vetted once a year. You arrive at our terminal, get on the plane, and

▸ **5.** Click the **Air Taxi** link to verify that the link to the Taxi.htm page works properly.

▸ **6.** Click the **Back** button (or the appropriate tab) in your browser to return to the FlightNew Web page.

Earlier, you created a link to an anchor on the same page. Now that you have shown Michael how to use links to other Web pages, you are ready to show him how to include a link to an anchor on a different Web page.

Linking to an Anchor on a Different Page

When you click a link to a different page, the first screen of that new page is displayed. If users do not find what they are looking for on that first screen, you force them to scroll through the rest of the page. You can eliminate the need for users to scroll through the rest of the page by first linking to a different page and then linking to an anchor on that page—a double link. You must code the anchors beforehand in the target page in the appropriate places. Generally, headings are good places to code anchors.

To link to an anchor on a different page, the value for the hypertext reference is composed of the following parts:

- The target page
- The flag character
- The anchor name

Note that the entire value appears together without any spaces, as shown in the following example:

```
<a href="taxi.htm#join">Air Taxi Club</a>
```

Now when the user clicks the words "Air Taxi Club," the first link displays the page named Taxi.htm, and then the second link to the anchor displays the screen where the anchor named *join* is located.

You could also link to an anchor on a page at another Web site, but to do so could be problematic. You have no control over that page, and if the code for that page should be revised and the anchors moved, renamed, or eliminated, your link to that anchor on that Web site would no longer work.

An anchor named join has already been included on the Taxi.htm page to the left of the h2 heading. The anchor looks like so:

```
<a id="join"></a><h2>Join the Air Taxi Club</h2>
```

You will now show Michael how to code the link to the anchor named join on the Taxi.htm Web page.

To add a link to an anchor on another page:

▶ **1.** Make sure the FlightNew HTML file is open in Notepad.

▶ **2.** In the last paragraph of the document, position the insertion point before the word "Air". Type the following bold code, which is also shown in red in Figure 6-9. Remember to code the end anchor tag </a> after the word "Club."

```
<p>Contact us today so you can join our
<a href="taxi.htm#join">Air Taxi Club</a> for even better
service. We'll fly you from your heliport to ours.</p>
```

Code for an anchor on another page ◀ **Figure 6-9**

```
<p>Contact us today so you can join our <a href="taxi.htm#join">Air Taxi Club</a> for  even better
service. We'll fly you from your heliport to ours.</p>

<p><a href="#top">Back to Top</a></p>
```

code for creating a link to the Air Taxi Club Web page

3. Save the FlightNew HTML file.

4. Refresh the FlightNew Web page in your browser, and then compare it to Figure 6-10 to verify that the link to the anchor *join* is now displayed.

Figure 6-10 ▶ **Link to the anchor in the browser**

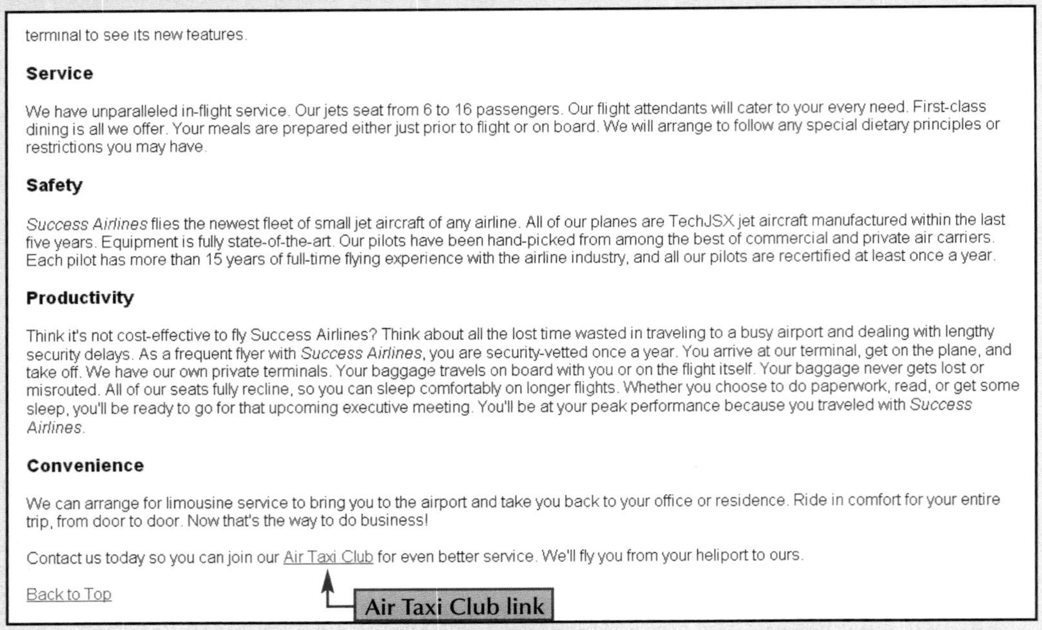

---

terminal to see its new features.

Service

We have unparalleled in-flight service. Our jets seat from 6 to 16 passengers. Our flight attendants will cater to your every need. First-class dining is all we offer. Your meals are prepared either just prior to flight or on board. We will arrange to follow any special dietary principles or restrictions you may have.

Safety

Success Airlines flies the newest fleet of small jet aircraft of any airline. All of our planes are TechJSX jet aircraft manufactured within the last five years. Equipment is fully state-of-the-art. Our pilots have been hand-picked from among the best of commercial and private air carriers. Each pilot has more than 15 years of full-time flying experience with the airline industry, and all our pilots are recertified at least once a year.

Productivity

Think it's not cost-effective to fly Success Airlines? Think about all the lost time wasted in traveling to a busy airport and dealing with lengthy security delays. As a frequent flyer with *Success Airlines*, you are security-vetted once a year. You arrive at our terminal, get on the plane, and take off. We have our own private terminals. Your baggage travels on board with you or on the flight itself. Your baggage never gets lost or misrouted. All of our seats fully recline, so you can sleep comfortably on longer flights. Whether you choose to do paperwork, read, or get some sleep, you'll be ready to go for that upcoming executive meeting. You'll be at your peak performance because you traveled with *Success Airlines.*

Convenience

We can arrange for limousine service to bring you to the airport and take you back to your office or residence. Ride in comfort for your entire trip, from door to door. Now that's the way to do business!

Contact us today so you can join our Air Taxi Club for even better service. We'll fly you from your heliport to ours.

Back to Top   **Air Taxi Club link**

---

5. Click the **Air Taxi Club** link text. Verify that the link works properly.

6. At the bottom of the TaxiNew page, click on the link text for *Home* to return to the FlightNew Web page.

Next, you'll examine how to link a page to a different Web site.

Linking to Another Web Site

To link to another Web site, you must include the complete URL of the site as the value for the href attribute. It is very important that you include the http:// protocol. If you do not, the link will not work. For example, if you want to create a link to weather.com, you would use the following code:

```
<a href="http://www.weather.com">Latest Weather</a>
```

Reference Window | **Creating a Link to an External Web Site**

- To create a link to an external Web site, use:
  ```
  <a href="http://www.domainname.suffix">linktext</a>
  ```
  where href is the hypertext reference attribute, www is the service, *domainname* is the domain name, *suffix* is the suffix, and *linktext* is the text that the user clicks to activate the link.

Michael wants to be sure that the airline's travelers know if there are going to be any weather-related problems. You will show Michael how to include a link to an external Web site, the weather.com site.

To code a link to an external Web site:

▶ 1. Make sure the FlightNew HTML file is open in Notepad.

▶ 2. On a blank line just below the last paragraph of the page, type the following code to create the link, which is also shown in red in Figure 6-11.

```
<p><a href="http://www.weather.com">Latest Weather</a></p>
```

Code for a link to an external Web site ◀ **Figure 6-11**

```
<p><a href="http://www.weather.com">Latest Weather</a></p>

<p><a href="#top">Back to Top</a></p>
```

code to link to the weather.com Web site

▶ 3. Save the FlightNew HTML file.

▶ 4. Refresh the FlightNew Web page in your browser, and then compare it to Figure 6-12 to verify that the link to the weather.com Web site is now displayed.

Link to an external Web site in the browser ◀ **Figure 6-12**

Service

We have unparalleled in-flight service. Our jets seat from 6 to 16 passengers. Our flight attendants will cater to your every need. First-class dining is all we offer. Your meals are prepared either just prior to flight or on board. We will arrange to follow any special dietary principles or restrictions you may have.

Safety

Success Airlines flies the newest fleet of small jet aircraft of any airline. All of our planes are TechJSX jet aircraft manufactured within the last five years. Equipment is fully state-of-the-art. Our pilots have been hand-picked from among the best of commercial and private air carriers. Each pilot has more than 15 years of full-time flying experience with the airline industry, and all our pilots are recertified at least once a year.

Productivity

Think it's not cost-effective to fly Success Airlines? Think about all the lost time wasted in traveling to a busy airport and dealing with lengthy security delays. As a frequent flyer with *Success Airlines*, you are security-vetted once a year. You arrive at our terminal, get on the plane, and take off. We have our own private terminals. Your baggage travels on board with you or on the flight itself. Your baggage never gets lost or misrouted. All of our seats fully recline, so you can sleep comfortably on longer flights. Whether you choose to do paperwork, read, or get some sleep, you'll be ready to go for that upcoming executive meeting. You'll be at your peak performance because you traveled with *Success Airlines*.

Convenience

We can arrange for limousine service to bring you to the airport and take you back to your office or residence. Ride in comfort for your entire trip, from door to door. Now that's the way to do business!

Contact us today so you can join our Air Taxi Club for even better service. We'll fly you from your heliport to ours.

Latest Weather ◀ Latest Weather link to weather.com

Back to Top

▶ 5. Click the **Latest Weather** link text. Verify that the link to the weather.com external Web site works.

▶ 6. Return to the FlightNew HTML page.

So far you have learned that there are several different types of links. Each page should have an anchor at the top of the page and a link at the bottom of the page that links back to the top of the page. You also have learned that you can create links to other pages at the same Web site, a link to an anchor at another page at the same Web site, and a link to another Web site. Now you will work with Michael on the page layout and show him how to set the style for the links.

| Review | **Session 6.1 Quick Check** |

1. What set of tags is used for both anchors and links?
2. What attribute must always be used with the anchor tag to create an anchor?
3. What attribute is used to create a link?
4. What is a referring page?
5. What is a target page?
6. What flag character is used when creating a link to an anchor?
7. Which code do you enter first: the anchors or the links?

Session 6.2

Planning the Page Layout

Michael would like the FlightNew Web page to have two columns. A sidebar, a narrow column on the left side of the screen, will be used for the links. The right side of the screen, which will be a much wider column, will be the main window. Because the sidebar will have several floated elements, you will also create a container box. You will show Michael how to create the container box now.

To create the container box:

► **1.** Make sure the FlightNew HTML file is open in Notepad.

► **2.** On a blank line after the body element style, type the following code to create the container box, which is also shown in red in Figure 6-13.

```
#container {
margin-left: auto;
margin-right: auto;
width: 780px; }
```

Figure 6-13 ▸ **Code for the container ID selector**

```
body {
font-family: arial,helvetica,sans-serif; }

#container {
margin-left: auto;          ← code to create
margin-right: auto;            the container
width: 780px; }

</style>
```

Now that the container ID selector has been created, you need to apply the container ID selector. You will show Michael how to do so. You also need to code the end </div> tag to indicate where this page division will end. You will show Michael where to code this tag.

To apply the container ID selector:

▶ **1.** On a blank line below the body tag, type the following code, which is also shown in red in Figure 6-14.

```
<div id="container">
```

Code to apply the container ID selector ◀ Figure 6-14

```
#container {
margin-left: auto;
margin-right: auto;
width: 780px; }

</style>
</head>
<a id="top"></a>
<body>
<div id="container">
```

▶ **2.** On a blank line above the </body> tag, type the following code, which is also shown in red in Figure 6-15.

```
</div>
```

The end </div> tag for the container ◀ Figure 6-15

```
<p><a href="#top">Back to Top</a></p>
</div>
</body>
</html>
```

▶ **3.** Save the FlightNew HTML file.

Creating the Sidebar for the Links

You will now show Michael how to create the sidebar box. You will use an ID selector named *sidebar* to do so.

To create the sidebar box:

▶ **1.** Make sure the FlightNew HTML file is open in Notepad.

▶ **2.** On a blank line after the container ID selector code, type the following code, which is also shown in red in Figure 6-16.

```
#sidebar {
font-size: 12pt;
width: 201px;
float: left;
color: white;
background-color: brown;
border: black thick solid;
text-align: center; }
```

Figure 6-16 ▶ **Code for the sidebar ID selector**

```
#container {
margin-left: auto;
margin-right: auto;
width: 780px; }

#sidebar {
font-size: 12pt;
width: 201px;
float: left;                    ← code to create
color: white;                     the sidebar
background-color: brown;
border: black thick solid;
text-align: center; }
```

Now that the sidebar ID selector has been created, you need to apply the sidebar ID selector. You will show Michael how to do so. You also need to code the end </div> tag to indicate where the sidebar division will end. You will show Michael where to code this tag.

To apply the sidebar ID selector:

▶ **1.** On a blank line below the code to apply the container ID selector, type the following code, which is also shown in red in Figure 6-17.

```
<div id="sidebar">
```

Figure 6-17 ▶ **Code to apply the sidebar ID selector**

```
</style>
</head>
<a id="top"></a>
<body>
<div id="container">
<div id="sidebar">
<a href="about.htm">About Us</a>
<a href="taxi.htm">Air Taxi</a>
<a href="cargo.htm">Cargo</a>
<a href="info.htm">Information</a>
<a href="reserve.htm">Reservations</a>
```

▶ **2.** On a blank line below the Reservations link, type the following code, which is also shown in red in Figure 6-18.

```
</div>
```

The end </div> tag for the sidebar ◄ Figure 6-18

```
<div id="container">
<div id="sidebar">
<a href="about.htm">About Us</a>
<a href="taxi.htm">Air Taxi</a>
<a href="cargo.htm">Cargo</a>
<a href="info.htm">Information</a>
<a href="reserve.htm">Reservations</a>
</div>
```

▶ **3.** Save the FlightNew HTML file.

▶ **4.** Refresh the FlightNew Web page in your browser, and then compare it to Figure 6-19 to verify that the sidebar box has been created.

Sidebar in the browser ◄ Figure 6-19

sidebar contains links to other pages

Are You Successful?

You know you are when you fly *Success Airlines*. We offer the finest on-demand service for the busiest and most successful executives in the country along the East Coast corridor, from Canada to Florida and the Caribbean. Pass your mouse over the map of our renovated New York terminal to see its new features.

Service

We have unparalleled in-flight service. Our jets seat from 6 to 16 passengers. Our flight attendants will cater to your every need. First-class dining is all we offer. Your meals are prepared either just prior to flight or on board. We will arrange to follow any special dietary principles or restrictions you may have.

Safety

Success Airlines flies the newest fleet of small jet aircraft of any airline. All of our planes are TechJSX jet aircraft manufactured within the last five years. Equipment is fully state-of-the-art. Our pilots have been hand-picked from among the best of commercial and private air carriers. Each pilot has more than 15 years of full-time flying experience with the airline industry, and all our pilots are recertified at least once a year.

Productivity

Think it's not cost-effective to fly Success Airlines? Think about all the lost time wasted in traveling to a busy airport and dealing with lengthy security delays. As a frequent flyer with *Success Airlines*, you are security-vetted once a year. You arrive at our terminal, get on the plane, and take off. We have our own private terminals. Your

Now that the sidebar for the links has been created, you are ready to show Michael how to style the links.

Don't assume that every sidebar you encounter on a Web page has been created by using CSS. A common design trick is to create a background image that mimics the appearance of a sidebar. The image is created in a graphics-editing program such as Photoshop. The designer creates an image 1000px (or more) wide and 1–3px high, so the image looks like a horizontal rule. The first 300 or so pixels of the image have a light color (such as beige). The next 10–20px have darker color, such as navy or black. This darker section will create the illusion of a vertical rule to the right of the sidebar when the image is displayed in the browser. The remainder of the rule is colored the background color of the main body window. The image is then used as a background image for the Web page. Because the default for a background image is to repeat the image horizontally and vertically, the image, although very small, fills the entire contents of the page. The downside to using this design trick is that you can't resize the box, change the color, or change the border widths using CSS. Because the sidebar is actually a background image, if you want to edit the background or the vertical rule, you must have access to the design program that originally created the background image or find someone who does have that design program to edit the image for you.

Styling Links

Links can be styled, just like any other element. To do so, you style the <a> element. Michael has decided to display the links in 12pt navy text. The code you create now will style all the links on the page whether they are links to anchors, to other pages at the same Web site, or to an external Web site. You will show Michael how to style the anchor element now.

To style the links:

1. Make sure the FlightNew HTML file is open in Notepad.

2. On a blank line after the sidebar ID selector code, type the following code to style the links, which is also shown in red in Figure 6-20.

```
a {
font-weight: bold;
font-size: 12pt;
color: navy; }
```

Figure 6-20 | **Code to style the anchor element**

```
text-align: center; }

a {
font-weight: bold;
font-size: 12pt;
color: navy; }

</style>
```

3. Save the FlightNew HTML file.

4. Refresh the FlightNew Web page in your browser, and then compare it to Figure 6-21 to verify that the links are now displayed in bold 12pt navy text.

The anchor element styled in the browser | Figure 6-21

all sidebar text
is now bold
and navy

Are You Successful?

You know you are when you fly *Success Airlines*. We offer the finest on-demand service for the busiest and most successful executives in the country along the East Coast corridor, from Canada to Florida and the Caribbean. Pass your mouse over the map of our renovated New York terminal to see its new features.

Service

We have unparalleled in-flight service. Our jets seat from 6 to 16 passengers. Our flight attendants will cater to your every need. First-class dining is all we offer. Your meals are prepared either just prior to flight or on board. We will arrange to follow any special dietary principles or restrictions you may have.

Safety

Success Airlines flies the newest fleet of small jet aircraft of any airline. All of our planes are TechJSX jet aircraft manufactured within the last five years. Equipment is fully state-of-the-art. Our pilots have been hand-picked from among the best of commercial and private air carriers. Each pilot has more than 15 years of full-time flying experience with the airline industry, and all our pilots are recertified at least once a year.

Productivity

Think it's not cost-effective to fly Success Airlines? Think about all the lost time wasted in traveling to a busy airport and dealing with lengthy security delays. As a frequent flyer with *Success Airlines*, you are security-vetted once a year. You arrive at our terminal, get on the plane, and take off. We have our own private terminals. Your

---

Right now, the page looks unbalanced, with too much space below the links. You will show Michael how to insert an image into the sidebar box, which will create a more balanced look to the page layout.

Inserting an Image into the Sidebar Box

The sidebar has quite a bit of space below the links. Michael has decided this would be a great place to insert an image of one of Success Airlines flight attendants. You will show Michael how to insert an image into the sidebar. This image will be displayed below the links.

To insert an image below the links in the sidebar:

▶ 1. Make sure the FlightNew HTML file is open in Notepad.

▶ 2. On a blank line after the link for Reservations (and above the </div> tag), type the following code to insert the image of the flight attendant, which is also shown in red in Figure 6-22.

```
<img src="attendant.jpg" alt="image of one of Success Airlines'
flight attendants" width="200" height="300" />
```

Figure 6-22

Code for the attendant.jpg image

```
<div id="container">
<div id="sidebar">
<a href="about.htm">About Us</a>
<a href="taxi.htm">Air Taxi</a>
<a href="cargo.htm">Cargo</a>
<a href="info.htm">Information</a>
<a href="reserve.htm">Reservations</a>
<img src="attendant.jpg" alt="image of one of Success Airlines' flight attendants" width="200"
height="300" />
</div>
```

▶ **3.** Save the FlightNew HTML file.

▶ **4.** Refresh the FlightNew Web page in your browser, and then compare it to Figure 6-23 to verify that the image of the flight attendant is now displayed below the links.

Figure 6-23

The attendant.jpg image in the browser

attendant image in the sidebar

Are You Successful?

You know you are when you fly *Success Airlines*. We offer the finest on-demand service for the busiest and most successful executives in the country along the East Coast corridor, from Canada to Florida and the Caribbean. Pass your mouse over the map of our renovated New York terminal to see its new features.

Service

We have unparalleled in-flight service. Our jets seat from 6 to 16 passengers. Our flight attendants will cater to your every need. First-class dining is all we offer. Your meals are prepared either just prior to flight or on board. We will arrange to follow any special dietary principles or restrictions you may have.

Safety

Success Airlines flies the newest fleet of small jet aircraft of any airline. All of our planes are TechJSX jet aircraft manufactured within the last five years. Equipment is fully state-of-the-art. Our pilots have been hand-picked from among the best of commercial and private air carriers. Each pilot has more than 15 years of full-time flying experience with the airline industry, and all our pilots are recertified at least once a year.

Productivity

Think it's not cost-effective to fly Success Airlines? Think about all the lost time wasted in traveling to a busy

Laptop computer users often rely on keyboard shortcuts rather than using a mouse, especially when the user is a passenger on a plane or train, where the use of a mouse is not practical. Laptop users in these situations often rely on keyboard shortcuts called **access keys**. The access key is a letter or number that corresponds to letters or numbers in the Windows menu bar at the top of the screen. The access key is activated by pressing the Alt key and a corresponding letter or number. To assign access keys on a Web page, within the link code, code the **accesskey attribute** and assign a keyboard shortcut using any letter or number, like so:

```
<a href="http:/www.successairlines.com" accesskey="s">Success
Airlines</a>
```

The user can then press the Alt key and the letter or number you have assigned as the shortcut value. In this instance, pressing Alt and the lowercase letter "s" selects the link.

For Firefox users, pressing Alt and the shortcut value activates the link. For Internet Explorer users, pressing Alt and the shortcut value gives the link the **focus**, which means that the link becomes the one that will be activated if the user presses the Enter key. An element that has the focus has a dotted border around it. You can see which link has the focus by viewing the status bar at the bottom of the screen. In most programs, a keyboard shortcut appears as an underscored letter or number on the screen. That is not true for browsers. There is no visual clue for shortcuts even if you make the link have a text-decoration property value of none.

Link keyboard shortcuts override browser keyboard shortcuts. For example, if you created a shortcut using this code: accesskey="v" it would override the browser shortcut to View a page. As such, use the accesskey attribute with caution.

Using Pseudo-Class Selectors

Earlier, you learned about pseudo-elements, such as :first-letter and :first-line. Remember, the word *pseudo* means "not genuine." In HTML, no elements are named *first-letter* or *first-line*. When you style the :first-letter and :first-line pseudo-elements, you are styling elements *that do not exist*. However, a pseudo-class selector is used to style an element *that does exist*; in this case, the anchor element. Although there are other pseudo-class selectors, four pseudo-class selectors are commonly used with links:

:link
:visited
:hover
:active

By default, most browsers indicate links by underlining the link text and displaying the text in blue. After you click a link, it becomes a visited link, and the text and underline appear in purple. CSS allows you more variety in choosing the appearance of links and visited links as well. In addition, CSS can add "mouse over" (rollover) effects, so that when the user passes the mouse pointer over a link, the link text can appear in a different color, background color, or font.

All of the following pseudo-class selectors are used together with the anchor element selector. The order of the pseudo-classes does matter. You don't have to use all of these pseudo-class selectors, but you must use them in the following order:

- **:link** is used to change the appearance of unvisited link text. You want your unvisited links to stand out. Use bright colors for unvisited links.
- **:visited** is used to change the appearance of the visited link text. You *don't* want your visited links to stand out, so use darker colors for visited links and remove text decoration.

> Tip
>
> Do not increase the font size in a rollover by more than 2pts. Using a larger font size is distracting.

> Tip
>
> To remember the correct order of these pseudo-class selectors, use the mnemonic "**love-ha**te relationship."

- **:hover** is used to change the appearance of the link when the user passes the mouse pointer over the link.
- **:active** is used to change the appearance of the link text when the user clicks the link.

InSight | **Clearing the Browser History**

In Firefox, the :visited pseudo-class will not work unless the Remember visited pages for the last __ days text box has a value greater than 0. (Look for this setting in the Options dialog box.)

The :visited pseudo-class selector works fine in Internet Explorer even if the Days to keep pages in history setting in the Options dialog box has a value of zero.

If you are testing visited links and want to refresh the screen, in Internet Explorer or Firefox, clear or delete the browsing history, and then refresh the window.

Understanding Specificity and Pseudo-Class Selectors

Specificity in pseudo-classes does matter. In your style sheets, style the anchor element first, and then style the four pseudo-class selectors *in this order*:

a
a:link
a:visited
a:hover
a:active

Because of specificity, any properties that you use in the anchor element should also be styled in any pseudo-class you create.

In styling your links, you use the anchor element selector to style anchor links. If you do not style the :link pseudo-class selector as well, all links will appear as you styled the anchor element. If you have styled both the anchor element and the a:link pseudo-class selector, then your anchor links will appear differently from all other links on the Web page. For example, in the following code, link text to anchors will appear in blue; all other link text on the page will appear in green:

```
a {
color: blue; }

a:link {
color: green; }
```

> **Tip**
>
> You can apply the a:hover pseudo-class to any block-level element.

Michael wants the links in the sidebar to be displayed differently from the other links on the page. Michael also wants to know if there is an easy way to display the links vertically rather than horizontally without having to enter code for each line. He knows he can make an unordered list for the links, or he could use the <p> </p> tags and several <br /> tags to format the links. However, he would like to avoid all that coding. You can use the display property and assign it a value of *block*. Doing so will arrange the links vertically without the need to create a list or insert paragraph and break tags.

Michael has decided to style the links in the sidebar using several of the pseudo-class selectors. You will show him how to code the :link and :visited pseudo-class selectors now.

To code the :link and :visited pseudo-class selectors:

▶ **1.** Make sure the FlightNew HTML file is open in Notepad.

▶ **2.** On a blank line below the code to style the anchor element, type the following code, which is also shown in red in Figure 6-24.

```
#sidebar a:link {
font-size: 12pt;
color: white;
background-color: brown;
padding: .5em;
text-align: center;
font-weight: bold;
display: block; }

#sidebar a:visited {
font-size: 12pt;
padding: .5em;
color: black;
text-decoration: none;
display: block; }
```

Code to style the :link pseudo-class selector and the :visited pseudo-class selector ◀ **Figure 6-24**

```
a {
font-weight: bold;
font-size: 12pt;
color: navy; }

#sidebar a:link {
font-size: 12pt;
color: white;
background-color: brown;        code to format
padding: .5em;                  the link text
text-align: center;
font-weight: bold;
display: block; }

#sidebar a:visited {
font-size: 12pt;
padding: .5em;                  code to format
color: black;                   visited links
text-decoration: none;
display: block; }
```

▶ **3.** Save the FlightNew HTML file.

▶ **4.** Refresh the FlightNew Web page in your browser, and then compare it to Figure 6-25 to verify that you have correctly set the style for the links in the sidebar. The link for Air Taxi, which you clicked earlier, should appear as a visited link.

▶ **5.** Follow the instructions in the "Clearing the Browser History" Insight to clear your browser history. (Make sure that the choice for Days to keep pages in history is set to 0.)

Figure 6-25	New styles reflected on the Web page

links now appear in a block as centered, bold, and white text

About Us

Air Taxi

Cargo

Information

Reservations

Are You Successful?

You know you are when you fly *Success Airlines*. We offer the finest on-demand service for the busiest and most successful executives in the country along the East Coast corridor, from Canada to Florida and the Caribbean. Pass your mouse over the map of our renovated New York terminal to see its new features.

Service

We have unparalleled in-flight service. Our jets seat from 6 to 16 passengers. Our flight attendants will cater to your every need. First-class dining is all we offer. Your meals are prepared either just prior to flight or on board. We will arrange to follow any special dietary principles or restrictions you may have.

Safety

Success Airlines flies the newest fleet of small jet aircraft of any airline. All of our planes are TechJSX jet aircraft manufactured within the last five years. Equipment is fully state-of-the-art. Our pilots have been hand-picked from among the best of commercial and private air carriers. Each pilot has more than 15 years of full-time flying experience with the airline industry, and all our pilots are recertified at least once a year.

Productivity

Michael wants to know if it is possible to create an interesting effect when the user passes the mouse pointer over a link in the sidebar. You will show Michael how to code the a:hover pseudo-class selector. The selector will be styled so that the font size is increased, the background color will change to black, and a white, solid, thin border will be displayed around the link text.

To code the a:hover pseudo-class selector

1. Make sure the FlightNew HTML file is open in Notepad.

2. On a blank line below the code to style the a:visited pseudo-class, type the following code to style the a:hover pseudo-class, which is also shown in red in Figure 6-26.

```
#sidebar a:hover {
font-size: 14pt;
font-weight: bold;
color: gold;
background-color: black;
text-decoration: underline;
border: white solid thin; }
```

Code to style the :hover pseudo-class selector ◀ **Figure 6-26**

```
#sidebar a:hover {
font-size: 14pt;
font-weight: bold;
color: gold;
background-color: black;
text-decoration: underline;
border: white solid thin; }

</style>
</head>
```

code to change the appearance of the links when you point to them

▶ **3.** Save the FlightNew HTML file.

▶ **4.** Refresh the FlightNew Web page in your browser.

▶ **5.** Point to each of the links to verify that the :hover pseudo-class is working, as is shown for the first link in Figure 6-27.

Revised sidebar displayed on the Web page ◀ **Figure 6-27**

hand pointer indicates you are pointing to a link

Tip

A group of links to other pages or sites is often called a *navigation bar*.

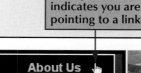

About Us
Air Taxi
Cargo
Information
Reservations

Succe$$ Airlines

Are You Successful?

You know you are when you fly *Success Airlines*. We offer the finest on-demand service for the busiest and most successful executives in the country along the East Coast corridor, from Canada to Florida and the Caribbean. Pass your mouse over the map of our renovated New York terminal to see its new features.

Service

We have unparalleled in-flight service. Our jets seat from 6 to 16 passengers. Our flight attendants will cater to your every need. First-class dining is all we offer. Your meals are prepared either just prior to flight or on board. We will arrange to follow any special dietary principles or restrictions you may have.

Safety

Success Airlines flies the newest fleet of small jet aircraft of any airline. All of our planes are TechJSX jet aircraft manufactured within the last five years. Equipment is fully state-of-the-art. Our pilots have been hand-picked from among the best of commercial and private air carriers. Each pilot has more than 15 years of full-time flying experience with the airline industry, and all our pilots are recertified at least once a year.

Productivity

Setting the Style for the Main Document Window

You have completed work on the sidebar. Now you want to turn your attention to the main window. The main window will also float left so that it is displayed alongside the sidebar. You will show Michael how to include the code for the main ID selector now.

To create the main ID selector:

▶ **1.** Make sure the FlightNew HTML file is open in Notepad.

▶ **2.** On a blank line after #sidebar a:hover code, type the following code to set the style for the main ID selector, which is also shown in red in Figure 6-28.

```
#main {
float: left;
width: 510px;
padding: 1em;
font-size: 11pt;
font-family: arial,helvetica,sans-serif;
color: black;
background-color: white;
border-left: navy solid 1em;
border-right: navy solid 1em;
background-color: wheat;
text-align: left; }
```

Figure 6-28 ▶ **Code for the main ID selector**

```
#main {
float: left;
width: 510px;
padding: 1em;
font-size: 11pt;
font-family: arial,helvetica,sans-serif;
color: black;
background-color: white;
border-left: navy solid 1em;
border-right: navy solid 1em;
background-color: wheat;
text-align: left; }

</style>
```

Now that the main ID selector has been created, you need to apply the main ID selector. You will show Michael how to do so. You also need to code the end </div> tag to indicate where the sidebar division will end. You will show Michael where to code this tag.

To apply the main ID selector:

▶ **1.** On a blank line above the code for Jet.gif, the Success Airlines logo image, type the following code, which is also shown in red in Figure 6-29.

```
<div id="main">
```

Code to apply the main ID selector ◄ Figure 6-29

```
<img src="attendant.jpg" alt="image of one of Success Airlines' flight attendants" width="200"
height="300" />
</div>
<div id="main">
<p><img src="jet.gif" alt="Success Airlines logo" width="440" height="100" /></p>
```

▶ **2.** On a blank line above the container end </div> tag near the bottom of the page, type the following code, which is also shown in red in Figure 6-30.

```
</div>
```

Code for the end </div> tag for the main selector ◄ Figure 6-30

```
<p><a href="#top">Back to Top</a></p>
</div>
</div>
```

▶ **3.** Save FlightNew.

▶ **4.** Refresh the FlightNew Web page in your browser, and then compare it to Figure 6-31 to verify that the main window has the correct style.

The main ID selector in the browser ◄ Figure 6-31

black text on a wheat background

About Us
Air Taxi
Cargo
Information
Reservations

Succe$$ Airlines

Are You Successful?◄

You know you are when you fly *Success Airlines*. We offer the finest on-demand service for the busiest and most successful executives in the country along the East Coast corridor, from Canada to Florida and the Caribbean. Pass your mouse over the map of our renovated New York terminal to see its new features.

Service

We have unparalleled in-flight service. Our jets seat from 6 to 16 passengers. Our flight attendants will cater to your every need. First-class dining is all we offer. Your meals are prepared either just prior to flight or on board. We will arrange to follow any special dietary principles or restrictions you may have.

Safety

Success Airlines flies the newest fleet of small jet aircraft of any airline. All of our planes are TechJSX jet aircraft manufactured within the last five years. Equipment is fully state-of-the-art. Our pilots have been hand-picked from among the best of commercial and private air carriers. Each pilot has more than 15 years of full-time flying experience with the airline industry, and all our pilots are recertified at least once a year.

Michael would also like to set the style for the h3 heading and the em elements in the main document window to draw more attention to these formatting elements. He would like h3 headings to appear in navy. He would like em elements to appear in brown and also be bold. You will show Michael how to do so now.

To style the h3 headings and the em elements:

▶ **1.** Make sure the FlightNew HTML file is open in Notepad.

▶ **2.** On a blank line after the main ID selector code, type the following code to style the h3 headings and em elements, which is also shown in red in Figure 6-32.

```
h3 {
color: navy; }

em {
color: brown;
font-weight: bold; }
```

Figure 6-32 ▶ **Code to set the style of the h3 and em selectors**

```
text-align: left; }

h3 {
color: navy; }

em {
color: brown;
font-weight: bold; }

</style>
```

▶ **3.** Save the FlightNew HTML file.

▶ **4.** Refresh the FlightNew Web page in your browser, and then compare it to Figure 6-33 to verify that h3 headings appear in navy and em elements appear in brown and are bold.

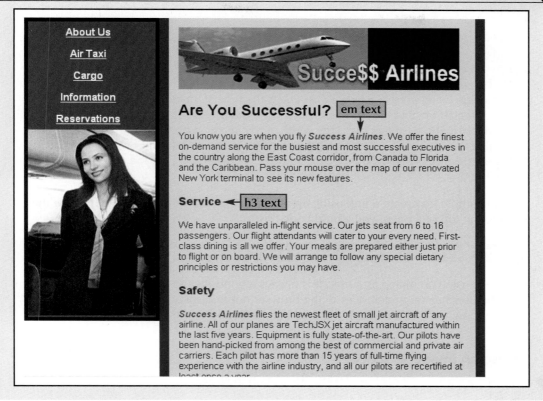

So far, you have used text as a link. You can also use an image as a link. Later, you will also see that a single image can link to several locations.

Using Images with Links

Instead of link text, you could use images with your links. Images such as arrows and pointers are commonly used as navigational icons. A graphic image, such as an upward-pointing or left-pointing arrow, often appears at the bottom of a Web page to serve as a link back to the top of the page, the previous page, or the home page. Any text or image code that falls between the start anchor tag and the end anchor tag can be clicked and used as a link in the browser.

Reference Window | **Using an Image as a Link**

- To use an image as a link, use the following code:
  ```
  <a href="filename.htm"><img src="imagename.filetype"
  alt="alternatetext" width="widthvalue"
  height="heightvalue">linktext</a>
  ```
  where <a is the start anchor tag, filename.htm is the name of the file you are linking to, img is the image element, src is the source attribute, imagename is the file name of the image being used as a link, filetype is the type of image file (such as .jpg or .gif), alt is the alt attribute, alternatetext is the description of the image, width is the width attribute, widthvalue is the width of the image in pixels, height is the height attribute, heightvalue is the height of the image in pixels, linktext is the text that the user will click to activate the link, and </a> is the end anchor tag.

For example, to create a link using an image that would link from the bottom of the page to the top of a page, you would code this:

```
<a href="#top"><img src="uparrow.jpg" alt="image of arrow pointing
upwards" width="40" height="40" />Back to Top</a>
```

If you are using an image as a link, it is always a good idea to have some link text, just in case the user has set preferences in the browser not to display images. You will show Michael how to insert an image that will link to the top of the page.

To use an image as a link:

1. Make sure the FlightNew HTML file is open in Notepad.

2. In the code for the link to the top of the page, position the insertion point to the right of the angle bracket (>) that follows the anchor code. Type the following code shown in bold, which is also shown in red in Figure 6-34.

   ```
   <p><a href="#top"><img src="uparrow.jpg" alt="image of arrow
   pointing upwards" width="40" height="40" />Back to Top</a></p>
   ```

Figure 6-34 **Code for the uparrow image used in the link to the anchor named top**

```
<p><a href="http://www.weather.com">Latest Weather</a></p>

<p><a href="#top"><img src="uparrow.jpg" alt="image of arrow pointing upwards" width="40"
height="40" />Back to Top</a></p>
</div>
</div>
```

3. Save the FlightNew HTML file.

4. Refresh the FlightNew Web page in your browser, and then compare it to Figure 6-35 to verify that the Uparrow image has now been displayed.

5. Click the image to verify that the link back to the top of the page works correctly.

carriers. Each pilot has more than 15 years of full-time flying experience with the airline industry, and all our pilots are recertified at least once a year.

Productivity

Think it's not cost-effective to fly Success Airlines? Think about all the lost time wasted in traveling to a busy airport and dealing with lengthy security delays. As a frequent flyer with *Success Airlines*, you are security-vetted once a year. You arrive at our terminal, get on the plane, and take off. We have our own private terminals. Your baggage travels on board with you or on the flight itself. Your baggage never gets lost or misrouted. All of our seats fully recline, so you can sleep comfortably on longer flights. Whether you choose to do paperwork, read, or get some sleep, you'll be ready to go for that upcoming executive meeting. You'll be at your peak performance because you traveled with *Success Airlines*.

Convenience

We can arrange for limousine service to bring you to the airport and take you back to your office or residence. Ride in comfort for your entire trip, from door to door. Now that's the way to do business!

Contact us today so you can join our **Air Taxi Club** for even better service. We'll fly you from your heliport to ours.

Latest Weather

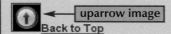 uparrow image
Back to Top

Now that you have shown Michael how to use an image as a link, you will show him how to troubleshoot typical problems that come from using an image as a link.

Setting the Border Style for an Image Used as a Link

When an image is used as a link, by default, a 1-pixel blue border is created around the image. Should you choose to do so, you can remove the blue border by creating a style for the img element selector. Use the border-width property and set its value to 0, as shown in the following dependent class for the img element selector code:

```
img.align {
border-width: 0; }
```

Working with White Space and Images

By default, no white space appears between an image and text that appears alongside an image. To create some white space between the text and the image, use the margin property and apply white space, as is shown in the following code:

```
img.align {
border-width: 0;
margin-right: 1em;
margin-bottom: 0; }
```

Using the vertical-align Property with Images

By default, the bottom of the image is aligned with a line of text alongside it. You can use the vertical-align property to position the image so that the image is centered vertically. In this instance, use the vertical-align property and assign the value of *middle*.

```
img.align {
border-width: 0;
margin-right: 1em;
margin-bottom: 0;
vertical-align: middle; }
```

Michael has noticed that the arrow image does not have any white space between the image and the link text alongside of the image. He also has noticed that the arrow image is not centered vertically alongside the link text. You will help Michael correct both of those problems. You will style all images on the Web page to have some white space. In addition, because you separately want to style only images that are used as links, you will also show Michael how to create and style a dependent class for the img element selector. You will name the dependent class *align*.

To style the images:

1. Make sure the FlightNew HTML file is open in Notepad.

2. On a blank line after the em element selector code, type the following code, which is also shown in red in Figure 6-36.

```
img {
margin-bottom: 1em;
border-width: 0; }

img.align {
border-width: 0;
margin-right: 1em;
margin-bottom: 0;
vertical-align: middle; }
```

Figure 6-36   **Code to style all images**

```
em {
color: brown;
font-weight: bold; }

img {
margin-bottom: 1em;
border-width: 0; }

img.align {
border-width: 0;
margin-right: 1em;
margin-bottom: 0;
vertical-align: middle; }

</style>
```

Now that the align dependent class has been created, you need to apply the align class to the image code for the Uparrow image. You will show Michael how to do so.

To apply the align dependent class to the Uparrow image:

▶ **1.** Within the code for the Uparrow image, type the following code shown in bold, which is also shown in red in Figure 6-37.

```
<p><a href="#top"><img src="uparrow.jpg" alt="image of arrow
pointing up" width="40" height="40" class="align" />Back to Top</
a></p>
```

Applying the align class ◀ **Figure 6-37**

```
<p><a href="#top"><img src="uparrow.jpg" alt="image of arrow pointing upwards" width="40"
height="40" class="align" />Back to Top</a></p>
```

▶ **2.** Save the FlightNew HTML file.

▶ **3.** Refresh the FlightNew Web page in your browser, and then compare it to Figure 6-38 to verify that the style for the image is correct.

The align class in the browser ◀ **Figure 6-38**

carriers. Each pilot has more than 15 years of full-time flying experience with the airline industry, and all our pilots are recertified at least once a year.

Productivity

Think it's not cost-effective to fly Success Airlines? Think about all the lost time wasted in traveling to a busy airport and dealing with lengthy security delays. As a frequent flyer with *Success Airlines*, you are security-vetted once a year. You arrive at our terminal, get on the plane, and take off. We have our own private terminals. Your baggage travels on board with you or on the flight itself. Your baggage never gets lost or misrouted. All of our seats fully recline, so you can sleep comfortably on longer flights. Whether you choose to do paperwork, read, or get some sleep, you'll be ready to go for that upcoming executive meeting. You'll be at your peak performance because you traveled with *Success Airlines*.

Convenience

We can arrange for limousine service to bring you to the airport and take you back to your office or residence. Ride in comfort for your entire trip, from door to door. Now that's the way to do business!

Contact us today so you can join our **Air Taxi Club** for even better service. We'll fly you from your heliport to ours.

Latest Weather

aligned image → **Back to Top**

If you have many images to show to your Web page visitors, it is neither wise nor practical to try to place all those images on one page. Fortunately, there is a solution. On the referring page, you can use a smaller image—called a thumbnail—that will serve as a link to the larger image on a target page. You will show Michael how to create these types of links now.

Using Thumbnails

Because of the potentially large byte size of an image, it is wise not to have too many large images on a page. Also, a page that has little text and several large images is not very informative or interesting; on the contrary, it looks amateurish.

If you have many images to display (such as a gallery of images), a useful strategy is to have a smaller image, called a **thumbnail** image, on the referring page. The thumbnail image serves as a link to the larger full-size image on the target page. The code on the referring page would be similar to this (note that the values for the width and the height attributes are an appropriately smaller size):

```
<a href="marie.htm"><img src="jacket.gif" width="75"
height="100" />Fashions from Marie</a>
```

Once the reader has opened the page with the full-size image, don't strand your reader. Code a link back to the referring page and code a link to the home page as well.

Creating an E-Mail Link

You probably are familiar with a link at the bottom of a Web page that asks you to contact the Webmaster or to e-mail your comments. The last type of link you will show Michael how to create is an e-mail link. An e-mail link does not link to another location on the same or different Web page. Instead, you use an e-mail link to open e-mail software, such as Microsoft Outlook, so that you can compose and send an e-mail message.

You create an e-mail link by using the *mailto:* protocol. When you use the mailto: protocol, you don't include the http:// protocol.

| Reference Window | **Creating a Link to an E-Mail Address** |

- To create a link to an e-mail address, use:
  `<a href="mailto:`*emailaddress@domainname.suffix*`">`*linktext*`</a>`
  where `<a` is the start anchor tag, `href` is the hypertext reference attribute, `mailto` is the protocol, *emailaddress* is the email address of the recipient, `@` is the @ symbol, *domainname* is the domain name, *suffix* is the suffix, `linktext` is the text that the user will click to activate the link, and `</a>` is the end anchor tag.

E-mail addresses are usually italicized, but they do not have to be. The <address> tag, which italicizes text, is commonly used when creating an e-mail link; however, you can still use the <em> tag if you want to italicize the text in the e-mail address. Note that you do not include a space between the colon in the mailto protocol and the e-mail address. The code for a hypertext link to an e-mail address would look similar to this:

```
<address>Contact us: <a href="mailto:customerservice@sucessairlines.
com">customerservice@sucessairlines.com</a></address>
```

The link text in the e-mail link has the complete e-mail address, rather than a shortened form. You can't assume that the visitor is accessing your site at home or at work and has access to an e-mail client, or program, on the computer. If the user is accessing the Internet at a local library, a hotel, or at school, the e-mail client on the user's computer may be disabled to prevent unauthorized or improper use of e-mail. If the visitor's computer does not have an e-mail client, at least the visitor can make note of the address and send e-mail from a different computer at a later time. You will show Michael how to include an e-mail link. The link will be placed between the link to weather.com and the link to the top of the page. The link also includes an image, and uses the *align* dependent class.

To create an e-mail link:

▶ **1.** Make sure the FlightNew HTML file is open in Notepad.

▶ **2.** On a blank line below the link to weather.com, type the following code to create an e-mail link, which is also shown in red in Figure 6-39.

```
<p><a href="mailto:customerservice@sucessairlines.com"><img
src="email.jpg" class="align" height="40" width="40">Contact
Us</a></p>
```

Code for an e-mail link ◀ Figure 6-39

e-mail address

```
<p><a href="http://www.weather.com">Latest Weather</a></p>

<p><a href="mailto:customerservice@sucessairlines.com"><img src="email.jpg" class="align"
height="40" width="40">Contact Us</a></p>

<p><a href="#top"><img src="uparrow.jpg" alt="image of arrow pointing upwards" width="40"
height="40" class="align" />Back to Top</a></p>
```

e-mail link text

▶ **3.** Save the FlightNew HTML file.

▶ **4.** Refresh the FlightNew Web page in your browser, and then compare it to Figure 6-40 to verify that the link is displayed on the screen.

E-mail link in the browser ◀ Figure 6-40

Productivity

Think it's not cost-effective to fly Success Airlines? Think about all the lost time wasted in traveling to a busy airport and dealing with lengthy security delays. As a frequent flyer with *Success Airlines*, you are security-vetted once a year. You arrive at our terminal, get on the plane, and take off. We have our own private terminals. Your baggage travels on board with you or on the flight itself. Your baggage never gets lost or misrouted. All of our seats fully recline, so you can sleep comfortably on longer flights. Whether you choose to do paperwork, read, or get some sleep, you'll be ready to go for that upcoming executive meeting. You'll be at your peak performance because you traveled with *Success Airlines*.

Convenience

We can arrange for limousine service to bring you to the airport and take you back to your office or residence. Ride in comfort for your entire trip, from door to door. Now that's the way to do business!

Contact us today so you can join our **Air Taxi Club** for even better service. We'll fly you from your heliport to ours.

Latest Weather

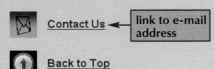 Contact Us ◀ link to e-mail address

Back to Top

▶ **5.** Test the link. When your e-mail program opens and displays a new message window, close the program.

You will now raise an issue of Web courtesy with Michael. When users click a link, they expect to see a different location in the browser. Users should be notified about any links that do not link to different locations in the browser.

Linking to Non-HTML Files

You can link to any file, not just HTML files, such as a Microsoft Word file, an Adobe PDF file, or a multimedia file such as a .wav file or a .swf file. You should always include some text on your page that identifies the file as being one that is not an HTML file. When visitors click a link, they expect to see another HTML page, not a page that may require a download or the installation of a plug-in that's necessary to view the page. In the link to a non-HTML file, include the file extension in the link text so that the visitor will know the link is not to another Web page or Web site, but to a file from another software program, like so:

`View the Word file:` <u>`anniversary.doc`</u>

In this session, you learned that it is possible to style links, just as you would style any other element. There are several pseudo-class selectors that can be used to style links. There are pseudo-classes to style unvisited links and visited links. You can also style links to create a hover effect, which means that the link will change its appearance when the mouse pointer hovers over the link. If you are using an image as a link, you learned that you can remove the border from an image used as a link. You also learned that you can align the image with a line of text alongside it. If you are linking to a file that is not an HTML file, always alert the reader that he or she is not linking to an HTML file.

Review | Session 6.2 Quick Check

1. What "navigational links" should be at the bottom of every page?
2. If you are using an image as a link, what else should you include in case the user has a browser that doesn't support images or has turned off images in his or her User Preferences.
3. Which pseudo-class selector affects the appearance of visited links?
4. Which pseudo-class selector affects the appearance of unvisited links?
5. Which pseudo-class selector affects the appearance of a link when the mouse pointer passes over a link?
6. What is a thumbnail link?
7. What should be put into code on every page used as a thumbnail page?
8. What protocol is used to establish an e-mail link?

Session 6.3

Organizing Files at Your Web Site

So far, the links you have written to other pages are straightforward. The assumption is that the HTML file and the file you are linking to both reside in the same file folder. This assumption is called relative file addressing. A **relative file address** is one where a file is linked in relation to another file at the same Web site and stored in the same folder on the same computer or on the same file server.

However, if the link is to a file on a different file server or at a different Web site, the link must contain an absolute file address, like so: *http://www.ford.com/index.html.* An **absolute file address** specifies the entire directory path to a linked file. For example, if you have stored an HTML file on your computer in a folder named Cities, and you are linking to a page in a folder named Towns, you cannot use this:

```
<a href="seaside.htm">Visit the town of Seaside</a>
```

You must instead use this:

```
<a href="towns/seaside.htm">Visit the town of Seaside</a>
```

If you are trying to manage your files for your personal Web page, it is not a problem to store all your files in the root directory on your hard drive or in a single folder on your hard drive or removable disk. But in the workplace, you might have to manage a site with thousands or tens of thousands of HTML, graphics, video, and sound files. If you placed all of those files in the root directory of the hard drive or in one file folder, it would be quite a challenge to locate and manage those files.

> **Tip**
>
> As a start, place all your image files in a folder named *images*.

Creating Parent and Child Folders

Your hard drive is divided into the root directory, folders, and subfolders. A **parent folder** is a folder that is at least one level higher in the directory structure. A **child folder** is a folder at least one level below the parent folder. If two folders are on the same level, they are referred to as **sibling folders**. Figure 6-41 shows this simple file structure involving a parent folder (Cities) and a child folder (Towns).

Parent folder (Cities) and child folder (Towns) | Figure 6-41

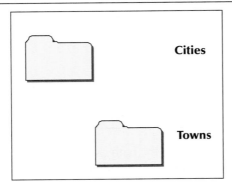

Of course, each folder can also contain some files. Suppose the parent folder (Cities) contains a file named *Miami.htm,* and the child folder (Towns) contains a file named *Seaside.htm.* The file structure would be similar to the one shown in Figure 6-42.

Figure 6-42 ▶ **Files in the Cities and Towns folders**

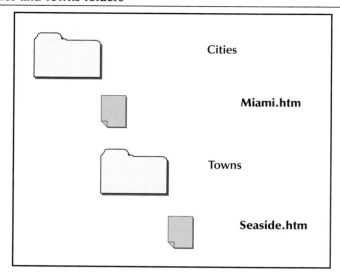

Moving Down One Level in the Directory Structure

Moving down in the directory structure is fairly simple. For example, suppose that in the file *Miami.htm*, you wanted to code a link to the file named *Seaside.htm. Seaside.htm* is in the child folder, which is *one folder down* in the directory structure. See Figure 6-43.

Figure 6-43 ▶ **Linking to a file in a child folder**

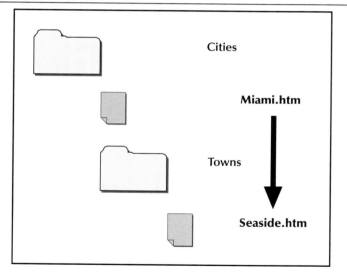

In this instance, you would specify the path as follows: (1) the folder named *Towns*, followed by a slash, and then (2) the file named *Seaside.htm*. You would use the following code for the link:

```
<a href="towns/seaside.htm">A quick tour of Seaside</a>
```

Moving Up One Level in the Directory Structure

Moving up in the directory structure is a different matter. Suppose that in the file named *Seaside.htm* in the *Towns* folder, you wanted to create a link to the file named *Miami.htm* in the *Cities* folder. The file *Miami.htm* is in the parent folder—*one level above* the current folder where *Seaside.htm* is stored. See Figure 6-44.

Linking to a file in a parent folder ◄ Figure 6-44

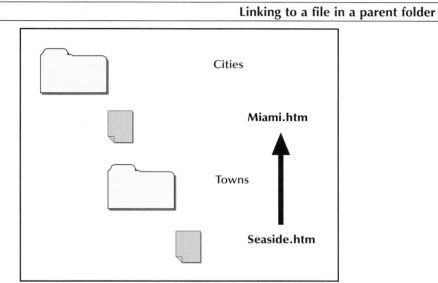

To link to a file that is in a folder one level above the current folder, you have to use the "dot dot" notation (../). You then specify the path to that file. Note the dots and the slash in the path:

```
<a href="../miami.htm">Let's look at Miami</a>
```

Now take it one step further. Add another folder (Hamlets) and another file (Smalltown.htm) to the directory structure, as shown in Figure 6-45.

Figure 6-45 | **Adding another child folder and file to the folder structure**

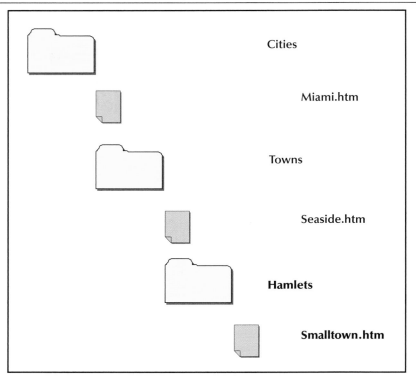

Moving Down Two Levels

Suppose that in the file *Miami.htm* in the *Cities* folder, you also want to link to the file named *Smalltown.htm* in the *Hamlets* folder. You are linking to a file down two levels in the directory structure, as shown in Figure 6-46.

Linking files in child folders | **Figure 6-46**

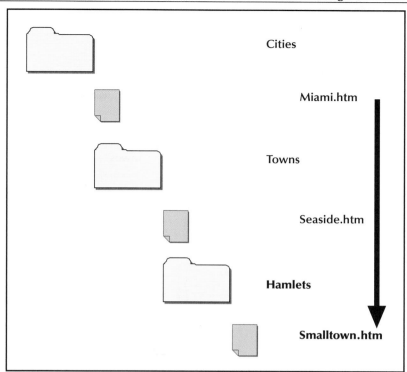

In this instance, the path would be put in code like so:

```
<a href="towns/hamlets/smalltown.htm">The Smalltown hamlet</a>
```

Moving Up Two Levels

Now suppose that in the file named *Smalltown.htm* in the *Hamlets* folder, you want to code a link to *Miami.htm* in the *Cities* folder. As shown in Figure 6-47, you have to go up *two levels*.

Figure 6-47 | **Linking to a file up two levels in the folder structure**

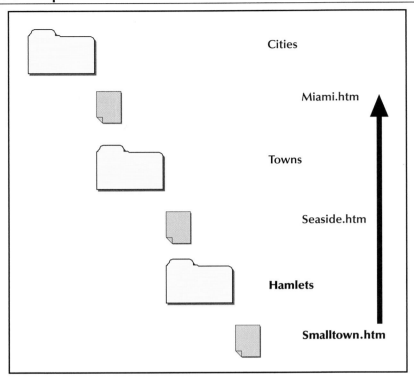

To do so, you code the *double dot* notation, and then specify the path like so:

```
<a href="../../miami.htm">Visit Miami</a>
```

InSight | **Setting the Tab Order for Links**

Computer users, particularly those who use a laptop computer, sometimes rely on using the Tab key to navigate among links. Pressing the Tab key repeatedly will cause the cursor to move from the Address box to the first link on the Web page. By default, the links are prioritized in the order they appear in the HTML code. You can override that sequence and prioritize the links in a different order by setting the Tab index. In the link code, use the tabindex attribute and assign a number as a value. The lower the number, the higher the priority. The code for the tabindex attribute would be like so:

```
<a href="http://www.airboomer.com" tabindex="3">Air Boomer</a>
<a href="http://www.successairlines.com" tabindex="1">Success
Airlines</a>
<a href="http://www.teenairlines.com" tabindex="2">Teen Airlines</a>
```

In the preceding code, when the user presses the Tab key, the focus will first go to the link for Success Airlines. The next time the user presses the Tab key, Teen Airlines will get the focus. The third time the user presses the Tab key, Air Boomer will get the focus. The accesskey attribute can be used together with the tabindex attribute, like so:

```
<a href="http://www.successairlines.com" accesskey="s" tabindex="1">
Success Airlines</a>
```

Depending on the browser and the browser version, pressing the Tab key might not move the cursor from the Address box to the first link. You might first encounter a search box or toolbar options. As such, you might have to press the Tab key several times to have the first link get the focus.

Creating Image Maps

Recall that you can use an image as a link. An **image map** is an image that is divided into sections that serve as two or more links. The areas of the image that are designated to be used as links are called **hotspots**. The image used as the image map can be any image—it doesn't have to be an image of a map, although that is commonly true. Success Airlines is promoting the renovation of its New York terminal and has provided Michael with an image named Terminal.gif, which is a map of the New York City terminal. The image will be divided into three hotspots, each of which will link to different anchors on another page named nyphotos.htm. The hotspots will be for the main concourse, the limousine service, and security.

Your first step is to enter the code for the image, as you normally would, like so:

```
<img src="terminal.gif" alt="map of New York terminal" width="200"
height="340" />
```

Coding the usemap Attribute

After you enter the image source code along with the usual alternate text value and other image attributes and values, you include the **usemap attribute**, which is used solely to identify the name of the image that will be used as the map. The value for the usemap attribute is the name of the image map. You can name the map whatever you want, but it should describe the image. The value of the usemap attribute is preceded by a flag character (#), like so:

```
<img src="terminal.gif" alt="map of New York terminal" width="200"
height="340" usemap="#terminal" />
```

Creating Code for the Image Map

The code for the image map involves two tags, the **<map>** tag and one or more **<area>** tags. The <map> tag is a paired tag; and the end </map> tag will follow all of the coding for the map. The <area> tag is an empty tag, so it ends with the space-slash combination.

Tip

It is good coding practice to place the image map code just above the code for the image map, though it is not required.

Coding the Map Tag

The start <map> tag identifies the name of the image that will be used as a map. The *name* attribute is always used with the start <map> tag. (You could also use the id attribute instead of the name attribute, but the id attribute in this instance is not yet fully supported.) The value of the name attribute is whatever value you gave to the usemap attribute in the <img> tag code.

Although the value (the map name) was preceded by a # symbol in the <img> tag code, the value is not preceded by a # symbol here:

```
<img src="terminal.gif" alt="map of New York terminal" width="200"
height="340" usemap="#terminal" />
<map name="terminal">
```

Coding the Area Tag

One or more <area> tags follow the <map> tag. You can have as many areas as are feasible, given the size of the image.

```
<img src="terminal.gif" alt="map of New York terminal" width="200"
height="340" usemap="#terminal" />
<map name="terminal">
<area
```

The <area> tag has three attributes: *shape, coords,* and *href.*

Determining the Shape

The shape attribute takes one of three values:
    rect
    circle
    poly
    Use *rect* for squares and rectangles, use *circle* for circles and ovals, and use *poly* for any irregular shape (basically, any other shape).
    The first shape used in this image map is a rectangle. To code the shape attribute and its value, you would code this:

```
<img src="terminal.gif" alt="map of New York terminal" width="200"
height="340" usemap="#terminal" />
<map name="terminal">
<area
    shape="rect"
```

Using the coordinates Attribute

The **coordinates attribute** is used to determine what part of your image will be used as a link. Think of your computer screen as a sheet of transparent graph paper with 800 columns across and 600 rows down. Each intersection of a column and a row represents a small box on the screen that can be assigned a coordinate value, such as 45 boxes across and 49 boxes down, which would be expressed as coordinate values of 45,49. The coordinate values for a rectangle indicate the upper left-hand and lower right-hand corners of the rectangle.
    Unfortunately, you can't determine the coordinates by using HTML. However, you can use specialized image map programs such as MapEdit, and you can use mapping utilities in HTML editors such as Dreamweaver, Fireworks, and Photoshop. You could also use Microsoft Paint to determine the coordinates, which is what you will show Michael how to use now.

To start Microsoft Paint:

▶ 1. Click the **Start** button 🪟 on the Windows taskbar.

▶ 2. Point to **All Programs**, and then click **Accessories**.

▶ 3. Click **Paint**. If you were to open the image that Michael has supplied, it would appear in Microsoft Paint as shown in Figure 6-48.

Image map in Microsoft Paint ◀ **Figure 6-48**

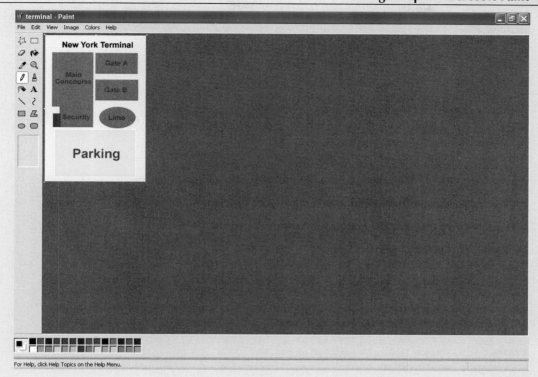

The first hotspot will be of the main concourse. To determine the coordinates for this hotspot, which is a rectangular hotspot, you need the coordinates of the upper-left corner and the coordinates for the lower-right corner. In Paint, you would position the mouse pointer in the upper-left corner of where the rectangle will begin. Look at the status bar in the lower-right portion of the screen. It will show the screen coordinates. In this instance, the coordinates are 16 and 34. Next, you would position the mouse pointer in the lower-right corner of the rectangle. This time the coordinates are 92 and 143.

All the coordinates that fall between those value pairs will become part of a clickable region of the image. In the <area> tag, you must enclose the coordinates within quotation marks and separate each coordinate value by commas:

```
<img src="terminal.gif" alt="map of New York terminal" width="200"
height="340" usemap="#terminal" />
<map name="terminal">
<area
    shape="rect"
    coords="16,34,92,143"
```

Coding the hypertext reference Attribute

The last attribute for the <area> tag is href. The href attribute identifies the link. In this instance, the link is to an anchor on another page that will display information about the main concourse. That page is nyphotos.htm. Enter the href value and then close the <area> tag with the space-slash combination.

```
<img src="terminal.gif" alt="map of New York terminal" width="200"
height="340" usemap="#terminal" />
<map name="terminal">
<area
    shape="rect"
    coords="16,34,92,143"
    href="nyphotos.htm#concourse" />
```

Coding the End Map Tag

After you have entered all the hotspots, close the image map code with the end </map> tag, like so:

```
<img src="terminal.gif" alt="map of New York terminal" width="200"
height="340"
usemap="#terminal" />
<map name="terminal">
<area
    shape="rect"
    coords="16,34,92,143"
    href="nyphotos.htm#concourse" />
</map>
```

You will be coding more hotspots later, but for now, you would like to have Michael include the first hotspot and then test to see if the hotspot works.

Tip

It is good coding practice to include the start <map> tag, its attributes and values, and the end </map> tag at the same time.

To code the rectangular hotspot:

▶ **1.** Make sure the FlightNew HTML file is open in Notepad.

▶ **2.** On a blank line below the code for attendant.jpg, and above the end </div> tag, type the following code to begin creating the image map. Figure 6-49 also shows this code in red.

```
<img src="terminal.gif" alt="map of New York terminal" width="200"
height="340" usemap="#terminal" />
<map name="terminal">
<area
    shape="rect"
    coords="16,34,92,143"
    href="nyphotos.htm#concourse" />
</map>
```

Figure 6-49	Initial code for the image map and the rect shape

```
<img src="attendant.jpg" alt="image of one of Success Airlines flight attendants" width="200"
height="300" />
<img src="terminal.gif" alt="map of New York terminal" width="200" height="340"        code for
usemap="#terminal" />                                                                    the image

<map name="terminal">
<area
    shape="rect"                                              code for
    coords="16,34,92,143"                                     the map
    href="nyphotos.htm#concourse" />
</map>
</div>
```

▶ **3.** Save the FlightNew HTML file.

▶ **4.** Refresh the FlightNew Web page in your browser, and then compare it to Figure 6-50 to verify that the image map is now displayed.

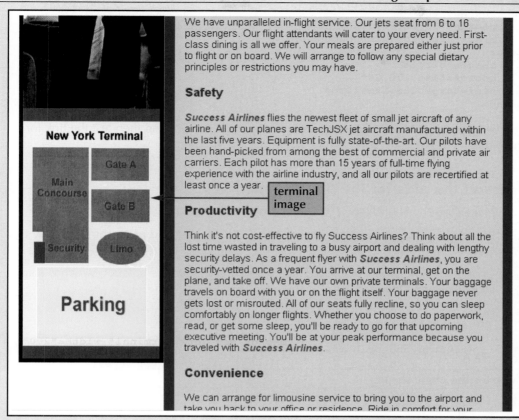

> **5.** Pass the mouse pointer over **Main Concourse** in the image map.

> **6.** Test the link. Then click the **Back** button (or the appropriate tab) in your browser to return to the FlightNew page.

Now that you have shown Michael how to code a rectangular hotspot, you will show him how to code a circle hotspot. The coordinate values for a circle are determined in a different manner from determining the coordinate values for a rectangle.

Creating Code for the Circle Hotspot

You include as many <area> tags as you want to have links. If you had more hotspots to create, you would just keep adding more <area> tags, which is what you will do here. You next want to create a hotspot for the limousine service. That shape is a circle. For a circle, the coordinate values designate the center of the circle and the size of its radius.

To determine the coordinate values for a circle, in Microsoft Paint, you first click the center of the circle and note the coordinate values, which in this instance are 145 and 170. Then you drag straight up to the edge of the circle. This time the coordinate values for the edge of the circle are now 145 and 146. It is the difference between that last coordinate value that represents the size of the radius, which in this instance is the difference between the coordinates 170 and 146. The difference between those two numbers is 24. The coordinate values for this circle are 145,170,24.

```
<img src="terminal.gif" alt="map of New York terminal" width="200"
height="340" usemap="#terminal" />
<map name="terminal">
<area
    shape="rect"
    coords="16,34,92,143"
    href="nyphotos.htm#concourse" />
<area
    shape="circle"
    coords="145,170,24"
    href="nyphotos.htm#limo" />
</map>
```

You will now show Michael how to include the circle hotspot and then test the link for the circle.

To insert the code for the circle hotspot:

▶ **1.** Make sure the FlightNew HTML file is open in Notepad.

▶ **2.** Position the insertion point before the end </map> tag and press the **Enter** key to create a new line.

▶ **3.** On a blank line, type the following code to create the circle hotspot, which is also shown in red in Figure 6-51.

```
<area
    shape="circle"
    coords="145,170,24"
    href="nyphotos.htm#limo" />
```

Figure 6-51	Code for the circle shape

```
<map name="terminal">
<area
    shape="rect"
    coords="16,34,92,143"
    href="nyphotos.htm#concourse" />
<area
    shape="circle"              ← sets the link for
    coords="145,170,24"            the Limo circle
    href="nyphotos.htm#limo" />
</map>
</div>
```

▶ **4.** Save the FlightNew HTML file.

▶ **5.** Refresh the FlightNew Web page in your browser.

▶ **6.** Pass the mouse pointer over the **Limo** circle in the image map.

▶ **7.** Test the link. Then click the **Back** button (or the appropriate tab) in your browser to return to the FlightNew page.

There is only one more shape to code. The last shape will be an irregular shape, which is a polygon.

Creating Code for the Polygon Hotspot

All other shapes are polygons, and the coordinate values represent each corner of the polygon. A polygon, therefore, will have many coordinate values depending on the level of detail and accuracy you want to have. The security area hotspot is a polygon.

```
<img src="terminal.gif" alt="map of New York terminal" width="200"
height="340" usemap="#terminal" />
<map name="terminal">
<area
    shape="rect"
    coords="16,34,92,143"
    href="nyphotos.htm#concourse" />
<area
    shape="circle"
    coords="145,170,24"
    href="nyphotos.htm#limo" />
<area
    shape="poly"
    coords="29,147,30,160,16,162,16,188,93,187,96,145"
    href="nyphotos.htm#security" />
</map>
```

You will now show Michael how to enter the code for the polygon hotspot.

Tip

Don't enter too large a string of coordinate values when you are creating a polygon shape. You are defining the polygon shape in general, not in exact detail.

To include the polygon hotspot:

▶ 1. Make sure the FlightNew HTML file is open in Notepad.

▶ 2. Position the insertion point before the end </map> tag and press the **Enter** key to create a new line.

▶ 3. On a blank line, type the following code to create the polygon hotspot, which is also shown in red in Figure 6-52.

```
<area
    shape="poly"
    coords="29,147,30,160,16,162,16,188,93,187,96,145"
    href="nyphotos.htm#security" />
```

Code for the polygon shape ◀ **Figure 6-52**

```
<area
    shape="circle"
    coords="145,170,24"
    href="nyphotos.htm#limo" />
<area
    shape="poly"
    coords="29,147,30,160,16,162,16,188,93,187,96,145"   ◀── sets the link for the
    href="nyphotos.htm#security" />                           security shape
</map>
```

▶ 4. Save the FlightNew HTML file.

▶ 5. Refresh the FlightNew Web page in your browser.

▶ 6. Pass the mouse pointer over the **Security** polygon in the image map.

▶ 7. Test the link. Then click the **Back** button (or the appropriate tab) in your browser to display the FlightNew page.

Michael notices that the sidebar column is not the same height as the main column. He would like to see the two columns to be of approximately the same height. You will show Michael how to add an image below the image map so that the columns are approximately the same height. The image will be that of a young, successful woman who is using the limousine service to arrive at the Success Airlines terminal.

To insert the code for the sidebar image:

▶ **1.** Make sure the FlightNew HTML file is open in Notepad.

▶ **2.** Position the insertion point below the end </map> tag and, if necessary, press the **Enter** key to create a new line.

▶ **3.** On a blank line, type the following code to insert the code for the image, which is also shown in red in Figure 6-53.

```
<img src="arrival.jpg" alt="image of young, successful woman
arriving in limo" width="200" height="310" />
```

Figure 6-53	Code for arrival.jpg

```
</map>
<img src="arrival.jpg" alt="image of young, successful woman arriving in limo" width="200"
height="310" />
</div>
```

▶ **4.** Save the FlightNew HTML file.

▶ **5.** Refresh the FlightNew Web page file in your browser, and then compare it to Figure 6-54 to verify that the image of the limo passenger is now displayed.

Figure 6-54	Arrival.jpg image in the browser

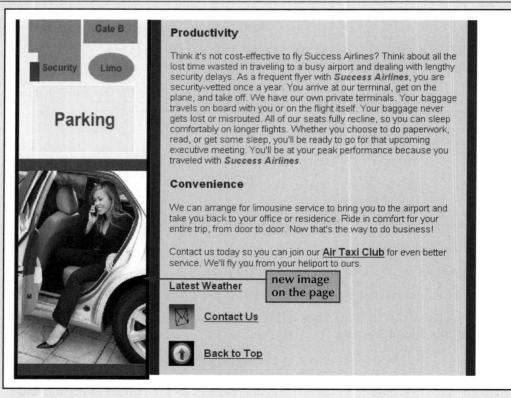

Michael would like the background color to be navy, rather than white. You will show him how to make this change to the document.

To change the background color:

▶ **1.** Make sure the FlightNew HTML file is open in Notepad.

▶ **2.** Position the insertion point before the } tag in the body element selector.

▶ **3.** Press the **Enter** key to insert a new line.

▶ **4.** On the new blank line, type the following bold code to insert the code to change the background color for the page, which is also shown in red in Figure 6-55.

```
body {
font-family: arial,helvetica,sans-serif;
background-color: navy; }
```

Code for the background color ◀ Figure 6-55

```
body {
font-family: arial,helvetica,sans-serif;
background-color: navy; }

#container {
```

▶ **5.** Save the FlightNew HTML file.

▶ **6.** Refresh the FlightNew Web page file in your browser, and then compare it to Figure 6-56 to verify the background color is now navy.

Revised FlightNew Web page in the browser ◀ Figure 6-56

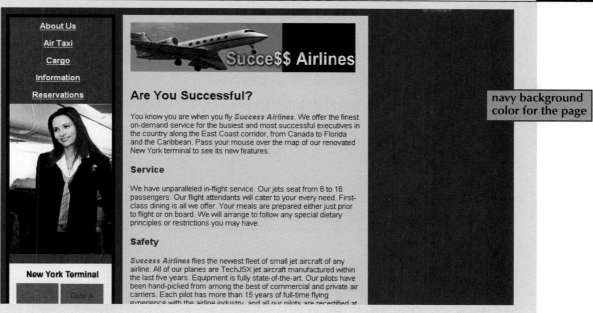

The last change that Michael wants to make is to center the document on the page. To do this, you will show Michael how to enter the code for an independent style, and then apply the independent style.

To insert the code for the independent style:

1. Make sure the FlightNew HTML file is open in Notepad.

2. Position the insertion point after the code to set the style for the align dependent class. Press the **Enter** key to create a new line.

3. On the new blank line, type the following code, which is also shown in red in Figure 6-57.

```
.center {
text-align: center; }
```

Figure 6-57	Creating an independent style for centering the document

```
img.align {
border-width: 0;
margin-right: 1em;
margin-bottom: 0;
vertical-align: middle; }

.center {
text-align: center; }

</style>
</head>
```

4. Save the FlightNew HTML file.

Now you will show Michael how to apply the center independent style.

To insert the code for the center independent style:

1. Make sure the FlightNew HTML file is open in Notepad.

2. Position the insertion point after the start <body> tag. Press the **Enter** key to create a new line.

3. On the new blank line, type the following code, which is also shown in red in Figure 6-58.

```
<div class="center">
```

Figure 6-58	Applying the center independent style

```
</style>
</head>
<a id="top"></a>
<body>
<div class="center">
<div id="container">
<div id="sidebar">
```

4. Position the insertion point before the end </body> tag.

5. Press the **Enter** key to create a new line.

6. On the new blank line, type the following code, which is also shown in red in Figure 6-59.

```
</div>
```

```
<p><a href="#top"><img src="uparrow.jpg" alt="image of arrow pointing upwards" width="40"
height="40" class="align" />Back to Top</a></p>
</div>
</div>
</div>
</body>
</html>
```

7. Save the FlightNew HTML file, and then compare it to Figure 6-60 to view the completed FlightNew Web page.

About Us

Air Taxi

Cargo

Information

Reservations

New York Terminal

Gate A

Main Concourse

Gate B

Security   Limo

Parking

Succe$$ Airlines

Are You Successful?

You know you are when you fly *Success Airlines*. We offer the finest on-demand service for the busiest and most successful executives in the country along the East Coast corridor, from Canada to Florida and the Caribbean. Pass your mouse over the map of our renovated New York terminal to see its new features.

Service

We have unparalleled in-flight service. Our jets seat from 6 to 16 passengers. Our flight attendants will cater to your every need. First-class dining is all we offer. Your meals are prepared either just prior to flight or on board. We will arrange to follow any special dietary principles or restrictions you may have.

Safety

Success Airlines flies the newest fleet of small jet aircraft of any airline. All of our planes are TechJSX jet aircraft manufactured within the last five years. Equipment is fully state-of-the-art. Our pilots have been hand-picked from among the best of commercial and private air carriers. Each pilot has more than 15 years of full-time flying experience with the airline industry, and all our pilots are recertified at least once a year.

Productivity

Think it's not cost-effective to fly Success Airlines? Think about all the lost time wasted in traveling to a busy airport and dealing with lengthy security delays. As a frequent flyer with *Success Airlines*, you are security-vetted once a year. You arrive at our terminal, get on the plane, and take off. We have our own private terminals. Your baggage travels on board with you or on the flight itself. Your baggage never gets lost or misrouted. All of our seats fully recline, so you can sleep comfortably on longer flights. Whether you choose to do paperwork, read, or get some sleep, you'll be ready to go for that upcoming executive meeting. You'll be at your peak performance because you traveled with *Success Airlines*.

Convenience

We can arrange for limousine service to bring you to the airport and take you back to your office or residence. Ride in comfort for your entire trip, from door to door. Now that's the way to do business!

Contact us today so you can join our **Air Taxi Club** for even better service. We'll fly you from your heliport to ours.

Latest Weather

 Contact Us

 Back to Top

▶ **8.** Close Notepad and close your browser.

In this session, you learned about absolute and relative links. To link to a file in a different folder, you must specify the path to that file. An image map uses a single image as the source for several links. Any image may be the source of an image map. A hotspot is an area of an image that serves as a link. A hotspot can be one of three general shapes—a rectangle, a circle, and a polygon, which is any shape other than a rectangle or a circle.

Review | **Session 6.3 Quick Check**

1. What tag is used to declare an image to be used as an image map?
2. What tag determines what part of an image will be used as a link?
3. What are the three values for the shape attribute?
4. What attribute determines the coordinates for the link?
5. How do you determine what the coordinates are?
6. If the shape of the area you want to define as a hotspot is a square, which value for the shape attribute would you use?
7. If the shape of the area you want to define as a hotspot is an irregular shape, which value for the shape attribute would you use?
8. If the shape of the area you want to define as a hotspot is oval, which value for the shape attribute would you use?

Review | **Tutorial Summary**

An anchor is a particular location on a Web page. The <a> tag (the anchor tag) is used for both anchors and links. The id attribute is used to give an anchor a name. Links can be made to an anchor on the same page, a different page, an anchor on a different page, a different Web site, or an e-mail address. The href attribute and its value specifies the target of a link. The referring page is the page with links to another page. The target page is the page that will be displayed when the user clicks a link in the referring page. If you are linking to another Web site, you must include the complete URL of that Web site as the value for the href attribute. A thumbnail is a smaller version of a much larger image. Use the mailto: protocol to establish an e-mail link. The pseudo-class selectors used with the anchor tag are :link, :visited, :hover, and :active. A hotspot is an area of an image that is used as a link. The usemap attribute is used to declare an image for use as a map. The <map> tag identifies the name of the image to be used. The <area> tag defines the general area of an image that can be used for links. The shape attribute takes one of three values: rect, circle, or poly. The coords attribute and its values specify the exact coordinates for the link. The coordinate values cannot be obtained within HTML; they must be obtained from graphics software or a graphical Web editor.

Key Terms

<area> tag
<map> tag
absolute file address
access key
accesskey attribute
anchor
child folder
client computer
coordinates attribute
file server
hotspot
hypertext reference
    attribute

hypertext transfer
    protocol (HTTP)
id attribute
image map
link
link text
packet
parent folder
placeholder character
placeholder page
protocol
pseudo-class selector

referring page
relative file address
sibling folder
suffix
target page
TCP/IP (Transmission Con-
    trol Protocol/Internet
    Protocol)
thumbnail
Uniform Resource
    Locator (URL)
usemap attribute

| Practice | **Review Assignments** |

Take time to practice the skills you learned in the tutorial using the same case scenario.

Data Files needed for this Review Assignment: Taxi.htm, Copters.htm, Copter.jpg, Hanger.jpg, and Pad.jpg

In addition to its charter jet services, Air Success runs a profitable helicopter taxi service. You have been asked to develop a Web Page that lists the features of the Air Success Air Taxi service. You will use an image that will serve as a link to another page that features larger photos of the types of helicopters that the Success Air Taxi service provides for its customers. Complete the following steps:

1. Use Notepad to open the **Taxi.htm** file located in your Tutorial.06\Review folder included with your Data Files. Save this file as **TaxiNew.htm** in the same folder.
2. You will be creating an embedded style sheet. In the head area below the page title, enter the code for the start <style> and the end </style> tags. In the start <style> tag, include the **media** attribute with a value of **screen**.
3. Below the start <style> tag, insert a comment that includes your first and last name as the author and today's date.
4. Set the style for the body to have a background color of wheat and to display the text in Verdana, a sans serif font.
5. Set the style for the <img> element selector to have an orange border with a border width of 10px.
6. Create an ID selector named **sidebar**. Set the style for this selector to float left, have a width of 210px, a height of 750px, and a background color of navy.
7. Create an ID selector named **main**. Set the style for this selector to display text in navy with a margin on the left of 250px.
8. Set the style for the h1 element selector to display text in Lucida calligraphy, a serif font. The text should be centered.
9. Set the style for the ul element selector so that bullets are displayed as squares and the position of the bullets is inside, rather than outside.
10. Set the style for the anchor element selector to display links in black, bold, and italic text.
11. On a blank line just above the start <body> tag, insert the code for an anchor with an ID named **top.**
12. Just below the start <body> tag, insert the code for a link to **Copters.htm**. The image Copter.jpg is used as the link. For the image's alternate text, use the words **image of helicopter icon**. The image has a width of 191px and a height of 247px.
13. On a blank line just above the code that links to the Copters HTML file, insert the code for a start <div> tag and apply the sidebar ID selector.
14. On a blank line below the code that links to the Copters HTML file, insert the code for an end </div> tag.
15. On a blank line above the h1 heading, "Success Airlines Air Taxi Services," insert the code for a start <div> tag and apply the main ID selector.
16. Just above the end </body> tag, insert the code for an end </div> tag.
17. On a blank line below the link to the FlightNew HTML file and within <p></p> tags, insert the code to link to the anchor named top. The link text should be **Back to Top.**
18. Save your TaxiNew HTML document, and then open it in your browser. The document should be similar to the one shown in Figure 6-61.

Figure 6-61

Success Airlines Air Taxi Services

Air Taxi for Routine or Urgent Business

We have regularly-scheduled flights from heliports in all the cities we serve. If you need an air taxi for an important business meeting within 100 miles of the heliport, we can make all flight arrangements for you.

We Offer:

- Affordable same-day charter service for recreation or business meetings.
- Flexible flight schedules. You arrange the drop-off and pick-up times for charter flights.
- Vetted security. Your identity is checked using your special Air Taxi ID. Our biometric scanners will handle your security issues in seconds, not hours, as it would be at a major regional or local airport.
- Flights with meal services and flight attendant service. These services are not available on flights under 60 minutes unless special arrangements are made at least one day in advance.

Private Charters for Your Business Needs

- Business meetings
- Sports events
- Vacation trips
- Private events
- Private parties
- Official corporate trips for groups

Join the Air Taxi Club

- Use Success Airlines Air Taxi to get you to the airport
- You'll arrive at the Air Success heliport
- Use Success Airlines Air Taxi to fly you from the airport

Home

Back to Top

19. Test all links.
20. Close all open windows.
21. Submit the results of the preceding steps to your instructor, either in printed or electronic form, as requested.

Apply | Case Problem 1

Use the skills you learned in the tutorial to create a Web page for a real estate firm.

Data Files needed for this Case Problem: Bath1.jpg, Bath2.jpg, Bed1.jpg, Bed2.jpg, Brad.gif, Bradford.htm, Ken.gif, Kensington.htm, Kit1.jpg, Kit2.jpg, Real.gif, and Real.htm

Real Estates   Real Estates is a real estate company that sells luxury properties. Real Estates only sells homes in the $1 million and higher category. Real Estates has two new properties it would like to showcase, Kensington Manor and the Bradford Estate. You have been asked to create a Web page for Real Estates. You will also work with two pages that showcase some of the rooms in Kensington Manor and the Bradford Estate. Complete the following steps:

1. Use Notepad to open the **Real.htm** file located in your Tutorial.06\Case1 folder included with your Data Files. Save this file as **RealNew.htm** in the same folder.
2. You will be creating an embedded style sheet. In the head area below the page title, enter the code for the start <style> and the end </style> tags. In the start <style> tag, include the **media** attribute with a value of **screen**.
3. Below the start <style> tag, insert a comment that includes your first and last name as the author and today's date.
4. Set the style for the <body> tag selector to display text as white with a background color of green.

5. Create an ID selector named **manorbox**. Position the box absolutely 15px from the top and 700px on the left. The box should be 280px wide. The box should have a border that is purple, solid, and 7px thick. Text in the box should be centered.

6. Create an ID selector named **estatebox**. Position the box absolutely 300px from the top and 700px on the left. The box should be 280px wide. The box should have a border that is purple, solid, and 7px thick. Text in the box should be centered.

7. Set the style for the <p> element selector to display text as bold and in the Arial font.

8. Create an ID selector named **links**. This will be a box for the navigation bar containing the links. Position the box absolutely on the page, 135px from the top and 10px from the left. The box should be 675px wide. The box should have a border that is navy, solid, and thin. The box should have a background color of black. Text in the box should be centered.

9. Set the style for the anchor element selector to display text as white, bold, and in the Arial font. There should be a padding of 0.3em.

EXPLORE 10. Set the style for the a:hover pseudo-class selector to display text in black with a background color of yellow.

EXPLORE 11. Set the style for the a:active pseudo-class selector to display text in red.

12. Set the style for the img element selector so that there is no border width.

13. Create an ID selector named **main**. Position the box absolutely on the page, 180px from the top. Text should be displayed in the Arial font. The box should float left. The box should be 650px wide.

14. In the body of the document, on a blank line above the five links for the navigation bar, insert the code for a start <div> tag and apply the links ID selector.

15. On a blank line below the five links for the navigation bar, insert the code for an end </div> tag.

16. On a blank line above the paragraph "Kensington Manor," insert the code to link to the Kensington.htm file. The link should also use an image named Ken.gif. The alternate text is **image of the Kensington manor**. The image has a width of 250px and a height of 150px.

17. On a blank line above the code to link to the Kensington HTML file, insert the code for a start <div> tag and apply the manorbox ID selector.

18. On a blank line below the code to link to the Kensington HTML file, insert the code for an end </div> tag.

19. On a blank line above the paragraph "Bradford Estate," insert the code for a link to the Bradford.htm file. The link also uses an image named Brad.gif. The alternate text is **image of the Bradford estate**. The image has a width of 250px and a height of 150px.

20. On a blank line above the code to link to the Bradford HTML file, insert the code for a start <div> tag and apply the estatebox ID selector.

21. On a blank line below the code to link to the Bradford HTML file, insert the code for an end </div> tag.

22. On a blank line above the first <h4> tag, insert the code for a start <div> tag and apply the main ID selector.

23. On a blank line above the end </body> tag, code an end </div> tag.

24. Between the <address></address> tags, insert the code for an e-mail link to realestates@comlink.com. Use the e-mail address as the link text.

25. Save your RealNew HTML document, and then open it in your browser. The document should be similar to the one shown in Figure 6-62.

Figure 6-62

26. Test the links to the Kensington Manor, the Bradford Estate, and realestates@comlink.com.
27. Close all open windows.
28. Submit the results of the preceding steps to your instructor, either in printed or electronic form, as requested.

Apply | Case Problem 2

Use the skills you learned in the tutorial to create and style a Web page for a minor league baseball team.

Data Files needed for this Case Problem: Cap.gif, Cloth.jpg, Glove.jpg, Hotdog.jpg, Kids.gif, News.htm, Pitcher.jpg, Roster.htm, Stadium.gif, Team.htm, Teamlogo.gif, Tickets.htm

The Palmetto Plovers The Palmetto Plovers are a new minor league team that is about to play its first season. Located in Palmetto Hills in the Florida panhandle, the team hopes to draw fans from the entire Gulf area, particularly those who do not want to make the long drive to Atlanta or Tampa Bay. Plover Field is the new stadium that has been built for the Palmetto Plovers. With a seating capacity of 8,000, it's one of the largest minor league stadiums in the region. You have been asked to compose several Web pages for the Palmetto Plovers. You will compose a home page, which will link to a page that lists ticket prices. The home page will also link to a page that lists the team roster and a page that gives details about team news. Complete the following steps:

1. Use Notepad to open the **Team.htm** file located in your Tutorial.06\Case2 folder included with your Data Files. Save this file as **TeamNew.htm** in the same folder.
2. You will be creating an embedded style sheet. In the head area below the page title, enter the code for the start <style> and the end </style> tags. In the start <style> tag, include the **media** attribute with a value of **screen**.
3. Below the start <style> tag, insert a comment that includes your first and last name as the author and today's date.

⊕ EXPLORE

4. Set the style for the body element selector to display text in the Arial font. Use the Cloth.jpg file as a background image for the page.
5. Set the style for the anchor element selector so that all links are displayed in bold, 14pt text. The background color should be brown, and there should be a left margin of 5px.
6. Use a pseudo-class selector to set the style for unvisited links to have a text color of white.
7. Use a pseudo-class selector to set the style for visited links to have a text color of navy and no underlining.
8. Use a pseudo-class selector to create a hover effect so that the link text is brown and the background color is white.
9. Create an ID selector named **links**. This will be a box for the navigation bar. The links box should be positioned absolutely 140px from the top edge of the screen and 50px from the left edge of the screen. The box should be 400px wide and have a padding of 5px. Set the box's z-index to 2. All text in the box should be centered.
10. Create an ID selector named **stadium**. This will be a box for the stadium image on the left. The box should be positioned absolutely 10px from the top of the screen and 50px from the left edge of the screen. The box should be 400px wide and have a border that is brown, solid, and thin.
11. Create an ID selector named **main**. This will be a box for the main window on the right. The box should be positioned absolutely 10px from the top of the screen and 470px from the left edge of the screen.

⊕ EXPLORE

12. Create a descendant selector for paragraphs for the main ID selector. The text should be displayed as 11pt, bold text.
13. Create an ID selector named **cap**. This will be a box for the image in the lower-left corner of the screen. The box should be positioned absolutely 400px from the top and 50px from the left edge of the screen. The box should have a border that is brown, solid, and thin.

14. Create an ID selector named **kids**. This will be a box for the image in the lower-right corner of the screen. The box should be positioned absolutely 400px from the top and 475px on the left. The box should have a border that is brown, solid, and thin.

15. Create an independent class named **center** that centers text.

16. In the body of the document, using the existing text as link text, create links to **Tickets.htm**, **Roster.htm**, and **News.htm**.

17. Above the links you just created, insert the code for a start <div> tag and apply the links ID selector; also insert the code for an end </div> tag below the links.

18. Above the code for Stadium.gif, insert the code for a start <div> tag and apply the stadium ID selector; also insert the code for an end </div> tag below the Stadium.gif image code.

19. Above the code for Cap.gif, insert the code for a start <div> tag and apply the cap ID selector; also insert the code for an end </div> tag below the Cap.gif image code.

20. Above the code for Kids.gif, insert the code for a start <div> tag and apply the kids ID selector; also insert the code for an end </div> tag below the Kids.gif image code.

21. Above the code for the Teamlogo.gif, code a start <div> tag and apply the main ID selector.

22. On a blank link line below the start <div> tag for the main ID selector and above code for the Teamlogo.gif, insert the code for another start <div> tag and apply the center class; also insert the code for an end </div> tag below the Teamlogo.gif image code.

23. Insert the code for an end </div> tag above the end </body> tag.

24. Save your TeamNew HTML document, and then open it in your browser. The document should be similar to the one shown in Figure 6-63.

Figure 6-63

25. Test all links.

26. Close all open windows.

27. Submit the results of the preceding steps to your instructor, either in printed or electronic form, as requested

---

Challenge | Case Problem 3

Use what you've learned, and expand your skills, to create and style a Web page for an outlet mall.

Data Files needed for this Case Problem: Clothing.jpg, Food.htm, Food.jpg, General.htm, General.jpg, Linens.htm, Linens.jpg, Mall.gif, Shoes.htm, Shoes.jpg, Shopping.gif, Victor.gif, and Victor.htm

Victor's Outlet Mall   Victor's Outlet Mall is a newly constructed outlet shopping experience that offers great variety at discounted prices. The mall consists of four major sections—a large area of shops that sells general merchandise, a mini-mall that sells clothing and shoes, a retail outlet that sells linens and bedding, and a food court. You have been asked to create a Web site for Victor's. You will include an image map of the mall and several pages that provide photos of the shopping experience at Victor's. Complete the following steps:

1. Use Notepad to open the **Victor.htm** file located in your Tutorial.06\Case3 folder included with your Data Files. Save this file as **VictorNew.htm** in the same folder.

2. You will be creating an embedded style sheet. In the head area below the page title, enter the code for the start <style> and the end </style> tags. In the start <style> tag, include the **media** attribute with a value of **screen**.

3. Below the start <style> tag, insert a comment that includes your first and last name as the author and today's date.

4. Set the style for the body element to have a background color of wheat. Text should appear in Verdana, a sans serif font.

5. Set the style for the anchor element selector to display text as navy and bold.

⊕ EXPLORE
6. Create an ID selector named **container**. This will be a container box for the imagebox and the mallbox. Style this box to have a width of 775px. Both the margin-left and margin-right properties should have a value of auto.

7. Create an ID selector named **imagebox**. Style this box to have a width of 300px and a height of 342px. The box should float right and have padding of 0.2em with a border that is brown, solid, and thin.

8. Create an ID selector named **mallbox**. This will be a box for the information about the mall. The box should have a width of 400px, float left, and have padding of 1em with a border on the right that is navy, solid, and thick.

⊕ EXPLORE
9. Create a dependent class named **center** for the <div> tag. This class centers text.

10. On a blank line just above the start <body> tag, insert the code for an anchor named **top**.

11. On a blank line just below the start <body> tag, insert the code for a start <div> tag and apply the container ID.

12. In the code for the Victor.gif image, position the insertion point to the right of the closing quotation mark following "victor.gif." Press the Spacebar and then apply the center class.

13. On a blank line just above the code for the Shopping.gif image, insert the code for a start <div> tag and apply the imagebox ID selector.

14. On a blank line following the paragraph that ends with the words "at very reasonable prices," insert the code for an end </div> tag.

15. On a blank line above the h3 heading that begins with the words, "Your One-Stop Shopping Solution," insert the code for a start <div> tag and apply the mallbox ID selector.

16. Below the comment "Code for image map begins here," insert the code for an image map as follows:
    - The source of the image used for the map is Mall.gif. For alternate text, use the words "image map of Victor's outlet mall." The map image has a width of 400px and a height of 332px.
    - For the usemap attribute, use the value of #victor.
    - Name the map "victor".
    - The image map has four areas. The general merchandise area is a polygon. The coordinates are 0,0,0,340,108,340,108,122,210,121,207,0.
    - This area should link to a file named **General.htm.**

⊕ EXPLORE 17. The food court area is a circle. The coordinates are 179,236,92. The area should link to a file named **Food.htm**.

⊕ EXPLORE 18. The shoes and clothing area is a rectangle. The coordinates are 258,0,397,168. The area should link to a file named **Shoes.htm**.

⊕ EXPLORE 19. The linens and bedding area is a rectangle. The coordinates are 256,166, 398,340. The area should link to a file named **Linens.htm**.

20. Below the rectangle area, insert the code for an end </map> tag.

21. Between the <p></p> tags and using the words, **Back to Top** as the link text, insert the code for a link to the anchor named top.

22. On a blank line below the code to link to the anchor named top, insert the code for an end </div> tag.

23. On a blank line above the end </body> tag, insert the code for another end </div> tag.

24. Save your VictorNew HTML document, and then open it in your browser. The document should be similar to the one shown in Figure 6-64.

Figure 6-64

Victor's Outlet Mall

Your One-Stop Shopping Solution for all the Family's Needs

Welcome to the home page for Victor's Outlet Mall. Looking for clothes and shoes at discount prices? We've got them! Looking for quality footwear for the whole family? We've got them — and at prices you can afford. Want linens and bedding for the home? Yes, we've got that, too, and you won't believe the selection you'll find at rock-bottom prices. Click on one of the stores in the store map below to learn more.

Victor's was established in 1998. We have more than two centuries' experience in serving you. We know what shoppers want in today's economy. You don't need us to tell you how hard it is to make end's meet. Let us help you balance your budget while providing your family with outstanding value and excellent service.

Our outlet mall is currently divided into four sections. We have over 20 shops that sell general merchandise, a mini-mall with six stores that sell clothing and shoes, and a retail outlet that sells linens and bedding. We also have a large food court and restroom facilities.

General Merchandise

Shoes and Clothing

Food Court and Central Mall

Linens and Bedding

Back to Top

Victor's has ample, free parking. We also have a trolley service that will take you from one end of the outlet mall to the other. There is no fee for this service. We have diaper-changing facilities available in all our restrooms. We have ample seating inside the mall, and we have adopted all entrances and exits for easy access for our handicapped customers.

Coming this fall, we will be opening our new sporting goods section. This new wing will be adjacent to the general merchandise area. We will be offering discounts on all types of sporting goods equipment. We will have all the top brands selling at vastly reduced prices. Some of these items will be closeouts, so be sure to get here early on the day the sporting goods section opens.

If you are hungry or just need a break from all that shopping, please drop by the food court. We have a fabulous variety of foods that are all sold at very reasonable prices.

25. Test all links.
26. Close all open windows.
27. Submit the results of the preceding steps to your instructor, either in printed or electronic form, as requested.

Create | **Case Problem 4**

Using the figures provided, create a Web page for a law firm.

Data Files needed for this Case Problem: Bios.htm, Forest.jpg, Greenlogo.gif, Lawyers.htm, Lawbooks.gif, and Team.gif

The Green Lawyers Group   The Green Lawyers Group is a new law firm that specializes in the field of environmental law. The Green Lawyers prosecute and defend cases involving land, sea, and air pollution. All of the lawyers in the Green Lawyers Group have a broad range of experience in environmental law. Rashif Jackson, the senior partner, has asked you to create a Web site for the Green Lawyers Group. You will create two pages for the site. The home page will have an image map that links to anchors on a biographies page. Complete the following steps:

1. Use Notepad to open the **Bios.htm** file located in your Tutorial.06\Case4 folder included with your Data Files. Save this file as **BiosNew.htm** in the same folder.
2. Below the start <style> tag, insert a comment that includes your first and last name as the author and today's date.
3. Just above the start <body> tag code an anchor named **top**.
4. Insert code for anchors just above the text for each lawyer's name. Use the first name of each lawyer as the name for each anchor.
5. At the bottom of the page, insert the code for a link back to the home page, which will be named **LawyersNew.htm**.
6. At the bottom of the page, also insert the code for a link to the anchor named top.
7. Save the BiosNew HTML file, and then close it.
8. Use Notepad to open the **Lawyers.htm** file located in your Tutorial.06\Case4 folder included with your Data Files. Save this file as **LawyersNew.htm** in the same folder.
9. Below the start <style> tag, insert the code for a comment that includes your first and last name as the author and today's date.
10. Within the <style></style> tags, type the code to set the style for the :link pseudo-class selector as you choose.
11. Type the code to set the style for the :visited pseudo-class selector as you choose.
12. Type the code to set the style for the :hover pseudo-class selector as you choose.
13. Using Microsoft Paint or other image-editing software, use the Team.gif image to create an image map.
14. Determine the coordinates for rectangular hotspots for each of the lawyers: Susan, Anthony, Sharon, Rashif, and Rosemarie.
15. In your LawyersNew HTML file, using the coordinates you determined in the preceding step, create links to each of the anchors you included on the BiosNew page.
16. Insert the code for the end </map> tag below the image map code.
17. At the bottom of the LawyersNew HTML page, type the code to link to the BiosNew page. Use the words "Lawyers' Biographies Page" as the link text.
18. Save your LawyersNew HTML document, and then open it in your browser. Test all links.
19. Close all open windows.
20. Submit the results of the preceding steps to your instructor, either in printed or electronic form, as requested.

Review	**Session 6.1 Quick Check Answers**

1. <a> </a>
2. id
3. the href attribute
4. the page with the links
5. the page that will be displayed when the user clicks the link text or image
6. the # symbol
7. Code the anchors first, then the links.

| Review | | Session 6.2 Quick Check Answers |

1. links back to the top of the page, the next page, the previous page, and the home page
2. some link text
3. a:visited
4. a:link
5. a:hover
6. When the user clicks a smaller image (the thumbnail image) used as a link, a different page with the larger image is displayed.
7. a link back to the referring page.
8. Mailto:

| Review | | Session 6.3 Quick Check Answers |

1. \<map\>
2. \<area /\>
3. rect, circle, and poly
4. coords
5. You can't do it in HTML. You must use a third-party software program such as Dreamweaver, Photoshop, or Microsoft Paint.
6. rect
7. poly
8. circle

Ending Data Files

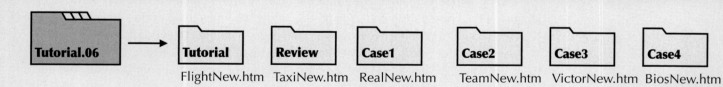

Tutorial.06 →	Tutorial	Review	Case1	Case2	Case3	Case4
	FlightNew.htm	TaxiNew.htm	RealNew.htm	TeamNew.htm	VictorNew.htm	BiosNew.htm
						LawyersNew.htm

Objectives

Session 7.1
- Discern the difference between data tables and layout tables
- Create a table to display and organize data
- Merge table columns or rows

Session 7.2
- Understand how to plan and use layout tables
- Create a table for layout
- Learn how to nest a data table within a layout table

Session 7.3
- Create styles to change the appearance of a table
- Position the cell contents vertically
- Position a table horizontally

Creating Tables

Using Tables to Display Data and Design Pages

Case | The Sound Bay Ferry Service

The Sound Bay Ferry serves as the primary transportation service between Sound Bay and Bay Island, which is about 40 miles northeast of Green Bay, Wisconsin. Operating from May through September, the Sound Bay Ferry is quite popular not only with local residents, but also with the many visitors who come to this region during the summer. Travelers find the ferry to be a relaxing and fairly inexpensive means of commuting to and from Bay Island, a popular summer resort area and nature preserve. Passengers also find the ferry to be a great way to enjoy the scenic beauty of the region. You are a summer intern working for George Chatham, the owner of the Sound Bay Ferry. He has asked for your assistance in creating a Web page for the Sound Bay Ferry. In particular, he wants to display the new ferry timetable prominently on the Web page. He hopes doing so will reduce his printing costs and let him quickly update the timetable when he starts running a new ferry next month. George is familiar with HTML, and he has created a Web page with some content describing the Sound Bay Ferry. You will begin by showing George how to use HTML tables to display and organize data. You will then show George how to use HTML tables for page layout. Finally, you will show George how to style tables using CSS.

Starting Data Files

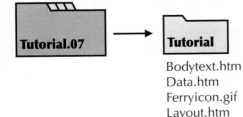

Tutorial.07 →

Tutorial
Bodytext.htm
Data.htm
Ferryicon.gif
Layout.htm
Seamist.jpg

Review
Cruiser.jpg
Foil.htm
Foilbanner.gif

Case1
Body.htm
Female.jpg
Female2.jpg
Female3.jpg
Male.jpg

Case2
Library.htm
Masthead.gif
Masthead2.gif

Case3
Baxter.htm
College.gif
Greer.htm
Greer.jpg
Student.jpg
Student2.jpg
Student3.jpg

Case4
Catdog.jpg
Catdog2.jpg
Catdog3.jpg
Petlogo.jpg
Pets.htm
Vet.jpg
Vet2.jpg

Session 7.1

Understanding the Limitations of HTML Tables

If you are familiar with the table feature of a word processing program, you know that you can use tables to create columns and rows to display data in an organized manner. You also know how easy it is to create tables using a word processing program's table "quick create" or "table draw" feature. However, HTML does not have these ease-of-use features for creating tables. If you've worked with tables in a word processing program, you know that a **cell** is the intersection of a column and row. Using HTML, however, you must enter the code for a table one row at a time and one cell at a time.

You might also be familiar with a spreadsheet program, such as Microsoft Office Excel, which similarly uses columns and rows to organize data. A spreadsheet program also has extensive math, formula creation, and charting features. HTML, however, does not have these features. Spreadsheet programs refer to cells by their cell addresses. For example, the intersection of Column C and Row 2 is referred to as cell address C2. Cell addresses do not exist in HTML. In HTML, when you refer to a cell, you must describe its location in the table. In this instance, what is cell C2 in a spreadsheet program is described in an HTML table as "the third cell in the second row."

Until recently, HTML tables were used both as a means for organizing data and creating page layout. While HTML tables are still used to organize data, CSS is now the preferred method for creating page layout. To organize data, you create a **data table**, which is a table used to align text and numbers in columns and rows. To design pages, you can create a **layout table**, which is a table intended solely for page layout. Any element can be placed inside a cell—text, images, and even another table. When you place a table inside another table, you are creating a **nested table**. You will first show George how to create a data table. Later you will copy the data table code into a page that has a layout table, creating a nested table.

George has sketched out how he would like the data table to appear. See Figure 7-1.

Figure 7-1 ▶ **Sketch of the data table**

Ferry Schedule			
Ferry	Departs	Arrives	Returns
Bayrunner	11 a.m.	12:15 p.m.	2 p.m.
Sound Skipper	12 p.m.	1:15 p.m.	Time
Sea Mist	2 p.m.	3:15 p.m.	Approximate

Creating a Table to Display and Organize Data

In addition to having several images and paragraph text, the Sound Bay Ferry page will have a data table that lists the ferry schedule for the summer season. Because you are creating this table to display schedule data in rows and columns, you'll create a data table. You will begin by opening a file where you will create the data table for the Sound Bay Ferry.

To view the original data table Web page:

▶ **1.** Use your text editor to open the file **Data.htm** from the Tutorial.07\Tutorial folder of your Data Files.

▶ **2.** Save the file as **DataNew** in the same folder.

Now you're ready to start entering the HTML code to create the table.

Entering the Table Code

Tables begin with the start <table> tag. The end </table> tag follows all the table code. Tables can be placed anywhere within the <body> </body> tags.

```
<body>
<table>
. . . table code goes here . . .
</table>
</body>
```

Table borders are the horizontal and vertical ruled lines both outside and inside the table. You use the border attribute and its value in pixels to create the table borders, which often are referred to as the table **gridlines** or the table grid. By default, a table does not show the gridlines. When you first create a data table, it's useful to display the gridlines because you can clearly see the alignment of the table cells. The border attribute with a value of 1 or greater will display the table gridlines in the browser. The code for the border attribute and its value would be entered like so:

```
<table border="1">
```

Creating a Table Border | Reference Window

- To create a table border, enter the following code:
    ```
    <table border="pixelvalue">
    ```
    where *border* is the border attribute and *pixelvalue* is the width of the border expressed in pixels. The higher the pixel value, the thicker the border.

Using the title Attribute and the summary Attribute

Include the **title attribute** and its value so that a ScreenTip appears when a user points to the table in the browser. The **summary attribute** and its value do not display a ScreenTip, nor does its value appear in the browser, but the value of the summary attribute does provide information to users with screen readers, which enhances the accessibility of your Web pages. As such, you should always include a summary in the start <table> tag.

Entering the Title and Summary Attributes

- To begin creating a table, enter the following code:
  ```
  <table title="tabletitle" summary="tablesummary">
  </table>
  ```
  where *table* is the start table tag, *title* is the title attribute, *tabletitle* is a brief description of the table to be used as a ScreenTip, *summary* is the summary attribute, *tablesummary* is a detailed description of the table content, and *</table>* is the end table tag on a separate line.

Tip

Always code the start <table> and end </table> tags at the same time so you don't forget to code the end </table> tag.

The summary should be more detailed than the title. For example, compare the title text to the more detailed summary text in the following code:

```
<table border="1" title="The Sound Bay Ferry Schedule" summary="The Sound
Bay Ferry runs from May through September. Extra service is provided on the
following days: Memorial Day, July 4, and Labor Day. Ample parking is
available at all ferry terminals.">

</table>
```

You will show George how to enter code for the start <table> tag, the border attribute and its value, the title attribute and its value, and the summary attribute and its value. You will also enter the code for the end </table> tag.

To enter code for the table tags and the start table tag's attributes and values:

▶ **1.** In the DataNew document, below the start <body> tag code, type the following code, which is also shown in red in Figure 7-2.

```
<table border="1" title="The Sound Bay Ferry Schedule"
summary="The Sound Bay Ferry runs from May through September.
Extra service is provided on the following days: Memorial Day,
July 4, and Labor Day. Ample parking is available at all ferry
terminals.">

</table>
```

Figure 7-2 ▶ **Code for the start table tag and the end table tag**

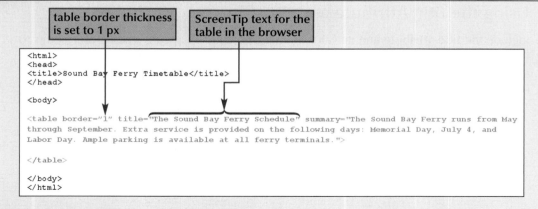

2. Save DataNew.

Now that you have entered the start and end table tags, you're ready to continue creating the table.

Creating a Caption

A **caption** is a brief description of the table contents. Unlike the summary attribute and its value, which are not displayed in the browser, the caption text is displayed in the browser. The caption text can be as brief as the words "Figure 1" or the caption text can be more descriptive, such as "Profit and Loss Statement for the Last Two Quarters of the Current Fiscal Year." A table caption is optional, but it helps in identifying the data in a table, especially if the table is complex and has a great deal of numeric data.

Creating a Table Caption | Reference Window

- To create a table caption, enter the following code:
    ```
    <caption>captiontext</caption>
    ```
    where *caption* is the start caption tag, *captiontext* is the text in the caption, and *</caption>* is the end caption tag. If you want to position the caption below the table, insert the align attribute into the caption tag and assign the value of bottom.

The <caption></caption> tags are used to create a table caption. If you do include a table caption, the caption tags must follow the start <table> tag. The caption text can be positioned above or below the table, but it is normally positioned below the table. By default, however, the caption appears above the table. If you choose to do so, you can omit the caption and enter text either above or below the table as you normally would. The caption is part of the table. If you set the style of the table to display text in 14pt Arial font, the caption text is also displayed with that style.

The <caption> tag centers the caption text and creates a blank line below the caption text. The end </caption> tag does not have to be placed on a separate line; it can follow the text, similar to the way you code the end </title> tag when you code the title text. Following is an example of a table caption.

```
<table border="1" title="The Sound Bay Ferry Schedule" summary="The Sound
Bay Ferry runs from May through September. Extra service is provided on the
following days: Memorial Day, July 4, and Labor Day. Ample parking is
available at all ferry terminals.">

<caption>May &ndash; September Timetable</caption>

</table>
```

Because of a lack of browser support, you still must use the deprecated **align attribute** to position the caption below the table. Use the align attribute with a value of *bottom* to position the caption below the table, as in the following code:

```
<table border="1" title="The Sound Bay Ferry Schedule" summary="The Sound
Bay Ferry runs from May through September. Extra service is provided on the
following days: Memorial Day, July 4, and Labor Day. Ample parking is
available at all ferry terminals.">

<caption align="bottom">May &ndash; September Timetable</caption>

</table>
```

InSight | **Using the Caption-side Property**

CSS does have a property called caption-side that you can use to position captions. Unfortunately, the caption-side property has little browser support. Until this property becomes widely supported, continue to use the deprecated align attribute to position the caption. The caption-side property takes these values:

- **left**: The caption is displayed to the left of the table.
- **right**: The caption is displayed to the right of the table.
- **top**: The default; the caption is displayed above the table and centered.
- **bottom**: The caption is displayed below the table and centered.

You will now show George how to enter the table caption.

To enter the table caption:

▶ 1. In your text editor, display the HTML code for DataNew.

▶ 2. On a blank line below the code for the start <table> tag code, type the following code, which is also shown in red in Figure 7-3.

```
<caption align="bottom">May &ndash; September Timetable</caption>
```

Figure 7-3 | **Code for the caption tag**

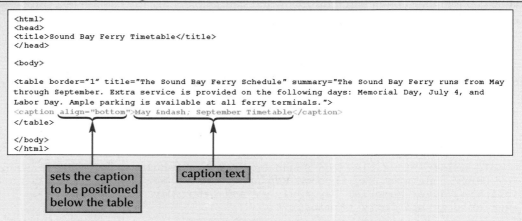

```
<html>
<head>
<title>Sound Bay Ferry Timetable</title>
</head>

<body>

<table border="1" title="The Sound Bay Ferry Schedule" summary="The Sound Bay Ferry runs from May
through September. Extra service is provided on the following days: Memorial Day, July 4, and
Labor Day. Ample parking is available at all ferry terminals.">
<caption align="bottom">May &ndash; September Timetable</caption>
</table>

</body>
</html>
```

sets the caption to be positioned below the table

caption text

▶ 3. Save DataNew. Open DataNew in your browser and refresh the screen to verify that the table caption is displayed. See Figure 7-4.

Figure 7-4 | **Caption on the Web page**

May – September Timetable

Next, you'll show George how to enter the rows in the table.

Creating Table Rows

Table rows are created by entering the code for the start table row tag <tr> and the end table row tag </tr>. It's good coding practice to type both the start <tr> tag and the end </tr> tag at the same time. By doing so, you don't have to remember to code the </tr> tag after all the table data has been entered into the row. Not including an end </tr> tag can cause significant problems when the table appears in the browser. To make the table row code easier to read, enter the code for the table row tags on their own lines, like so:

```
<tr>

table data tags will go here ...

</tr>
```

Entering the Table Data

The data for each cell is entered between the table data tags, <td> and </td>. The table data tags contain the cell contents for each cell in the row. When entering the table data tags, it is common practice to indent the table data code by at least two spaces. Doing so makes it easier to see the start and end of each row.

Creating Table Rows | Reference Window

- To create table rows, enter the following code:
  ```
  <tr>
    <td>tabledata</td>
  </tr>
  ```
  where *<tr>* is the start table row tag, *td* is the start table data tag, *tabledata* is the data for the cell, *</td>* is the end table data tag, and *</tr>* is the end table row tag.

The data table initially will consist of five rows, each with four columns. Later, you will combine some of the cells, but for now, you must enter code so that the data table has five rows and four columns, a total of 20 cells. All cells must have some content. For now, you will code the   special character to insert a space character in cells where there is no data, such as the cells to the right of the cell with words "Ferry Schedule" in the first row of the table.

Displaying Cells Without Data | InSight

An **empty cell** is a cell without any data. CSS has an **empty-cells property**, which takes these values: *show*, whereby a border is drawn around the empty cell, and *hide*, whereby no border is drawn around the empty cell. To set the style for table data cells to always show a border even if the cell has no content, you set the style for the td element selector similar to this:
```
td {
empty-cells: show; }
```
By setting the style for the td element to always show borders, you don't have to include the code   in each empty cell.

You will show George how to enter the table data for the first row.

To enter the table data for the first row:

▶ **1.** In your text editor, display the HTML code for DataNew.

▶ **2.** Position the insertion point below the code after the </caption> tag, and then press the **Enter** key to create a new line.

▶ **3.** Type the following code, which is also shown in red in Figure 7-5. Press the **Enter** key after you type the </tr> tag.

```
<tr>
   <td>Ferry Schedule</td>
   <td> </td>
   <td> </td>
   <td> </td>
</tr>
```

Figure 7-5	Code for the first table row

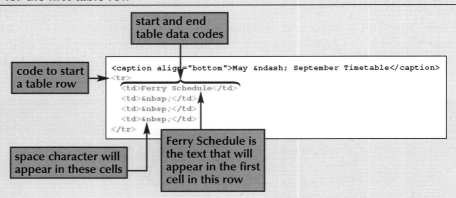

▶ **4.** Save DataNew. In your browser, refresh the screen to verify that the first row in the table is displayed. See Figure 7-6.

Figure 7-6	First table row on the Web page

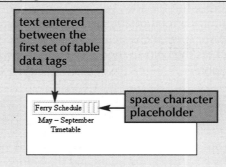

Tip

Any element can be placed into a table cell, including an image, a horizontal rule, a heading, links, or paragraph text.

George wants to include column headings for each column in the table. You'll show him how to create these table headers next.

Creating Table Headers

Most HTML tables have one or more rows used for the column headers, which by default make the text in the header centered and bold. Use the optional table header tags, <th> and </th>, to create **table headers**. To make the table header code more readable, it's common practice to indent the table header code, just as you did already with the <td></td> tags. The code for a table header row would be entered like so:

```
<tr>
  <th></th>
</tr>
```

The second row of the table will be a table header row. The header row contains information about the ferry name, the departure time, the arrival time, and the return time. You will now show George how to enter the table header row.

To enter the data for the table header row:

▶ **1.** In your text editor, display the HTML code for DataNew.

▶ **2.** On a blank line below the code for the first table row, type the following code, which is also shown in red in Figure 7-7. Press the **Enter** key after you type the </tr> tag.

```
<tr>
  <th>Ferry</th>
  <th>Departs</th>
  <th>Arrives</th>
  <th>Returns</th>
</tr>
```

Code for the table header row ◀ **Figure 7-7**

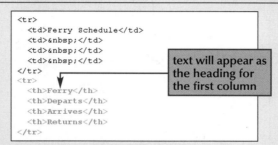

▶ **3.** Save DataNew. In your browser, refresh the screen to verify that the table header row is displayed. See Figure 7-8.

Table header row on the Web page ◀ **Figure 7-8**

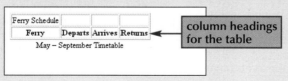

You will now show George how to code the remaining three rows of the table. The ferry schedule table has three table data rows, one for each ferry.

To enter the table data for the remaining rows:

▶ **1.** In your text editor, display the HTML code for DataNew.

Tip

To reduce coding errors, type a complete set of table row and table data tags and then copy and paste the code for each row in the table.

▶ **2.** On a blank line after the </tr> tag for the table header row, type the following code, which is also shown in red in Figure 7-9.

```
<tr>
   <td>Bayrunner</td>
   <td>11 a.m.</td>
   <td>12:15 p.m.</td>
   <td>2 p.m.</td>
</tr>

<tr>
   <td>Sound Skipper</td>
   <td>12 p.m.</td>
   <td>1:15 p.m.</td>
   <td>Time Approximate</td>
</tr>

<tr>
   <td>Sea Mist</td>
   <td>2 p.m.</td>
   <td>3:15 p.m.</td>
   <td> </td>
</tr>
```

Figure 7-9 **Code for the remaining table data rows**

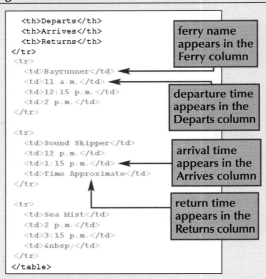

▶ **3.** Save DataNew. In your browser, refresh the screen to verify that the table data rows are displayed in the browser. See Figure 7-10.

Figure 7-10 **Table data rows on the Web page**

Ferry Schedule			
Ferry	**Departs**	**Arrives**	**Returns**
Bayrunner	11 a.m.	12:15 p.m.	2 p.m.
Sound Skipper	12 p.m.	1:15 p.m.	Time Approximate
Sea Mist	2 p.m.	3:15 p.m.	
May – September Timetable			

George notices that some table cells don't display data, such as in the first row. He'd like to combine those cells into a single cell. You'll show him how to do so by merging the cells.

Merging Cells in Columns

Note that the Ferry Schedule row has a cell with data (the words "Ferry Schedule") and three cells without data. Those are the four cells you will merge (combine). HTML uses the **colspan attribute** to merge cells across columns. Within a <th> or a <td> tag, you indicate the number of columns to merge, or span across the columns.

Spanning Cells Across Columns | Reference Window

- To span a cell across columns, enter the following code:
  ```
  <td colspan="value">
  ```
  where *colspan* is the colspan attribute and *value* is the number of columns that will be spanned. The colspan attribute and its value must be placed in the cell in which the colspan should begin. All empty spanned table data cells should be deleted.

The following code merges cells across four columns:

```
<td colspan="4">Ferry Schedule</td>
```

In the Sound Bay Ferry data table, the first row will span four columns. You always enter the colspan attribute and its value in the cell where the cells begin to merge. The code for the first <td> tag in the first row needs to be edited to appear like so:

```
<tr>
  <td colspan="4">Ferry Schedule</td>
  <td> </td>
  <td> </td>
  <td> </td>
</tr>
```

The Ferry Schedule table no longer needs the cells with the   special character, which has been serving as placeholders. You need to delete the <td></td> tags and the   special character for each of those cells.

You will now show George how to merge the cells in the Ferry Schedule row.

To merge the cells in the Ferry Schedule row:

▶ 1. In your text editor, display the HTML code for DataNew.

▶ 2. In the start <td> tag for "Ferry Schedule," position the insertion point to the left of the angle bracket (>).

▶ 3. Press the **Spacebar**, and then type **colspan="4"** (without a period).

▶ 4. Delete the three table data cells containing the   placeholder data. Your code should now look similar to the code shown in red in Figure 7-11.

Figure 7-11 ▶ **Code for the colspan in the first row**

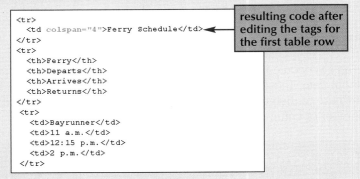

```
<tr>
  <td colspan="4">Ferry Schedule</td>
</tr>
<tr>
  <th>Ferry</th>
  <th>Departs</th>
  <th>Arrives</th>
  <th>Returns</th>
</tr>
<tr>
  <td>Bayrunner</td>
  <td>11 a.m.</td>
  <td>12:15 p.m.</td>
  <td>2 p.m.</td>
</tr>
```

resulting code after editing the tags for the first table row

▶ **5.** Save DataNew. In your browser, refresh the screen to verify that the cells in the Ferry Schedule row have been merged across columns. See Figure 7-12.

Figure 7-12 ▶ **Merged cells on the Web page**

Ferry Schedule			
Ferry	Departs	Arrives	Returns
Bayrunner	11 a.m.	12:15 p.m.	2 p.m.
Sound Skipper	12 p.m.	1:15 p.m.	Time Approximate
Sea Mist	2 p.m.	3:15 p.m.	

May – September Timetable

first row in the table now appears as a single column

George also wants to merge cells to eliminate the blank cell in the lower-right corner of the table. You'll show him how to merge cells in rows to do so.

Merging Cells in Rows

Note that there is only placeholder data (the   special character) in the last cell in the Sea Mist row. The Returns time is shown as "Time Approximate" because the departure times vary, based on the number of passengers who want to return and the afternoon weather conditions, which can be quite stormy in summer. You will merge the last two cells in the Sound Skipper and Sea Mist rows so that the Time Approximate cell spans two rows.

Reference Window | **Merging Cells in Rows**

- To span a cell across rows, enter the following code:
  ```
  <td rowspan="value">
  ```
  where *rowspan* is the rowspan attribute and *value* is the number of rows that will be spanned. The rowspan attribute and its value must be placed in the cell in which the rowspan should begin. All empty spanned table data cells should be deleted. If a row containing a rowspan is formatted, the row will include all the cells horizontally and the merged cells vertically.

Tip

The text in the cell for the rowspan is automatically centered vertically.

The **rowspan attribute** is used to merge cells in rows. You will be spanning two cells, so the value for the rowspan attribute in this instance will be 2. The rowspan attribute and its value are always entered in the cell where the merge will begin. As such, the

Sound Skipper table data should be edited to insert the rowspan attribute and its value into the last cell in the Sound Skipper row, like so:

```
<tr>
  <td>Sound Skipper</td>
  <td>12 p.m.</td>
  <td>1:15 p.m.</td>
  <td rowspan="2">Time Approximate</td>
</tr>
```

In the Sea Mist row, you no longer need the cell with the   character, so you can delete that cell. You will now show George how to merge the cells in the Sound Skipper row.

To merge the cells across the rows:

▶ **1.** In your text editor, display the HTML code for DataNew.

▶ **2.** In the last cell of the Sound Skipper row, in the start <td> tag for "Time Approximate," position the insertion point to the left of the angle bracket (>). Press the **Spacebar**.

▶ **3.** Type **rowspan="2"** (without a period).

▶ **4.** Delete the **<td> </td>** tags in the Sea Mist row. Your code should now look similar to the code shown below and shown in red in Figure 7-13.

Code for the rowspan ◀ **Figure 7-13**

```
<tr>
  <td>Sound Skipper</td>
  <td>12 p.m.</td>
  <td>1:15 p.m.</td>
  <td rowspan="2">Time Approximate</td>  ◀── resulting code after
</tr>                                          editing the tags in the
<tr>                                           Sound Skipper table row
  <td>Sea Mist</td>
  <td>2 p.m.</td>
  <td>3:15 p.m.</td>
</tr>
</table>
```

▶ **5.** Save DataNew. In your browser, refresh the screen to verify that the cells have been merged across rows. See Figure 7-14.

Merged cells spanning one row on the Web page ◀ **Figure 7-14**

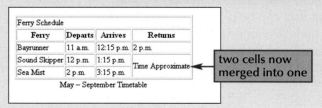

two cells now merged into one

Ferry Schedule			
Ferry	Departs	Arrives	Returns
Bayrunner	11 a.m.	12:15 p.m.	2 p.m.
Sound Skipper	12 p.m.	1:15 p.m.	Time Approximate
Sea Mist	2 p.m.	3:15 p.m.	

May – September Timetable

Tip

When you set the style for a row with cells merged by rowspan, you format all the cells in the row, including the merged cell. The "row" includes cells horizontally *and* vertically.

InSight		Planning the Table

Because tables involve a considerable amount of code, it can be difficult to debug a problem in your table code. Here's a good strategy for creating tables:

- Sketch out the table on paper. Give each cell a number, starting with cell 1 in the upper left-hand corner and continue numbering each cell from left to right and top to bottom.
- In your text editor, type the code for the first row of the table. Use placeholder data in the cells. (You can type anything in the cell, such as the word "placeholder.")
- Name and save the file.
- Open the file in the browser. Observe the result. Debug as necessary.
- When you are certain the code for the first table row is correct, copy this first table row code and paste it once in each remaining row.
- If cells are to be merged, perform one merge at a time. Save and replace the file after each merge. View the result. Debug as necessary.
- When you are satisfied that the table structure is correct, delete the placeholder data. You can use your text editor's Find and Replace feature to find all instances of the word "placeholder" and replace it with nothing.
- Type the actual table data in each cell.

You have now learned that tables can be used for two purposes. A data table is used to organize data. A layout table is used for page layout. The table tag takes several attributes. Among them are the border attribute, which can be used to display table grid-lines, the title attribute, which provides text for a ScreenTip, and the summary attribute, which provides a description of the table that will not display in the browser, but is used by screen readers. An optional caption tag can be used to provide the table with a description that will display in the browser. Table rows are created by entering a pair of <tr> </tr> tags. The <td> </td> or the <th> </th> tags are used to enclose the contents of a cell within a row. The table header tags make text bold and centered. You can combine cells by using the colspan attribute to merge across columns or the rowspan attribute to merge across rows. Now that the data table is complete, you will next show George how to use a layout table to control the page layout.

Review		Session 7.1 Quick Check

1. How does a data table differ from a layout table?
2. How does the table title differ from the table summary?
3. What is the purpose of a table caption?
4. What types of data can be placed into a table cell?
5. How does a table header cell differ from a table data cell?
6. What is an empty cell?
7. What attribute is used to merge columns? What attribute is used to merge rows?

Session 7.2

Using Tables for Layout

Today, Web developers typically use CSS for page layout. However, because that was not true several years ago, many existing Web sites still rely on tables for layout, so you should know how to create a page layout using tables. George has sketched a design for the Web page he wants, which will feature a banner row at the top of the page. The data table you created in Session 7.1 will appear below the banner. Below the data table will be an image of the Sea Mist, one of the Sound Bay ferries. To the right will be a column for the body text, and at the bottom of the table, a footer row will appear with address and contact information. The design looks like Figure 7-15.

Sketch for the layout table | Figure 7-15

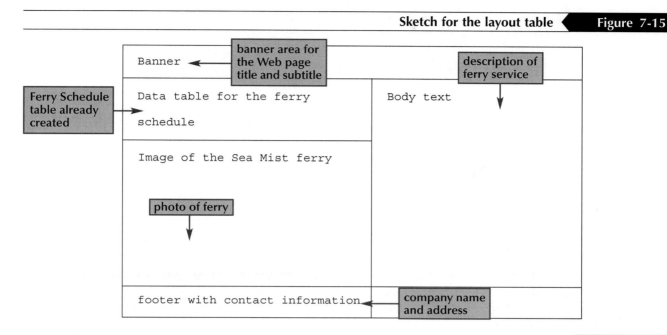

In the layout table, you will use the colspan attribute in the banner row and in the footer row to merge cells across columns. You will merge rows to establish the body text column. Because this is a layout table, you do not need to enter the code for the title attribute and a value, or for a summary attribute and a value. During the design process, it is helpful to see the table gridlines, so you will enter the code for the border attribute with a value of 1 in the start <table> tag. You will first have George enter a comment to identify the author and the creation date of the file.

To create the comment:

1. Use your text editor to open the **Layout.htm** file located in the Tutorial.07\Tutorial folder included with your Data Files. Save this file as **LayoutNew.htm** in the same folder.

2. On a blank line below the start <style> tag, type the following code to create a comment, which is also shown in red in Figure 7-16.

    ```
    /* Your First Name Your Last Name
    Today's Date */
    ```

Comment code | Figure 7-16

```
<html>
<head>
<title>The Sound Bay Ferry</title>

<style type="text/css" media="all">

/* Your First Name Your Last Name
Today's Date */

</style>
</head>
```

3. Save the LayoutNew file.

You will show George how to enter code for the layout table and some placeholder data.

To enter the code and placeholder text for the layout table:

▶ **1.** In your text editor, display the HTML code for LayoutNew.

▶ **2.** Below the start body tag, type the following code and placeholder text, which is also shown in red in Figure 7-17.

```
<table border="1">
<tr>
  <td colspan="2">Banner</td>
</tr>

<tr>
  <td>Data table for the ferry schedule</td>
  <td rowspan="2">Body text</td>
</tr>

<tr>
  <td>Image of the Sea Mist ferry</td>
</tr>

<tr>
  <td colspan="2">Footer with contact information</td>
</tr>
</table>
```

Figure 7-17 ▶ **The code for the layout table**

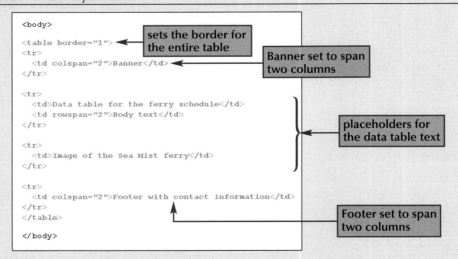

▶ **3.** Save LayoutNew. In your browser, open LayoutNew and compare your screen with the one shown in Figure 7-18.

Figure 7-18 **Layout table and placeholder text on the Web page**

Banner	
Data table for the ferry schedule	Body text
Image of the Sea Mist ferry	
Footer with contact information	

Using the pre Tag | InSight

In the earliest versions of HTML, tables were created by using the <pre></pre> tags to create what is known as preformatted text. The <pre></pre> tags indicate to the browser that the exact appearance of the text—including spaces—must be preserved. Preformatted text is displayed in a Courier font. In those early days, tables were created by typing the text for the first entry in the first column, pressing the Spacebar as many times as necessary to position the insertion point for the second column, typing the first entry in the second column, and so on. As such, it was tedious to create tables, and it was very difficult to edit them. Today, the <pre></pre> tags are seldom used in HTML, but the <pre></pre> tags are used in programming languages such as JavaScript, and they are still used to format text for electronic transmission to the Securities and Exchange Commission.

Now that you have established the table layout, you need content to replace the placeholder text. You will start with the banner row. You will show George how to delete the placeholder text and code an h1 heading and some text for the banner row.

To enter the h1 heading for the banner:

▶ 1. In your text editor, display the HTML code for LayoutNew.

▶ 2. Position the insertion point to the left of the letter B in the word "Banner" in the first table data tag of the table.

▶ 3. Delete the word **Banner**.

▶ 4. Type the following text below, which is also shown in red in Figure 7-19.

```
<h1>THE SOUND BAY FERRY SERVICE
<br />Serving Sound Bay for Over 50 Years</h1>
```

Code for the banner row ◀ Figure 7-19

```
<body>

<table border="1">

<tr>
  <td colspan="2"><h1>THE SOUND BAY FERRY SERVICE
<br />Serving Sound Bay for Over 50 Years</h1></td>
</tr>
                                        h1 heading to appear
                                        in the banner area
<tr>
  <td>Data table for the ferry schedule</td>
  <td rowspan="2">Body text</td>
</tr>

<tr>
  <td>Image of the Sea Mist ferry</td>
</tr>

<tr>
  <td colspan="2">Footer with contact information</td>
</tr>
```

▶ 5. Save LayoutNew. In your browser, refresh the screen to verify that the h1 heading is displayed. See Figure 7-20.

Figure 7-20 ▶ **The h1 heading in the banner row on the Web page**

table width expands
to accommodate
the banner text

Next, you will show George how to copy the table code from the data table you created earlier and paste it into the cell with the placeholder words "Data table for the ferry schedule." Recall that placing a table within a table is called nesting a table.

To copy and paste the data table code:

▶ 1. In your text editor, switch to the DataNew file. (Open the file if necessary.)

▶ 2. Position the insertion point to the left of the start <table> code for the data table.

▶ 3. Select all the code through the end </table> tag.

▶ 4. Press the **Ctrl+C** keys to copy the selected text.

▶ 5. Close the DataNew file. (If you are prompted to save changes, click **No**.)

▶ 6. In your text editor, switch to the LayoutNew file.

▶ 7. In the table cell for the data table contents, delete the words **Data table for the ferry schedule**.

▶ 8. Press the **Ctrl+V** keys to paste the code from the DataNew data table.

▶ 9. Save LayoutNew. In your browser, refresh the screen to verify that the data table is displayed. See Figure 7-21.

Figure 7-21 ▶ **Nested data table on the Web page**

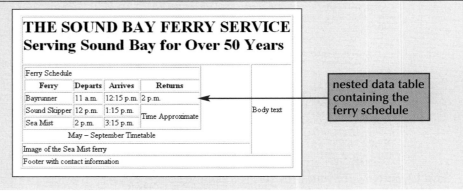

nested data table
containing the
ferry schedule

George uses interns every summer and wants to be sure that other interns can edit the Web page as necessary. You'll show him how to include comments in the table to inform others who work with the page.

Inserting Comments into the Table

It's a good idea to document where a nested table begins and ends. That will help you, and anyone else who works with the code, to find where the nested data table is located within the layout table. You will show George how to insert the necessary comments into the layout table.

To enter the comment above and below the data table:

▶ **1.** In your text editor, display the HTML code for LayoutNew.

▶ **2.** Position the insertion point to the left of the start <table> tag for the data table.

▶ **3.** Press the **Enter** key four times to create several blank lines.

▶ **4.** Press the **Up Arrow** key twice.

▶ **5.** On a blank line, type the following text, which is also shown in red in Figure 7-22.

```
<!-- nested data table begins here -->
```

Code for the comment above the data table ◀ **Figure 7-22**

```
<body>

<table border="1">

<tr>
  <td colspan="2"><h1>THE SOUND BAY FERRY SERVICE
<br />Serving Sound Bay for Over 50 Years</h1></td>
</tr>

<tr>
  <td>

<!-- nested data table begins here -->

<table border="1" title="The Sound Bay Ferry Schedule" summary="The Sound Bay Ferry runs from May
through September. Extra service is provided on the following days: Memorial Day, July 4, and
Labor Day. Ample parking is available at all ferry terminals.">
<caption align="bottom">May &ndash; September Timetable</caption>
<tr>
  <td colspan="4">Ferry Schedule</td>
</tr>
<tr>
  <th>Ferry</th>
  <th>Departs</th>
```

> comment to note the beginning of the nested table

▶ **6.** Position the insertion point after the end </table> tag for the data table.

▶ **7.** On a blank line, type the following text, which is also shown in red in Figure 7-23.

```
<!-- nested data table ends here -->
```

Code for the data table comment ◀ **Figure 7-23**

```
</tr>
</table>

<!-- nested data table ends here -->

</td>
```

> comment to note the end of the nested table

▶ **8.** Save LayoutNew.

> **Tip**
>
> Use comments only when necessary. Too many comments can defeat the purpose of calling the Web developer's attention to a particular line or area of code.

The layout table is now starting to take shape. George has already created a Web document that has the body text for the right column. You will show him how to copy and paste that text into the appropriate cell in the layout table.

To copy and paste the body text code:

1. Open a new session of your text editor.

2. Open the file **Bodytext.htm** from the Tutorial.07\Tutorial folder of your Data Files.

3. Select all the code in the file.

4. Press the **Ctrl+C** keys.

5. Close the Bodytext file. (If you are prompted to save changes, click **No**.)

6. In your text editor, switch to the LayoutNew file.

7. In the table cell for the body text contents, delete the words **Body text**.

8. Between the <td></td> tags, press the **Ctrl+V** keys to paste the code from the Bodytext file.

9. Save LayoutNew. In your browser, refresh the screen to verify that the body text is now displayed in the right-hand column of the table. See Figure 7-24.

| Figure 7-24 | Body text in the right column on the Web page |

Next, you will code the image of the Sea Mist, the most popular of the Sound Bay ferries. George has provided you with an image file of the Sea Mist. You'll show him how to enter code into the layout table to include this image.

> **Tip**
>
> When using images in a table cell, scale the image to be slightly larger than the table cell so the image completely occupies the cell.

To enter code for the Sea Mist ferry image:

1. In your text editor, display the HTML code for LayoutNew.

2. Position the insertion point in the cell that contains the placeholder text "Image of the Sea Mist ferry."

3. Delete the placeholder text.

4. Between the <td></td> tags, type the following code, which is also shown in red in Figure 7-25.

```
<img src="seamist.jpg" alt="image of the Sea Mist ferry"
width="450" height="360" />
```

Code for the Sea Mist ferry image **Figure 7-25**

```
<tr>
  <td><img src="seamist.jpg" alt="image of the Sea Mist ferry" width="450" height="360" /></td>
</tr>

<tr>
  <td colspan="2">Footer with contact information</td>
```

5. Save LayoutNew. In your browser, refresh the screen to verify that the image of the Sea Mist ferry is displayed. See Figure 7-26.

Image of the Sea Mist ferry on the Web page **Figure 7-26**

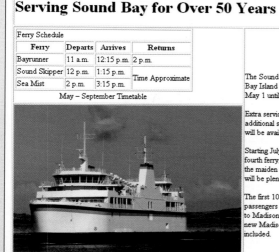

Last, George wants to replace the placeholder text in the footer with the actual address of the Sound Bay Ferry. You will show him how to do so now.

To enter the contact information:

▶ **1.** In your text editor, display the HTML code for LayoutNew.

▶ **2.** Position the insertion point in the cell that contains the placeholder text "Footer with contact information."

▶ **3.** Delete the placeholder text.

▶ **4.** Between the <td></td> tags, type the following code, which is also shown in red in Figure 7-27.

```
Sound Bay Ferry Service &middot; 121 Bay Avenue &middot Sound
Bay, WI 54000
```

Figure 7-27 ▶ **Code for the contact information**

```
<tr>
  <td><img src="seamist.jpg" alt="image of the Sea Mist ferry" width="450" height="360" /></td>
</tr>

<tr>
  <td colspan="2">Sound Bay Ferry Service &middot; 121 Bay Avenue &middot Sound Bay, WI 54000</td>
</tr>
</table>
```

company name
and address

▶ **5.** Save LayoutNew. In your browser, refresh the screen to verify that the contact information is displayed in the footer row. See Figure 7-28.

Figure 7-28 ▶ **Contact information on the Web page**

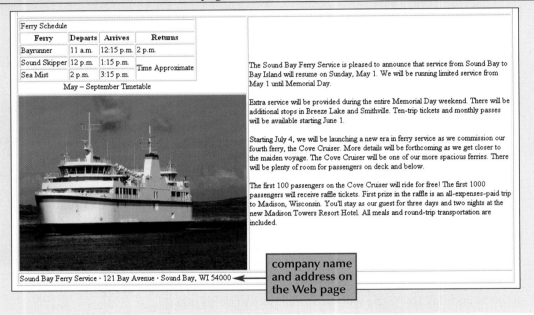

company name
and address on
the Web page

Tip

Eliminating the borders in a table is often referred to as giving the table a seamless border.

Now that the placeholder text has been replaced with actual data, you no longer need to display the nested data table border. You will show George how to delete the border attribute and its value.

To delete the layout table border:

▶ **1.** In your text editor, display the HTML code for LayoutNew.

▶ **2.** Just below the start body tag, position the insertion point in the start table tag for the layout table.

▶ **3.** Delete the code **border="1"**. Your code should be similar to the code shown in red in Figure 7-29.

The border attribute and value deleted from the layout table ◄ Figure 7-29

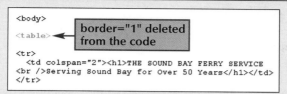

```
<body>
<table>        border="1" deleted
               from the code
<tr>
  <td colspan="2"><h1>THE SOUND BAY FERRY SERVICE
<br />Serving Sound Bay for Over 50 Years</h1></td>
</tr>
```

▶ **4.** Save LayoutNew. In your browser, refresh the screen to verify that the borders for the layout table no longer are displayed. The borders for the data table remain. See Figure 7-30.

Table borders no longer appear on the Web page ◄ Figure 7-30

THE SOUND BAY FERRY SERVICE
Serving Sound Bay for Over 50 Years

table borders have been deleted

Ferry Schedule			
Ferry	**Departs**	**Arrives**	**Returns**
Bayrunner	11 a.m.	12:15 p.m.	2 p.m.
Sound Skipper	12 p.m.	1:15 p.m.	Time Approximate
Sea Mist	2 p.m.	3:15 p.m.	

May – September Timetable

The Sound Bay Ferry Service is pleased to announce that service from Sound Bay to Bay Island will resume on Sunday, May 1. We will be running limited service from May 1 until Memorial Day.

Extra service will be provided during the entire Memorial Day weekend. There will be additional stops in Breeze Lake and Smithville. Ten-trip tickets and monthly passes will be available starting June 1.

Starting July 4, we will be launching a new era in ferry service as we commission our fourth ferry, the Cove Cruiser. More details will be forthcoming as we get closer to the maiden voyage. The Cove Cruiser will be one of our more spacious ferries. There will be plenty of room for passengers on deck and below.

The first 100 passengers on the Cove Cruiser will ride for free! The first 1000 passengers will receive raffle tickets. First prize in the raffle is an all-expenses-paid trip to Madison, Wisconsin. You'll stay as our guest for three days and two nights at the new Madison Towers Resort Hotel. All meals and round-trip transportation are included.

In this session, you learned that tables can be used to arrange page layout. When tables are used for page layout, most of the formatting is controlled by the table element, not the body element. You also learned how to nest a data table within a layout table. You learned how to eliminate the borders between cells once the layout has been finalized. Now you will learn how to apply CSS styles to table elements.

Session 7.2 Quick Check | Review

1. What is the first step in planning a layout table?
2. If you are creating a layout table, where would you code the start <table> tag?
3. When you create a layout table, do you code the table first or do you first code the contents for the Web page?
4. What is a nested table?
5. What would you code to document that a nested table exists in the layout table?
6. When using tables for layout, is it common to eliminate the borders?

Session 7.3

Tip

Because the table will occupy the entire page, you should focus your attention on setting the style for the table element in a layout table, not for the body element.

Using CSS with Tables

Normally, when you style a document, you can control the appearance of the entire document by styling the body element selector. In a layout table, you enter the code for the start <table> tag just below the start <body> tag, and you code the end </table> tag just above the end </body> tag. Because the layout table occupies the entire body section, almost all styles you create for the table will supersede any styles you create for the body.

You should, however, always set the style for the background color or background image for the page. If the table does not occupy the entire screen width and height, the background color or background image will appear in those areas where the table does not appear. You will show George how to set the style for the body element to change the background color of the page.

To change the background color of the page:

▶ **1.** In your text editor, display the HTML code for LayoutNew.

▶ **2.** Position the insertion point below the CSS comment code.

▶ **3.** Type the following code, which is also shown in red in Figure 7-31.

```
body {
background-color: tan; }
```

Figure 7-31	Code to style the body element

```
<html>
<head>
<title>The Sound Bay Ferry</title>

<style type="text/css" media="all">

/* Your First Name Your Last Name
Today's Date */

body {
background-color: tan; }
```

sets the background color of the body section to tan

▶ **4.** Save LayoutNew. In your browser, refresh the screen to verify that the background color of the page is now tan. See Figure 7-32.

THE SOUND BAY FERRY SERVICE
Serving Sound Bay for Over 50 Years

Ferry Schedule			
Ferry	**Departs**	**Arrives**	**Returns**
Bayrunner	11 a.m.	12:15 p.m.	2 p.m.
Sound Skipper	12 p.m.	1:15 p.m.	Time Approximate
Sea Mist	2 p.m.	3:15 p.m.	

May – September Timetable

background of the layout table is now tan

The Sound Bay Ferry Service is pleased to announce that service from Sound Bay to Bay Island will resume on Sunday, May 1. We will be running limited service from May 1 until Memorial Day.

Extra service will be provided during the entire Memorial Day weekend. There will be additional stops in Breeze Lake and Smithville. Ten-trip tickets and monthly passes will be available starting June 1.

Starting July 4, we will be launching a new era in ferry service as we commission our fourth ferry, the Cove Cruiser. More details will be forthcoming as we get closer to the maiden voyage. The Cove Cruiser will be one of our more spacious ferries. There will be plenty of room for passengers on deck and below.

The first 100 passengers on the Cove Cruiser will ride for free! The first 1000 passengers will receive raffle tickets. First prize in the raffle is an all-expenses-paid trip to Madison, Wisconsin. You'll stay as our guest for three days and two nights at the new Madison Towers Resort Hotel. All meals and round-trip transportation are included.

George wants to fine-tune the text and other elements of the table. You'll show him how to change the appearance of the entire layout table next.

Changing the Appearance of the Entire Table

When a layout table has a nested table, the formatting of each table can at first be at odds with each other. To solve this problem, you will set the style for the layout table, and then you will set style for the data table to resolve any formatting conflicts. George would like to display the table text in 12pt Arial type. He also wants to give the table a neutral background color that is lighter than the tan background color. You will show George how to set the style for the layout table now.

To style the layout table:

▶ **1.** In your text editor, display the HTML code for LayoutNew.

▶ **2.** Position the insertion point below the start code for the body style.

▶ **3.** Type the following code, which is also shown in red in Figure 7-33.

```
table {
width: 775px;
margin-left: auto;
margin-right: auto;
font-size: 12pt;
font-family: arial,helvetica,sans-serif;
background-color: wheat; }
```

Figure 7-33 | **Code to set the style for the table element**

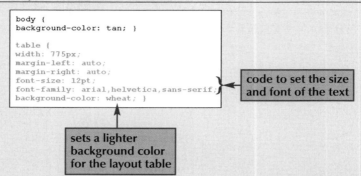

```
body {
background-color: tan; }

table {
width: 775px;
margin-left: auto;
margin-right: auto;
font-size: 12pt;
font-family: arial,helvetica,sans-serif;
background-color: wheat; }
```

code to set the size and font of the text

sets a lighter background color for the layout table

▶ 4. Save LayoutNew. In your browser, refresh the screen to verify that the background color of the page is now wheat. Don't be alarmed about the size of the data table. See Figure 7-34.

Figure 7-34 | **Layout table on the Web page**

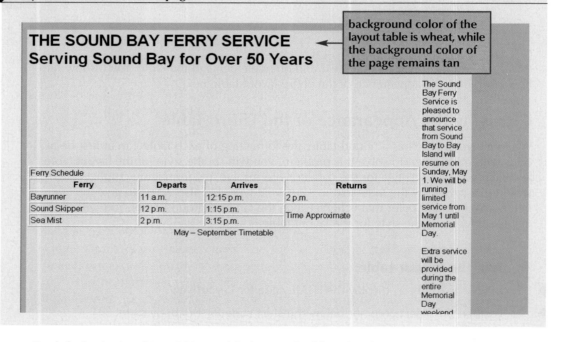

THE SOUND BAY FERRY SERVICE
Serving Sound Bay for Over 50 Years

background color of the layout table is wheat, while the background color of the page remains tan

The Sound Bay Ferry Service is pleased to announce that service from Sound Bay to Bay Island will resume on Sunday, May 1. We will be running limited service from May 1 until Memorial Day.

Extra service will be provided during the entire Memorial Day weekend

Ferry Schedule

Ferry	Departs	Arrives	Returns
Bayrunner	11 a.m.	12:15 p.m.	2 p.m.
Sound Skipper	12 p.m.	1:15 p.m.	Time Approximate
Sea Mist	2 p.m.	3:15 p.m.	

May – September Timetable

By default, the borders within a table have a double rule. If you want to change the double rule to a single rule, use the **border-collapse property** and set its value to *collapse*. For example:

```
table {
border-collapse: collapse; }
```

Setting the Style for the Nested Data Table

George would also like to set the style for the nested data table. He asks you how you can change the style, since you have already set the style for the table element. You explain that you could use inline styles, but you do not want to embed code into the Web page. You'd rather have all the style codes at the top of the page where they are organized and easy to find. To set the style for the nested table, you will create three dependent ID selectors. You will have a dependent selector named *data*, which will set the style for the table. A dependent selector named *green* will set the style for the data table caption, and a dependent selector named *header* will set the style for table header rows. You will now show George how to create these three dependent selectors to style the data table.

To style the data table:

▶ **1.** In your text editor, display the HTML code for LayoutNew.

▶ **2.** Position the insertion point below the code to style the table element selector.

▶ **3.** On a blank line, type the following code, which is also shown in red in Figure 7-35.

```
table#data {
background-color: lightblue;
width: 100%;
border: black solid thick;
border-collapse: collapse; }

caption#green {
color: white;
background-color: green;
font-weight: bold; }

td#header {
font-size: 16pt;
text-align: center; }
```

Code to set the style for the nested data table ◀ **Figure 7-35**

```
table {
width: 775px;
margin-left: auto;
margin-right: auto;
font-size: 12pt;
font-family: arial, helvetica, sans-serif;
background-color: wheat; }

table#data {
background-color: lightblue;
width: 100%;
border: black solid thick;
border-collapse: collapse; }

caption#green {
color: white;
background-color: green;
font-weight: bold; }

td#header {
font-size: 16pt;
text-align: center; }
```

data selector sets the style for the table

green selector sets the style for the data table caption

header selector sets the style for the table header rows

▶ **4.** Save LayoutNew.

Now that you have created the dependent selectors, you have to apply the selectors. You will show George how to apply the data, green, and header dependent ID selectors.

To apply the data, green, and header dependent ID selectors:

▶ **1.** In your text editor, display the HTML code for LayoutNew.

▶ **2.** Type the following code shown in bold, which is shown in red in Figure 7-36.

```
<td><table border="1" id="data" title="The Sound Bay Ferry Schedule">
<caption id="green" align="bottom">May &ndash; September
Timetable</caption>

<tr>
  <td id="header" colspan="4">Ferry Schedule</td>
```

Figure 7-36

Applying the data, green, and header dependent selectors

```
<!-- nested data table begins here -->

<table border="1" id="data" title="The Sound Bay Ferry Schedule" summary="The Sound Bay Ferry runs
from May through September. Extra service is provided on the following days: Memorial Day, July 4,
and Labor Day. Ample parking is available at all ferry terminals. ">
<caption id="green" align="bottom">May &ndash; September Timetable</caption>
<tr>
  <td id="header" colspan="4">Ferry Schedule</td>
</tr>
```

▶ **3.** Save LayoutNew. In your browser, refresh the screen to verify that the style for the data table has been set correctly. See Figure 7-37.

Figure 7-37

Data table on the Web page

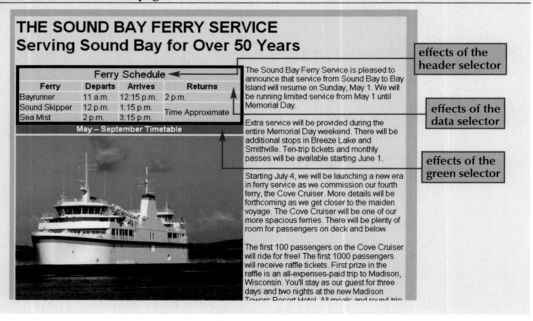

George also thinks using an alternating background color for the rows of the table would make the information easier to read. You'll show him how to create this effect in a table.

Striping Rows

Tip

A common naming convention for striping rows is to name one selector "odd" and the other "even." You apply the odd selector to odd-numbered rows and the even selector to the even-numbered rows.

Many tables mimic the appearance of computer printout where each row has an alternating background color, making the rows easier to locate and read. This effect is called **row striping** and is accomplished using CSS. You can set the style for the tr element selector once and then apply that style to every other row. You could also create two dependent styles for the tr selector and alternatively apply styles to each row in the table.

George would like to stripe the Sound Skipper row to create some contrast between that row and the other rows. Because there is also a rowspan in this row, the striping will continue across the row and then down the cells where the rowspan has been created.

To create the style for the Sound Skipper row:

▶ **1.** In your text editor, display the HTML code for LayoutNew.

▶ **2.** Position the insertion point below the code for the td#header dependent ID selector.

▶ **3.** On a blank line, type the following code, which is also shown in red in Figure 7-38.

```
tr#navy {
color: white;
background-color: navy; }
```

Code to create the style for the Sound Skipper row ◀ **Figure 7-38**

```
td#header {
font-size: 16pt;
text-align: center; }

tr#navy {
color: white;
background-color: navy; }
```

navy ID selector specifies white text on a navy background

▶ **4.** Save LayoutNew.

Now you must apply the navy ID selector to the row that will have a background color of navy. You will show George how to apply the navy dependent class.

To apply the navy dependent ID selector:

▶ **1.** In your text editor, display the HTML code for LayoutNew.

▶ **2.** Position the insertion point to the left of the angle bracket (>) in the start <tr> tag for the Sound Skipper row.

▶ **3.** Press the **Spacebar**.

▶ **4.** Type the following code shown in bold, which is also shown in red in Figure 7-39.

```
<tr id="navy">
  <td>Sound Skipper</td>
  <td>12 p.m.</td>
  <td>1:15 p.m.</td>
  <td rowspan="2">Time Approximate</td>
</tr>
```

Applying the navy dependent ID selector ◀ **Figure 7-39**

```
<tr id="navy">
  <td>Sound Skipper</td>
  <td>12 p.m.</td>
  <td>1:15 p.m.</td>
  <td rowspan="2">Time Approximate</td>
</tr>
```

▶ **5.** Save LayoutNew. In your browser, refresh the screen to verify that the data table has been styled. See Figure 7-40.

Figure 7-40 ▶ Sound Skipper row striped on the Web page

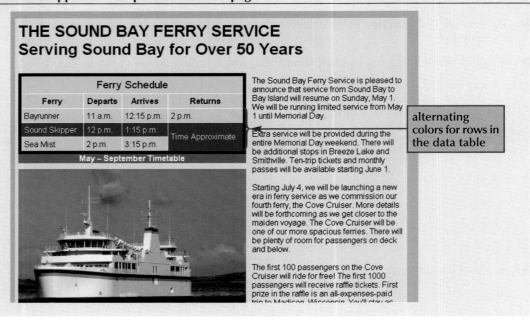

You've finished fine-tuning the data table, so George wants to work on the layout table.

Changing the Appearance of the Layout Table Cells

Now that you've changed the appearance of the data table, you can turn your attention to showing George how to change the style of the layout table. You can easily control the appearance of all the cells in the layout table by setting styles for the td and th element selectors. For example, right now, the text in each cell is too close to the edges of the cells. You'd like to give the cells some padding to provide white space around the contents of the cells. George also wants the text in the paragraph column to appear at the top of the column, not centered, where it is now by default. Because you have already created a style for the td element selector, you will have to create a dependent class for the td element selector to vertically align the text in one particular cell. You will show George how to style all the cells in the table and then apply the *align* dependent class, which will vertically align the text in the right column.

To enter the code to style the table cells:

▶ 1. In your text editor, display the HTML code for LayoutNew.

▶ 2. Position the insertion point below the code for the tr#navy dependent style.

▶ 3. On a blank line, type the following code, which is also shown in red in Figure 7-41.

```
td, th {
padding: .3em; }

td.align {
vertical-align: top; }
```

Code to set the style for the layout table cells ◀ Figure 7-41

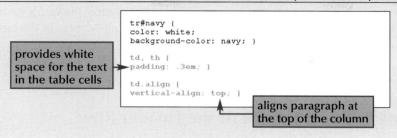

```
tr#navy {
color: white;
background-color: navy; }

td, th {
padding: .3em; }

td.align {
vertical-align: top; }
```

provides white space for the text in the table cells →

aligns paragraph at the top of the column →

Now that you have created the dependent class, you also need to apply the class. You will show George how to do that now.

To apply the align class:

▶ **1.** If necessary, in your text editor, display the HTML code for LayoutNew.

▶ **2.** Position the insertion point to the right of the close quote in the code `<td rowspan="2">`, which is just below the comment "nested data table ends here."

▶ **3.** Press the **Spacebar**. Type the following code, which is also shown in red in Figure 7-42.

```
<td rowspan="2" class="align">
```

Code for the align dependent class ◀ Figure 7-42

```
<td rowspan="2" class="align"><p>The Sound Bay Ferry Service is pleased to announce that service
from Sound Bay to Bay Island will resume on Sunday, May 1. We will be running limited service from
May 1 until Memorial Day.</p>
```

▶ **4.** Save LayoutNew. In your browser, refresh the screen to verify that the text in the right-hand column now appears beginning at the top of the cell. See Figure 7-43.

Text aligned at the top of the right column on the Web page ◀ Figure 7-43

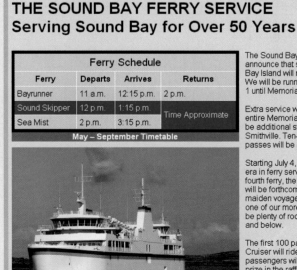

THE SOUND BAY FERRY SERVICE
Serving Sound Bay for Over 50 Years

Ferry Schedule			
Ferry	Departs	Arrives	Returns
Bayrunner	11 a.m.	12:15 p.m.	2 p.m.
Sound Skipper	12 p.m.	1:15 p.m.	Time Approximate
Sea Mist	2 p.m.	3:15 p.m.	

May – September Timetable

The Sound Bay Ferry Service is pleased to announce that service from Sound Bay to Bay Island will resume on Sunday, May 1. We will be running limited service from May 1 until Memorial Day.

Extra service will be provided during the entire Memorial Day weekend. There will be additional stops in Breeze Lake and Smithville. Ten-trip tickets and monthly passes will be available starting June 1.

Starting July 4, we will be launching a new era in ferry service as we commission our fourth ferry, the Cove Cruiser. More details will be forthcoming as we get closer to the maiden voyage. The Cove Cruiser will be one of our more spacious ferries. There will be plenty of room for passengers on deck and below.

The first 100 passengers on the Cove Cruiser will ride for free! The first 1000 passengers will receive raffle tickets. First prize in the raffle is an all-expenses-paid trip to Madison, Wisconsin. You'll stay as

If there are no data tables on the page and you are using tables for layout, you probably want to eliminate all table borders. Table borders come from two different sources. The outside borders are controlled by the table element selector; the inside borders are controlled by the td and th element selectors. To eliminate all borders in the table, style these elements like so:

```
table, td, th {
border: 0; }
```

Changing the Appearance of the Header Row

George would also like to change the appearance of the header row to have the text stand out. He has supplied you with an image to be used as a background for the h1 heading. The image is of a ferryboat icon. George would also like the heading centered and have a bottom border, which will serve to divide the banner from the rest of the page. To close up space between the h1 heading and the table, he also doesn't want any white space following the heading. You will show George how to set the style for the h1 heading now.

To set the style for the h1 heading:

1. In your text editor, display the HTML code for LayoutNew.

2. Position the insertion point below the code for td.align dependent class.

3. Type the following code, which is also shown in red in Figure 7-44.

```
h1 {
width: 775px;
height: 125px;
font-size: 20pt;
font-family: "bernhardmod BT",serif;
padding: 15 15 0 40;
background-image: url(ferryicon.gif);
background-repeat: no-repeat;
text-align: center;
border-bottom: groove thick;
margin-bottom: 0; }
```

Figure 7-44 — Code to set the style for the h1 heading

```
td.align {
vertical-align: top; }

h1 {
width: 775px;
height: 125px;
font-size: 20pt;
font-family: "bernhardmod BT",serif;       inserts an ferry
padding: 15 15 0 40;                        icon image
background-image: url(ferryicon.gif);
background-repeat: no-repeat;
text-align: center;                         centers the text
border-bottom: groove thick;
margin-bottom: 0; }
```

4. Save LayoutNew. In your browser, refresh the screen to verify that the h1 heading has been styled. See Figure 7-45.

ferry icon image

THE SOUND BAY FERRY SERVICE
Serving Sound Bay for Over 50 Years ← centered text

Ferry Schedule			
Ferry	Departs	Arrives	Returns
Bayrunner	11 a.m.	12:15 p.m.	2 p.m.
Sound Skipper	12 p.m.	1:15 p.m.	Time Approximate
Sea Mist	2 p.m.	3:15 p.m.	
May – September Timetable			

The Sound Bay Ferry Service is pleased to announce that service from Sound Bay to Bay Island will resume on Sunday, May 1. We will be running limited service from May 1 until Memorial Day.

Extra service will be provided during the entire Memorial Day weekend. There will be additional stops in Breeze Lake and Smithville. Ten-trip tickets and monthly passes will be available starting June 1.

Starting July 4, we will be launching a new era in ferry service as we commission our fourth ferry, the Cove Cruiser. More details will be forthcoming as we get closer to the maiden voyage. The Cove Cruiser will be one of our more spacious ferries. There will be plenty of room for passengers on deck and below.

The first 100 passengers on the Cove Cruiser will ride for free! The first 1000 passengers will receive raffle tickets. First prize in the raffle is an all-expenses-paid trip

Your next task is to position the entire layout table on the page.

Positioning the Entire Table

Currently, the table is positioned at the left margin. You can center the table by using the <div> </div> tags and applying a style to center the table, just as you have already done to center an image.

If you want to have the table in the body of a document along with text, you can float a table left or right, similar to the way you floated images left or right. George wants to center the table. You will show him how to create an independent style and then apply the style.

Tip

If the table width is less than 100%, you can center a table in the Firefox browser only by using the margin-left and the margin-right properties and assigning each property the value of *auto*.

To enter the code for the center independent class:

▶ **1.** If necessary, in your text editor, display the HTML code for LayoutNew.

▶ **2.** Position the insertion point below the code to style the h1 heading.

▶ **3.** Type the following code, which is also shown in red in Figure 7-46.

```
.center {
text-align: center; }
```

Figure 7-46 ⟩ **Code for the center independent class**

```
h1 {
width: 775px;
height: 125px;
font-size: 20pt;
font-family: "bernhardmod BT",serif;
padding: 15 15 0 40;
background-image: url(ferryicon.gif);
background-repeat: no-repeat;
text-align: center;
border-bottom: groove thick;
margin-bottom: 0; }

.center {
text-align: center; }
```

Now that you have created the independent class, you will show George how to apply the class.

To apply the center class:

▶ **1.** If necessary, in your text editor, display the HTML code for LayoutNew.

▶ **2.** Position the insertion point below the start <body> tag.

▶ **3.** Type the following code, which is also shown in red in Figure 7-47.

   `<div class="center">`

Figure 7-47 ⟩ **Applying the center independent class**

```
.center {
text-align: center; }

</style>
</head>

<body>
<div class="center">        ◀── centers the layout
                               table on the page
<table>
```

▶ **4.** Position the insertion point above the end </body> tag.

▶ **5.** Type the following code, which is also shown in red in Figure 7-48.

   `</div>`

Figure 7-48 ⟩ **Including the end div tag**

```
</tr>
</table>
</div>
</body>
</html>
```

▶ **6.** Save LayoutNew. In your browser, refresh the screen to verify that the table is now centered in the browser. See Figure 7-49.

Layout table centered on the Web page ◀ **Figure 7-49**

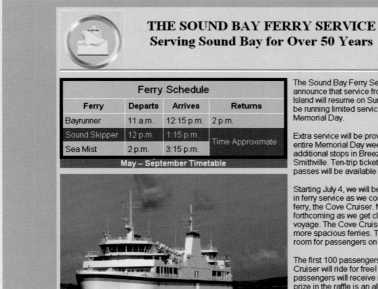

Formatting Columns with the col Tag | InSight

The <col /> tag is used to format several columns or individual columns. The <col /> tag is an empty element, so close it with the "space slash" combination. You begin by entering the <col /> tag after the <table> and <caption> tags (if there is a caption). If you want to format more than one column, use the span attribute and assign a value equal to the number of columns you want to style. You can also apply different formatting to individual columns. You code inline styles for the columns, adding as many <col /> tags as you need. Note the empty <col /> tag below:

```
<table>
<caption>Figure A (Quarterly Sales Leaders)</caption>
<col style="font: 14pt arial; text-align: center; color: green;
background-color: yellow;" />
<col />
<col style="font: 18pt arial; text-align: right; color: navy;
background-color: ivory;" />
```

George would also like the footer text to capture the reader's attention even though it is at the bottom of the page. George suggests centered, bold, white text on a black background for the footer row. Because you want to style this row uniquely and not affect the appearance of the other rows in the table, you will show George how to create a dependent ID selector to set the style for only the footer row.

To set the style for the footer row:

▶ **1.** In your text editor, display the HTML code for LayoutNew.

▶ **2.** Position the insertion point below the code for the center independent class.

3. On a blank line, type the following code, which is also shown in red in Figure 7-50.

```
tr#black {
color: white;
background-color: black;
font-weight: bold;
text-align: center; }
```

Figure 7-50 ▷ **Code for the black dependent ID selector**

```
.center {
text-align: center; }

tr#black {         creates a dependent ID
color: white;      selector named black that
background-color: black;   displays centered white text
font-weight: bold;   on a black background
text-align: center; }
```

Last, you have to apply the black dependent ID selector to the footer row. Doing so will give that row a background color of black. You will show George how to apply the black dependent ID selector.

To apply the black dependent ID selector:

▶ **1.** If necessary, in your text editor, display the HTML code for LayoutNew.

▶ **2.** Position the insertion point to the left of the angle bracket (>) in the start <tr> tag for the footer row.

▶ **3.** Press the **Spacebar**.

▶ **4.** Type the following code shown in bold, which is also shown in red in Figure 7-51.

```
<tr id="black">
  <td colspan="2">Sound Bay Ferry Service &middot;
121 Bay Avenue &middot Sound Bay, WI</td>
</tr>
```

Figure 7-51 ▷ **Applying the black dependent selector**

```
<tr id="black">
  <td colspan="2">Sound Bay Ferry Service &middot; 121 Bay Avenue &middot Sound Bay, WI 54000</td>
</tr>
```

▶ **5.** Save LayoutNew. In your browser, refresh the screen to verify that the black dependent ID selector has been applied to the completed Web page. See Figure 7-52.

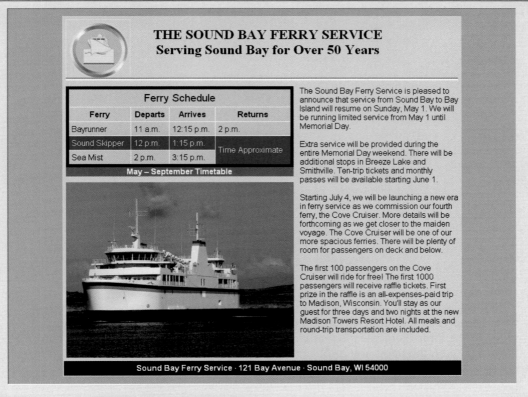

THE SOUND BAY FERRY SERVICE
Serving Sound Bay for Over 50 Years

Ferry Schedule

Ferry	Departs	Arrives	Returns
Bayrunner	11 a.m.	12:15 p.m.	2 p.m.
Sound Skipper	12 p.m.	1:15 p.m.	Time Approximate
Sea Mist	2 p.m.	3:15 p.m.	

May – September Timetable

The Sound Bay Ferry Service is pleased to announce that service from Sound Bay to Bay Island will resume on Sunday, May 1. We will be running limited service from May 1 until Memorial Day.

Extra service will be provided during the entire Memorial Day weekend. There will be additional stops in Breeze Lake and Smithville. Ten-trip tickets and monthly passes will be available starting June 1.

Starting July 4, we will be launching a new era in ferry service as we commission our fourth ferry, the Cove Cruiser. More details will be forthcoming as we get closer to the maiden voyage. The Cove Cruiser will be one of our more spacious ferries. There will be plenty of room for passengers on deck and below.

The first 100 passengers on the Cove Cruiser will ride for free! The first 1000 passengers will receive raffle tickets. First prize in the raffle is an all-expenses-paid trip to Madison, Wisconsin. You'll stay as our guest for three days and two nights at the new Madison Towers Resort Hotel. All meals and round-trip transportation are included.

Sound Bay Ferry Service · 121 Bay Avenue · Sound Bay, WI 54000

▶ **6.** Close your text editor and close your browser.

Avoiding Deprecated Attributes

The following attributes should be avoided in the table tag or table data tags because they are deprecated, are proprietary, have poor browser support, or their purpose can be better achieved by using CSS. See Figure 7-53.

Figure 7-53 | **Deprecated table attributes**

Attribute	Purpose	CSS Use
align	Positions the table left, center, or right	Deprecated; use the CSS text-align property; for now, continue to use this attribute only with the caption tag
bordercolorlight	Applies a color to the top and the left outside borders of a table; Internet Explorer only	Use the CSS border properties instead
bordercolordark	Applies a color to the right and the bottom outside borders of a table; Internet Explorer only	Use the CSS border properties instead
bgcolor	A table, row, and cell attribute that applied background color	Deprecated; use the CSS background-color property instead
cellpadding	A table attribute; adds padding to a cell	Use CSS padding properties instead
cellspacing	A table attribute; increases the distance between cells	Use the CSS border-spacing property, which currently works only in Firefox
valign	Aligns an image or text vertically in a cell	Deprecated; use the CSS vertical-align property instead

In this session, you learned how to style data tables and layout tables. You learned which properties should be styled in the body element and which properties should be styled in the table element. You learned that it's common to position the table centered horizontally on the page. You also learned that if there is a nested table, you need to code dependent ID selectors to style just the elements in the nested table.

Review | **Session 7.3 Quick Check**

1. In a layout table, what properties should always be styled in the body element?
2. Is it common to position a table? If so, where is the table positioned?
3. What properties are commonly used to format table cells?
4. What is the purpose of the border-collapse property?
5. What property and what value are used to align the cell contents so that the text begins at the top of the cell?
6. What is the purpose of striping rows?

HTML lacks many of the word processor features for creating and formatting tables. Tables have been used to arrange data. In the past, tables were also used for page layout, but this usage is now discouraged. A good strategy for coding tables is to code the table first, using placeholder data to do so. If you need to merge columns or rows, perform each merge and then view the document in the browser to observe the result. Once you have determined the table code is correct, delete the placeholder data and enter the actual table data. The <table> tag begins each table and the </table> tag ends each table. A table caption, which provides a description of the table, is optional. The tags to create a table row are <tr> and </tr>. The tags to create table data are <td> and </td>. You use the colspan attribute to merge columns and the rowspan attribute to merge rows. You can use the float property to position a table at the left or the right of the screen. The border-collapse property is used to change the default ruling of a table from a double line to a single line. If you are coding a data table, it's best to first code the table in a separate document, and then copy the table code into the document that will contain the data table.

Key Terms

align attribute	empty cell	row striping
border-collapse property	empty-cells property	summary attribute
caption	gridline	table border
cell	layout table	table header
colspan attribute	nested table	title attribute
data table	rowspan attribute	

| Practice | **Review Assignments** |

Data Files needed for the Review Assignments: Cruiser.jpg, Foil.htm, and Foilbanner.gif

The Sound Bay Ferry Service plans to introduce a new high-speed ferry service using a hydrofoil. The hydrofoil ferry will cut the commuting time to Bay Island in half. In addition to speeding the journey along the bay, the hydrofoil comes with a full set of amenities not found on most other ferries. The ferry will have dining facilities to serve a light breakfast or lunch. Passengers will be able to have wireless laptop connectivity and watch television on wide-screen plasma screens. The main seating area has comfortable padded seats, not the hardwood bench seats installed on the ferries currently in operation. You have been asked to compose a Web page that announces the arrival of the hydrofoil service. You have decided to create a table layout with a banner row on top, which will include an image and a horizontal rule. The left column will contain the promotional copy; the right column will display an image of the hydrofoil. A footer row will appear at the bottom of the page with the address of the Sound Bay Ferry Service. Jessica Doyle, a publicist for the hydrofoil manufacturer, has written some promotional copy for you, which you will incorporate into the table. Complete the following steps:

1. Use your text editor to open the **Foil.htm** file located in your Tutorial.07\Review folder included with your Data Files. Save this file as **FoilNew.htm** in the same folder.

2. You will be creating an embedded style sheet. In the head area below the page title, enter the code for the start <style> and the end </style> tags. In the start <style> tag, include the **media** attribute with a value of **all**.

3. Below the start <style> tag, enter a comment that includes your first and last name as the author and today's date.

4. Create grouped selectors to style the table element selector and the table data element selector to have a background color of cadetblue. Text should be displayed as bold, 12pt, and in Verdana, a sans serif font. Set the table to have no borders and a padding of 0.5em.

5. Create an independent class named **center** that centers text.

6. Set the style for the hr element selector to display a gold rule with a height of 5px. The background-color should be gold.

7. Set the style for the img element selector to have a border that is black, solid, and medium.

8. Create an ID selector named **aligntop** that vertically aligns elements at the top of a cell.

9. Create an ID selector named **footer**. Set the style for this ID selector to display white centered text on a black background with a padding of 0.5em.

10. In the body section and below the comment "Create your table here," create a table with three rows and two columns (a total of six cells). Remember to code the end </table> tag at the end of the table. Type the word **placeholder** in each cell.

11. Save your FoilNew HTML document, and then open it in your browser. Make corrections as necessary.

12. In your text editor, insert the necessary code to have the first <td> cell of the first row span two columns. Delete extra cells.

13. Insert the necessary code to have the first <td> cell of the third row span two columns. Delete extra cells.

14. Save your FoilNew HTML document, and then open it in your browser. Make corrections as necessary.

15. In your text editor, delete all placeholder text.

16. In the first <td> tag of the table, apply the center class.

17. In the second cell of the second row, in the <td> tag, apply the aligntop ID selector so that the Cruiser.jpg image will align at the top of the cell.

18. In the <td> tag for the last row, apply the footer ID selector.

19. Cut and paste code and text as directed in the comments.

20. Delete all comments.

21. Save your FoilNew HTML document, and then open it in your browser. The document should be similar to the one shown in Figure 7-54.

Figure 7-54

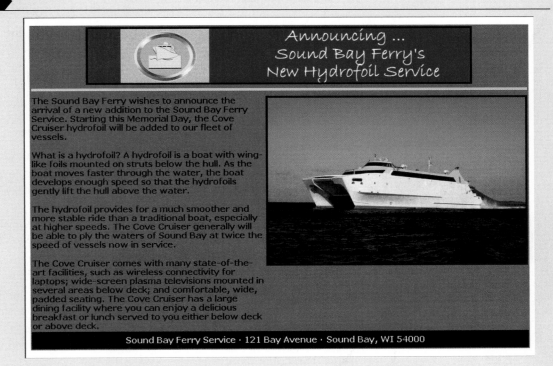

22. Close all open windows.

23. Submit the results of the preceding steps to your instructor, either in printed or electronic form, as requested.

| Apply | **Case Problem 1** |

Use the skills you learned in the tutorial to create a Web page for a fitness center.

Data Files needed for this Case Problem: Body.htm, Female.jpg, Female2.jpg, Female3.jpg, and Male.jpg

Body by You Joan Gardner, the owner of a large fitness center, has approached you about creating a Web page about her business, Body by You. Body by You has a different approach to offering fitness. While most health clubs and fitness centers have adults as customers, Body by You offers fitness classes for all ages. Although all age groups are welcome to the club, each day is devoted to focusing on one particular age group. Of keen interest to Joan is helping children and teens maintain proper health and fitness. Special classes are also arranged for baby boomers and seniors who do not want to live a sedentary lifestyle in their golden years. You will create table styles and apply those styles to a table that highlights the activities offered weekly at Body by You. Complete the following steps:

1. Use your text editor to open the **Body.htm** file located in your Tutorial.07\Case1 folder included with your Data Files. Save this file as **BodyNew.htm** in the same folder. If necessary, scroll down to see the entire page contents.

2. An embedded style has been created for you. Below the start <style> tag, insert a comment that includes your first and last name as the author and today's date.

⊕ **EXPLORE**

3. Below the code for the body element selector and the comment below it, set the style of the table element selector as follows:
   - Have the border of the table appear as black, thin, and solid.
   - Position the table absolutely on the screen, 20px from the top and 600px from the left.
   - The width of the table should be 200px; the height of the table should also be 200px.
   - The overflow property should have a value of auto.
   - The text should be displayed as bold text.
   - The border-collapse property should have a value of collapse.
   - The table should float right. The margin on the right, bottom, and left should be 1em.

4. Create a style for table cells so that they have a padding of 0.5em.

5. Create a style for table headers that centers text and displays text as gold with a background color of navy. The text should appear in all uppercase letters (use a style to do so).

6. Create a dependent class for table rows named **blue**. This style should have text appear as black text on a lightblue background.

7. Create a dependent class for table rows named **navy**. This style should have text appear as white text on a navy background.

8. In the body of the document, scroll through the text and locate the start <table> tag for the data table. (It's right after the comment "The data table starts here.")

9. In the table header tag for the first row of the data table, (the cell with the words "A Special Day for Each Day of the Week") apply the attribute and value to have that cell span two columns.

10. Beginning with the table row tag for the Mondays row and ending with the table row tag for the last row, which has information about a Holiday Special, alternatively apply the blue and the navy classes to each table row tag in the table to create a striped row effect.

11. Save your BodyNew HTML document, and then open it in your browser. The document should be similar to the one shown in Figure 7-55.

Figure 7-55

Body by You
A Lifetime of Fitness

At *Body by You*, you don't have to be in your 20's to look great. We believe age is just a number. Here at *Body by You*, even 80 is the new 40!

Got an overweight child? *Body by You* will strive to have your child maintain an appropriate weight that will restore your child's confidence and good health. All our exercises are coupled with classes on making smart, healthful, and nutritional choices for your children.

Had a baby? We can get you back into shape in just a few weeks. We have a nursery service right here at *Body by You*. We'll take care of your baby while you work yourself back into shape.

At *Body by You* we feel your senior days should be spent swimming in our Olympic-size pool, doing low-impact or non-impact exercises, Yoga, Pilates, and gentle cardio-vascular conditioning.

We've designed programs for every age group from 6 to 106. Come join the fun at *Body by You*. It's *your* body; make the most of it.

Body by You
28 San Palmetto Way
Alhambra, CA 91801
646 744-1230

A SPECIAL DAY FOR EACH DAY OF THE WEEK	
Mondays	Kids Central (grades K-3)
Tuesdays	Tweens and Teens Time (grades 4-8 and grades 9-12) in separate groups
Wednesdays	Active Adults (ages 19-49)
Thursdays	BoomerVille (ages 50-69)
Fridays	Senior City (ages 70+)
Saturdays	Boys, Girls, Tweens and Teens Gymnastics
Sundays	Slimnastics

Holiday Special. Just Announced! Tweens can join for an extra six months and get two months' membership for free!

12. Close all open windows.

13. Submit the results of the preceding steps to your instructor, either in printed or electronic form, as requested.

Apply | **Case Problem 2**

Use the skills you learned in the tutorial to create and style a Web page for a library.

Data Files needed for this Case Problem: Library.htm, Masthead.gif, and Masthead2.gif

The Sharon City Library The Sharon City, Kansas, public library has undergone a major renovation. The building itself has been almost completely rebuilt. The Sharon City library now considers itself to be more of a cybrary, a computer-enhanced library. The library emphasizes computer use at the library more than it does lending books and periodicals. The library has done away with its paper-based card catalog and now solely uses computer terminals for visitors to search its databases, all of which are now online. The library has several multimedia rooms where visitors can listen to or watch various types of media. The most popular addition has been a large coffee and snack shop. Visitors are pleased that they no longer have to leave the building to get something to eat or drink. Roger Ramos, the head librarian, has asked you to revise the library's home page. All of the other pages at the Web site are formatted with tables, so you will use a layout table on the revised home page as well. Roger has already created some copy for you, which you will use in your new table. Complete the following steps:

1. Use your text editor to open the **Library.htm** file located in your Tutorial.07\Case2 folder included with your Data Files. Save this file as **LibraryNew.htm** in the same folder.

2. You will be creating an embedded style sheet. In the head area below the page title, enter the code for the start <style> and the end </style> tags. In the start <style> tag, include the **media** attribute with a value of **all**.

3. Below the start <style> tag, insert a comment that includes your first and last name as the author and today's date.

⊕ EXPLORE   4. Below the comment code, set the style for the table element selector as follows:
   - The width of the table should be 750px.
   - The left margin should have a value of auto.
   - The right margin should have a value of auto.
   - The text should be 10pt and in the Arial font.

5. Create a style for the table data cells. The width should be 33%. The border should be black, groove, and thin. Use the border-collapse property to collapse the borders. The contents of the cells should be vertically aligned at the top. Each cell should have a padding of 0.3em.

6. Create a style for the h2 element selector that centers text and displays text in blue.

7. Create an independent class named **center** that centers text.

8. Create a style for the address element selector. Text should appear as centered, bold, and white on a blue background. The text should also be capitalized (use a style to do so) with a padding of 0.5em.

9. In the body section, below the comment "Create the table here," create a table with four rows and three columns (a total of 12 cells). Type the word **placeholder** into each of the 12 cells. (*Hint*: Create the table code for the first row and then copy and paste the code three times to create the code for the other rows.) Remember the end </table> tag at the end of the table.

10. Save your LibraryNew HTML document, and then open it in your browser. Make corrections as necessary.

⊕ EXPLORE   11. In your text editor, enter code for the table as follows:
   - In the first row of the table, insert the code in the first <td> tag to have a column span of three columns. Delete cells in the first row as necessary.
   - In the second row of the table, insert the code in the first <td> tag to have a column span of three columns. Delete cells in the second row as necessary.
   - In the last row of the table, insert the code in the first <td> tag to have a column span of three columns. Delete cells in the last row as necessary.

12. Save your LibraryNew HTML document, and then open it in your browser. Make corrections as necessary.

13. In your text editor, when you are sure the table structure is correct, delete all placeholder text. (*Hint*: Use the Find and Replace tool to do so.)

14. Above the start <table> tag, insert a start <div> tag and apply the center class.

15. Below the end </table> tag, insert an end </div> tag.

16. Follow the instructions in the comments to cut and paste code and text into the appropriate cells in the LibraryNew data table.

17. After you have completed cutting and pasting text, delete all comments.

18. Save your LibraryNew HTML document, and then open it in your browser. The document should be similar to the one shown in Figure 7-56.

Figure 7-56

19. Close all open windows.
20. Submit the results of the preceding steps to your instructor, either in printed or electronic form, as requested.

Challenge	**Case Problem 3**

Use what you've learned, and expand your skills, to create and style a Web page for the Education Department at a community college.

Data Files needed for this Case Problem: Baxter.htm, College.gif, Greer.htm, Greer.jpg, Student.jpg, Student2.jpg, Student3. jpg

Baxter Lake Community College Baxter Lake Community College is a small, public college located in eastern Colorado. The college grants a two-year Associates Degree in Education. Nearly all the graduates transfer to four-year public or private institutions to obtain a degree in Education. Dr. Anandami Greer, the department chair of the Education Department, has approached you about updating the department's home page, which is formatted using a table layout. Dr. Greer wants the page to focus on the department's philosophy of education. She wants to ensure that Baxter Lake Community College is attracting the type of student who believes in a similar philosophy or would like to learn how to adopt such a philosophy. Complete the following steps:

1. Use your text editor to open the **Baxter.htm** file located in your Tutorial.07\Case3 folder included with your Data Files. Save this file as **BaxterNew.htm** in the same folder.
2. You will be creating an embedded style sheet. In the head area below the page title, enter the code for the start <style> and the end </style> tags. In the start <style> tag, include the **media** attribute with a value of **all**.
3. Below the start <style> tag, insert a comment that includes your first and last name as the author and today's date.

4. Below the comment you just entered, set the style for the table element selector as follows:
   - The text should be 12pt and in the Book Antiqua font, a serif font.
   - The width of the table should be 100%.

EXPLORE

5. Create a dependent class named **contact** for the table data element selector. Set the width to 25%. Have the cell contents vertically aligned to the top of the cell. Include a border on the right that is black, inset, and thick.

EXPLORE

6. Create a dependent class named **main** for the table data element selector. Set the width to 75%. Have the cell contents vertically aligned to the top of the cell. The margin on the left should be 1em; the padding on the left should be 2em.

7. Create a style for the anchor element selector. The font size should be 12pt and the text color should be brown.

8. Create a style for the a:hover pseudo-class. The hover effect should display the text in navy with a background color of orange.

EXPLORE

9. Create a style for the h1 element selector as follows:
   - The font should be Times New Roman, a serif font.
   - The background image should be College.gif.
   - The image should not repeat.
   - The image should be positioned in the center of the element (*Hint*: Use **center center**.)
   - The background color should be navy.
   - Text should be centered.
   - The height should be 150px and the width 100%.
   - Include padding on the top of 25px.
   - Include a bottom border that is black, inset, and thick.

10. Create an independent class named **center** that centers text.

11. Create a style for the address element selector that displays text as bold.

12. Create a style for the hr element selector. The color of the rule should be brown. The background color should be brown.

13. In the body section, below the comment, "Create the table here," create a table with two rows and two columns (a total of four cells). Type the word **placeholder** into each cell. Remember to code the end </table> tag at the end of the table.

14. Save BaxterNew. Open the file in the browser, and then return to your text editor to make corrections as necessary.

15. In your text editor, in the first row of the table, insert the code to have a column span of two columns. Delete cells in the first row as necessary. Delete all placeholder text.

16. Above the start <table> tag, insert a start <div> tag and apply the center class. Below the end </table> tag, insert an end </div> tag.

17. In the first cell of the second row, apply the contact class to the table data cell. In the second cell of the second row, apply the main class to the table data cell. Cut and paste code and text as directed in each comment. After you have completed cutting and pasting text, delete all comments.

18. Below the start <body> tag, insert an anchor named **top**.

19. Enter contact information as follows:
    - On a separate line and below the paragraph text for "Do You Want to be This Type of Teacher?," include an e-mail link to admissions@baxterlake.edu. Use the e-mail address as the link text. Insert the code for the e-mail link within the <address></address> tags.
    - On a separate line and below the e-mail link, insert a link to Dr. Greer's home page, greer.htm. Use **Department Chair** as the link text.
    - On a separate line and below the link to Dr. Greer's home page, insert a link to an external Web site: nea.org. Use **National Education Association** as the link text.
    - On a separate line and below the link to the National Education Association, insert a link to the anchor named, top. Use **Back to Top** as the link text.
20. Save your BaxterNew HTML document, and then open it in your browser. Test all links. The document should be similar to the one shown in Figure 7-57.

Figure 7-57

Baxter Lake Community College
The College for Education

Department Chair

Dr. Anandami Greer

Faculty

- Dr. Morton E. Greenburg
- Dr. Tony Romanelli
- Dr. Cynthia Fong
- Dr. Sharim Khan
- Dr. Ted McBride
- Dr. Shanique Umbasha
- Dr. Maria Perez
- Dr. Wanda O'Toole

Location

The Bremsen Building
Main Campus

OUR PHILOSOPHY OF TEACHING

The faculty are dedicated to creating a learning environment that fosters academic achievement and mutual respect for the rights, ideas, and opinions of others. These are the primary methodologies employed:

Use a Variety of Teaching Methods

We do not presuppose that all students have the same learning styles. Some students learn through memorizing or through explanation or demonstration; others, by reading and drawing their own conclusions. For example, these are some common learning styles:

- Preference for learning alone, in small groups, or in large groups.
- Preference for observation vs. participation.
- Preference for immersion.
- Use of visuals.

Cognizant of the differences in student learning styles and being aware that each student acquires information differently, we take learning differences into account by varying the methods and approaches used. An eclectic teaching methodology must, therefore, prevail – to teach one way is the wrong way. Common principles followed here include:

- Breaking the subject matter into its smallest components (granularized instruction).
- Modify the teaching level to "fit" the class/students.
- Rearrange as need be, and then present material in the logical progression that begins with the simple and ends with the more complex.
- Add variety in all aspects of instruction; using lecture, group discussion, simulation, and modeling.

Encourage Ongoing Student-Teacher Dialogue

Faculty make every effort to provide time for discussion of class problems. There is a student-teacher dialogue. The students, therefore, work in partnership with the professor to clarify, explain, and better organize the content of the course. By discussing common problems with the students before the lesson begins, students see that others make errors and that making errors should not lead to a lessening of self-esteem. Instead, they learn that it is normal to occasionally encounter difficulty and there are strategies that can be used to overcome these difficulties.

Maintain Good Student Rapport

Faculty strive at all times to encourage thinking as opposed to memorization. Memorization is required only when necessary. Instead, students are taught cognitive problem solving. When these students enter the business workforce, they will be required to exhibit creativity, to show the ability to solve problems, and to demonstrate sound decision making. Because of these impending job requirements, students must learn how to extrapolate what has been learned in the classroom so that they can apply their current learning to new situations. Students learn not to be teacher-dependent for the right answers because they can apply a transfer of existing learning that will give them the 'knowledge tools' for solving future problems.

Establish Fair, Measurable, and Attainable Goals

Each student knows what is expected of him or her and the time and manner of evaluation. Evaluation represents a fair, semester-long sample of a student's work, taking into account that a student's ability on a given day in a certain subject can be prone to negative outside variables – illness, family problems, fatigue, etc. Testing is done in moderation, and the results of each question in each exam are analyzed to improve instruction. Student feedback is used to improve future exams to reduce the number of questions that may be deemed by the students to be ambiguous or peripheral. The fairness and clarity of each question is always under review.

Motivate Students to Learn

Faculty are generous with deserved praise for a job well done; as a result, students get a sense of achievement, belonging, and a feeling of satisfaction.

Students are constantly reminded of the relevance of the day's lesson to future work goals. Students are told what they are going to learn today and why it is important. The proper amount of practice is provided, and the students perform an abbreviated example of the lesson. This practical application of instruction reinforces productive behavior that promotes learning and effects retention. Until the student has applied what has been taught, neither the student nor the teacher can really be certain that there has been successful instruction on the part of the teacher and complete learning on the part of the student.

Maintain a Well-Managed Classroom Environment

The classroom itself represents a planned, organized atmosphere. A work-oriented feeling prevails in the class right from the beginning. This self-directed activity is the pattern expected by a prospective employer; thus, the students are learning good job habits as well. Student anxiety is low because openness is the norm. Faculty try to maintain a positive, non-threatening, humanistic climate at all times.

Do You Want to be This Type of Teacher?

If the answer is yes, please contact our Admissions Office, located in Sandler Hall, Room 212.

admissions@baxterlake.edu

Department Chair
National Education Association
Back to Top

21. Close all open windows.
22. Submit the results of the preceding steps to your instructor, either in printed or electronic form, as requested.

| Create | **| Case Problem 4** |

Using the figures provided, create a Web page for a pet store.

Data Files needed for this Case Problem: Catdog.jpg, Catdog2.jpg, Catdog3.jpg, Petlogo.jpg, Pets.htm, Vet.jpg, and Vet2.jpg

Pets Furr You   Pets Furr You is a pet store that specializes in the sale of cats and dogs. Pets Furr You stocks an unusually wide variety of cats and dogs. In addition to the sale of pets, the store also does a brisk business in selling pet food. Pets Furr You also has a pet-sitting service. The store is conveniently located next to a veterinary hospital. Both businesses complement each other and frequently refer customers to each other. Hanna Riley, the owner of Pets Furr You, has asked you to update the home page for Pets Furr You. Complete the following steps:

1. Use your text editor to open the **Pets.htm** file from your Tutorial.07\Case4 folder of your Data Files. Save the file as **PetsNew.htm** in the same folder.
2. Below the start <style> tag, insert a comment that includes your first and last name as the author and today's date.
3. In PetsNew, create a table of at least three rows and two columns.
4. Set the style of the <table> element to change the font, background color, and width of the table.
5. Set the style of the <td> or <th> element selectors.
6. Create ID selectors, dependent or independent styles, as needed.
7. Apply selectors and classes as needed.
8. Illustrate the use of either colspan or rowspan.
9. Incorporate at least one image from the images provided. Scale the image, if necessary.
10. Save your PetsNew HTML document, and then open it in your browser.
11. Close all open windows.
12. Submit the results of the preceding steps to your instructor, either in printed or electronic form, as requested.

| Review | **| Quick Check Answers** |

Session 7.1

1. A data table is used to arrange data in columns and rows. A layout table is designed solely for page layout.
2. The title should be a brief description of the table. The title appears as a ScreenTip when the user points to the table. The summary does not appear in the browser, but is useful for screen readers. The summary gives a more detailed description of the table than does the title.
3. A caption is an optional part of the table. The caption appears in the browser either above or below the table. The caption gives a brief description of the purpose of the table. The caption is part of the table.
4. any element, such as text, a list, images, or links

5. A table header will make text in the cell centered and bold.
6. a cell with no data in it
7. colspan; rowspan

Session 7.2

1. Create a sketch of the layout table.
2. just below the start <body> tag
3. You would code the layout table first, and then add the contents to the cells.
4. a table within a table
5. a comment above and below the nested table
6. yes, thereby creating seamless borders

Session 7.3

1. the background-color, the background-image property, or both
2. yes; the table is usually centered horizontally
3. the padding property and the border property
4. The borders would have a single ruling, rather than a double ruling.
5. vertical align with a value of top
6. By contrasting the difference between the rows, it makes the rows more readable.

Ending Data Files

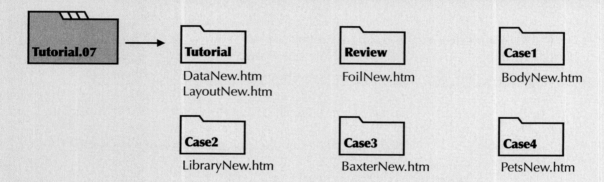

Tutorial.07 → **Tutorial**
DataNew.htm
LayoutNew.htm

Review
FoilNew.htm

Case1
BodyNew.htm

Case2
LibraryNew.htm

Case3
BaxterNew.htm

Case4
PetsNew.htm

Tutorial 8

Session 8.1
• Create an HTML form
• Create fields for text
• Create text boxes

Session 8.2
• Choose an appropriate form control
• Create radio buttons, check boxes, and list boxes
• Create menus in a group

Session 8.3
• Create methods for sending data and clearing forms
• Create command buttons
• Organize Windows controls

Creating Forms

Using Forms to Capture Data

Case | Wardrobe Wonderful

Wardrobe Wonderful is a successful clothing company that markets its merchandise to professional men and women. The company only sells business attire, such as men's and women's suits, dresses, shirts and blouses, ties and scarves, belts, and leather dress shoes. Based in Beaumont, Montana, the company began operating 20 years ago as a mail-order catalog company. The company enjoyed immediate success. Over the last few years, however, Wardrobe Wonderful has seen declining sales. The cost of printing and distributing catalogs has risen sharply. Competitors who have turned to the Web to market their products are increasingly taking away customers from Wardrobe Wonderful. As such, the company is considering moving most—if not all—of its business to the Web. You work as an assistant to Kirsten Barnes, the marketing director at Wardrobe Wonderful. Kirsten has asked for your help in creating and designing several pages for the company's new Web site. You will show Kirsten how to create a Web form that will gather the information needed to complete an online transaction.

Starting Data Files

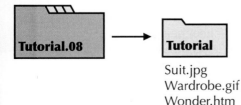

Tutorial.08 →	Tutorial	Review	Case1	Case2	Case3	Case4
	Suit.jpg	Order.htm	No.gif	Balloon.jpg	Boy.gif	Bride.jpg
	Wardrobe.gif	Wardrobe.gif	Ok.gif	Candle.jpg	Bunch.htm	Hall.gif
	Wonder.htm		Onloin.gif	Candy.jpg	Bytelogo.gif	Hall.htm
			Onloin.htm	Flo.gif	Girl.gif	
				Flowers.htm		

Session 8.1

Creating an HTML Form

Prior to taking a course in HTML, you may not have had much experience in creating Web pages, but you certainly had considerable experience in working with forms. You have completed paper forms to apply for college, financial aid, or a job, and to complete a survey. If you've ever shopped online, you have entered data into a form that was presented in the browser and created using HTML. Similar to a paper-based form, an HTML **form** is used to gather data from a user.

The HTML code within a form is used to create Windows controls. A **Windows control** is any object in a window or dialog box. Examples of Windows controls are a text box, a radio button, or a check box. A Windows control could also be a command button, which is used to execute or reject a user action. Examples of command buttons are the OK and Cancel buttons.

Reference Window | **Creating a Form**

- To create a form, enter the following code:
  ```
  <form method="methodtype" action="scripturl"></form>
  ```
  where *methodtype* is either get or post, and *scripturl* is the location on the file server where the script will be run when the form is submitted.

HTML form elements are commonly contained within an HTML table. The table aligns the form elements horizontally and vertically. If you decide to use a table to contain the form elements, sketch out the form design on paper, and then use your design as a guide when you enter the code for the HTML table. You should enter the table code and make necessary corrections to the table first. Once you are certain the table structure is correct, you can then add the form elements to the table.

The HTML form only serves to gather data. You still need a means to send the data in the form to a file server and then process that data on the server. The acronym CGI stands for Common Gateway Interface, a standard developed for communicating with Web servers. A CGI script is a series of instructions written in a scripting language, such as Perl. As you will see, the HTML action attribute is used to execute (run) a script on the server that will process the form data.

Tip

On a file server, CGI bin (cgi-bin) is often the name of the directory that contains CGI programs.

Using Windows Controls

An HTML form contains a number of Windows controls—text areas, radio buttons, check boxes, drop-down list items, and command buttons. You will use HTML to create these Windows controls. You can align the form controls on a Web page in a number of ways. You can enter the code for the controls between <p></p> tags, you can use CSS to position the controls, or you can create an HTML data table to align the form elements within table cells.

You have decided to use an HTML data table with 12 rows and 2 columns to align the form elements. The Web page will also have a picture of the item being ordered, which in this instance is a woman's suit. You have already created several styles for the document and the table. You will now have Kirsten open the document you have created, enter a comment to document her work, and have her examine the HTML code that has been written so far.

To create the comment:

▶ 1. Use your text editor to open the **Wonder.htm** file located in the Tutorial.08\Tutorial folder included with your Data Files. Save this file as **WonderNew.htm** in the same folder.

▶ 2. On a blank line below the start <style> tag, create a comment using your name and today's date, as shown in the following code and is displayed in red in Figure 8-1.

```
/* Your First Name Your Last Name
Today's Date */
```

The comment code ◀ | Figure 8-1

```
<html>
<head>
<title>Wardrobe Wonderful</title>

<style type="text/css" media="all">

/* Your First Name Your Last Name
Today's Date */

body {
background-color: cadetblue; }
```

▶ 3. Save the file. Observe the existing styles and table code in the document.

Next, you'll show Kirsten how to format the table that will contain the form controls.

Setting the Style for the Form

Recall that in earlier tutorials, you have set the style for boxes and the HTML table element. Similarly, you can also set the style for the form element. In the Wardrobe Wonderful Web page, an image will appear on the left side of the page, and the form will be positioned to the right of the image. In addition, you will show Kirsten how to set the styles for several text properties and specify a background color for the form.

Every form begins with the start <form> tag. If you are using a table to align the form elements, the start <form> tag must be entered before the start <table> tag. The start <form> tag looks like this:

```
<form
```

Every form must have a name. Use the name attribute to specify a name that describes the information the form gathers or is similar to the name of the database that will be receiving the data. Several forms can be used in the same Web page or Web site. In this instance, you have decided to name the form *transaction* because that describes the purpose of the form.

```
<form name="transaction">
```

The form tag also contains a few lines of scripting code. The **action attribute** and its value identify the location on the server and the name of the script that will run when the user clicks the Submit button in the form. For example:

```
<form name="transaction"
action="http://mywebsite.com/cgi-bin/myscript.cgi">
```

> **Tip**
> A Web page can have more than one form.

The **method attribute** and its value follow the action attribute and its value. The method attribute has only two possible values: *get* or *post*. Because there is a strict limit to the amount of data that can be sent using get, you will use post as the value for the method attribute when you create this HTML form. For example:

```
<form name="transaction"
action="http://mywebsite.com/cgi-bin/myscript.cgi" method="post">
```

| InSight | | **Collecting Data by Using E-Mail** |

Microsoft Access 2007 has a new feature that allows for data collection using e-mail. Once the Access database has been created, you can use an HTML form that you have created to collect data. The form is e-mailed to the clients from whom you are seeking responses. When the completed forms are e-mailed back to the sender, the data in the form is extracted from the e-mail message and transferred to the appropriate database on your computer. You have the option of automating the transfer to the database, or you can choose to manually transfer the data when you want.

You will show Kirsten how to enter the form element and its attributes and values.

To enter the form element code:

▶ **1.** In your text editor, display the HTML code for WonderNew.

▶ **2.** Above the start <table> tag, type the following code, which is also shown in red in Figure 8-2.

```
<form name="transaction"
action="http://mywebsite.com/cgi-bin/myscript.cgi"
method="post">
```

| Figure 8-2 | Code for the form element |

```
<div class="center">

<form name="transaction" action="http://mywebsite.com/cgi-bin/myscript.cgi" method="post">
```

form code with name, action, and method attributes

▶ **3.** Save WonderNew.

You also need to include the end </form> tag. You will show Kirsten where to insert that tag next.

To enter the end form tag:

▶ **1.** In your text editor, display the HTML code for WonderNew.

▶ **2.** On a blank line below the end </table> tag, type the following code, which is also shown in red in Figure 8-3.

```
</form>
```

Code for the end form tag | Figure 8-3

```
<!-- command buttons -->

<tr>
  <td class="center" colspan="2"></td>
</tr>
</table>
</form>
</div>
```

enter the end form tag after the end table tag

▶ **3.** Save WonderNew.

You can format a form element the same way you format any Web page element. Now that the form has been created, you will show Kirsten how to set the style for the form element.

To enter the code to set the style for the form:

▶ **1.** In your text editor, display the HTML code for WonderNew.

▶ **2.** On a blank line below the comment, type the following code, which is also shown in red in Figure 8-4.

```
form {
font-size: 12pt;
font-family: verdana,sans-serif;
position: absolute;
left: 360px;
top: 10px;
width: 60%;
background-color: wheat; }
```

Code to set the style for the form | Figure 8-4

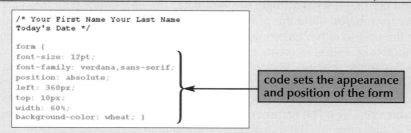

```
/* Your First Name Your Last Name
Today's Date */

form {
font-size: 12pt;
font-family: verdana,sans-serif;
position: absolute;
left: 360px;
top: 10px;
width: 60%;
background-color: wheat; }
```

code sets the appearance and position of the form

▶ **3.** Save WonderNew. Refresh the file in your browser. Compare your screen with the one shown in Figure 8-5 to verify that the form is displayed correctly.

Figure 8-5 The form document displayed in the browser

Now that you have set the style for the form, you are ready to add controls to the form that let you collect data.

Creating Input Fields

Recall that a field represents a single piece of data. The user enters data into each of the fields in the form based upon the **prompting text**, which is a description of the data you are asking the user to either enter into a text field or select from a Windows control.

The <input> tag is used to create a variety of form objects. The type attribute and its values determine the specific type of form object that is created. The <input> tag is an empty tag, so it must be closed with the space-slash combination. Note that following the <form> tag, the table structure begins. Each of the form controls will be entered into a pair of table data tags. The first set of table data tags contains the prompting text. The second set of tags contains the forms code. For example:

```
<table>
<tr>
  <td>Last Name</td>
  <td><input
```

The input type determines what Windows control will be created in the form. Each control has different attributes and values. See Figure 8-6.

Input types ◄ **Figure 8-6**

Value	Attribute(s)	Purpose
text		Creates a text box
	size	Sets the size of the box
	maxlength	Sets the maximum number of characters that will be accepted
password		Creates a text box where asterisks are displayed no matter what is entered
radio		Creates a radio button (also known as an option button)
	value	Determines what data will be sent to the database if the user selects a particular radio button
	checked	Sets a particular radio button as the default
checkbox		Creates a check box
	value	Determines what data will be sent to the database if the user selects a particular check box
	checked	Sets a particular check box as the default
reset		Creates a Reset button (clears the form)
	value	Determines what text is displayed on the Reset button
submit		Creates a Submit button (sends the data to the server)
	value	Determines what text is displayed on the Submit button
button		Creates a button (with any description)

The type attribute would be entered like this:

```
<table>
<tr>
  <td>Last Name</td>
  <td><input type=
```

Figure 8-7 illustrates different types of Windows controls created by using the input element.

Windows controls on the Web page ◄ **Figure 8-7**

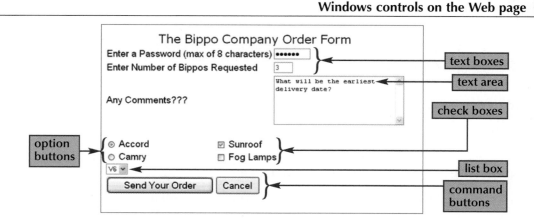

Creating Text Boxes

Text boxes are used when you want the user to type **alphanumeric** data (letters, numbers, or symbols) into a single line in a form. The type attribute with a value of *text* creates a one-line text box.

Reference Window | **Creating Text Boxes**

- To create a text box, use the following code:
  ```
  <input type="text_type" id="label" value="initialvalue"
  size="sizewidth" maxlength="maxwidth" />
  ```
  where *text_type* is either `text` or `password`, *label* is the text that identifies the input data, *initialvalue* is the default data that will be shown in the field, *sizewidth* is the width of the box in pixels, and *maxwidth* is the maximum number of characters that can be typed in the field.

For example:

```
<table>
<tr>
  <td>Last Name</td>
  <td><input type="text" />
```

Text boxes are also used to create password fields, where the user is asked to log on with a password. If you want the text field to be a password field, change the value of the type attribute to *password*. As the user enters text into the field, asterisks, or bullets are displayed instead of the numbers or letters the user is actually typing. These types of text boxes are useful when you need to authenticate a user.

Using Names and IDs

When creating a text box, you must also give the field a name so that when the data is sent to the server, the data is sent to the corresponding field in the database. With the exception of radio buttons, you can use either the id or the name attribute to name a field.

The id or name attribute corresponds to the field name in the database that will be receiving the data. The name attribute is deprecated, so the id attribute is preferred. The field id or name in the form should also match the case used in the database. For example, *zipcode* and *ZIPCODE* are two different field names. The id attribute and its value would be entered like this:

```
<table>
<tr>
  <td>Last Name</td>
  <td><input type="text" id="lastname" />
```

Controlling the Text Box Width

You can control the width of the text box by using the size attribute and assigning a value that corresponds to the number of characters that will be displayed in the box. The default width is 20. The size attribute and its value would be entered after the id or name attribute and its value, like so:

```
<table>
<tr>
  <td>Last Name</td>
  <td><input type="text" id="lastname" size="25" />
```

Using the maxlength Attribute

When you use the size attribute and its value, the value only determines the width of the box in characters on the screen. If you were to continue typing more characters into the box, the field would still accept input and the text box would keep scrolling to the right. You can, however, use the **maxlength attribute** to set a strict limit on the number of characters that can be typed in a text box. For example, if you set the maxlength to 25 characters, the text box will not continue to scroll; it will cease accepting input into the box after the 25th character has been entered. For example:

```
<table>
<tr>
  <td>Last Name>
  <td><input type="text" id="lastname" size="25" maxlength="25" />
```

Using the value Attribute

If you want to have the text field display a value by default, use the *value* attribute and assign the most commonly used value, like this:

```
<table>
<tr>
  <td>State</td>
  <td><input type="text" id="state" size="20" maxlength="20"
  value="New York" /></td>
</tr>
```

You will now show Kirsten how to create all of the text boxes. You will enter code to create text boxes for the last name, the first name, the address line, and the city, state, and zip code.

To enter the text boxes for the form:

▶ 1. In your text editor, display the HTML code for WonderNew.

▶ 2. In the body area, below the comment "text boxes," type the following code shown below in bold, which is also shown in red in Figure 8-8.

```
<tr>
  <td class="left">Last Name</td>
  <td class="right"><input type="text" id="lastname"
size="25" maxlength="30" /></td>
</tr>
<tr>
  <td>First Name</td>
  <td><input type="text" id="firstname" size="25"
maxlength="30" /></td>
</tr>
<tr>
  <td>Address</td>
  <td><input type="text" id="address" size="25" /></td>
</tr>
<tr>
  <td>City</td>
  <td><input type="text" id="city" size="25" /></td>
</tr>
<tr>
  <td>State</td>
  <td><input type="text" id="state" size="2" /></td>
</tr>
<tr>
  <td>Zip</td>
```

```
    <td><input type="text" id="zipcode" size="5" /> -
    <input type="text" id="plusfour" size="4" /></td>
    </tr>
```

Figure 8-8 ▶ **Code for the text boxes**

```
<!-- textboxes -->

<tr>
  <td class="left">Last Name</td>
  <td class="right"><input type="text" id="lastname" size="25" maxlength="30" /></td>
</tr>
<tr>
  <td>First Name</td>
  <td><input type="text" id="firstname" size="25" maxlength="30" /></td>
</tr>
<tr>
  <td>Address</td>
  <td><input type="text" id="address" size="25" /></td>
</tr>
<tr>
  <td>City</td>
  <td><input type="text" id="city" size="25" /></td>
</tr>
<tr>
  <td>State</td>
  <td><input type="text" id="state" size="2" /></td>
</tr>
<tr>
  <td>Zip</td>
  <td><input type="text" id="zipcode" size="5" /> - <input type="text" id="plusfour" size="4" />
  </td>
</tr>
```

> text box for the Last Name is 25 characters wide by default, but can expand to 30 characters

▶ **3.** Save WonderNew. Refresh the file in your browser. Compare your screen with the one shown in Figure 8-9 to verify that the code for the text boxes has been entered correctly.

Figure 8-9 ▶ **Text boxes on the Web page**

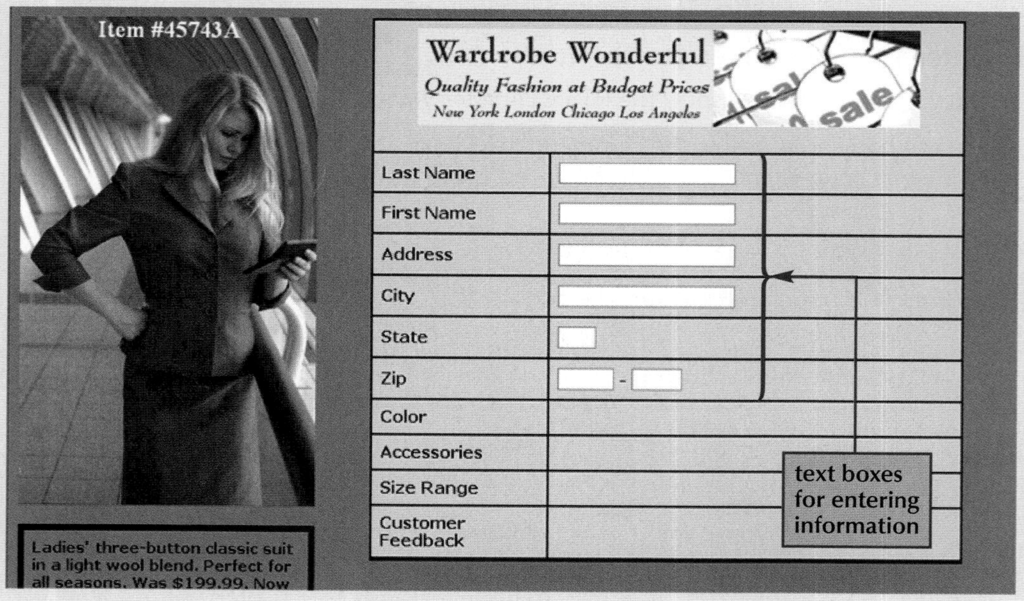

Item #45743A

Wardrobe Wonderful
Quality Fashion at Budget Prices
New York London Chicago Los Angeles

Last Name		
First Name		
Address		
City		
State		
Zip		
Color		
Accessories		
Size Range		
Customer Feedback		

text boxes for entering information

Ladies' three-button classic suit in a light wool blend. Perfect for all seasons. Was $199.99. Now

In this first session, you learned HTML is used to create the user interface and gather information for a form. In addition to the HTML form, you need to create and name fields in a database program. You also need to use a script to transfer data that has been gathered in an HTML form to the database. Add text boxes to the form when you want the user to enter text. You can control the size of the text box as it is displayed on the screen. You can also set the maximum number of characters that can be entered into the text box. You can make a text box into a password field by changing the value of the input type to password. Prompting text is a suggestion of what you want the user to enter into the text box field. In the next session, you will see how Windows controls are used to make selections.

Session 8.1 Quick Check | Review

1. What are the three components needed for a Web database?
2. What tags start and end forms?
3. What input type would you use to create a text box?
4. What does the maxlength attribute do?
5. Is it possible to display more characters than are specified by the maxlength attribute?
6. What input type would you use to create a password field?

Session 8.2

Creating Radio Buttons

So far, you have used text boxes to input alphanumeric text. Windows also has a control that allows the user to make a single choice from a list of choices.

Use a **radio button** when you want the user to choose only one item from a list of choices. Give the radio button a name that corresponds to the same field name in the database. When creating radio buttons, use the name attribute, not the id attribute.

Creating Radio Buttons | Reference Window

- To create radio buttons, enter the following code:
  ```
  <input type="radio" name="button_name"
  value="data" />display_text
  ```
  where *radio* is the value for the type attribute, *button_name* identifies the button selected, *data* is the data that will be sent to the server if the button is selected, and *display_text* is the text that will appear to the right of the radio button.
- Optionally, the attribute and value of `checked="checked"` may be used to identify a single default choice.

For example:

```
<td><input type="radio" name="color"
```

Tip

Radio buttons are also called option buttons.

Using the value Attribute

The *value* attribute and its value describe the data that will be sent to the database. Each value corresponds to a different radio button. For example:

```
<td><input type="radio" name="color" value="gray" />
```

If you want to specify a certain radio button as the default choice (usually the first choice in the list), then add the checked attribute and value of *checked*. For example:

```
<td><input type="radio" name="color" value="gray"
checked="checked" /></td>
```

The text that follows the <input> tag is the text that will appear to the right of the radio button in the form. For example, the following code creates a radio button labeled Gray that is selected by default:

```
<td><input type="radio" name="color" value="gray"
checked="checked" />Gray</td>
```

You will now show Kirsten how to enter the radio button code into the form.

To enter the code for the radio buttons:

▶ **1.** In your text editor, display the HTML code for WonderNew.

▶ **2.** Below the comment "radio buttons; gray is selected," type the following code shown in bold, which is also shown in red in Figure 8-10.

```
<tr>
  <td>Color</td>
  <td><input type="radio" name="color" value="gray"
checked="checked" />Gray <input type="radio" name="color"
value="navy" />Navy <input type="radio" name="color"
value="taupe" />Taupe</td>
</tr>
```

Figure 8-10 ▷ **Code for the radio buttons**

```
<!-- radio buttons; gray is selected -->

<tr>
  <td>Color</td>
  <td><input type="radio" name="color" value="gray" checked="checked" />Gray <input type="radio"
name="color" value="navy" />Navy <input type="radio" name="color" value="taupe" />Taupe</td>
</tr>
```

code creates three radio buttons labeled Gray, Navy, and Taupe

▶ **3.** Save WonderNew. Refresh the file in your browser. Compare your screen with the one shown in Figure 8-11 to verify that the code for the radio buttons has been entered correctly.

Another way to provide a set of choices to users is to create check boxes, which you'll show Kirsten how to do next.

Creating Check Boxes

Include a **check box** on a form when you want the user to choose *one or more* items from a list of items. The input type for check boxes is *checkbox*.

Creating Check Boxes | Reference Window

- To create check boxes, enter the following code:

```
<input type="checkbox" id="box_name"
value="data" />display_text
```
where *checkbox* is the value for the type attribute, *box_name* identifies the box being selected, *data* is the data that will be sent to the server if the check box is selected, and *display_text* is the text that will appear to the right of the check box.
- Optionally, the attribute and value of checked="checked" may be used to identify a default choice.

Tip

In code, write checkbox as one word. In standard English, use two words: check box.

The following code creates a check box control:

```
<tr>
  <td><input type="checkbox"
```

Again, you should include an id attribute for the field that corresponds to the appropriate field in the database. For example:

```
<tr>
  <td><input type="checkbox" id="scarf" /></td>
</tr>
```

The value attribute and its value describe the data that will be sent to the database. Each value corresponds to a different check box. For example:

```
<tr>
  <td><input type="checkbox" id="scarf" value="scarf" /></td>
</tr>
```

Using the checked Attribute

If you want, you can have one of the boxes checked by default when the form opens. Just as you did in selecting a radio button to have a default choice, you use the **checked attribute** and assign it a value of checked. For example:

```
<tr>
  <td><input type="checkbox" id="scarf" value="scarf"
checked="checked" /></td>
</tr>
```

The text that appears following the <input> tag is the text that will be displayed to the right of the check box in the form. For example, the following code creates a selected check box labeled "Scarf":

```
<tr>
  <td><input type="checkbox" id="scarf" value="scarf"
checked="checked" />Scarf</td>
</tr>
```

You will now show Kirsten how to enter the code for the check boxes.

To enter the code for the check boxes:

▶ 1. In your text editor, display the HTML code for WonderNew.

▶ 2. Below the comment "checkboxes, scarf is selected," type the following code shown in bold, which is also shown in red in Figure 8-12.

```
<tr>
  <td>Accessories</td>
  <td><input type="checkbox" id="scarf" value="scarf"
checked="checked" />Black Scarf <input
type="checkbox" id="jewelry" value="jewelry" />#34 Lapel Pin
<input type="checkbox" id="brooch" value="brooch" />#56
Brooch</td>
</tr>
```

Figure 8-12	Code for the check boxes

```
<!-- checkboxes; scarf is selected -->

<tr>
  <td>Accessories</td>
  <td><input type="checkbox" id="scarf" value="scarf" checked="checked" />Black Scarf <input
type="checkbox" id="jewelry" value="jewelry" />#34 Lapel Pin <input type="checkbox" id="brooch"
value="brooch" />#56 Brooch></td>
</tr>
```

3. Save WonderNew. Refresh the file in your browser. Compare your screen with the one shown in Figure 8-13 to verify that the code for the check boxes has been entered correctly.

Check boxes on the Web page | Figure 8-13

check boxes for selecting one or more accessories

Besides selecting check boxes and radio buttons, users can also select items by clicking them in a list. You'll show Kirsten how to include these types of controls next.

Creating List Boxes and Drop-Down List Boxes

List boxes are used to show a list of items to choose from. When you want to show one item in the list and require the user to click a list arrow to display the contents of the list, the box is called a **drop-down list box**. Drop-down list boxes are useful when you are trying to conserve screen space.

Tip

A drop-down list is commonly used when the list of choices is long, such as a list of states.

Reference Window | **Creating Drop-Down List Boxes**

- To create a drop-down list box, enter the following code:
  ```
  <select id="label" size="number"><optionA>...
  </optionZ></select>
  ```
  where *label* identifies the data that will be sent to the server, *number* is the number of items to display (a value of 1 creates a drop-down list box), *optionA* is the first option in the list, and *optionZ* is the last option in the list.
- Optionally, use `multiple="multiple"` to allow more than one item in the list to be chosen.
- Optionally, use `selected="selected"` to make an item the default choice.

Using the select Tag

You create a list box by using the `<select></select>` tags. You generally precede the list box with prompting text, suggesting the user choose one or more items. Again, give the field an id attribute that matches the corresponding field name in the database. For example:

```
<tr>
  <td>Size</td>
  <td><select id="suit">
```

Using the size Attribute

Tip

You should always include the size attribute even if you want to use the default value of 1. Setting the size attribute and value clearly states your intention to make this a drop-down list box.

The *size* attribute indicates the number of list items that are shown in the list box when the form opens. If you have more list items than you indicate in the size, scroll bars are automatically created. If you limit the size to 1, then the user will see a drop-down list box. Depending on where the box is on the screen, the drop-down list box might pop up instead of dropping down. By default, the *size* attribute is set to 1. For example:

```
<tr>
  <td>Suit Size</td>
  <td><select id="suit" size="1">
```

InSight | **XML and Data**

XML is an acronym for Extensible Markup Language. XML describes data, while HTML formats and displays the same data. You create your own XML tags. As such, XML allows Web page developers to define their own tags to document the structure of the data. An XML document would be structured as follows, with a single root element and multiple child and subchild elements:

```
<ledger>
  <payment>
    <invoice></invoice>
  </payment>
</ledger>
```

Since the turn of the century, XML has rapidly gained popularity because it works on all hardware and software platforms. Once you have completed your study of HTML and CSS, it would be well worth your while to explore all that XML has to offer.

Using the option Tags

The <option> </option> tags are used to identify each item in the list. The value assigned to the option determines which field in the database will receive the data. You follow the list with the </select> tag. For example:

```
<tr>
<td>Suit Size</td>
  <td><select id="suit" size="1">
  <option>petite</option>
  <option>small</option>
  <option>medium</option>
  <option>large</option>
  </select>
</td>
</tr>
```

To have an option in the list selected as the default choice, use the *selected* attribute with the value of *selected*. For example:

```
<option selected="selected">medium</option>
```

Using the multiple Attribute

If you want the user to be able to click (and thereby select) more than one item in the list by using CTRL+click or SHIFT+click, use the **multiple attribute** by entering the code multiple="multiple," like so:

```
<select multiple="multiple"
```

You will now show Kirsten how to create a drop-down list.

To enter the code for the drop-down list:

▶ **1.** In your text editor, display the HTML code for WonderNew.

▶ **2.** Below the comment "drop-down list box," type the following code shown in bold, which is also shown in red in Figure 8-14.

```
<tr>
   <td>Size Range</td>
   <td><select id="range" size="1">
<option>choose a size</option>
<option>4P</option>
<option>6P</option>
<option>8P</option>
<option>10P</option>
<option>12P</option>
<option selected="selected">6</option>
<option>8</option>
<option>10</option>
<option>12</option>
<option>14</option>
<option>16</option>
<option>16W</option>
<option>18W</option>
<option>20W</option>
<option>22W</option>
<option>24W</option>
</select> (Petites, Misses, or Women's)</td>
</tr>
```

Figure 8-14 ▶ **Code for the drop-down list**

```
<!-- drop down list box -->

<tr>
  <td>Size Range</td>
  <td><select id="range" size="1">
<option>choose a size</option>
<option>4P</option>
<option>6P</option>
<option>8P</option>
<option>10P</option>
<option>12P</option>
<option selected="selected">6</option>
<option>8</option>
<option>10</option>
<option>12</option>
<option>14</option>
<option>16</option>
<option>16W</option>
<option>18W</option>
<option>20W</option>
<option>22W</option>
<option>24W</option>
</select> (Petites, Misses, or Women's)</td>
</tr>
```

▶ **3.** Save WonderNew. Refresh the file in your browser. Compare your screen with the one shown in Figure 8-15 to verify that the code for the drop-down list has been entered correctly.

Figure 8-15 ▶ **Drop-down list on the Web page**

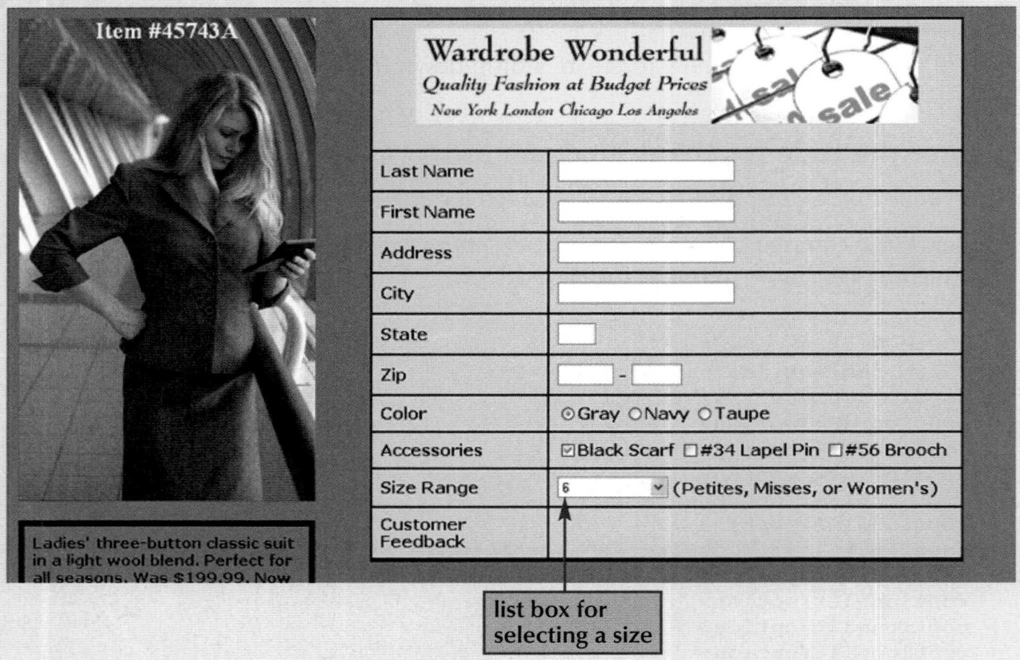

list box for selecting a size

If you have a drop-down list with many options, you can organize the items into option groups. You'll show Kirsten how to do so next.

Creating Option Groups

You can organize the items in a selection list by dividing the options into groups, called **option groups**. You use the <optgroup></optgroup> tags to do so. The label attribute serves as the heading for the option group.

- To create an option group, enter the following code:

    ```
    <optgroup label="heading"> options . . . </optgroup>
    ```
    where *heading* is the name of the heading for the option group, and *options* are the options in the option list.

Kirsten wants the groups to be based on three categories of clothing: Petites, Misses, and Women's. You will show Kirsten how to include the option groups now.

To enter the code for the option groups in the drop-down list:

▶ **1.** In your text editor, display the HTML code for WonderNew.

▶ **2.** In the code for the drop-down list, type the following code shown in bold, which is also shown in red in Figure 8-16.

```
<tr>
  <td>Size Range</td>
  <td><select id="range" size="1">
<option>choose a size</option>
<optgroup label="Petites">
<option>4P</option>
<option>6P</option>
<option>8P</option>
<option>10P</option>
<option>12P</option>
</optgroup>
<optgroup label="Misses">
<option selected="selected" >6</option>
<option>8</option>
<option>10</option>
<option>12</option>
<option>14</option>
<option>16</option>
</optgroup>
<optgroup label="Women's">
<option>16W</option>
<option>18W</option>
<option>20W</option>
<option>22W</option>
<option>24W</option>
</optgroup>
</select> (Petites, Misses, or Women's)</td>
</tr>
```

Figure 8-16 ▸ Code for the option groups

```
        <td><select id="range" size="1">
<option>choose a size</option>
<optgroup label="Petites">
<option>4P</option>
<option>6P</option>
<option>8P</option>
<option>10P</option>
<option>12P</option>
</optgroup>
<optgroup label="Misses">
<option selected="selected" >6</option>
<option>8</option>
<option>10</option>
<option>12</option>
<option>14</option>
<option>16</option>
</optgroup>
<optgroup label="Women's">
<option>16W</option>
<option>18W</option>
<option>20W</option>
<option>22W</option>
<option>24W</option>
</optgroup>
</select> (Petites, Misses, or Women's)</td>
</tr>
```

▸ **3.** Save WonderNew. Refresh the file in your browser. Compare your screen with the one shown in Figure 8-17 to verify that the code for the option groups has been entered correctly.

Figure 8-17 ▸ Option groups on the Web page

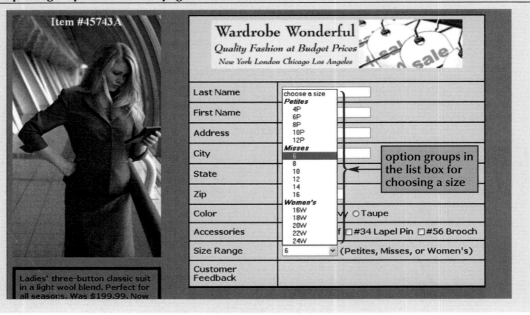

To let users enter comments or other text, you can create a text area, which you'll show Kirsten how to create next.

Creating a Text Area

Recall, you created a text box to create a one-line field for alphanumeric input. You can use the <textarea> </textarea> tags if you want the user to enter multiple lines of text. You must also give the field an id attribute and value so that when the data is sent to the server, the data will be entered into the database in the corresponding field.

Creating Text Areas | Reference Window

- To create text areas, enter the following code:

  ```
  <textarea id="label" rows="height" cols="width"></textarea>
  ```
  where *label* is the text that identifies the input data to the server, *height* is the number of rows expressed as a number, and *width* is the character width of the text area expressed as a number.

The textarea tag, the id attribute, and a value would be entered like so:

```
<tr>
  <td>Comments?</td>
  <td><textarea id="feedback"
```

Using the cols and rows Attributes

You must specify a width and a height for the text area. You control the width of the text area by using the **cols attribute**; you control the height of the text area by using the **rows attribute**. Assign as a value the number of characters wide you want the text area to be; assign as a value the number of rows you want the text area to be.

If you enter text between the start <textarea> and end </textarea> tags, that text will be displayed in the text area.

You will show Kirsten how to add a text area to obtain customer feedback about Wardrobe Wonderful's products and services.

> **Tip**
>
> Although the default values for a text area are 20 characters and 2 rows, it is always a good idea to include the rows and cols attributes and values for a text area.

> **Tip**
>
> Text areas are often used to create an area for customer feedback or suggestions to the Webmaster.

To enter the code for the text area:

▶ 1. In your text editor, display the HTML code for WonderNew.

▶ 2. Below the comment "textarea," type the following code shown in bold, which is also shown in red in Figure 8-18.

```
<tr>
  <td>Customer Feedback</td>
  <td><textarea id="feedback" value="feedback" rows="5"
cols="50"></textarea></td>
</tr>
```

Code for the text area ◀ Figure 8-18

```
<!-- textarea -->

<tr>
  <td>Customer Feedback</td>
  <td><textarea id="feedback" rows="5" cols="50"></textarea></td>
</tr>
```

> sets the size of the text area to five rows and 50 columns and allows the text to wrap

▶ **3.** Save WonderNew. Refresh the file in your browser. Compare your screen with the one shown in Figure 8-19 to verify that the code for the text area has been entered correctly.

Figure 8-19 ▶ **Text area on the Web page**

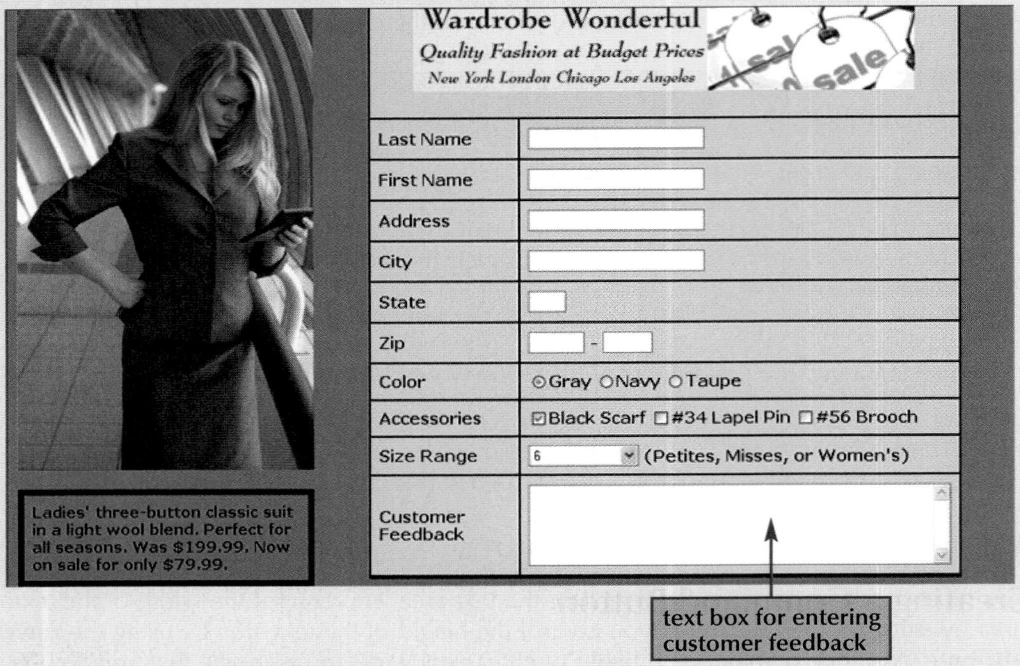

text box for entering customer feedback

In this session, you learned that forms have controls that allow the user to select from one or more options. Create radio buttons if you want the user to select only one choice from a list of choices. Create check boxes if you want the user to select one or more items from a list of choices. You can create option groups so that the choices in a drop-down list are divided into logical groups. A text area is a text box that is several lines long. Text areas are very commonly used to obtain user feedback or comments. You will now learn how to organize fields for the browser window and how to either accept or reject the input for the form.

Review | **Session 8.2 Quick Check**

1. What value for the type attribute would you use to create a radio button?
2. What value for the type attribute would you use to create a check box?
3. What attribute and value would make a radio button the default choice?
4. What attribute and value would make a check box the default choice?
5. What tags create a drop-down list?
6. What attribute controls the number of items in the list?
7. What tags create choices in a list?

Session 8.3

Accepting or Rejecting Data

After a user enters all the data in the form, you need to provide a mechanism for submitting the data to the database. You also need to provide a mechanism to clear the data should the user decide to start over or cancel the operation.

Recall, a command button is a Windows control; in this instance, it is a button, such as the OK or Cancel button, that is used to either execute or reject a user action. In an HTML form, the input type of *submit* is used to accept the data and transmit the data to the database, as shown in the following code:

```
<input type="submit" />
```

The value attribute determines what text appears on the button. In the following example, the words "Continue with Order" will appear on the submit button.

```
<input type="submit" value="Continue with Order" />
```

You also need to provide a button to give the user an opportunity to start over or cancel the operation entirely. To do so, the input type takes a value of *reset*, as shown in the following code:

```
<input type="reset" value="Cancel" />
```

Creating a Command Button

The advantage of using the input type with a value of submit or reset lies in its simplicity. You don't have to do very much to create a button. As an alternative to using the input attribute with a value of submit or reset, you can create buttons using the <button> </button> tags. The advantage of doing so is that you can set a style for the button. For example, you can use any of the font, text, and color properties to set the button style. You can place an image on the button or use an image as a background for the button using the background-image property.

> **Tip**
>
> When using an image with the button, create a dependent class for the image element selector, include margin space around the image, and position the image vertically.

Creating a Button | Reference Window

- To create a button, enter the following code:
  ```
  <button type="buttontype">buttontext</button>
  ```
  where *buttontype* is either submit or reset, and *buttontext* is the text that will be displayed on the button.
- Optionally, you may include an image with alternate text, the vertical-align property, and the width and height properties.
- If you are using an image with text, you may have the image appear to the left or the right of the button text.
- You can also use a background image for the button.

Following are some examples of styling the button element:

```
button {
padding-top: .1em;
margin-left: 2em;
font-weight: bold;
color: black;
background-color: orange; }
```

```
img.button {
margin-right: 1em;
vertical-align: middle; }
```

In the following code, the submit button uses the image Ok.gif and the reset button uses the image No.gif. The button class vertically aligns the image in the middle. The code for the button would look similar to this:

```
<tr>
<td><button type="submit"><img src="ok.gif" class="button">
Submit Order</button> <button type="reset"><img src="no.gif"
class="button">Cancel</button></td>
</tr>
```

You will show Kirsten how to enter the code for the submit and reset command buttons, and then you will set the style for the buttons.

To enter the code for the command buttons:

1. In your text editor, display the HTML code for WonderNew.

2. Below the comment "command buttons," type the following code shown in bold, which is also shown in red in Figure 8-20.

```
<tr>
  <td class="center" colspan="2">
  <button type="submit">Submit Order</button>
  <button type="reset">Cancel</button>
  </td>
</tr>
```

Figure 8-20 **Code for the command buttons**

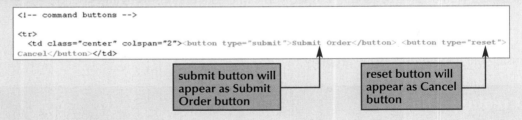

```
<!-- command buttons -->

<tr>
  <td class="center" colspan="2"><button type="submit">Submit Order</button> <button type="reset">
Cancel</button></td>
```

submit button will appear as Submit Order button

reset button will appear as Cancel button

3. Save WonderNew. Refresh the file in your browser. Compare your screen with the one shown in Figure 8-21 to verify that the code for the submit and reset command buttons has been entered correctly.

Command buttons on the Web page ◀ **Figure 8-21**

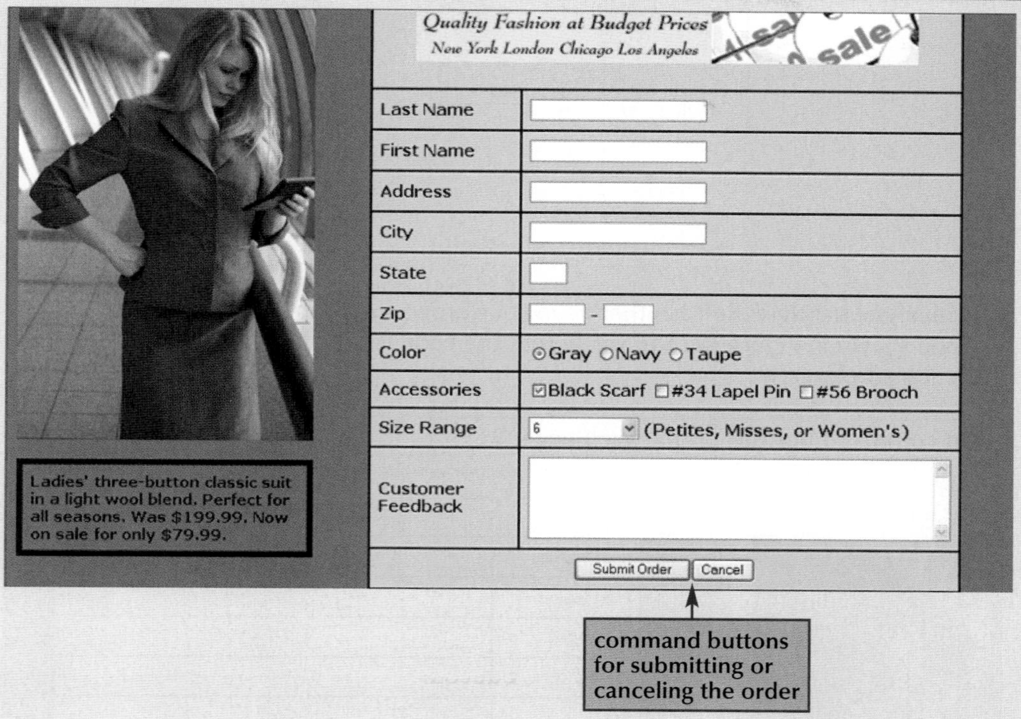

command buttons
for submitting or
canceling the order

The buttons are currently displayed in the default style, which is black text on a silver background. To make the buttons stand out on the screen, you will show Kirsten how to set the style for the button element.

To set the style for the button element:

▶ 1. In your text editor, display the HTML code for WonderNew.

▶ 2. On a blank line below the code to set the style for the form, type the following code, which is also shown in red in Figure 8-22.

```
button {
color: white;
background-color: navy;
border: silver outset thick;
margin-right: .5em;
text-align: center;
font-weight: bold;
font-size: 12pt;
font-family: arial,helvetica,sans-serif; }
```

Figure 8-22 ▶ **Code to set the style for the button element**

```
button {
color: white;
background-color: navy;
border: silver outset thick;
margin-right: .5em;
text-align: center;
font-weight: bold;
font-size: 12pt;
font-family: arial,helvetica,sans-serif; }

body {
background-color: cadetblue; }
```

▶ **3.** Save WonderNew. Refresh the file in your browser. Compare your screen with the one shown in Figure 8-23 to verify that the code for the button style has been entered correctly.

Figure 8-23 ▶ **Styled command buttons on the Web page**

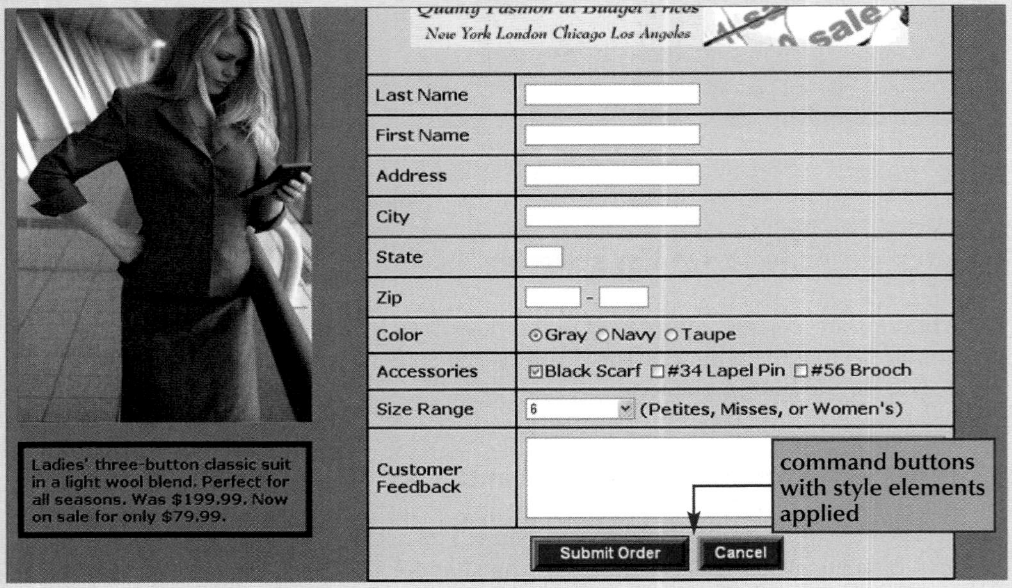

You and Kirsten have finished creating the controls on the form. Now you can fine-tune the form to make it appealing and useful by organizing the controls.

Organizing Form Controls

Although the Wardrobe Wonderful form is fairly simple, it's always a good idea to organize the form controls so that they are displayed in the browser in related groups. Doing so clearly identifies which Windows controls are part of the same group. For example, the text boxes could be organized into one group. The radio buttons and the check boxes could be organized into a second group, and the command buttons could be a third group. The following tags are used to organize form controls:

• Fieldset
• Legend

Using the fieldset Tags

The <fieldset></fieldset> tags draw a box around form elements when displayed in the browser.

Organizing Form Elements

- To organize form elements using the fieldset and legend tags, enter the following code:

```
<fieldset><legend>legendtext</legend>form_elements
</fieldset>
```

where *legendtext* is the text for the legend and *form_elements* are the controls you want in the fieldset.

For example, to draw attention to the Accessories check boxes, you could change the text color, the background color, and the border color, style, and width. To do so, you would set the style for the fieldset tag like so:

```
fieldset {
color: navy;
background-color: orange;
border: navy inset thick; }
```

You will show Kirsten how to set the style for the fieldset element selector now.

To enter the code to set the style for the fieldset:

▶ **1.** In your text editor, display the HTML code for WonderNew.

▶ **2.** On a blank line below the code to set the style for the button element, type the following code, which is also shown in red in Figure 8-24.

```
fieldset {
color: navy;
background-color: orange;
border: navy inset thick; }
```

Code to set the style for the fieldset ◀ **Figure 8-24**

```
fieldset {
color: navy;
background-color: orange;
border: navy inset thick; }

body {
background-color: cadetblue; }
```

▶ **3.** Save WonderNew.

Because this fieldset will be used to group the items in the check boxes, the fieldset tags will be entered in the check box row. For example:

```
<tr>
  <td>Accessories</td>
  <td><fieldset><input type="checkbox" name="scarf" value="scarf"
checked="checked" />Black Scarf <input type="checkbox" name="jewelry"
value="jewelry" />#34 Lapel Pin <input type="checkbox" name="brooch"
value="brooch" />#56 Brooch</fieldset></td>
</tr>
```

You will show Kirsten how to insert the fieldset tags.

To enter the fieldset tags:

▶ 1. In your text editor, display the HTML code for WonderNew.

▶ 2. In the table cell for the check boxes, type the following code, which is also shown in red in Figure 8-25.

```
<tr>
  <td>Accessories</td>
  <td><fieldset><input type="checkbox" id="scarf"
value="scarf" checked="checked" />Black Scarf <input
type="checkbox" id="jewelry" value="jewelry" />#34 Lapel Pin
<input type="checkbox" id="brooch" value="brooch" />#56
Brooch</fieldset></td>
</tr>
```

Figure 8-25	Code for the fieldset tags

```
<!-- checkboxes; scarf is selected -->

<tr>
  <td>Accessories</td>
  <td><fieldset><input type="checkbox" id="scarf" value="scarf" checked="checked" />Black Scarf
<input type="checkbox" id="jewelry" value="jewelry" />#34 Lapel Pin <input type="checkbox"
id="brooch" value="brooch" />#56 Brooch></fieldset></td>
</tr>
```

▶ 3. Save WonderNew. Refresh the file in your browser. Compare your screen with the one shown in Figure 8-26 to verify that the fieldset tags have been entered correctly.

Figure 8-26	The fieldset on the Web page

In addition to grouping the controls using a fieldset, you can include descriptive text using the legend tags.

Using the legend Tags

The <legend></legend> tags are used to display some descriptive text for the fieldset. You can also set the style for the legend tag. In this instance, Wardrobe Wonderful is giving away accessories if the purchaser buys today, so Kirsten wants you to use the <legend> </legend> tags to call attention to that part of the form. You will show her how to enter those tags.

To enter the code to set the style for the legend tags:

▶ **1.** In your text editor, display the HTML code for WonderNew.

▶ **2.** On a blank line below the code to set the style for the fieldset, type the following code, which is also shown in red in Figure 8-27.

```
legend {
color: red;
background-color: white;
border: navy solid thin;
padding: .1em;
margin-left: 2em; }
```

Code to set the style for the legend ◀ Figure 8-27

```
fieldset {
color: navy;
background-color: orange;
border: navy inset thick; }

legend {
color: red;
background-color: white;
border: navy solid thin;
padding: .1em;
margin-left: 2em; }
```

▶ **3.** Save WonderNew.

The text that Kirsten wants to emphasize are the words, "$3.99 Each if You Buy Today." The start <legend> tag should precede those words and the end </legend> tag should follow those words.

You will now show Kirsten where to enter the <legend></legend> tags.

Tip

Limit the legend text to not more than one line.

To use the legend tags:

▶ **1.** In your text editor, display the HTML code for WonderNew.

▶ **2.** In the table cell where you previously entered the <fieldset> tag, type the following code shown below in bold, which is also shown in red in Figure 8-28.

```
<tr>
  <td>Accessories</td>
  <td><fieldset><legend>$3.99 Each if You Buy
Today!</legend><input type="checkbox" id="scarf"
value="scarf" checked="checked" />Black Scarf <input
type="checkbox" id="jewelry" value="jewelry" />#34 Lapel Pin
<input type="checkbox" id="brooch" value="brooch" />#56
Brooch</fieldset></td>
</tr>
```

Figure 8-28 **Code for the legend tags**

```
<!-- checkboxes; scarf is selected -->

<tr>
  <td>Accessories</td>
  <td><fieldset><legend>$3.99 Each if You Buy Today!</legend><input type="checkbox" id="scarf"
value="scarf" checked="checked" />Black Scarf <input type="checkbox" id="jewelry"
value="jewelry" />#34 Lapel Pin <input type="checkbox" id="brooch" value="brooch" />#56 Brooch>
</fieldset></td>
  </tr>
```

▶ **3.** Save WonderNew. Refresh the file in your browser. Compare your screen with the one shown in Figure 8-29 to verify that the legend tags have been entered correctly and to view the completed Web page.

Figure 8-29 **The completed Web page**

▶ **4.** Close your text editor and close your browser.

You can also group controls on a form using graphic elements such as horizontal rules, which you'll explore next.

Using Horizontal Rules with Forms

Another means of grouping items in the form is to divide a group of objects with a horizontal rule. If, for example, the form were within a table, use the *colspan* attribute to span the width of the columns. For example:

```
<tr>
  <td colspan="2"><hr /></td>
</tr>
```

Using the label Tags | InSight

The `<label></label>` tags are used to eliminate sets of `<tr></tr>` tags for each radio button or check box entry. The `<label>` tags must have the attribute *for*. Another advantage to using `<label>` tags is that the tags can be styled to change the appearance of the corresponding text label. The disadvantage is that the Windows form controls will not be aligned as they would if you were using a table structure. Set the value of the for attribute equal to the value of the id or the name attribute of the related element. Examples:

```
<label for="lastname">Last Name:</label>
<input type="text" id="lastname" />
<br />
<input type="text" id="firstname" />

<input type="radio" name="size" id="small" />
<label for="small">Small</label>
<br />
<input type="radio" name="size" id="large" />
<label for="large">Large</label>

<input type="checkbox" id="sendmail">
<label for="sendmail">Send me Mail</label>
```

Figures 8-30 and 8-31 summarize the form elements and form attributes and values.

Form elements ◄ **Figure 8-30**

Tag(s)	Use	Comment
`<form> </form>`	Begins and ends a form	No limit on the number of forms in a document
`<input>`	Creates form objects	
`<textarea>`	Creates a multiple-line field for text	
`<option>`	Creates entries for a list	
`<fieldset>`	Organizes form elements	
`<legend>`	Creates descriptive text for a form	
`<select>`	Creates a list	

Form attributes ◄ **Figure 8-31**

Attribute	Use	Comment
Action	Identifies the location on the server where the database resides	
Maxlength	Determines the maximum number of characters that will be accepted into a text field	
Password	Creates ***** on the screen instead of displaying text in a text box	
Type	Determines the type of control	Value of *radio* creates a radio button; value of *checkbox* creates a check box
Size	Determines the number of entries in the list	

Review | **Session 8.3 Quick Check**

1. What input type would be used to create a button that would erase the entries in all the fields?
2. What input type would be used to create a button that sends data to a database?
3. What tag is used to organize form elements?
4. What does that tag do?
5. What tag creates caption text for a form?
6. What tag is used to create dividers within the form?

Review | **Tutorial Summary**

To create a form, you need to create a database, run a script, and create a form for input. The tags to start and end the form are <form> and </form>. You can have more than one set of <form> tags within the body of the document. The method attribute is used to run a script. The <input> tag is used to create a variety of form objects. Text boxes are areas of the screen in which the user can input text. The size and maxlength attributes control the size of the text box and how many characters will be accepted for input. The password attribute creates a password field. The <textarea> tag creates a multiple-line text entry field. Radio buttons are used to select only one item from a list of choices. Check boxes are used to select one or more items from a list of choices. The <select> tag is used to create a default choice in a list. The <option> tag is used to identify items in a menu. The submit command button is used to send information to the database; the reset command button is used to clear the form. You can use the <button> tag to set a style for the command buttons. You can organize the form elements by using the <fieldset> and the <legend> tags.

Key Terms

action attribute
alphanumeric
CGI (Common Gateway
    Interface)
check box
checked attribute
cols attribute

drop-down list box
form
maxlength attribute
method attribute
multiple attribute
option group

prompting text
radio button
rows attribute
script
scripting language
Windows control

Practice	**Review Assignments**

Take time to practice the skills you learned in the tutorial using the same case scenario.

Data Files needed for the Review Assignments: Order.htm and Wardrobe.gif

Kirsten Barnes was pleased with the Web page you created for her, which allowed customers to choose an item and then add it to the shopping cart. Now Kirsten wants you to create a form that will gather information about the customer and record the transaction. Complete the following:

1. Use your text editor to open the **Order.htm** file in your Tutorial.08/Review folder of your Data Files. Save the file as **OrderNew.htm** in the same folder.

2. Below the start style tag, insert a comment that includes your first and last name as the author and today's date.

3. Below the comment, create a style for the form element to have a width of 60% and a background color of wheat.

4. In the body section, just above the start <table> tag, insert the start <form> tag. Name the form order. The value for the action attribute will be: http://mywebsite.com/cgi-bin/myscript.cgi. The form method will be post. Insert the end </form> tag above the </div> tag.

5. In the second row of the table, create a text field with the id of email. Set the size to 30. E-mail Address is the prompting text.

6. In the third row of the table, create three text fields with the ids of area code, exchange, and extension. Set the size and maxlength of the area code to 3. Set the size and maxlength of the exchange to 3. Set the size and maxlength of the extension to 4. Phone is the prompting text.

7. In the next three rows, create text fields with the ids of billaddress1, billaddress2, and city. Each field will have a size of 20. Use Billing Address 1, Billing Address 2, and City as the prompting text.

8. In the next row, create a text field with the id of state. The size and the maxlength will be 2. State is the prompting text.

9. In the next row, create two text fields with the ids of zip and zipfour. The size and the maxlength of the zip field will be 5; the size and the maxlength of the zipfour field will be 4. Zip is the prompting text.

10. In the next row, create a text field with the id of country. The size will be 20. Country is the prompting text.

11. In the next row, create a text field with the id of customer_name. Set the size to 20. Name as it Appears on Credit Card is the prompting text.

12. Below the row for the customer_name text field, create an option list. The id will be credit. The size will be 1. The options should be Choose a credit card, Visa, Mastercard, Discover, and American Express. Credit Card Name is the prompting text.

13. Below the row for the credit card name option list, create another option list. The id will be month. The size will be 1. The 13 options should be month, and the numbers 01 through 12. Expiration Date Month is the prompting text.

14. Below the row for the month option list, create another option list. The id will be year. The size will be 1. The eight options should be the word "year" and the years 2010 through 2016. Expiration Date Year is the prompting text.

15. Below the option list for the year option list, create a text field. The id will be number. The size will be 20. Card Number is the prompting text.

16. In the row below the text field for the Card Number, create three radio buttons. The name for all three buttons will be shipping. The values will be standard, rush, and nextday. Have the choice for rush as the default choice. Shipping Method is the prompting text.

17. In the row below the radio buttons, create three check boxes. The name for all three check boxes will be handling. The values for the check boxes will be giftwrap, ribbon, and bow. Make ribbon the default choice. Special Handling (Check all that apply) is the prompting text.

18. Below the check boxes, in the last row of the table, create a submit button with the value Send Your Order. Create a reset button with the value Start Over.

19. Save your OrderNew HTML document, and then open it in your browser. The document should be similar to the one shown in Figure 8-32.

Figure 8-32

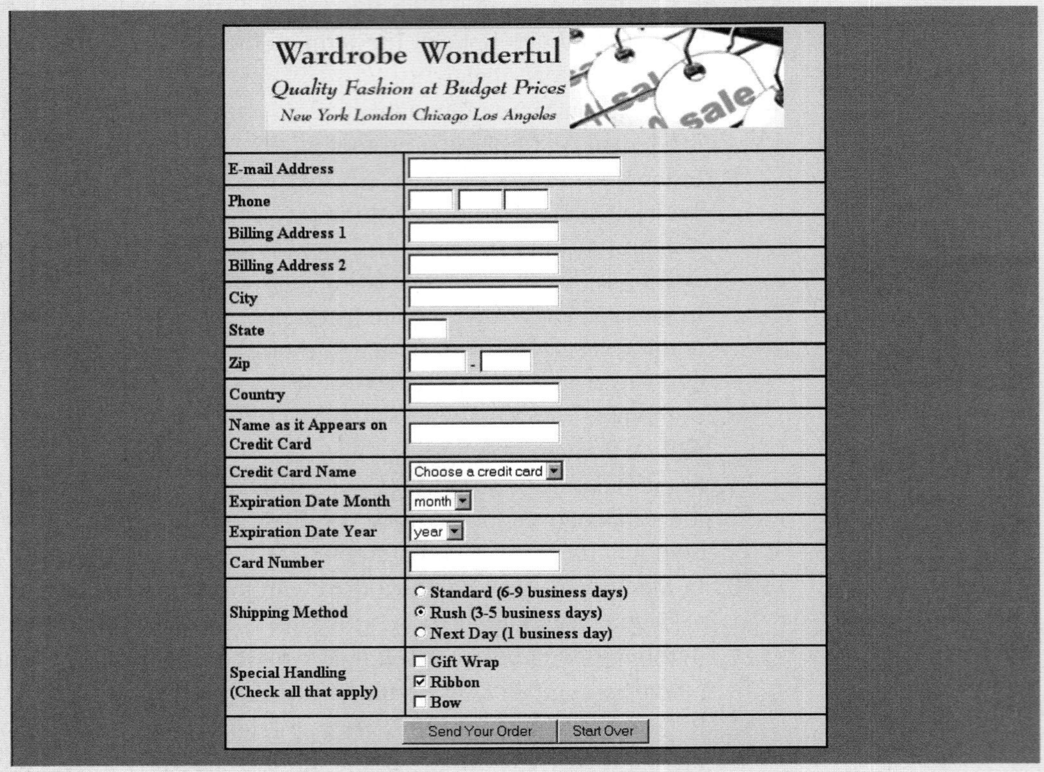

20. Close all open windows.

21. Submit the results of the preceding steps to your instructor, either in printed or electronic form, as requested.

Apply | **Case Problem 1**

Use the skills you learned in the tutorial to create a Web page for a Meat and Poultry distribution company.

Data Files needed for this Case Problem: No.gif, Ok.gif, Onloin.gif, and Onloin.htm

OnLoin Meat and Poultry Products OnLoin Meat and Poultry Products supply many of the nation's finest restaurants with top-quality meats and poultry. The company sells its products exclusively on the Web and uses its rapid, national distribution channels to ship its products within hours after orders are received. Gus Tyrell, the chief marketing manager, has asked you to create a new form for ordering their products. Complete the following:

1. Use your text editor to open the **Onloin.htm** file from your Tutorial.08/Case1 folder of your Data Files. Save the file as **OnloinNew.htm** in the same folder.

2. Below the start style tag, insert a comment that includes your first and last name as the author and today's date.

3. Below the comment and above the existing styles, create a style for the form element. Style the form to have a width of 70% and a background color of lightblue. Text should be in Arial font. There should be padding on the left of 1em.

4. Create a style for the button element. The style should have 0.1em of padding on the top, a left margin of 2em, and bold, black text on a yellow background. The button should have a border that is black, solid, and thin.

5. Create a dependent style for the image element named vertical. The style should create a margin on the right of 1em and vertically align an image in the middle.

6. In the body section, just above the start <table> tag, insert the start <form> tag. Name the form purchases. The value for the action attribute will be: http://mywebsite.com/cgi-bin/myscript.cgi. The form method will be post. Enter the end </form> tag above the </div> tag.

7. In the second row of the table, create a password field with an id of password and a size of 15. Password is the prompting text.

8. In the third row of the table, create another password field with an id of passwordconfirm and a size of 15. Confirm Password is the prompting text.

9. Below the second password field, create a check box field. The id should be shipping. This check box should be checked by default. Check here if the billing and the shipping address are the same is the prompting text.

10. Below the check box field, create a drop-down list. The id should be title. The size should be 1. The four options should be: (No title), Mr., Mrs., and Ms.

11. Below the options list, create a text field with an id of phone and a size of 12. The field should have a maximum length of 15. Phone is the prompting text.

12. Below the text field for the phone number, create a text field with an id of companyname and a size of 20. Company/Business Name is the prompting text.

13. Below the text field for the company name, create two text fields. The id for the first field should be address1; the id for the second field should be address2. Each field should have a size of 20. Address Line 1 is the prompting text for the first field. Address Line 2 is the prompting text for the second field.

14. Below the address line fields, create a text field with an id of city and a size of 20. City is the prompting text.

15. Below the city field, create a text field with an id of state and a size of 2. The maximum length should be 2. State is the prompting text.

16. Below the state field and in the same table cell, create a text field with an id of zip and a size of 5. The maximum length for this field should be 5. Type a space, dash, and space, and then create a second text field with an id of zipfour and a size of 4. The maximum length should be 4. Zip is the prompting text.

17. Below the zipfour field, create a text field with an id of country and a size of 20. Country is the prompting text.

18. Below the country field, create a text field with an id of email and a size of 25. E-mail is the prompting text.

19. Below the email field, create a check box field. The id should be offers. The check box should be checked by default. The prompting text is "I would like to receive special offers via e-mail."

EXPLORE

20. Below the cell containing the horizontal rule, create a button using the button tags. This will be a submit button. The label text is Submit Order. The submit button uses the image Ok.gif. Apply the vertical class to the image. Use the button tags to create a reset button with the label text of Cancel. The reset button uses the image No.gif. Apply the vertical class to the image.

21. Save your OnloinNew HTML document, and then open it in your browser. The document should be similar to the one shown in Figure 8-33.

Figure 8-33

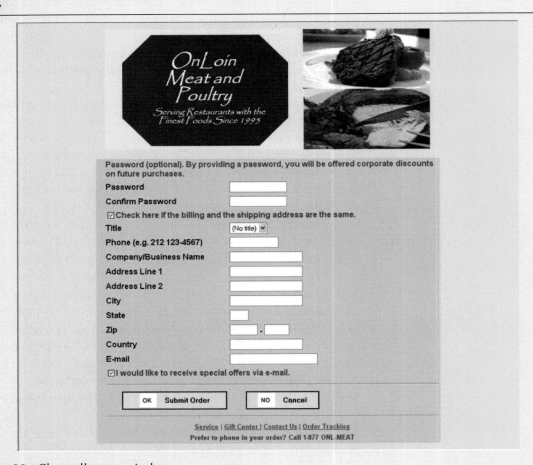

22. Close all open windows.

23. Submit the results of the preceding steps to your instructor, either in printed or electronic form, as requested.

| Apply | | Case Problem 2 |

Use the skills you learned in the tutorial to create and style a Web page for a florist.

Data Files needed for this Case Problem: Balloon.jpg, Candle.jpg, Candy.jpg, Flo.gif, and Flowers.htm

Flo's Florist   Flo Stein is the owner of a small chain of florist shops. She has a well-established online business, but she has approached you about an idea to expand her business to new markets. In addition to selling flowers online, Flo also wants to expand her product line to include other gift items. Your form will allow the customer to purchase other items in addition to flowers. Flo also wants the customers to create a personalized card that can be sent along with the order as a gift. Complete the following:

1. Use your text editor to open the **Flowers.htm** file from your Tutorial.08/Case2 folder of your Data Files. Save the file as **FlowersNew.htm** in the same file folder.
2. Below the start style tag, insert a comment that includes your first and last name as the author and today's date.
3. Below the comment, create a style for the form element. Style the form to have a width of 775px, a background color of peach. The font should be Arial. There should be padding on the left of 1em.

⊕ EXPLORE
4. Create a style for the button element. The style should have 0.1em of padding on the top, a left margin of 2em, bold, and white text on a navy background. The button element should have a border that is silver, outset, and 0.5em.
5. Create a style for the fieldset element. Style the fieldset to have a border that is black, solid, and thin. There should be padding of 0.3em.
6. Create a style for the legend element. Style the legend to have text displayed in 14pt, bold, pink, and in the Garamond (a serif) font. There should be a background color of black and padding of 0.2em.
7. In the body section, just above the start <table> tag, insert the start <form> tag. Name the form gifts. The value for the action attribute will be: http://mywebsite.com/cgi-bin/myscript.cgi. The form method will be post. Enter the end </form> tag above the end </div> tag following the end </table> tag for the second table.
8. In the first cell of the third row of the table, type the code for three radio buttons. Use candles as the value for the name attribute. The values for each radio button will be: red, white, and purple. The text to be displayed is Red, White, and Purple.
9. In the second cell of the third row of the table, type the code for three radio buttons. Use candy as the value for the name attribute. The values for each radio button will be 8oz, 16oz, and 32oz. The text to be displayed for the radio buttons will be 8 oz, 16 oz, and 32 oz.
10. In the third cell of the third row of the table, type the code for five radio buttons. Use balloon as the value for the name attribute. The values for each radio button will be as follows: birthday, congrats, wishes, anniversary, and getwell. The text to be displayed will be as follows: Happy Birthday, Congratulations, Best Wishes, Happy Anniversary, and Get Well Soon.

⊕ EXPLORE
11. In the fourth row of the table, you will be creating three drop-down list boxes. In the first cell of the third row, use candle_num as the value for the id. The size should be 1. The options will be 1, 2, 3, and 4. The prompting text is Quantity.
12. In the second cell of the fourth row, use candy_num as the value for the id. The size should be 1. The options will be 1, 2, 3, and 4. The prompting text is Quantity.
13. In the third cell of the fourth row, use balloon_num as the value for the id. The size should be 1. The options will be 1, 2, 3, 4, 6, and 12. The prompting text is Quantity.

14. In the first cell of the first row of the second table, create a text area. The id should be note. There should be 10 rows and the text area should be 50 characters wide.

◈ EXPLORE

15. In the second cell of the first row of the second table, create a button using the button tags. This will be a submit button. The label text is Continue Order.

16. In the third cell of the first row of the second table, create another button using the button tags. This will be a reset button. The label text is Cancel.

17. In the table cell for the candle radio buttons, include a fieldset and a legend. The text for the legend will be Scented Candles. Insert an end </fieldset> tag before the </td> tag for that cell.

18. In the table cell for the candy radio buttons, include a fieldset and a legend. The text for the legend will be Box of Chocolates. Insert an end </fieldset> tag before the </td> tag for that cell.

19. In the table cell for the balloon radio buttons, include a fieldset and a legend. The text for the legend will be Balloon Bouquet. Insert an end </fieldset> tag before the </td> tag for that cell.

20. Save your FlowersNew HTML document, and then open it in your browser. The document should be similar to the one shown in Figure 8-34.

Figure 8-34

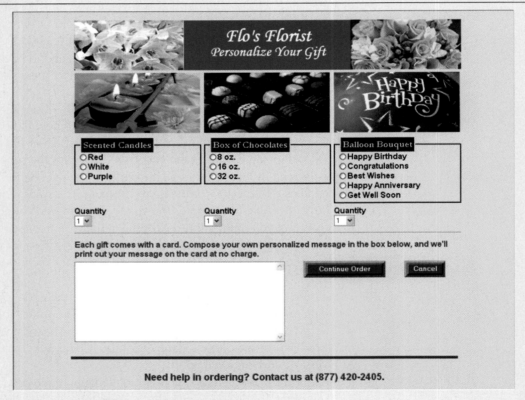

21. Close all open windows.

22. Submit the results of the preceding steps to your instructor, either in printed or electronic form, as requested.

Challenge | Case Problem 3

Use what you've learned, and expand your skills, to create and style a Web page for a computer repair service.

Data Files needed for this Case Problem: Boy.gif, Bunch.htm, Bytelogo.gif, and Girl.gif

The Byte Bunch   The Byte Bunch is a company that sells discounted software to programmers from beginner to expert. The company also derives revenue by selling training materials such as books, training manuals, and videos on DVDs. The Byte Bunch has found that it makes as much money on these supplementary materials as it does from the sales of software. To target its audience for the types of materials they might be interested in purchasing, it is important to know the level of programming experience of its customers. Leona Lee, the sales manager at the Byte Bunch, has asked you to create a Web page that will gather background information about their customers. Leona has asked that the Web page have as little code as possible, so you will create the page using three id class selectors for the content, rather than organize the data using a table structure. Complete the following:

1. Use your text editor to open the **Bunch.htm** file from your Tutorial.08/Case3 folder of your Data Files. Save the file as **BunchNew.htm** in the same file folder.

2. Below the start style tag, include a comment with your first and last name as the author and today's date.

✥ **EXPLORE** 3. Create a style for the legend tag selector. Have text be displayed in orange with a background color of black. There should be padding of 0.3em.

✥ **EXPLORE** 4. Create a style for the fieldset tag selector. There should be padding of 0.3em.

5. In the body section, just below the comment "the form starts here," enter the code for the start <form> tag. Name the form info. The value for the action attribute will be: http://mywebsite.com/cgi-bin/myscript.cgi. The form method will be post. Enter the end </form> tag above the comment, "the form ends here."

6. To the right of the prompting text for the First Name and Last Name, create two text boxes, one for the first name and one for the last name. The id for the text box for the first name should be firstname. The id for the text box for the last name should be lastname.

7. Create two other text boxes, one for E-mail and one for Phone. The id for the E-mail text box should be email. The id for the Phone text box should be phone. For the phone text box, use the value attribute and assign a value of xxx xxx-xxxx.

8. Below the prompting text, "Programming Expertise," insert the code for four radio buttons. Use expert as the value for the name attribute. The values for each radio button will be: beginner, intermediate, experienced, and pro. The text to display for each radio button is Beginner, Intermediate, Experienced, and Real Pro.

✥ **EXPLORE** 9. Just below the start <form> tag, create a fieldset and a legend. The text for the legend is "Tell Us About Yourself." Insert an end </fieldset> tag after the code for the radio button for Real Pro.

10. Below the prompting text, "Software Used," create three check boxes. The id for all three check boxes is used. The values will be C++, VB, and Java. The text to display will be C++, Visual Basic, and Java.

11. Below the prompting text, "What Are You Spending Your Time Developing Now?", insert a text area. The text area id should be time. The text area should be 10 rows high and 50 columns wide.

12. Below the text area, include two command buttons: a submit button whose value is Submit Form, and a reset button whose value is Reset.

13. Save your BunchNew HTML document, and then open it in your browser. The document should be similar to the one shown in Figure 8-35.

Figure 8-35

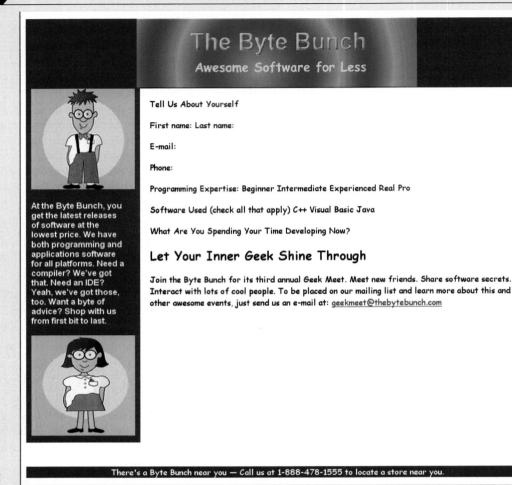

14. Close all open windows.
15. Submit the results of the preceding steps to your instructor, either in printed or electronic form, as requested.

| Create | **Case Problem 4** |

Using the figures provided, create and style a Web page for a caterer.

Data Files needed for this Case Problem: Bride.jpg, Hall.gif, and Hall.htm

LaFleur Caterers   LaFleur Caterers is a large catering hall that specializes in arranging events for 50 to 500 people. LaFleur makes all the arrangements for invitations, flowers, limousines, portrait photography, videography, live or recorded music with a DJ, and tuxedo or gown rentals. LaFleur also runs a travel agency, primarily for newlyweds to plan and book their honeymoon vacations. LaFleur offers choices for wait staff, personal bridal attendants, directional cards, coat check, and a gazebo garden ceremony. Limousine service offers choices from 6, 8, 10, or 12-passenger limousine, antique Rolls Royce, or even a horse and buggy. Brenda McNair, the new manager of LaFleur Caterers, has asked you to create a Web-based form that will allow customers to choose from among all of the services available. You have decided to organize the data using a table structure for the form. Complete the following:

1. Use your text editor to open the **Hall.htm** file from your Tutorial.08/Case4 folder of your Data Files. Save the file as **HallNew.htm** in the same file folder.

2. Below the start style tag, enter a comment that includes your first and last name as the author and today's date.

3. Below the comment, "enter your form code here," enter the code for a form that includes examples of each of the following:

   a. radio buttons (have one of the radio buttons selected)

   b. check boxes (have one of the boxes checked)

   c. a fieldset (set a style for this element)

   d. a legend (set a style for this element)

   e. a drop-down list box (have one of the options selected)

   f. a text area

   g. submit and reset command buttons (set a style for the button element)

4. Save your HallNew HTML document, and then open it in your browser. Figure 8-36 illustrates an example of how your Web page for La Fleur Caterers might look.

Figure 8-36

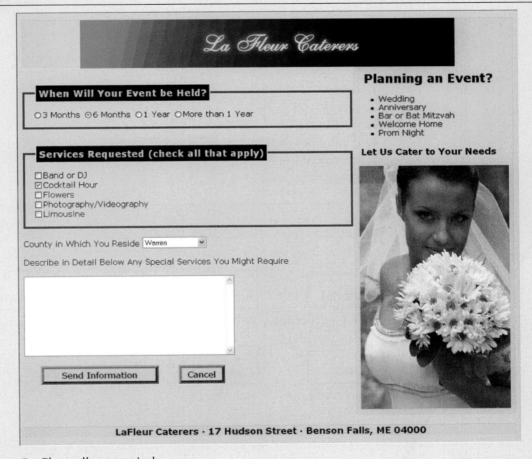

5. Close all open windows.

6. Submit the results of the preceding steps to your instructor, either in printed or electronic form, as requested.

Review | Quick Check Answers

Session 8.1

1. a database, a script, and an HTML form
2. <form> and </form>
3. text
4. controls the maximum number of characters that can be entered into a text field
5. no
6. password

Session 8.2

1. radio
2. checkbox
3. checked="checked"
4. checked="checked"
5. <select></select>
6. size
7. <option></option>

Session 8.3

1. reset
2. submit
3. <fieldset>
4. draws lines around a group of form elements
5. <legend>
6. <hr />

Ending Data Files

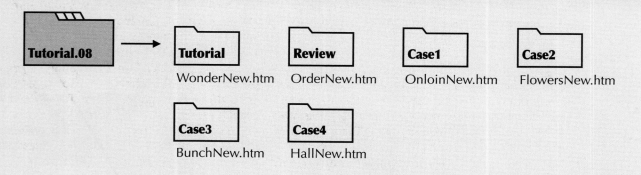

Tutorial.08 → Tutorial — WonderNew.htm

Review — OrderNew.htm

Case1 — OnloinNew.htm

Case2 — FlowersNew.htm

Case3 — BunchNew.htm

Case4 — HallNew.htm

Objectives

Session 9.1
- Decide when to use frames for a Web site
- Learn the components of framesets
- Create a frameset document
- Size frameset windows
- Target individual frame windows

Session 9.2
- Identify the purpose of inline frames
- Create an inline frame
- Target an inline frame window
- Use the meta tag to create a slide show

Creating Frames
Using Frames for Page Layout

Case | Stormm's Coffee

Stormm's Coffee is a chain of coffee shops located in the states of Indiana, Ohio, and Pennsylvania. Stormm's shies away from using elaborate names for its products as some of its competitors do. Instead, Stormm's product descriptions are stated in simple, understandable terms. Stormm's has learned that its customers want great-tasting products, not great-sounding products. Stormm's also sells a full line of baked goods and pastry items to attract customers to their coffee shops both day and night, and offers ice cream and fountain drinks to retain its customer base during the warmer months. Sal Tangello, the marketing manager for Stormm's, has asked for your help in updating the Stormm's Web site, which was created using HTML frames. You will work with Sal to show him how frames are created and how they function.

Starting Data Files

Tutorial.09 → **Tutorial**

Tutorial
Atlanta.htm
Banner.htm
Chicago.htm
Club.htm
Coffees.htm
Content.htm
Employment.htm
Environmental.htm
Frameset.htm
Franchises.htm
Gear.htm
Gift.htm
Harry.htm
Jane.htm
Links.htm
Links2.htm
Locator.htm
London.htm
NewYork.htm
Staff.htm
Tamira.htm
Welcome.htm
+ 9 graphic files

Review
Baked.htm
Banner2.htm
Cookies.htm
Croissant.htm
Danish.htm
Doughnuts.htm
Flan.htm
Footer.htm
Layercake.htm
More.htm
+ 8 graphic files

Case1
Biking.htm
Double.htm
Golf.htm
Hiking.htm
Pines.htm
Pinesbanner.htm
Pinesfooter.htm
Pineslinks.htm
Pinesviews.htm
Pool.htm
Restaurant.htm
Sailing.htm
Single.htm
Tennis.htm
Walkway.htm
+ 12 graphic files

Case2
Cave.htm
Mountain.htm
One.htm
Pole.htm
Rain.htm
Sail.htm
Shark.htm
Travel.htm
Volcano.htm
+ 8 graphic files

Case3
Motorbanner.htm
Motorframe.htm
Motormain.htm
Slide1.htm
Slide2.htm
Slide3.htm
+ 7 graphic files

Case4
Smile1.htm
Smile2.htm
Smile3.htm
Smile4.htm
Smile5.htm
Tottsbanner.htm
Tottscontent.htm
Tottsframeset.htm
Tottslinks.htm
+ 8 graphic files

Session 9.1

Using Frames on a Web Page

Recall in the tutorials on links and tables, you divided a Web page into regions, such as a sidebar on the left side of the page that was used to group links. If you clicked a link to another page, that Web page opened in a new browser window and replaced the page you were viewing. Frames, on the other hand, divide a Web page into several windows, called **frames**. Each frame allows you to see a different Web page in the *same* browser window. Typically, the frames display a banner logo document across the top of the screen and a list of links in a sidebar document on the left side of the screen. The largest window, usually to the right of the sidebar, is used to display the content document. In a frames layout, if the user clicks a link in the sidebar, the target page opens in the content document window to the right of the sidebar, not in a new browser window. The original banner document and the original sidebar document remain displayed on the screen.

In the late 1990s and the early part of this century, many Web developers created Web sites designed with frames. Over time, however, users became less enthusiastic about using frames. Users found that a frames layout can be difficult to bookmark and difficult to print. Users also preferred to have the documents displayed in the entire browser window, not just a smaller content window. Several years ago, first Firefox and then Internet Explorer introduced **tabbed browsing**, which is the ability to keep several Web pages open at the same time. To see a page you already have viewed, you click the page tab at the top of the browser screen. Because of all of these reasons, frames will become deprecated in XHTML 2.0, the next version of XHTML.

So why learn about frames? Some Web sites still rely on frames for page layout. It would not be a wise decision to create a new Web site using frames, but you need to know about frames in order to maintain those Web sites that still use frames for page layout.

To create frames, you first need to create a **frameset document**, which is the document that determines the number and size of the frames. The frameset document does not have any text or images; it only contains the HTML code that establishes the page layout for the frames. You also need to create the documents that will be displayed in the frames. It's best to create these documents first because it is the height and width of those documents that you will use to determine the size and number of the frames.

Using the frameset Tags

Frames are similar to tables in that frames establish rows and columns, but instead of typing text into a table cell, you use a frameset to determine the number and size of the rows and columns. A frameset layout can have windows that divide the screen only horizontally into rows or only vertically into columns. You can also divide the screen into both rows and columns. To do so, you have to place a frameset within another frameset, which is called a **nested frameset**. It is very common to have nested framesets. You will be creating a frameset for the rows and another frameset for the columns, which will result in a nested frameset.

The frameset document uses the <frameset> </frameset> tags. The <frameset> </frameset> tags replace the <body> </body> tags. You do not include any <body> tags in a frameset document. You'll begin by showing Sal how to enter an HTML comment into the document to identify the author and the creation date of the file.

To enter the document comment:

▶ 1. Use your text editor to open the **Frameset.htm** file located in the Tutorial.09\Tutorial folder included with your Data Files. Save this file as **FramesetNew.htm** in the same folder.

▶ 2. On a blank line below the end </head> tag, create an HTML comment using your name and today's date as shown below and in red in Figure 9-1.

```
<!-- Your First Name Your Last Name
Today's Date -->
```

HTML comment code ◄ **Figure 9-1**

```
<html>
<head>
<title>Stormm's Coffee &ndash; Simple Talk, Complex Coffee</title>
</head>

<!-- Your First Name Your Last Name
Today's Date -->

</html>
```

▶ 3. Save the FramesetNew file.

Tip
The frameset element is one of the few elements that cannot be styled by using Cascading Style Sheets.

You begin the frameset document by entering the start <frameset> tag, like so:

```
<html>
<head>
<title>Stormm's Coffee &ndash; Simple Talk, Complex Coffee</title>
</head>
<frameset
```

Creating Rows in a Frameset Document

You'll first show Sal how to create the rows frameset. The rows frameset uses the rows attribute. You need to decide the number of rows you want and the height of the rows. The row height is expressed as a percentage of the entire screen. The values are enclosed in quotes.

Creating a Rows Frameset | Reference Window

- To create a rows frameset, enter the following code:
  ```
  <frameset rows="value1, value2, ..."></frameset>
  ```
  where *value1* is the height of the first row, *value2* is the height of the second row, and so forth. The values should be expressed as a percentage.
- Optionally, use the (*) wildcard character as the last value or if the rows will be of equal height.

For example, to divide the screen into two frames with the top frame occupying 20 percent of the screen height and the bottom frame occupying 80 percent of the screen height, you would enter this code for the rows attribute and its percentage values:

```
<frameset rows="20%, 80%">
```

Note that the percentage values for the rows attribute are separated by a comma. All the percentage values together, not the individual values, are enclosed in quotes, so there should be only one start quote and one end quote for all the percentage values. For example, this code, with two sets of quotes, is incorrect. The frames would not be displayed correctly:

```
<frameset rows="20%," "80%">
```

You could also use pixel values for the row and column widths, but it's better to use percentages because percentage values are always displayed the same way irrespective of the screen resolution. You can also use the asterisk (*) as a wildcard character. In the preceding example, you could have entered the following code and achieved the same result, but with less code:

```
<frameset rows="20%, *">
```

If the rows are of equal size, you can use all wildcards if you want to. For example, to have three rows of equal size, you would enter this code:

```
<frameset rows="*, *, *">
```

The wildcard character can also be used as an instruction to fill the remaining screen space. Because browsers differ in the way they display a page, it's always a good idea to use at least one wildcard character in specifying the size of the frames. In that way, the wildcard value ensures that the entire screen height or width is occupied. It's a good coding practice to use the wildcard character as the last value, like so:

```
<frameset rows="33%, 33%, *">
```

You will show Sal how to enter the start <frameset> code now.

Tip

A space after each comma in the percentage values of wildcards is optional; just be consistent. The comma is required, the space is optional.

To enter the start frameset code:

▶ **1.** In your text editor, display the code for FramesetNew.htm.

▶ **2.** On a blank line below the comment, type the following code, which is also shown in red in Figure 9-2.

```
<frameset rows="20%, *">
```

Figure 9-2 ▶ **Code for the start frameset tag**

```
<html>
<head>
<title>Stormm's Coffee &ndash; Simple Talk, Complex Coffee</title>
</head>

<!-- Your First Name Your Last Name
Today's Date -->

<frameset rows="20%, *">   ◄——  start frameset tag

</html>
```

▶ **3.** Save the FramesetNew file.

After entering the frameset code, you enter the <frame /> tag, which you'll show Sal how to do next.

Using the frame Tag

The <frame /> tag identifies which document should be displayed in a frame. Although you could create and test the frameset without creating the documents to be displayed in the frames, you can get a better idea of whether your frame layout is correct if you first create the documents to be displayed in the frames. The <frame /> tag is an empty tag, so it must be ended with the space-slash combination. Similar to the <img /> tag, the <frame /> tag uses the src attribute. In this instance, however, the value of the src attribute is the document that will be displayed in the frame window, not an image file.

Creating Frames | Reference Window

- To create frames, enter the following code:

    ```
    <frame src="filename.htm" name="framename" />
    ```
    where *filename* is the name of the file that will be displayed in the frame and *framename* is the name of the frame.

So far, the screen has been divided into two rows, one that is 20 percent of the screen height and another row that is the remainder of the screen height. The top row will be the banner row. Although you can name the frame source file whatever you want, it's good coding practice to name the file based on its location or purpose. The frame source file for the banner will be a file named banner.htm, which has an image file of the Stormm's Coffee logo. The frame tag code would be entered like so:

```
<frameset rows="20%, *">
  <frame src="banner.htm" />
```

Similar to the <frameset> tag, the <frame /> tag is one of the few tags that cannot be styled by using Cascading Style Sheets.

Tip

Indent the frame tag code by two or three spaces to make the code more readable and easier to locate.

Planning for Browsers That Do Not Support Frames | InSight

To accommodate users with browsers or devices that do not support frames, use the <noframes> </noframes> tags in the frameset document. Text entered between these tags will be displayed in the browser window. In the noframes text, let the user know that their browser does not support frames. The noframes code looks like so:

```
<noframes>
<body>
<p>Your browser or device needs to support frames in order to view
this page.</p>
</body>
</noframes>
```

Note the use of the <body> tags within the <noframes> tags. This is the only instance where you would use <body> tags in a frameset document.

You will show Sal how to enter the code for the banner frame.

To enter the code for the banner frame:

▶ **1.** In your text editor, display the HTML code for FramesetNew.

▶ **2.** On a blank line below the start frameset tag, type the following bold code, which is also shown in red in Figure 9-3.

```
<frameset rows="20%, *">
  <frame src="banner.htm" />
```

Figure 9-3	Code for the frame source for the banner file

```
<html>
<head>
<title>Stormm's Coffee &ndash; Simple Talk, Complex Coffee</title>
</head>

<!-- Your First Name Your Last Name
Today's Date -->

<frameset rows="20%, *">
  <frame src="banner.htm" />        frame source is
                                    banner.htm

</html>
```

▶ **3.** Save FramesetNew. Open the FramesetNew Web page in your browser, and then compare your screen with the one shown in Figure 9-4 to verify that the banner file is displayed correctly.

Figure 9-4	The banner file in the frameset displayed on the Web page

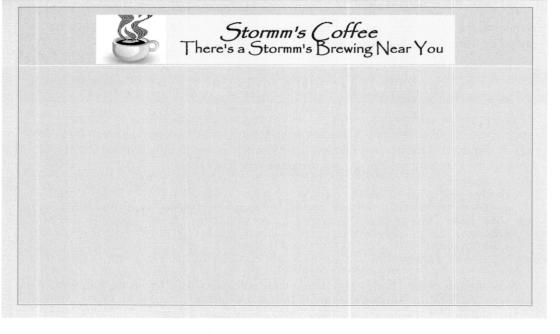

Now that you have shown Sal how to create the rows frameset, you will show him how to create the code for the columns frameset. This columns frameset will have two columns. There will be a fairly narrow column at the left for the links frame. There also will be a much wider column on the right, which will be the frame for the main document content.

Creating Columns in a Frameset Document

Within a <frameset> tag, use the cols attribute to divide the screen vertically into columns. For example, to divide the screen into two frames, one that is 25 percent of the screen vertically and the other that is the remainder of the screen vertically, you would enter this code:

```
<frameset cols="25%, *">
```

Creating a Columns Frameset | Reference Window

- To create a columns frameset, enter the following code:
  ```
  <frameset cols="value1, value2, etc."></frameset>
  ```
  where *value1* is the width of the first column, and *value2* is the width of the second column, and so forth. The values should be expressed as a percentage.
- Optionally, use the (*) wildcard character as the last value or if the columns will be of equal width.

The two documents that have been created to be displayed in the columns frames are links.htm and content.htm. Once again, you use the <frame /> tag to identify the document that will initially be displayed in the frame. The code for the two <frame /> tags would be entered like this:

```
<frameset cols="25%, *">
    <frame src="links.htm" />
    <frame src="content.htm" />
```

Every frameset must be followed by the end </frameset> tag. In this instance you have created two framesets, one for the rows and one for the columns. You must now enter two end </frameset> tags—one to end the columns frameset you just created and one to end the rows frameset you entered code for earlier. Because you are entering code for a frameset within a frameset (a nested frameset), it is good coding practice to indent each line of the second frameset. It's also a good coding practice to leave a blank line before and after the nested frameset, which makes the code for the nested frameset stand out. You will show Sal how to enter the code for the nested frameset and then enter the code for the two end </frameset> tags.

To enter the nested frameset and the end frameset tags:

1. In your text editor, display the HTML code for FramesetNew.

2. On a blank line below the frame source for the banner.htm file, type the following bold code, which is also shown in red in Figure 9-5.

```
<frameset rows="20%, *">
  <frame src="banner.htm" />

    <frameset cols="25%, *">
      <frame src="links.htm" />
      <frame src="content.htm" />
    </frameset>

</frameset>
```

Figure 9-5 ▶ **Code for the nested frameset and the end frameset tags**

```
<frameset rows="20%, *">
  <frame src="banner.htm" />

     <frameset cols="25%, *">
        <frame src="links.htm" />        }  nested frames
        <frame src="content.htm" />
     </frameset>

</frameset>

</html>
```

▶ **3.** Save FramesetNew. Refresh the FramesetNew Web page in your browser, and then compare your screen with the one shown in Figure 9-6 to verify that the framesets are displayed correctly. (Scroll bars may or may not appear, depending on your screen resolution.)

Figure 9-6 ▶ **Framesets displayed on the Web page**

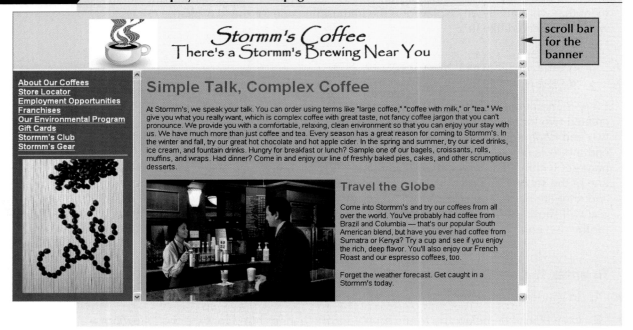

scroll bar for the banner

Recall that the links frame will be a sidebar on the left containing a list of links. Ordinarily, when a user clicks a link, the target document opens in a new browser window. That's not what you want here. You want to have the user click a link in the links frame and have that page open in the content frame at the right, not in a new browser window. Next, you will show Sal how to enter the code to have each of the links open in the content frame.

Opening a Document in a Specific Frame

By default, a link in a frameset document will open in the same frame. That poses a problem because when the user clicks a link in the links frame, you want the links.htm file to remain on the screen and have the referring document open in the target frame (content. htm) to the right. There are two steps to solve this problem. First, in the frame source code, you have to give the target frame a name. It's good coding practice to give the target frame the same name as the document name, like so:

```
<frameset rows="20%, *">
    <frame src="banner.htm" />

        <frameset cols="25%, *">
            <frame src="links.htm" />
            <frame src="content.htm" name="content" />
        </frameset>

</frameset>
```

Both the links frame and the content frame will be the targets for links, so you will need to give names to both of those windows. You will show Sal how to enter the name attribute and values for those frames now.

To enter the name attribute and its value:

▶ **1.** In your text editor, display the HTML code for FramesetNew.

▶ **2.** Position the insertion point after the close quote in each frame source filename, press the **Spacebar**, and type the following bold code, which is also shown in red in Figure 9-7.

```
<frameset cols="25%, *">
    <frame src="links.htm" name="links" />
    <frame src="content.htm" name="content" />
</frameset>
```

Code for the name attribute and its value ◀ **Figure 9-7**

```
<frameset rows="20%, *">
    <frame src="banner.htm" />          name values for the
                                        nested frameset
        <frameset cols="25%, *">
            <frame src="links.htm" name="links" />
            <frame src="content.htm" name="content" />
        </frameset>

</frameset>

</html>
```

▶ **3.** Save FramesetNew.

Now that the frames have been named, you can address the second step to have the link open in a target frame. You will show Sal how to use the target attribute.

Using the target Attribute

To specify a particular frame for a link to display, use the target attribute. The value for the target attribute determines which frame in the frameset will display the contents of the linked document, like so:

```
<a href="gifts.htm" target="content">Purchase Gifts</a>
```

Now that the frame has been named in the frame tag and a target frame has been specified in the link code, when the user clicks the link text for "Purchase Gifts," the Gifts.htm file will open in the content frame, not in a new browser window.

Using Magic Targets

Although there is nothing magical about them, several target values have special meaning in HTML and are referred to as **magic targets**. For example, to break out of frames completely and not open a new browser window, specify the target as **_top** like so:

```
<a href="links2.htm" target="_top">About Our Coffees</a>
```

Note the underscore in the target "_top."
    To open the link in a new browser window, specify the target as **_blank** like so:

```
<a href="links2.htm" target="_blank">About Our Coffees</a>
```

Note the underscore in the target "_blank."
    When you use the magic target _blank, the link will open in a new browser window, but the other browser window will remain open. Now you will have two browser windows open, not one, as there would be if the magic target had been _top.
    To open a document in the same frame as the link, specify the target as **_self** like so:

```
<a href="links2.htm" target="_self">About Our Coffees</a>
```

Note the underscore in the target "_self." The target of _self is often used to create a cascading menu in the links frame. It will appear as though the menu has opened a submenu, but actually, all that has occurred is that a different page has opened in the same frame. In the Links.htm file, the link to About Our Coffees links to a file named Links2.htm, which has another list of links and creates the illusion of a submenu.

Using the base Tag

You can automate the process of targeting the links. Instead of typing the target attribute and a value for each link, just use the <base /> tag, the target attribute, and its value in the <head> section of the links document, like so:

```
<head>
<title></title>
<base target="content" />
</head>
```

Because you have specified a base target, when the user clicks any link in the links file, the document will open in the target frame, which in this instance is the content frame. You do not need to enter the code target="content" in each link.

Using the scrolling Attribute

If you do not want scroll bars to appear for a frame, the **scrolling attribute** (with a value of *no*) will eliminate scroll bars in the browser. For example, if you have sized the banner frame correctly, you should not need scroll bars. To eliminate the scroll bars in the banner frame, the code for the banner frame would be modified like so:

```
<frame src="banner.htm" scrolling="no" />
```

Using the noresize Attribute

The noresize attribute prevents the user from resizing a window frame. This is a useful feature for the banner frame, which contains the Stormm's Coffee logo. Because you always want the Stormm's logo to be displayed, you don't want the user to be able to resize the banner frame window. To prevent resizing of a window, use the noresize attribute and assign a value of noresize, like so:

```
<frame src="banner.htm" noresize="noresize" />
```

If you want, you can use both the scrolling and the noresize attributes together, like so:

```
<frame src="banner.htm" scrolling="no" noresize="noresize" />
```

Controlling Scrollbars and the Frame Size | Reference Window

- To control the appearance of scrollbars and the size of a frame, enter the following code:
  ```
  <frame src="filename.htm" scrolling="scroll_value"
  noresize="noresize" />
  ```
  where *scroll_value* is either auto, yes, or no, and *noresize* has a value of noresize to disable screen resizing.

Sal would like the visitors to the Web site not to be able to adjust the scrolling and size of the banner. You will show him how to enter the code for the scrolling and the resize attributes now.

To enter the scrolling and noresize attributes:

1. In your text editor, display the HTML code for FramesetNew.

2. Position the insertion point to the right of the close quote in the code for the frame source for the banner.htm file. Press the **Spacebar**. Type the following bold code, which is also shown in red in Figure 9-8.

   ```
   <frameset rows="20%, *">
     <frame src="banner.htm" scrolling="no" noresize="noresize" />
   ```

Figure 9-8 ▶ **Code for the scrolling and noresize attributes**

```
<frameset rows="20%, *">
  <frame src="banner.htm" scrolling="no" noresize="noresize" />

     <frameset cols="25%, *">
        <frame src="links.htm" name="links" />
        <frame src="content.htm" name="content" />
     </frameset>

</frameset>
```

▶ **3.** Save FramesetNew. Refresh the FramesetNew Web page in your browser, and then compare your screen with the one shown in Figure 9-9 to verify that the banner frame does not have scroll bars. Point to the bottom edge of the banner frame to verify that the frame cannot be resized.

Figure 9-9 ▶ **Frameset without scroll bars for the banner**

Now that the appearance of the banner frameset has been addressed, Sal wonders how you can control the display of the borders between frames. You will show Sal how to do so in the frameset document.

The border Attribute

You can also disable resizing by adding the border attribute to the frameset tag and assigning a value of zero. When borders are set to zero, no borders are displayed; therefore, there are no window borders to resize. From a design standpoint, eliminating borders also creates a less cluttered look to the screen, a look that is called **seamless frames**. For example:

```
<frameset rows="20%, *" border="0">
<frameset cols="25%, *" border="0">
```

Sal would like to have seamless frames in the document, so you will show him how to enter the code to do so now.

To enter the code to control the display of borders:

▶ **1.** In your text editor, display the HTML code for FramesetNew.

▶ **2.** For each frameset tag, position the insertion point to the right of the close quote for the percentage values. Press the **Spacebar**. Type the following bold code, which is also shown in red in Figure 9-10.

```
<frameset rows="20%, *" border="0">
  <frame src="banner.htm" scrolling="no" noresize="noresize" />

    <frameset cols="25%, *" border="0">
      <frame src="links.htm" links="links" />
      <frame src="content.htm" name="content" />
    </frameset>

</frameset>
```

Code to create seamless frames ◀ Figure 9-10

```
<frameset rows="20%, *" border="0">◀───  border attribute
  <frame src="banner.htm" scrolling="no" noresize="noresize" />   set to 0 to create
                                                                  seamless frames
    <frameset cols="25%, *" border="0">
      <frame src="links.htm" name="links" />
      <frame src="content.htm" name="content" />
    </frameset>

</frameset>
```

▶ **3.** Save FramesetNew. Refresh the FramesetNew Web page in your browser, and then compare your screen with the one shown in Figure 9-11 to verify that the framesets no longer have borders.

Figure 9-11   Frameset displayed without borders on the Web page

Now that you have eliminated the frame borders, it's often useful to add white space to increase the distance between the content of one frame and its neighboring frame. You use the marginheight and the marginwidth attributes to add white space around the frame contents. You will show Sal how to use these two attributes.

The marginheight and marginwidth Attributes

The marginheight attribute adds white space above and below the frame contents; the marginwidth attribute adds white space to the left and right of the frame contents. The value is determined in pixels, like so:

```
<frame src="banner.htm" marginheight="2" marginwidth="5" />
```

The banner contains a centered image, so you do not need to change the margin width, but Sal would like to add some margin height to the banner frame. You will show him how to do so and complete the FramesetNew Web page.

To increase the margin height:

▶ 1. In your text editor, display the HTML code for FramesetNew.

▶ 2. In the frame source code for the banner.htm file, position the insertion point to the right of the close quote for the "noresize" value. Press the **Spacebar**. Type the following bold code, which is also shown in red in Figure 9-12.

```
<frameset rows="20%, *" border="0">
<frame src="banner.htm" scrolling="no"
noresize="noresize" marginheight="10" />
```

Code for the marginheight attribute ◄ **Figure 9-12**

```
<frameset rows="20%, *" border="0">
  <frame src="banner.htm" scrolling="no" noresize="noresize" marginheight="10"/>

    <frameset cols="25%, *" border="0">
      <frame src="links.htm" name="links" />
      <frame src="content.htm" name="content" />
    </frameset>

</frameset>
```

> marginheight attribute set to 10

▶ **3.** Save FramesetNew. Refresh the FramesetNew Web page in your browser, and then compare your screen with the one shown in Figure 9-13 to verify that the margin height has been increased.

Frameset with margin height increased on the completed Web page ◄ **Figure 9-13**

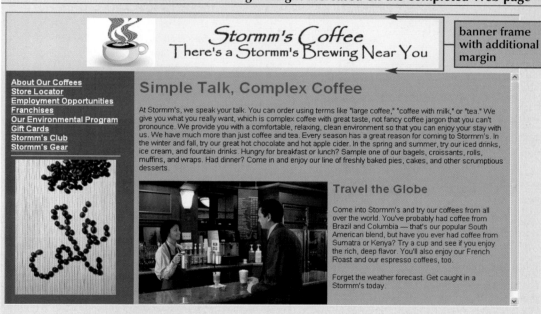

> banner frame with additional margin

▶ **4.** Click each of the links in the links frame to test that the links are working correctly and are opening in the content frame. The About Our Coffees link will display a submenu of links that will open in the content frame.

▶ **5.** Close your text editor. Close your browser.

Figure 9-14 lists the frameset properties.

Figure 9-14   **Frameset attributes and values**

Frames

Tags	Use	Comments
<frameset> </frameset>	The controlling document for frames	Cannot be styled using CSS
<frame />	Creates a window in a frame	Cannot be styled using CSS; this is an open tag
<base />	Used with the target attribute to specify a particular window where all links will open	The target frame must have a name; this is an empty element
<noframes> </noframes>	Used to contain text that will be displayed if the user's browser does not support frames	

Attributes

Tags	Use	Comments
rows	Determines the number of rows for the frameset	Use at least one wildcard character when determining percentages
cols	Determines the number of columns for the frameset	Use at least one wildcard character when determining percentages
src	Determines the source file for the <frame> tag	Required
name	Gives a frame window a name	
target	Identifies which named window will open when the user clicks on a link in a frame	
scrolling	Enables or disables scrolling	Default is yes
noresize	Disables the user from being able to resize frame windows	Takes only one value, noresize.
border	Increases or eliminates the default border between frames	Default is 2px
marginheight	Controls white space at the top and bottom of frames	
marginwidth	Controls white space at the left and right of frames	

Magic Targets

Tags	Use	Comments
target="_self"	Opens a link in the same frame window	Note the underscore in the target value of _self
target="_top"	Breaks out of frames completely; displays the file in the same browser window; one browser window remains open	Note the underscore in the target value of _top
target="_blank"	Opens a link in a new browser window; original browser window remains open; two browser windows will now be open	Note the underscore in the target value of _blank

In this session, you learned that a frameset is a controlling document that determines the layout of the frames documents. Although frames will be deprecated in the next version of HTML/XHTML, a working knowledge of frames is beneficial because many Web sites were created using frames for page layout. The rows attribute determines the number and the height of the rows in the frameset. The cols attribute determines the number and the width of the columns in the frameset. A frameset within another frameset is a nested frameset. The frames element is used to identify which file will be displayed in a particular frame. To have frame windows without scroll bars, use the scrolling attribute and set its value to no. To eliminate resizing in a frames window, use the noresize attribute with a value of noresize. To eliminate borders in a frameset, use the border attribute with a value of zero. You can control the margin height and margin width of a frame to add additional white space to the frame.

Session 9.1 Quick Check | Review

1. What set of tags is used to create a frameset?
2. What tag creates a frame?
3. What attribute is used to create columns?
4. What attribute is used to create rows?
5. What character is the wildcard character?
6. What value of the target attribute will have the link open in the same window?
7. What value of the target attribute will break out of frames completely and not open a new browser window?
8. What attribute is used to determine whether scroll bars will be displayed?
9. What attribute will disable window resizing?

Session 9.2

Inline Frames

Inline frames create a frame window within a document without your having to create a frameset. Inline frames are a powerful and easy way to view multiple documents within the same document. Inline frames use the <iframe> </iframe> tags.

Creating Inline Frames | Reference Window

- To create an inline frame, enter the following code:
  ```
  <iframe src="filename" name="target_name">
  </iframe>
  ```
  where *filename* is the name of the file that will initially be displayed in the inline frames window and *target_name* is the name of the inline frames window.

The inline frame is contained within the body of an HTML document. There is no frameset document. Inline frames can be used with or without tables. In the <iframe> tag, you determine the source of a **placeholder document**, the one that will initially be displayed in the frame, just as you would in the <frame /> tag in a frameset document. When you click a link, the contents of the placeholder document will be replaced by a new document. The inline frame begins with the start <iframe> tag. For example:

```
<iframe
```

The src attribute and its value will display the placeholder document, the document that will initially be displayed in the inline frame. For example:

```
<iframe src="welcome.htm"
```

The name attribute and its value are used to specify the name of a target frame where documents will be displayed. Once again, it's a good idea to name the frame based on the placeholder document's name. For example:

```
<iframe src="welcome.htm" name="welcome">
```

The end </iframe> follows the code for the inline frame. For example:

```
<iframe src="welcome.htm" name="welcome">
</iframe>
```

Tip

Place the end </iframe> tag on a separate line so that it stands out.

In the links code, you target the frames using the target attribute, as in the following code:

```
<a href="jane.htm" target="welcome">Jane Jeffries</a>
<a href="tamira.htm" target="welcome">Tamira Thomas</a>
<a href="harry.htm" target="welcome">Harry Thompson</a>
```

You must give the inline frame a width and a height; this can be done in one of two ways. Within the <iframe> tag, you could use the width and height attributes and specify values for each attribute, like so:

```
<iframe src="welcome.htm" name="welcome" width="40%" height="40%">
</iframe>
```

You could also style the iframe element to have a width and height by using the width and height properties, which is what you will now show Sal how to do.

Styling the iframe Element

Unlike the <frameset> element, which you cannot style, you can style the <iframe> element. Use the height and the width properties to determine the height and width of the inline frame. Once again, it's best to use percentages, rather than pixel values, for the height and the width. For example:

```
iframe {
width: 40%;
height: 40%;
```

The scrolling attribute and its value determine whether or not you want to include scroll bars in your inline frame. The most common value used with an inline frame is auto, which adds scroll bars to the inline frame only if necessary. For example:

```
iframe {
width: 40%;
height: 40%;
scrolling: auto;
```

You can also float the inline frame either left or right so that text can wrap around the inline frame. Some margin space may be necessary to create some white space between the inline frame and the text that wraps around the inline frame. For example:

```
iframe {
width: 40%;
height: 40%;
scrolling: auto;
float: left;
margin-right: 1em; }
```

You have created several documents for the inline frames. Staff.htm is the document that will contain the inline frame. Welcome.htm is the placeholder document that is initially displayed in the iframe window. All of the links in Staff.htm will be targeted to open in this window.

You will now show Sal how to enter the links code and establish a target for the links.

To enter the links code and set the target for the inline frame:

▶ **1.** Use your text editor to open the **Staff.htm** file located in the Tutorial.09\Tutorial folder included with your Data Files. Save this file as **StaffNew.htm** in the same folder.

▶ **2.** On a blank line below the h3 heading in the document body, type the following code, which is also shown in red in Figure 9-15.

```
<a href="jane.htm" target="welcome">Jane Jeffries</a>
<a href="tamira.htm" target="welcome">Tamira Thomas</a>
<a href="harry.htm" target="welcome">Harry Thompson</a>
```

Code for the links and the targets for the inline frame ◀ Figure 9-15

```
<h1>Jaroud Associates &mdash; New Staff Biographies Page</h1>

<h3>Click below to learn more about our new corporate hires.</h3>

<a href="jane.htm" target="welcome">Jane Jeffries</a>
<a href="tamira.htm" target="welcome">Tamira Thomas</a>
<a href="harry.htm" target="welcome">Harry Thompson</a>

<hr />
```

▶ **3.** Save StaffNew. Open the StaffNew file in your browser to verify that the page is displayed correctly as is shown in Figure 9-16.

StaffNew file with the links on the Web page ◀ Figure 9-16

Jaroud Associates — New Staff Biographies Page

Click below to learn more about our new corporate hires.

Jane Jeffries
Tamira Thomas   } ← links to staff Web pages
Harry Thompson

From Mr. Peters:

Please join me in welcoming Jane, Tamira, and Harry to our corporate staff.

We know that they will be making valuable contributions to the firm in the years to come.

I know we all wish them the best of luck.

— John Peters, Managing Partner

The next step is to create the inline frame. You will show Sal how to enter the code to do so and make sure that he enters the code for the end </iframe> tag on a separate line.

To enter the code for the inline frame:

▶ **1.** In your text editor, display the HTML code for StaffNew.

▶ **2.** On a blank line below the <hr /> tag, type the following code, which is also shown in red in Figure 9-17.

```
<iframe src="welcome.htm" name="welcome">
</iframe>
```

Figure 9-17 ▶ **Code for the inline frame**

```
<a href="jane.htm" target="welcome">Jane Jeffries</a>
<a href="tamira.htm" target="welcome">Tamira Thomas</a>
<a href="harry.htm" target="welcome">Harry Thompson</a>

<hr />

<iframe src="welcome.htm" name="welcome">     ◀ code to set the
</iframe>                                          inline frame
```

▶ **3.** Save the StaffNew file. Refresh the StaffNew Web page in your browser, and then compare your screen with the one shown in Figure 9-18 to verify that the inline frame is displayed correctly.

Figure 9-18 ▶ **Inline frame on the Web page**

Tip

An inline frame can be included in a document that is a frameset document.

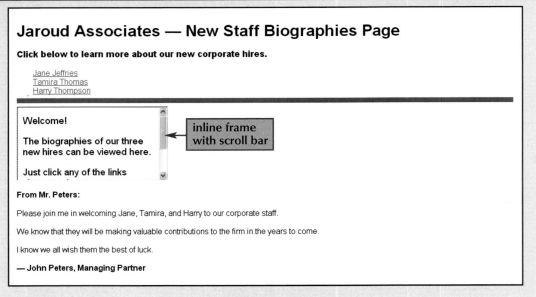

Jaroud Associates — New Staff Biographies Page

Click below to learn more about our new corporate hires.

Jane Jeffries
Tamira Thomas
Harry Thompson

Welcome!   ◀ inline frame
                              with scroll bar
The biographies of our three
new hires can be viewed here.

Just click any of the links

From Mr. Peters:

Please join me in welcoming Jane, Tamira, and Harry to our corporate staff.

We know that they will be making valuable contributions to the firm in the years to come.

I know we all wish them the best of luck.

— John Peters, Managing Partner

Now that the inline frame has been created, you can show Sal how to enter a CSS comment for the document and set the style for the inline frame.

To enter a comment and set the style for the inline frame:

▶ **1.** In your text editor, display the HTML code for StaffNew.

▶ **2.** On a blank line below the start <style> tag, type the following code, which is also shown in red in Figure 9-19.

```
/* Your First Name Your Last Name
Today's Date */

iframe {
width: 70%;
height: 70%;
scrolling: auto;
float: left;
margin-right: 1em; }
```

Comment code and the code for the inline frame ◀ Figure 9-19

```
<html>
<head>
<title>New Staff Biographies Page</title>

<style type="text/css" media="all">

/* Your First Name Your Last Name
Today's Date */

iframe {
width: 70%;
height: 70%;
scrolling: auto;                    sets the style for
float: left;                        the inline frame
margin-right: 1em; }
```

▶ **3.** Save the StaffNew file. Refresh the StaffNew Web page in your browser, and then compare your screen with the one shown in Figure 9-20 to verify that the inline frame has been styled correctly.

▶ **4.** Click each of the three links to verify that the links are displayed in the inline frame.

Document Type Definitions | InSight

Above the <html> tag, you will now often see an optional Document Type Definition, which provides information about the structure of an HTML/XHTML document. There are three document type definitions: Strict, Transitional, and Frameset.

Strict — The document is declared as using all HTML 4.01 tags except deprecated tags and frame tags, like so:
```
<!DOCTYPE html PUBLIC "-//W3C//DTD XHTML 1.1 Strict//EN"
"http://www.w3.org/TR/xhtml1/DTD/xhtml1-strict.dtd">
```

Transitional — The document is declared as using all HTML 4.01 tags including the deprecated tags, but not frame tags, like so:
```
<!DOCTYPE html PUBLIC "-//W3C//DTD XHTML 1.1 Transitional//EN"
"http://www.w3.org/TR/xhtml1/DTD/xhtml1-transitional.dtd">
```

Frameset — The document is declared as using all HTML 4.01 tags including the deprecated tags and the frame tags, like so:
```
<!DOCTYPE html PUBLIC "-//W3C//DTD XHTML 1.1 Frameset//EN"
"http://www.w3.org/TR/xhtml1/DTD/xhtml1-frameset.dtd
```

Figure 9-20 | **Styled inline frame on the Web page**

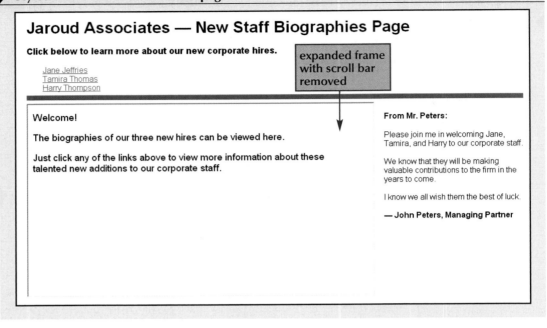

One of the more interesting aspects of inline frames is that you can have as many inline frames in a document as you want. You will use a second inline frame, which will serve as the container for a unique feature of the <meta> tag, which is the ability to have more than one document, in rotation, display in the same inline frame or frames window, which creates a slide show effect. You will show Sal how to have a slide show appear in the upper right-hand corner of the StaffNew document.

Using the meta Tag to Create a Slide Show

Tip

The code for the slide show could be entered in the document body, but <meta /> tags should be placed in the <head> area.

You probably have seen slide shows in banner ads and sidebars in pages on the Web. Within the <head></head> tags, you can use the <meta /> tag to enter the code to create a slide show. The "slides" are documents you have created that will be displayed in a frame—but only for a short duration, usually just a few seconds. The slide show code uses the <meta /> tag and the http-equiv attribute with a value of refresh, like so:

```
<meta http-equiv="refresh"
```

Reference Window | **Using the meta Tag to Create a Slide Show**

- To create a slide show, enter the following code:
  ```
  <meta http-equiv="refresh" content="number_seconds; url=filename">
  ```
  where *number_seconds* is the number of seconds you want as the interval until the next file is displayed and *filename* is the name of the next file to be displayed in the slide show.

The content attribute and its value determine the interval between the slides. The value is the interval (in seconds) before the next slide is displayed. In the example below, the interval is set to display the next slide in three seconds:

```
<meta http-equiv="refresh" content="3;
```

The url attribute and its value specify which file will be the next one to be displayed in the slide show. In the following example, a file named Atlanta.htm is the next file to be displayed:

```
<meta http-equiv="refresh" content="3; url=atlanta.htm" />
```

The punctuation in each attribute and value is critical:

- Note the hyphen between "http" and "equiv".
- The content value is preceded by a quotation mark and followed by a semicolon.
- The url attribute is not preceded by a quotation mark but is followed by a quotation mark.

Here's what happens during the slide show. The first document opens. After three seconds, the second document opens, and so forth. To automatically repeat (loop) the slide show, the <meta /> tag code in the last document in the slide show should have a url value that is the first document in the slide show.

Four documents have been created for the slide show: London.htm, Atlanta.htm, Chicago.htm, and NewYork.htm. Each document has the <meta /> tag code to load the next document in the slide show.

You will show Sal how to enter the code for a second inline frame, which will serve as a container for the slide show.

Tip

There is no means to run the show a set number of times. It loops continuously.

To enter the code for the second inline frame:

▶ **1.** In your text editor, display the HTML code for StaffNew.

▶ **2.** On a blank line below the h1 heading, type the following code, which is also shown in red in Figure 9-21:

```
<iframe src="london.htm">
</iframe>
```

Code for the second inline frame ◀ **Figure 9-21**

```
<body>

<h1>Jaroud Associates &mdash; New Staff Biographies Page</h1>

<iframe src="london.htm">
</iframe>

<h3>Click below to learn more about our new corporate hires.</h3>
```

▶ **3.** Save the StaffNew file.

Because there already is an inline frame in the document, you will have to create an ID selector to style the second inline frame. You will name the ID *slideshow*. You will show Sal how to set the style for the ID, and then you will show him how to apply the style. This slideshow ID selector will also set the height and the width for the second iframe.

To set the style for the inline frame:

▶ **1.** In your text editor, display the HTML code for StaffNew.

▶ **2.** On a blank line below the iframe style, type the following code, which is also shown in red in Figure 9-22.

```
#slideshow {
width: 25%;
height: 11%;
scrolling: no;
float: right;
border: orange solid thin; }
```

Figure 9-22 ▶ **Code for the slideshow ID selector**

```
iframe {
width: 70%;
height: 70%;
scrolling: auto;
float: left;
margin-right: 1em; }

#slideshow {
width: 25%;
height: 11%;
scrolling: no;
float: right;
border: orange solid thin; }
```

sets the style for the slide show

▶ **3.** Save the StaffNew file.

Although the scrolling property was used here, depending on your browser and browser version, you may have to enter the code for the scrolling attribute within the iframe element and set the scrolling value to "no" to eliminate scroll bars in the iframe. Now you will show Sal how to apply the slideshow ID selector.

To apply the style for the inline frame:

▶ **1.** In your text editor, display the HTML code for StaffNew.

▶ **2.** Position the insertion point to the right of the letter "e" in the start iframe tag. Press the **Spacebar** and type the following bold code, which is also shown in red in Figure 9-23.

```
<iframe id="slideshow" src="london.htm">
</iframe>
```

Figure 9-23 ▶ **Code to apply the slideshow ID selector**

```
</style>
</head>

<body>

<h1>Jaroud Associates &mdash; New Staff Biographies Page</h1>

<iframe id="slideshow" src="london.htm">
</iframe>
```

3. Save the StaffNew file. Refresh the StaffNew Web page in your browser, and then compare your screen with the one shown in Figure 9-24 to verify that the inline frame has been created correctly on the completed StaffNew Web page. Also verify that the slide show is running and loops back to the first document, London.htm.

Styled slideshow inline frame on the Web page ◀ **Figure 9-24**

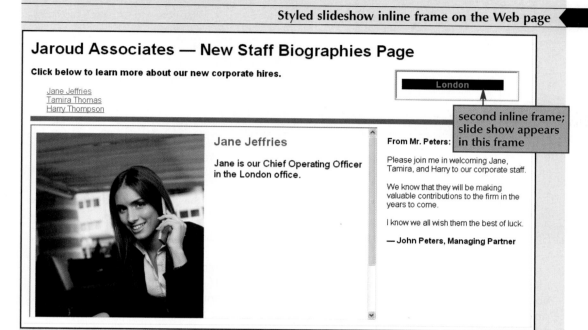

4. Close your text editor. Close your browser.

The Future of Frames | InSight

Frames have been around for more than a decade, so your knowledge of frames will still be useful for several years to come. However, it is best to use CSS for page layout, not frames, for the following reasons:

- Many search engines cannot index a specific page at a Web site created with frames.
- Visitors need to take further steps to print the correct frame document.
- Refreshing and reloading a frameset page may cause the original frameset, not the current page, to be displayed.
- Navigation, particularly using the Back button, can be tricky.
- You can't bookmark a frame; you can only bookmark the frameset URL.
- Frames will become deprecated in the next version of XHTML.

Figure 9-25 lists the iframes attributes.

Figure 9-25 The iframe attributes

Tags, Attributes, and Properties	Use	Comments
<iframe></iframe>	Start and end tags for iframe document	Place the end </frame> tag on its own line
src	Attribute used to identify the initial placeholder document for the iframe	Must be included
name	Gives the target iframe a name	Use name instead of id, which does not work in all browsers
target	Used in the link to direct the link to the target iframe	
height, width	Sets the height and width of the iframe	Use percentages so that the size of the frame is unchanged irrespective of screen resolution. Must be included either within the iframe tag or as a style for the iframe element
scrolling	Creates scroll bars if necessary	Use a value of *auto*

In this session, you learned that inline frames create a frame window within a document without your having to create a frameset. The inline frame is contained within the body of an HTML document. There is no frameset document. Inline frames use the <iframe> tag. The source attribute in the <iframe> tag determines the source of the document that will initially be displayed in the frame. When you click a link in the inline frame, the contents of the placeholder document will be replaced by a new document. The <meta /> tag can be used to create a looping slide show. The content attribute and its value determine the interval between the slides. The url attribute and its value execute the appearance of the next slide in the show.

Review | **Session 9.2 Quick Check**

1. What is the purpose of inline frames?
2. What tag is used to create inline frames?
3. Is that tag paired or empty?
4. What must you give to the inline frame window?
5. What two properties must be present to display the inline frame window?
6. What attribute must be present in the link to the inline frame?
7. What tag can be used to create a slide show?
8. What value is given the http-equiv attribute in the slide show?

Tutorial Summary | Review

Frames split the browser window into multiple windows. The frameset document is the controlling document for frames. The <frame /> tag is used to declare the source file for a frame. The cols and rows attributes determine the number of columns and the number of rows a frameset document will have. The wildcard character is the asterisk. The wildcard character is used as an instruction to fill any remaining space in columns or rows. The name attribute is used to give a window a name so that it can later be used as a target for a link. The target attribute directs a link to open in a specific frame window. The <base /> tag and the target attribute are used to select a window where all the links will be displayed. To open a link in the same window, specify a target="_self". To break out of frames and remain in the same browser window, specify a target="_top". To open a new browser window (and not close the current browser window), specify a target="_blank". To enable or disable scrolling, use the scrolling attribute. To disable window resizing, use the noresize attribute with a value of noresize. To eliminate borders in frames, set the border value to zero. To add white space to the left and the right of frames, use the marginwidth property. To add white space to the top and the bottom of frames, use the marginheight property. Use the <noframes> </noframes> tags to create text that the viewer will see in case his or her browser does not support frames. Inline frames can take the place of regular frames. You can have more than one inline frame in a document. The <meta /> tag and the http-equiv attribute can be used to create a slide show.

Key Terms

_blank target	frameset document	scrolling attribute
_self target	magic targets	seamless frames
_top target	nested frames	tabbed browsing
frame	placeholder document	

Practice	**Review Assignments**

Data Files needed for the Review Assignment: Baked.htm, Banner2.htm, Coffeelogo.gif, Cookies.htm, Cookies.jpg, Croissant.htm, Croissant.jpg, Danish.htm, Danish.jpg, Dessert.gif, Doughnuts.htm, Doughnuts.jpg, Flan.htm, Flan.jpg, Footer.htm, Layercake. htm, Layercake.jpg, and More.htm

Sal was very pleased with the update of the Stormm's Coffee home page. He would now like you to create a Web page that highlights some of the other products that Stormm's sells. He is particularly interested in promoting Stormm's line of breads and other baked goods. He wants you to create a page that will exhibit the variety of items that customers may choose from. Complete the following:

1. Use your text editor to open the **Baked.htm** file from your Tutorial.09\Review folder of your Data Files. Save the file as **BakedNew.htm** in the same folder.
2. Below the </head> tag, enter the code for an HTML comment that includes your first and last name as the author and today's date.
3. Below the comment, create a frameset with three rows. The row heights should be 30 percent, 60 percent, and the remainder of the screen. In the frameset tag, insert the attribute and value that will create seamless frames.
4. The frame source for the first row is **Banner2New.htm**.
5. The frame source for the second row is **More.htm**. Name this frame **more**.
6. The frame source for the third row is **FooterNew.htm**.
7. Insert the end </frameset> tag at the bottom of the frameset.
8. Save the BakedNew file, and then close it.
9. Use your text editor to open the **Footer.htm** file from your Tutorial.09\Review folder of your Data Files. Save the file as **FooterNew.htm** in the same folder.
10. In the link to BakedNew.htm, enter the code for the magic target that will break out of frames completely *and remain in the same browser window*.
11. Save the FooterNew file, and then close it.
12. Use your text editor to open the **Banner2.htm** file from your Tutorial.09\Review folder of your Data Files. Save the file as **Banner2New.htm** in the same folder.
13. In the <head> section and just below the page title, use the <base /> tag and code the attribute and value that will ensure that each link in the Banner2New file will be displayed in a frame named *more*.
14. Save the Banner2New file, and then close it.
15. Open the BakedNew file in your browser. The document should be similar to the one shown in Figure 9-26.

Figure 9-26

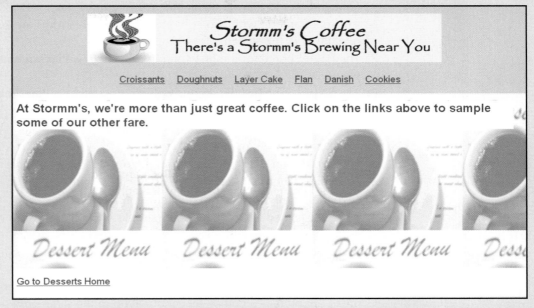

16. Test the link for Croissants. Use the link in the footer document to return back to the Desserts Home page. Test the five other links for the remaining pastry products.
17. Close all open windows.
18. Submit the results of the preceding steps to your instructor, either in printed or electronic form, as requested.

Apply | Case Problem 1

Use the skills you learned in the tutorial to create a Web page for a mountain resort lodge.

Data Files needed for this Case Problem: Biking.htm, Biking.jpg, Double.htm, Double. jpg, Golf.htm, Golf.jpg, Hiking.htm, Hiking.jpg, Needles.jpg, Pines.htm, Pinesbanner. htm, Pinesfooter.htm, Pineslinks.htm, Pineslogo.gif, Pinesviews.htm, Pool.htm, Pool.jpg, Restaurant.htm, Restaurant.jpg, Sailing.htm, Sailing.jpg, Single.htm, Single.jpg, Tennis. htm, Tennis.jpg, Walkway.htm, and Walkway.jpg

The Inn at Soaring Pines The Inn at Soaring Pines (better known as The Inn) is a sprawling, 400-room lodge nestled in the Rocky Mountains near Pine Valley, Colorado. The Inn markets itself as a place where visitors have two options: they can spend their stay engaged in quiet relaxation, or they can spend their time participating in a variety of leisure activities. Among the activities available are walking, hiking, sailing, golf, and tennis. The Inn has three restaurants that cater to just about everyone's taste. Sofia Ingerson, the manager of The Inn, has asked you to revise the home page for The Inn's Web site. Complete the following:

1. Use your text editor to open the **Pines.htm** file from your Tutorial.09\Case1 folder of your Data Files. Save the file as **PinesNew.htm** in the same folder.
2. Below the end </head> tag, enter the code for an HTML comment that includes your first and last name as the author and today's date.
3. Below the comment, create a frameset with three rows. The row heights are 25 percent, 65 percent, and the remainder of the screen.
4. The frame source for the first row in the rows frameset is **Pinesbanner.htm**.

5. A nested frameset will serve as the contents for the second row. Press the Enter key enough times to leave a blank line after the frame tag for Pinesbanner.htm.

6. Create a frameset with two columns. The column widths are 70 percent and the remainder of the screen.

7. The frame source for the first column document is **Pinesviews.htm**. Name this frame **views**.

8. The frame source for the second column document is **Pineslinksnew.htm**.

9. Enter the end </frameset> tag to end the columns frameset.

10. Press the Enter key enough times to create a blank line after the end </frameset> tag for the nested column frameset.

11. The frame source for the last row of the rows frameset is **Pinesfooter.htm**.

12. Enter the end </frameset> tag to end the rows frameset.

13. Save the PinesNew file, and then close it.

14. Use your text editor to open the **Pineslinks.htm** file from your Tutorial.09\Case1 folder of your Data Files. Save this file as **PineslinksNew.htm** in the same folder.

15. In the head area of PineslinksNew.htm and just below the page title, use the <base /> tag so that all links are set to target the frame named *views*.

⊕ EXPLORE 16. At the bottom of the page, in the link to PinesNew, insert the magic target that will break out of frames completely and remain in the same browser window.

17. Save the PinelinksNew file, and then close it.

18. Open the PinesNew file in your browser. The document should be similar to the one shown in Figure 9-27.

Figure 9-27

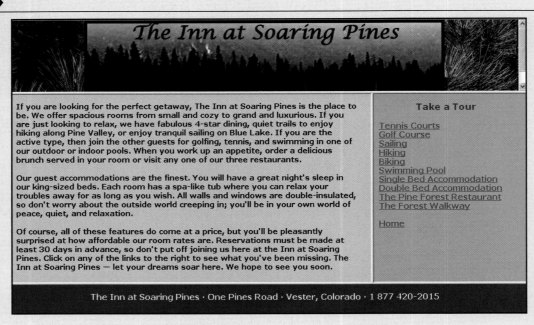

19. Test the links for all 10 of the activities and the link for the home page.

20. Close all open windows.

21. Submit the results of the preceding steps to your instructor, either in printed or electronic form, as requested.

Apply | Case Problem 2

Use the skills you learned in the tutorial to create and style a Web page for a travel adventure agency.

Data Files needed for this Case Problem: Cave.htm, Cave.jpg, Map.gif, Mountain.htm, Mountain.jpg, One.htm, Pole.htm, Pole.jpg, Rain.htm, Rain.jpg, Sail.htm, Sail.jpg, Shark.htm, Shark.jpg, Travel.htm, Volcano.htm, and Volcano.jpg

One to One Travel One to One Travel is a travel agency that specializes in unusual, exotic travel requests. Initially created as an agency that would train actors for roles in upcoming action movies, One to One Travel has expanded its clientele to anyone who can afford to spend considerable time and expense in the pursuit of a fantasy adventure. One to One hires local trainers and guides to take the adventurer step-by-step to not only provide an adventure tour, but also to prepare the traveler for what lies ahead. Based upon the time and success of the training, One to One plans a trip designed to match the skill level of the traveler. The traveler then sets out on his or her adventure with one or more guides—or an entire crew—to fulfill the traveler's dreams of adventure. Bill Catterson, president of One to One Travel, has asked you to update the company's Web site. He wants you to feature some of the more recent adventures his travelers have experienced. You have decided that an inline frame would be a good feature to add to his Web site. Complete the following:

1. Use Notepad to open the **One.htm** file from your Tutorial.09\Case2 folder of your Data Files. Save the file as **OneNew.htm** in the same folder.
2. In the <head> section, enter the code for a CSS comment that includes your first and last name as the author and today's date.

⊕ EXPLORE

3. In the <head> section of OneNew and just below the page title, use the <base /> tag to target a frame named **shark**.

⊕ EXPLORE

4. In the <head> section and below the a:hover style, create a style for the <iframe> element. Set the style for the iframe to have a width of 50 percent and a height of 70 percent. Scrolling should be set to auto. The inline frame should float at the left edge of the screen so that text can wrap to the right of the inline frame. Create 1em of white space to the right of the inline frame.
5. In the body section and below the comment for "insert iframe code here," insert the start <iframe> tag. The source document for the iframe is **Shark.htm**. Name this frame **shark**.
6. Place the end </iframe> tag on its own line.
7. Save the OneNew file, and then close it.
8. Open the OneNew file in your browser. The document should be similar to the one shown in Figure 9-28.

Figure 9-28

One to One Travel

If you are a writer, novelist, or screenwriter seeking background for a project; if you are an actor studying a role; or if you are just a plain adventurer at heart, One to One Travel will make your dreams come true. Have you ever wanted to scale Mt. Everest? hunt for shark? explore a labyrinth of caves? One to One Travel will not only make all the arrangements for your trip, we also will prepare you for an adventure of a lifetime.

If you have one month to one year, we will work with you to make sure your travel dreams come true. We have contracted with guides from all over the globe who will train you for your adventure. We'll gauge your learning and experience and then embark — one to one — on your travel adventure. Our clients come from all walks of life, — doctors, lawyers, athletes, entertainers, writers, actors, politicians, and more. If you seek action, excitement, some degree of danger, and the challenge of physical endurance, we will provide you with a once-in-a-lifetime adventure you will remember and treasure always. Click on the links below to sample some of the adventures that await you. Call us at 817 420-2010 for more information.

Shark Fishing

Shark Fishing off Australian Reefs
Exploration of Live Volcanic Eruption in Hawaii
Trekking through Cave Labyrinth in North Dakota
Climbing Mt. Hood
TransPacific Sail
Trekking the North Pole
Amazon Rain Forest Tour

9. Test the links for all seven of the activities.

10. Close all open windows.

11. Submit the results of the preceding steps to your instructor, either in printed or electronic form, as requested.

Challenge	**Case Problem 3**

Use what you've learned, and expand your skills, to create and style a Web page for an auto repair service.

Data Files needed for this Case Problem: Careers.jpg, Engine.gif, Mechanic.gif, Motorbanner.htm, Motorframe.htm, Motorlogo.gif, Motormain.htm, Rental.jpg, Slide1. htm, Slide2.htm, Slide3.htm, Tires.gif, and Tow.gif

The Motor Guys The Motor Guys is a chain of auto repair service shops. Serving cities primarily in Oregon, Washington, and Montana, the Motor Guys have built their reputation on being able to service just about any vehicle on the road. Because they have been able to offer car repair as a commodity, the Motor Guys franchise is becoming more popular every day. Presently, the Motor Guys Web site has a frames layout. Marsha Case, the general manager of the Motor Guys, has asked you to update the home page for the Motor Guys Web site. Complete the following:

1. Use your text editor to open the **Motorframe.htm** file from your Tutorial.09\Case3 folder of your Data Files. Save the file as **MotorframeNew.htm** in the same folder.

2. Below the \<head> section, enter the code for an HTML comment that includes your first and last name as the author and today's date.

⊕ **EXPLORE**

3. Below the comment, create a frameset with two rows. The row heights are 20 percent and the remainder of the screen. Enter the code so this frameset has no borders.

⊕ EXPLORE

4. The frame source for the first row in the rows frameset is Motorbanner.htm. Enter the code so that the frame cannot be resized. Enter the code so that there will be no scrollbars.

5. Below the frame source for the first row, create a nested frameset with two columns. The column widths are 60 percent and the remainder of the screen.

6. The frame source for the first column document is Motormain.htm.

7. The frame source for the second column document is Slide1New.htm.

8. Insert an end </frameset> tag to end the columns frameset.

9. Insert an end </frameset> tag to end the rows frameset.

10. Save the MotorframeNew file, and then close it.

⊕ EXPLORE

11. Use your text editor to open the **Slide1.htm** file from your Tutorial.09\Case3 folder of your Data Files. Save this file as **Slide1New.htm** in the same folder.

12. In the head area of Slide1New.htm and below the page title, enter the code for the <meta /> tag to create a slide show that will link this slide to the Slide2New.htm file. Have a delay of 7 seconds before the Slide2New file will be displayed. Save and close this file.

13. Use your text editor to open the **Slide2.htm** file from your Tutorial.09\Case3 folder of your Data Files. Save this file as **Slide2New.htm** in the same folder.

14. In the head area of Slide2New.htm and below the page title, enter the code for the <meta /> tag to create a slide show that will link this slide to the Slide3New.htm file. Have a delay of 7 seconds before the Slide3New file will be displayed. Save and close this file.

15. Use your text editor to open the **Slide3.htm** file from your Tutorial.09\Case3 folder of your Data Files. Save this file as **Slide3New.htm** in the same folder.

16. In the head area of Slide3New.htm and below the page title, enter the code for the <meta /> tag to create a slide show that will link this slide to the Slide1New.htm file. Have a delay of 7 seconds before Slide1New will be displayed. Save and close this file.

17. Open the MotorframeNew file in your browser. The document should be similar to the one shown in Figure 9-29. (Note that a vertical scroll bar might appear depending on the resolution of your monitor.)

Figure 9-29

The Motor Guys
Auto Repair and Service

Bring Your Car to the Motor Guys

Towing Service

If you need your engine tuned or repaired, come on in to the Motor Guys. We'll diagnose what ails your car and have it running right in no time. Need brakes? We can have them installed in under two hours.

Need an engine tune up? Let the Motor Guys take care of that, too. Can't get the car out of the driveway? Let the Motor Guys tow in your car. We offer tow hook and flatbed towing at very reasonable rates. If we can't fix a towed car in the first day, we don't charge for storage. We'll order the parts you need the same day so you can get back on the road in no time.

Call 1-800-645-9090
Day or Night

We stock every major brand of tire. If you need tires, we've got your brand in your size and at your price. We stock tires for passenger cars, SUV's, vans, and trucks. No matter what tire you need, we've got it in stock or we'll get the tires you need that same day.

How are your brakes? Your brakes are one of the most critical components of your car, and it's important that they always be in top shape. We can check your brakes, brake fluid levels, and make all necessary repairs and replacement. Don't let a brake problem go unrepaired. Come to the Motor Guys today so we can ensure that you always drive safely.

Get your name on our mailing list. We're always offering promotional items and service. We have a complete catalog of parts that will save you money on everything you purchase. You can shop brand names or off brand — we stock them all. We'll automatically let you know when it's time to bring in your car for service. Qualify for discounts, coupons, and free gifts — all from the men and women at the Motor Guys.

18. Observe the MotorframeNew file to see if the slide show is running correctly.
19. Close all open windows.
20. Submit the results of the preceding steps to your instructor, either in printed or electronic form, as requested.

Create	**Case Problem 4**

Using the files provided, create and style a Web page for a dental office.

Data Files needed for this Case Problem: Braces.jpg, Dentist.jpg, Smile1.jpg, Smile1. htm, Smile2.htm, Smile2.jpg, Smile3.htm, Smile3.jpg, Smile4.htm, Smile4.jpg, Smile5. htm, Smile5.jpg, Tottsbanner.htm, Tottscontent.htm, Tottsframeset.htm, Tottslinks.htm, and Tottslogo.gif

Tott's Dentistry Tott's Dentistry has been practicing dentistry and orthodontics for more than 25 years. Tott's Dentistry performs the usual repair for tooth decay, but most of its practice is devoted to orthodontics and cosmetic dentistry. LeAnne Tott, the owner of Tott's Dentistry, wants to update the Tott's Dentistry Web site, and she has asked your help in doing so. Complete the following:

1. Use your text editor to open the **Tottsbanner.htm** file from your Tutorial.09\Case4 folder of your Data Files. Save the file as **TottsbannerNew.htm** in the same folder.
2. In the <head> section, enter the code for a CSS comment that includes your first and last name as the author and today's date.
3. Set styles for the text in the document as you want.
4. Save your changes and then close TottsbannerNew.htm.
5. Use your text editor to open the **Tottscontent.htm** file from your Tutorial.09\Case4 folder of your Data Files. Save the file as **TottsContentNew.htm** in the same folder.
6. In the <head> section, enter the code for a CSS comment that includes your first and last name as the author and today's date.
7. Set styles for the text in the document as you want.
8. Save your changes and then close TottsContentNew.htm.
9. Use your text editor to open the **Tottslinks.htm** file from your Tutorial.09\Case4 folder of your Data Files. Save the file as **TottslinksNew.htm** in the same folder.
10. In the <head> section, enter the code for a CSS comment that includes your first and last name as the author and today's date.
11. In the TottslinksNew file, create five links to the following files (and for each of the links, the target attribute will be equal to "content"): Smile1.htm, Smile2.htm, Smile3.htm, Smile4.htm, and Smile5.htm.
12. Save your changes and then close TottslinksNew.htm.
13. Use your text editor to open the **Tottsframeset.htm** file from your Tutorial.09\Case4 folder of your Data Files. Save the file as **TottsframesetNew.htm** in the same folder.
14. Below the </head> tag, enter the code for an HTML comment that includes your first and last name as the author and today's date.
15. Create a frameset with two rows. You determine the row heights. Within the rows frameset, nest a second frameset for the columns. You determine the column widths.
16. The frame source for the banner frame should be TottsbannerNew.htm. Enter the code to ensure that the frame can't be resized. The frame should not have scrollbars.
17. The frame source for the links frame should be TottslinksNew.htm.
18. The frame source for the content frame should be TottscontentNew.htm. Name the frame **content**.
19. Enter the code for both end frameset tags.
20. Save the TottsframesetNew file.
21. Open the TottsframesetNew file in your browser. Test the links in the links frame.
22. Close all open windows.
23. Submit the results of the preceding steps to your instructor, either in printed or electronic form, as requested.

Review | **Quick Check Answers**

Session 9.1

1. <frameset> and </frameset>
2. <frame />
3. cols
4. rows
5. the asterisk
6. _self
7. _top
8. scrolling
9. noresize

Session 9.2

1. to create a frame window without the need for a frameset
2. <iframe>
3. paired
4. a name
5. height and width
6. the target attribute
7. the meta tag
8. refresh

Ending Data Files

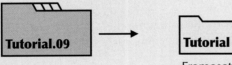

Tutorial.09 →

Tutorial
FramesetNew.htm
StaffNew.htm

Review
BakedNew.htm
Banner2New.htm
FooterNew.htm

Case1
PinesNew.htm
PineslinksNew.htm

Case2
OneNew.htm

Case3
MotorFrameNew.htm
Slide1New.htm
Slide2New.htm
Slide3New.htm

Case4
TottsbannerNew.htm
TottscontentNew.htm
TottsframesetNew.htm
TottslinksNew.htm

Reality Check

Now that you have learned how to create Web pages, it's time to create Web pages for your personal use. Increasingly, job applicants are submitting their resumes using the Web. One way to differentiate yourself from other job candidates, who might be submitting their résumé as a word processing document, is to send your résumé as an HTML file.

The Web site for your résumé should consist of at least two pages, one for your résumé and at least one other page, which might contain an image file or other supplementary material. Your Web pages do not have to be about yourself, but can be about any person, living or dead, or a completely fictional character. You might create a résumé for Mark Twain applying for a job as a newspaper columnist; Thomas Edison applying for a job as an inventor; or Eleanor Roosevelt applying for a job in government. The job you are applying for can be at either a real or a fictional company that sells a product or provides a service.

The contents of your Web pages must be original work—something that you yourself have created for this project alone, not the work of others. Your Web pages should meet the requirements of your campus acceptable computer use policy and not be offensive to anyone.

Note: Please be sure *not* to include any personal information of a sensitive nature in the Web pages you create to be submitted to your instructor for this exercise. Later on, you can update the Web pages with such information for your personal use.

1. Using embedded style sheets to format your Web pages, create Web pages that have the following components:
   - An anchor at the top of the page (used for a link to the bottom of the page)
   - A link at the bottom of the page back to the anchor at the top of the page
   - At least two section headings of different sizes (such as <h1> or <h2>)
   - Examples of bold text and italic text
   - At least five paragraphs of text
   - At least one image that is not a link
   - At least one image that is a link
   - A link to another page
   - A link to an anchor on another page
   - At least three external links to some of your favorite Web sites
   - An ordered or unordered list (change the list style type or use a list style image)
   - The <div> </div> tags and a class applied to the <div> tag
   - A table with a minimum of three columns and three rows, including a colspan or a rowspan
   - An independent class named **very** that changes the appearance of text to 14pt, italic, and red. Apply this class to several words on your home page.

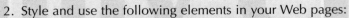

2. Style and use the following elements in your Web pages:
   - `<h1>`, `<h2>`, or `<h3>`
   - `<em>`
   - `<strong>`
   - `<p>`
   - a:link
   - a:visited
   - a:hover

3. Save your file as a file named *yourlastname*_resume.htm. Save all other files using a similar naming convention.

4. Submit your completed file and printouts to your instructor as requested.

Colors by Name and Hexadecimal Value

In the following table, the 17 Web-safe colors are in bold.

Named Color	Hexadecimal Code	Named Color	Hexadecimal Code
aliceblue	#F0F8FF	darkseagreen	#8FBC8F
antiquewhite	#FAEBD7	darkslateblue	#483D8B
aqua	**#00FFFF**	darkslategray	#2F4F4F
aquamarine	#7FFFD4	darkturquoise	#00CED1
azure	#F0FFFF	darkviolet	#9400D3
beige	#F5F5DC	deeppink	#FF1493
bisque	#FFE4C4	deepskyblue	#00BFFF
black	**#000000**	dimgray	#696969
blanchedalmond	#FFEBCD	dodgerblue	#1E90FF
blue	**#0000FF**	firebrick	#B22222
blueviolet	#8A2BE2	floralwhite	#FFFAF0
brown	#A52A2A	forestgreen	#228B22
burlywood	#DEB887	**fuchsia**	**#FF00FF**
cadetblue	#5F9EA0	gainsboro	#DCDCDC
chartreuse	#7FFF00	ghostwhite	#F8F8FF
chocolate	#D2691E	gold	#FFD700
coral	#FF7F50	goldenrod	#DAA520
cornflowerblue	#6495ED	**gray**	**#808080**
cornsilk	#FFF8DC	**green**	**#008000**
crimson	#DC143C	greenyellow	#ADFF2F
cyan	**#00FFFF**	honeydew	#F0FFF0
darkblue	#00008B	hotpink	#FF69B4
darkcyan	#008B8B	indianred	#CD5C5C
darkgoldenrod	#B8860B	indigo	#4B0082
darkgray	#A9A9A9	ivory	#FFFFF0
darkgreen	#006400	khaki	#F0E68C
darkkhaki	#BDB76B	lavender	#E6E6FA
darkmagenta	#8B008B	lavenderblush	#FFF0F5
darkolivegreen	#556B2F	lawngreen	#7CFC00
darkorange	#FF8C00	lemonchiffon	#FFFACD
darkorchid	#9932CC	lightblue	#ADD8E6
darkred	#8B0000	lightcoral	#F08080
darksalmon	#E9967A	lightcyan	#E0FFFF

Named Color	Hexadecimal Code	Named Color	Hexadecimal Code
lightgoldenrodyellow	#FAFAD2	palegreen	#98FB98
lightgreen	#90EE90	paleturquoise	#AFEEEE
lightgray	#D3D3D3	palevoiletred	#DB7093
lightpink	#FFB6C1	papayawhip	#FFEFD5
lightsalmon	#FFA07A	peachpuff	#FFDAB9
lightseagreen	#20B2AA	peru	#CD853F
lightskyblue	#87CEFA	pink	#FFC0CB
lightslategray	#778899	plum	#DDA0DD
lightsteelblue	#B0C4DE	powderblue	#B0E0E6
lightyellow	#FFFFE0	**purple**	**#800080**
lime	**#00FF00**	**red**	**#FF0000**
limegreen	#32CD32	rosybrown	#BC8F8F
linen	#FAF0E6	royalblue	#4169E1
magenta	#FF00FF	saddlebrown	#8B4513
maroon	**#800000**	salmon	#FA8072
mediumaquamarine	#66CDAA	sandybrown	#F4A460
mediumblue	#0000CD	seagreen	#2E8B57
mediumorchid	#BA55D3	seashell	#FFF5EE
mediumpurple	#9370DB	sienna	#A0522D
mediumseagreen	#3CB371	**silver**	**#C0C0C0**
mediumslateblue	#7B68EE	skyblue	#87CEEB
mediumspringgreen	#00FA9A	slateblue	#6A5ACD
mediumturquoise	#48D1CC	slategray	#708090
mediumvioletred	#C71585	snow	#FFFAFA
midnightblue	#191970	springgreen	#00FF7F
mintcream	#F5FFFA	steelblue	#4682B4
mistyrose	#FFE4E1	tan	#D2B48C
moccasin	#FFE4B5	**teal**	**#008080**
navajowhite	#FFDEAD	thistle	#D8BFD8
navy	**#000080**	tomato	#FF6347
oldlace	#FDF5E6	turquoise	#40E0D0
olive	**#808000**	violet	#EE82EE
olivedrab	#6B8E23	wheat	#F5DEB3
orange	#FFA500	**white**	**#FFFFFF**
orangered	#FF4500	whitesmoke	#F5F5F5
orchid	#DA70D6	**yellow**	**#FFFF00**
palegoldenrod	#EEE8AA	yellowgreen	#9ACD32

Named Character Entities

The following table lists the name, syntax, and description of the named character entities. If the browser does not support the named character entity, use the numerical character entity in its place (see Appendix C).

Name	Syntax	Description
	´	Acute accent
	&	Ampersand
	¦	Broken vertical bar
	¸	Cedilla
	¢	Cent sign
	©	Copyright symbol
	¤	General currency symbol
	°	Degree sign
	½	Fraction one-half
	¼	Fraction one-quarter
	&fract34;	Fraction three-fourths
	>	Greater than sign
	&iexcl	Inverted exclamation mark
	¿	Inverted question mark
	«	Left angle quotation mark
	<	Less than sign
	&macron;	Macron
	µ	Micro sign
	·	Middle dot
		Non-breaking space
	¬	Not sign
	&Ordf;	Feminine ordinal
	º	Masculine ordinal
	¶	Paragraph sign
	±	Plus minus symbol
	"	Double quotation mark
	»	Right angle quotation mark
	®	Registered trademark
	§	Section sign
	­	Soft hyphen
	¹	Superscript 1
	²	Superscript 2

Name	Syntax	Description
	&sup3;	Superscript 3
	&trade;	Trademark symbol
	&uml;	Umlaut
	&yen;	Yen sign
Aacute	&Aacute;	Capital A, acute accent
Agrave	&Agrave;	Capital A, grave accent
Acirc	&Acirc;	Capital A, circumflex accent
Atilde	&Atilde;	Capital A, tilde
Aring	&Aring;	Capital A, ring
Auml	&Auml;	Capital A, dieresis or umlaut mark
AElig	&AElig;	Capital AE, dipthong (ligature)
Ccedil	&Ccedil;	Capital C, cedilla
Eacute	&Eacute;	Capital E, acute accent
Egrave	&Egrave;	Capital E, grave accent
Ecirc	&Ecirc;	Capital E, circumflex accent
Euml	&Euml;	Capital E, dieresis or umlaut mark
Capital I, acute accent	&Igrave;	Capital I, grave accent
Icirc	&Icirc;	Capital I, circumflex accent
Iuml	&Iuml;	Capital I, dieresis or umlaut mark
ETH	&ETH;	Capital ETH, Icelandic
Ntilde	&Ntilde;	Capital N, tilde
Oacute	&Oacute;	Capital O, acute accent
Ograve	&Ograve;	Capital O, grave accent
Ocirc	&Ocirc;	Capital O, circumflex accent
Otilde	&Otilde;	Capital O, tilde
Ouml	&Ouml;	Capital O, dieresis or umlaut mark
Oslash	&Oslash;	Capital O, slash
Uacute	&Uacute;	Capital U, acute accent
Ugrave	&Ugrave;	Capital U, grave accent
Ucirc	&Ucirc;	Capital U, circumflex accent
Uuml	&Uuml;	Capital U, dieresis or umlaut mark
Yacute	&Yacute;	Capital Y, acute accent
szlig	&szlig;	Small sharp s, German (sz ligature)
aacute	&aacute	Small a, acute accent
agrave	&agrave	Small a, grave accent
acirc	&acirc;	Small a, circumflex accent
atilde	&atilde;	Small a, tilde
auml	&auml;	Small a, dieresis or umlaut mark
aelig	&aelig;	Small ae dipthong (ligature)
ccedil	&ccedil;	Small c, cedilla
eacute	&eacute;	Small e, acute accent
egrave	&egrave;	Small e, grave accent
ecirc	&ecirc;	Small e, circumflex accent
euml	&euml;	Small e, dieresis or umlaut mark

Name	Syntax	Description
iacute	í	Small i, acute accent
igrave	ì	Small i, grave accent
icirc	î	Small i, circumflex accent
iuml	ï	Small i, dieresis or umlaut mark
eth	ð	Small eth, Icelandic
ntilde	ñ	Small n, tilde
oacute	ó	Small o, acute accent
ograve	ò	Small o, grave accent
ocirc	ô	Small o, circumflex accent
otilde	õ	Small o, tilde
ouml	ö	Small o, dieresis or umlaut mark
oslash	ø	Small o, slash
uacute	ú	Small u, acute accent
ugrave	ù	Small u, grave accent
ucirc	û	Small u, circumflex accent
uuml	ü	Small u, dieresis or umlaut mark
yacute	ý	Small y, acute accent
thorn	þ	Small thorn, Icelandic
yuml	ÿ	Small y, dieresis or umlaut mark

Numeric Character Entities

The following table lists the numeric character references and corresponding descriptions.

Reference	Description
&#00;–&#08;	Unused
&#09;	Tab
&#10;	Line feed
&#11;–&#31;	Unused
&#32;	Space
&#33;	Exclamation mark
&#34;	Quotation mark (does not work in IE)
&#35;	Number (pound) sign
&#36;	Dollar sign
&#37;	Percent sign
&#38;	Ampersand
&#39;	Apostrophe
&#40;	Left parenthesis
&#41;	Right parenthesis
&#42;	Asterisk
&#43;	Plus sign
&#44;	Comma
&#45;	Hyphen
&#46;	Period
&#47;	Forward slash
0–9	Digits 0–9
&#58;	Colon
&#59;	Semicolon
&#60;	Less than symbol
&#61;	Equals sign
&#62;	Greater than
&#63;	Question mark
&#64;	Commercial at sign
A–Z	Letters A–Z
&#91;	Left square bracket
&#92;	Backslash
&#93;	Right square bracket
&#94;	Caret

Reference	Description
&#95;	Horizontal bar (underscore)
&#96;	Acute accent
a–z	Letters a–z
&#123;	Left curly brace
|	Vertical bar
&#125;	Right curly brace
&#126;	Tilde
&#127;–	Unused
&#130;	Comma
&#131;	Function sign (florin)
&#132;	Quotation mark (curly)
&#133;	Ellipsis
&#134;	Dagger
&#135;	Double dagger
&#136;	Circumflex
&#137;	Permille
&#138;	Capital S with hacek
&#139;	Left single angle
&#140;	Capital OE ligature
–	Unused
&#145;	Single beginning quote
&#146;	Single ending quote
&#147;	Double beginning curly quote
&#148;	Double ending curly quote
&#149;	Bullet
&#150;	En dash
&#151;	Em dash
&#152;	Tilde
&#153;	Trademark (tm)
&#154;	Small s with hacek
&#155;	Right single angle
&#156;	Lowercase oe ligature
–ž	Unused
&#159;	Capital Y with umlaut

Reference	Description	Reference	Description
	Non-breaking space	Í	Capital I, acute accent
¡	Inverted exclamation	Î	Capital I, circumflex accent
¢	Cent sign	Ï	Capital I, umlaut
£	Pound sterling	Ð	Capital ETH, Icelandic
¤	General currency sign	Ñ	Capital N, tilde
¥	Yen sign	Ò	Capital O, grave accent
¦	Broken vertical bar	Ó	Capital O, acute accent
§	Section sign	Ô	Capital O, circumflex accent
¨	Umlaut (dieresis)	Õ	Capital O, tilde
©	Copyright	Ö	Capital O, umlaut
ª	Feminine ordinal	×	Multiplication sign
«	Left angle quote	Ø	Capital O, slash
¬	Not sign	Ù	Capital U, grave accent
­	Soft hyphen	Ú	Capital U, acute accent
®	Registered trademark (R)	Û	Capital U, circumflex accent
¯	Macron accent	Ü	Capital U, umlaut
°	Degree sign	Ý	Capital Y, acute accent
±	Plus or minus	Þ	Capital Thorn, Icelandic
²	Superscript two	ß	Small sharp s, German (sz ligature)
³	Superscript three	à	Small a, grave accent
´	Acute accent	á	Small a, acute accent
µ	Micro sign	â	Small a, circumflex accent
¶	Paragraph sign	ã	Small a, tilde
·	Middle dot	ä	Small a, tilde
¸	Cedilla	å	Small a, ring
¹	Superscript one	æ	Small ae, (ligature)
º	Masculine ordinal	ç	Small c, cedilla
»	Right angle quote	è	Small e, grave accent
¼	Fraction one-fourth	é	Small e, acute accent
½	Fraction one-half	ê	Small e, circumflex accent
¾	Fraction three-fourths	ë	Small e, umlaut
¿	Inverted question mark	ì	Small i, grave accent
À	Capital A, grave accent	í	Small i, acute accent
Á	Capital A, acute accent	î	Small i, circumflex accent
Â	Capital A, circumflex accent	ï	Small i, umlaut
Ã	Capital A, tilde	ð	Small eth, Icelandic
Ä	Capital A, umlaut	ñ	Small n, tilde
Å	Capital A, ring	ò	Small o, grave accent
Æ	Capital AE, (ligature)	ó	Small o, acute accent
Ç	Capital C, cedilla	ô	Small o, circumflex accent
È	Capital E, grave accent	õ	Small o, tilde
É	Capital E, acute accent	ö	Small o, umlaut
Ê	Capital E, circumflex accent	÷	Division sign
Ë	Capital E, umlaut	ø	Small o, slash
Ì	Capital I, grave accent		

Reference	Description
&#249;	Small u, grave accent
&#250;	Small u, acute accent
&#251;	Small u, circumflex accent
&#252;	Small u, umlaut

Reference	Description
&#253;	Small y, acute accent
&#254;	Small thorn, Icelandic
&#255;	Small y, umlaut

HTML Elements

The following table lists the HTML elements by name and provides a description of each.

Name	Description
a	Anchor
abbr	Abbreviated form
acronym	Abbreviated form
address	By convention, the italicized address of the Web site or Webmaster
area	Client-side image map area
b	Bold text
base	Designates a default target
blockquote	Block-level element for a long quotation
body	Document body
br	Forced line break
button	Button
caption	Table caption
center	Center text (deprecated)
cite	Citation
code	Computer code
col	Table column
colgroup	Table column group
dd	Definition description
div	Generic style container
dl	Definition list
dt	Definition term
em	Emphasis
fieldset	Form control group
form	Interactive form
frame	Identifies window frame document
frameset	Window division
h1	Heading level 1
h2	Heading level 2
h3	Heading level 3
h4	Heading level 4
h5	Heading level 5

Name	Description
h6	Heading level 6
head	Document head
hr	Horizontal rule
html	Document root element
iframe	Inline frame
img	Embedded image
input	Form control
kbd	Monospace type
label	Form field label text
legend	Fieldset legend
li	List item
link	A media-independent link
map	Client-side image map
meta	Generic meta information
noframes	Designates substitute text for frames
object	Generic embedded object
ol	Ordered list
optgroup	Option group
option	Selectable choice
p	Paragraph
pre	Preformatted text
q	Short, inline quotation
samp	Sample program output
select	Option selector
span	Generic language/style container
strong	Strong emphasis (bold)
style	Style information
sub	Subscript
sup	Superscript
table	Document table
tbody	Table body
td	Table data cell
textarea	Multiline text field

Name	Description
tfoot	Table footer
th	Table header cell
thead	Table header
title	Document title
tr	Table row

Name	Description
tt	Teletype (monospaced text)
u	Underlined text (deprecated)
ul	Unordered list
var	Variable

CSS 2.1 Properties and Values

The following table lists the CSS 2.1 properties and the values available for each property. In the Values column, the default value is shown in bold. The Group column lists the group the property is a member of.

Property	Description	Values	Group
background	Shorthand property for setting all background properties	background-attachment background-color background-image background-position background-repeat	background
background-attachment	Sets the position of a background image as fixed or scrolls as the insertion point moves down the page	fixed **scroll**	background
background-color	Sets the background color of an element	rgb value hex value short hex value named value **transparent**	background
background-image	Sets an image as the background	url(filename) **none**	background
background-position	Sets the position of a background image	top left top center top right center left **center center** center right bottom left bottom center bottom right x% y%	background
background-repeat	Determines whether a background image will be repeated	**repeat** repeat-x repeat-y no-repeat	background
border	The shorthand property for setting all of the border properties	border-width border-style border-color	border
border-bottom	The shorthand property for setting all of the properties for the bottom border	border-bottom-width border-style border-color	border
border-bottom-color	Sets the color of the bottom border	border-color	border
border-bottom-style	Sets the style for the bottom border	border-style	border

Property	Description	Values	Group
border-bottom-width	Sets the width for the bottom border	thin **medium** thick length (in ems)	border
border-collapse	Determines whether a table border has a single or double rule	collapse **separate**	table
border-color	Sets the color for all four borders	rgb value hex value short hex value named value	border
border-left	The shorthand property for setting all of the properties for the left border	border-left-width border-style border-color	border
border-left-color	Sets the color for the left border	border-color	border
border-left-style	Sets the style for the left border	border-style	border
border-left-width	Sets the width for the left border	thin **medium** thick length (in ems)	border
border-right	The shorthand property for setting all of the properties for the right border	border-right-width border-style border-color	border
border-right-color	Sets the color for the right border	border-color	border
border-right-style	Sets the style for the right border	border-style	border
border-right-width	Sets the width for the right border	thin **medium** thick length (in ems)	border
border-style	Sets the style of the four borders	**none** hidden dotted dashed double groove inset outset ridge solid	border
border-top	The shorthand property for setting all of the properties for the top border	border-top-width border-style border-color	border
border-top-color	Sets the color for the top border	border-color	border
border-top-style	Sets the style for the top border	border-style	border
border-top-width	Sets the width for the top border	thin **medium** thick length (in ems)	border
border-width	A shorthand property for setting the width of the four borders in one declaration; can have from one to four values	thin **medium** thick length (in ems)	border

Property	Description	Values	Group
bottom	Determines how far from the bottom edge an element is from its parent element	**auto** length (in ems) %	positioning
caption-side	Determines the position of the table caption	**top** bottom left right	table
clear	Positions an element below another element	left right both none	classification
color	Determines text color	color in RGB, hex, short hex, or named values	text
display	Sets how and if an element is to be displayed	block inline list-item **none**	classification
empty-cells	Determines whether to show a table without content in a table	**hide** show	table
float	Positions an element in relation to another element	left right **none**	classification
font	The shorthand property for setting all of the properties for a font	font-style font-variant font-weight font-size/line-height font-family	font
font-family	A list of font family names from specific to generic	font-family name generic-family name	font
font-size	Sets the size for the font	xx-small x-small small medium large x-large xx-large smaller pt values em values	font
font-style	Sets the style for the font	**normal** italic oblique	font
font-variant	Displays text in small caps or in a normal font	**normal** small caps	font

Property	Description	Values	Group
font-weight	Sets the weight of a font	**normal** bold bolder lighter 100 200 300 400 500 600 700 800 900	font
height	Sets the height of an element	**auto** length (in ems) %	dimension
left	Determines how far from the left edge an element is from its parent element	**auto** length (in ems) %	positioning
letter-spacing	Increase or decrease the space between characters	**normal** length (in ems)	text
line-height	Determines the white space between lines	**normal** number length (in ems) %	text
list-style	The shorthand property for setting all of the list-style properties	list-style-type list-style-position list-style-image	list
list-style-image	Sets an image to be used as a list-style marker	**none** url	list
list-style-position	Determines where the list-item marker will be positioned	inside **outside**	list
list-style-type	Determines the type of the list-item marker	circle decimal decimal-leading-zero **disc** lower-alpha lower-roman none square upper-alpha upper-roman	list
margin	The shorthand property for setting the margin properties	margin-top margin-right margin-bottom margin-left	margin
margin-bottom	Sets the bottom margin for an element	auto length (in ems) %	margin
margin-left	Sets the left margin for an element	auto length (in ems) %	margin

Property	Description	Values	Group
margin-right	Sets the right margin for an element	auto length (in ems) %	margin
margin-top	Sets the top margin for an element	auto length (in ems) %	margin
overflow	Determines the visibility of an element should content not fit into its contents	auto hidden scroll **visible**	positioning
padding	The shorthand property for setting all of the padding properties	padding-top padding-right padding-bottom padding-left	padding
padding-bottom	Sets the bottom padding for an element	length (in ems) %	padding
padding-left	Sets the left padding for an element	length (in ems) %	padding
padding-right	Sets the right padding for an element	length (in ems) %	padding
padding-top	Sets the top padding for an element	length (in ems) %	padding
position	Positions an element	**static** relative absolute fixed	classification
position	Positions an element	absolute fixed relative **static**	positioning
right	Determines how far from the right edge an element is from its parent element	**auto** length (in ems) %	positioning
text-align	Aligns the text in an element horizontally	center justify **left** right	text
text-decoration	Adds a line above, through, or under text	line-through overline **none** underline	text
text-indent	Indents the first line of text in an element	length (in ems) %	text
text-transform	Determines the capitalization of text	capitalize lowercase **none** uppercase	text

Property	Description	Values	Group
top	Determines how far from the top edge an element is from its parent element	**auto** length (in ems) %	positioning
vertical-align	Sets the vertical alignment of an element	**baseline** bottom middle sub super text-bottom text-top top length %	positioning
visibility	Determines whether an element is visible	collapse hidden **visible**	classification
width	Sets the width of an element	**auto** % length (in ems)	dimension
word-spacing	Increases or decreases the space between words	**normal** length (in ems)	text
z-index	Determines the stacking order of an element (the greater the number, the higher the element is in the stack)	**auto** number	positioning

Pseudo-Classes

Pseudo-Class	Purpose
:active	Determines the style when a link is clicked
:focus	Determines the style when a link has the focus
:hover	Determines the style for mouse-over effect
:link	Determines the style for links that have not yet been visited
:visited	Determines the style for links that have been visited

Pseudo-Elements

Pseudo-Element	Purpose
:first-letter	Formats just the first letter of a word
:first-line	Formats just the first line of a paragraph
:before	Inserts white space before an element
:after	Inserts white space after an element

Glossary

:first-letter The pseudo-element that formats only the first letter of a word.

:first-line The pseudo-element that formats only the first line of a paragraph.

_blank target The magic target that opens a linked document in another browser window.

_self target The magic target that opens a linked document in the same frame window.

_top target The magic target that opens a linked document in the same browser window.

<area> tag The tag that is used to specify an image map's shape, coordinates, and hypertext reference.

<map> tag The tag that is used to create an image map.

<span> The tag that is used to format a section of text inline.

<style> tag The tag entered in the head section or in the document body that specifies properties and values for a style.

A

abbreviation The tag, which when used with the title attribute, produces a ScreenTip for an abbreviation.

absolute file address A link in which the precise address—including the path—is specified.

absolute positioning The method used to position an element using absolute values.

access key A keystroke combination of Ctrl and a letter or a number used to access a choice from the keyboard or from a menu.

accesskey attribute The attribute used to create an access key combination.

acronym The tag, which when used with the title attribute, produces a ScreenTip for an acronym.

action attribute In an HTML form, the attribute used to identify the name of the file to which you want to send content.

align attribute A deprecated attribute that is still used with table captions to position the caption below the table.

alpha filter A filter that creates a gradient fill.

alphanumeric Characters including letters, numbers, or both.

anchor A place within a document that is used as the target of a link.

ascender Part of a character, such as the letter "d," that appears above the baseline.

aspect ratio Maintaining the height and width proportions of an image to prevent the image from appearing distorted.

attribute A word or value that provides more information about or describes an element.

B

background-attachment property The property that specifies whether an image file scrolls with the insertion point.

background-color property The property that determines the background color of an element.

background-image property The property that specifies whether an image appears behind an element or as the background for the document's body.

background-position property The property that specifies a position, stated in keywords or in percentages, of an image.

background-repeat property The property that specifies whether an image repeats horizontally or vertically across the screen.

banner A document, text, or image that is designed to appear at the top of the page; usually used for either advertising or to display a corporate logo.

block-level element Any element that generates a blank line above and below its contents and is capable of having a padding, margins, and a border.

blur filter A filter that makes text appear out of focus.

border property The shortcut property that specifies the color, style, and width of an element's border.

border-collapse property The property that determines whether the table has single or double-ruled lines.

border-color property The shortcut property that specifies a border's color.

border-style property The shortcut property that specifies a border's style.

border-width property The shortcut property that specifies a width for a border.

bottom property The property used to determine an element's position from the bottom of the page.

C

caption Text that describes the contents of a table.

cascade The order in which a style will take effect; the specific overrides the more general.

Cascading Style Sheets (CSS) A style sheet language that separates format from content.

cell The intersection of a column and a row.

CGI (Common Gateway Interface) A set of rules that describes how a CGI program interacts with a Web server.

character reference Referring to a special character by the character's position in the ISO (the International Standards Organization) character set (e.g., ®).

check box A Windows control that allows the user to select one or more items from a list of choices.

checked attribute The attribute that creates a default choice in a list of radio buttons or check boxes.

child folder A folder within another folder.

client computer The computer that receives files or runs applications from a file server.

color property The property that determines the foreground color of an element.

cols attribute In an HTML form, the attribute used to determine the width of a text area.

colspan attribute The attribute that is used to merge columns.

compressed A means of encoding information using fewer bits; the compressed file is often referred to as zip file.

container box The invisible box that surrounds a block level element that controls an element's internal padding, border, and external margin.

contextual selector A selector within another selector, also known as a descendant selector.

coordinates attribute The attribute that determines a shape's coordinate values in an image map.

cross-browser support The concept of writing HTML code that will be displayed the same irrespective of the browser used to view the Web page.

D

data table A table whose primary purpose is to display data in columns and rows.

database An organized collection of facts.

declaration In a CSS rule, the property and the value; also known as a definition.

defined term In a definition list, the term that is being defined.

definition data In a definition list, the definition for the word that is being defined.

dependent class A class that sets the style for only one selector.

deprecated tag A tag that the World Wide Web Consortium has declared no longer should be used.

descender A character, such as the letter "g," that appears below the baseline.

display property The property that determines how and if an element will be displayed.

drop shadow filter A filter that casts a second separate shadow behind text.

drop-down list box A Windows control that by default initially displays only one choice in a list of choices.

E

element Any structural part of an HTML document.

element type declaration Declaring an element based on its start tag, content, and its end tag.

embedded style A style whose code is contained on the Web page itself in the head section of a document.

empty cell A cell without any content.

empty element An element that does not have any content; e.g., <br />.

empty-cells property The property that is used to display the grid lines surrounding a cell even if the cell does not have any data.

Extensible Hypertext Markup Language (XHTML) The standardized version of HTML.

external style A style written in a separate document that can be linked to one or more documents.

F

field The smallest element of data in a database.

file server A powerful computer that manages files, applications, and devices.

filter Proprietary code that adds special effects to the appearance of text.

flag character A special character, usually the octothorpe character (#), that serves as a directive for an HTML instruction.

float property The property that positions an element either left or right, permitting text to wrap around the element.

font list A list in descending order of the fonts that are to be used as the value for the font or font-family property.

font property The shortcut property that determines the font weight, font style, and font family.

font-family property The property that determines the font to be used for an element.

font-size property The property that determines the size of type.

font-style property The property that determines whether text appears as italic.

font-variant property The property that determines whether text appears in a small caps font.

font-weight property The property that determines whether text appears as bold text.

footer Text, an image, or a document designed to appear at the bottom of the page.

form An HTML structure that is used to gather data.

formatting tag A tag that serves to change the appearance of the contents of an element.

frame A horizontal or vertical division of the browser window.

frameset document The controlling document that determines how a browser window is divided into separate windows and what documents populate those windows.

G

glow filter A filter that creates an irregular shaped, colored shadow behind text.

Graphics Interchange Format (GIF) The standardized file format for files that contain line art.

gridline A ruled line that surrounds a table cell.

H

hanging indent A formatting technique where the first line of text of a paragraph appears at the left edge of the screen and the remaining lines are indented.

header Text, an image, or a document designed to appear at the top of the page.

heading tag Any one of the six heading tags that control the size of type from 8pt to 24pt.

height attribute The attribute that determines the height of an element.

height property The property that determines an element's height.

hexadecimal value A value, usually used for the color or background-color property, that is expressed in the hexadecimal numbering system.

hidden The value used with the visibility property to hide an element.

horizontal rule The empty tag that by default draws a gray or silver line across the entire screen width.

hotspot A place on a Web page that when the mouse passes over, becomes the source for a link.

href attribute The attribute whose value identifies the source of a link.

hypertext Text that serves as a link to another document.

Hypertext Markup Language (HTML) The standardized language for creating Web pages.

hypertext reference attribute The attribute whose value identifies the source of a link.

hypertext transfer protocol (HTTP) The set of communication rules used to transfer data on the Internet.

I

id attribute The attribute that identifies the name of an anchor element.

image map A single image that can be used as the source for several links.

image tag The empty element used to identify an image file and to provide descriptive information about its content and its size.

independent class A class that can style any element.

inline style A style that is entered into the body of the document.

Internet The global network of networks that exchanges information using standardized protocols.

J

Joint Photographic Experts Group (JPG or JPEG) The standardized file format for files that contain photographic content.

L

layering The concept of having elements positioned on top of each other.

layout table A table whose primary purpose is to align elements horizontally and vertically on the Web page.

left property The property used to determine an element's position from the left edge of the page.

line-height property The property that determines the line spacing of text.

link text The text that when clicked, serves as a link.

link Text or an image that when clicked, displays another location on the same page, a different Web page, or a different Web site.

list-style property The shortcut property that determines the bullet's type, style, and position.

list-style-image property The property that determines whether an image is used as the bullet marker.

list-style-position property The property that determines whether bullets appear indented in a list.

list-style-type property The property that determines what type of marker is used for an unordered or ordered list.

logical tag Those tags that do not implicity state how they format an element; e.g., <strong>.

M

magic targets The group of special targets that determines where a linked document will be displayed.

main The main document window.

margin property The shortcut property that determines the width of the external margins of an element.

markup The printer's marks that indicate how a document should be edited or display when printed.

maxlength attribute The attribute that limits the number of characters that can be entered into a text field.

media attribute The attribute that determines what type of media should be used with a style sheet; generally, the screen, a printer, or both.

metadata Code that provides information about the document itself.

method attribute The attribute used to identify the form method, usually get or post.

multiple attribute The attribute that allows more than one item in a drop-down list to be selected.

N

named entity reference The method used to refer to a special character by suggesting the character's name (e.g., ®).

nested frameset A frameset within another frameset.

nested table A table within another table cell.

normal flow The normal flow of elements in the document.

O

option group A means of visually grouping similar choices in a form.

ordered list A list using an alphanumeric character as the marker in which the order of the entries does matter.

overflow property The property that determines what should happen if an element's contents do not fit inside its container.

P

packet The process of breaking a communication into smaller components to be routed over a network.

padding property The shortcut property that determines the width of the internal padding of an element.

parent folder The highest level in a particular subdirectory.

physical tag An element that explicitly describes its purpose; e.g., <b>.

placeholder character A character, usually the octothorpe or pound (#) symbol, that serves to represent a hypertext reference in a link.

placeholder document The document that is intially displayed in a frames window.

placeholder icon An icon that is displayed when there is an error in the image tag code or if the path to the image file is incorrectly or not specified.

positioning properties The properties used to position an element in relation to the left, right, top, or bottom edges of a page.

print style A style whose purpose is to accommodate the printing of a Web page.

prompting text The text that describes to the user what data should be entered into a field or chosen by using a Windows control.

property Any one of the more than 100 CSS properties that affect the appearance and positioning of an element.

proprietary code Code that is specific to one vendor.

protocol A series of agreed-to standards for sending voice, video, and data over communciations lines.

pseudo-class selector A selector for which there is no HTML equivalent.

R

radio button A Windows control that allows the user to make only one choice from several choices.

referring page The page that serves as the source of a link.

rel attribute The attribute that identifies the relationship between the current document and the target of the URL.

relative file address A URL that does not specify the full path to the document.

relative positioning The concept of positioning an element in relation to the other elements on the page.

RGB triplet The shorthand notation, usually used with the color or background-color property, to express the values for the strength of red, green, and blue.

RGB value A value, usually used with the color or background-color property, that is expressed as the strength of either of the colors red, green, or blue.

right property The property used to determine an element's position from the right edge of the page.

row striping The process whereby alternate rows have different background colors, making the rows easier to differentiate and read.

rows attribute In an HTML form, the attribute used to determine the height of a text area.

rowspan attribute The attribute used to merge rows.

rule The CSS selector, the property, and the value.

S

scaling To size an image either larger or smaller.

ScreenTip A small rectangular area that displays information when the mouse passes over text or an image.

script A short program, written in a scripting language, used to execute a procedure.

scripting language A language designed to create a series of instructions that transfer the data gathered in an HTML form to the database stored on a PC or on a file server.

scroll A value used with the overflow property that displays scroll bars when the content of the box exceeds its boundaries.

scrolling attribute The attribute that determines whether a frames window has scroll bars.

seamless frame No border between frames.

search engine Any application that helps users find information.

selector The element or ID that will be changed.

shadow filter A filter that casts a single shadow behind text.

sibling folder A folder on the same level in the same file directory.

sidebar Text or images that are displayed in a narrow column, usually on the left or the right of the screen.

special character A character that cannot be entered by using the keyboard.

style A rule or a collection of rules.

style sheet A collection of styles.

suffix In a URL, another name for a top-level domain.

summary attribute A longer description of the contents of data table.

T

tabbed browsing The ability of contemporary browsers to keep open more than one page at a time.

table border The horizontal and vertical ruled lines within and outside table cells.

table header A row that is to appear at the top of a data table.

target page The page that is the object of a link.

TCP/IP Acronym for Transmission Control Protocol/Internet Protocol, the internationally agreed to protocol for transmitting communications over the Internet.

thumbnail A smaller image that usually is used as a link to a page that contains a much larger instance of the same image.

title attribute The attribute used to provide a brief description of an element.

top property The property used to determine an element's position from the top of the page.

type attribute The attribute that is used to specify the media type.

U

Uniform Resource Locator (URL) The complete address of the Web page you are viewing.

unordered list A list using a bullet character in which the order of the entries does not matter.

usemap attribute The attribute that identifies which image is used as the image map.

V

value The extent to or the manner in which an attribute or property will be changed.

visible The value used with the visibility property to make an element visible.

W

wave filter A filter that bends text.

Web browser A software program that is used to access the World Wide Web.

width attribute The attribute that defines the width of an element.

width property The property that is used to determine an element's width.

Windows control An object that enables user interaction or input, displays information, or sets values, such as radio buttons or check boxes.

World Wide Web (Web) The graphical user interface used to access the Internet.

World Wide Web Consortium (W3C) The international committee that sets standards for many Web programming languages.

Z

z-index property The property used to determine the stacking order of layered elements; the higher the element is in the stack, the more visible it is.

Index